This
apparitions, hauntings, astral projection, clairvoyance, and premonitions
is the first systematic work of its kind.
It was originally published in England in two separate volumes — **Real
Ghost Stories** and **More Ghost Stories**
— as Christmas and New Year numbers of **Review of Reviews**, 1891-92.
It was subsequently published as one
volume in 1897 under the title **Real
Ghost Stories.**

William Thomas Stead, the author of
Borderland, was an illustrious social
reformer and one of the most famous
journalists of the nineteenth century.
He was renowned for his brilliant

(continued on back flap)

ing psychic powers, having accurate
premonitions of future events. He experimented with automatic writing,
and produced clear, rational, prophetic communications from a deceased former colleague, Miss Julia
Ames.

Long out of print and exceedingly
rare, **Borderland** is a monumental
accomplishment — of immense historical worth and popular interest.
As a sourcebook for investigators of
the occult sciences, the present edition is an enjoyable and invaluable
compilation of most remarkable case
histories of supernatural phenomena.

BORDERLAND

A Casebook of
True Supernatural Stories

By W. T. STEAD

Introduction to American Edition by

Leslie Shepard

UNIVERSITY BOOKS New Hyde Park, New York

INTRODUCTION TO
NEW AMERICAN EDITION

This famous collection of true cases of apparitions, hauntings, astral projection, clairvoyance, and premonitions has pride of place as the first systematic work of its kind.

It first appeared in 1891-92, barely a decade after the founding of the British Society for Psychical Research, and a couple of years before publication of the Society's famous *Census of Hallucinations*. Although less bulky than that important work, it is easier reading, and more positive in its conclusions.

The man responsible for this book was one of the most famous British journalists of the nineteenth century. He was a passionately sincere social reformer and also had extraordinary psychic gifts of premonition and automatic writing.

WILLIAM THOMAS STEAD was born July 5, 1849, at Embleton, Northumberland, England, son of a Congregationalist minister. He was first educated by his father, and later attended Silcoates School, Wakefield. In 1863 he left school to be apprenticed as office boy in a merchant's countinghouse at Newcastle-on-Tyne. At the age of eighteen he was much impressed by the poems of James Russell Lowell, and resolved to dedicate his life to helping other people. He wrote: "The idea that everything wrong in the world was a divine call to use your life in righting it sank deep into my soul." He did valuable social work and campaigned for the founding of a Charity Organisation Society. About this time he had his first clairvoyant experience, during a holiday in Scotland. The story of this visit to a haunted castle is told in Chapter I of the second part of the present book.

In the 1860's, Stead began to write for the *Northern Echo* newspaper, and in 1871 he was appointed editor. He remained a journalist for the rest of his life, and became famous for his brilliant innovations, and for his powerful support of important causes. In 1880 he was appointed assistant editor to John Morley at the famous *Pall Mall Gazette,* and in 1883 he became sole editor. In 1890 he left this journal to found the *Review of Reviews.* He is credited with inventing the "New Journalism," which brought a wide range of important topics in bright, colorful prose to the man in the street. He introduced the interview technique and illustrations into the British daily press. He was also a pioneer of cheap reprints for mass sale in the form of penny pamphlets.

His amazing grasp of political realities made him the confidant of leading public figures of the day all over the world. It was Stead's interview with General Gordon at Southampton which resulted in the mission to Khartoum. A pacifist and close friend of empire-builder Cecil Rhodes, he campaigned against British policy in the Boer War. His exposure of the weaknesses of the British navy in 1884 had the direct result of stimulating Britain's revival of naval supremacy. He traveled the world, interviewing great leaders, and publicizing the true issues of international politics.

As a dedicated social reformer, he became respected and feared for his courage and absolute integrity. In defense of his principles, he even went to prison on one celebrated occasion. In 1885 the Chamberlain of the city of London confided in Stead that the confusion following the defeat of Gladstone's government had imperiled the passing of a new bill to strengthen the law against procuring children for prostitution. He said: "All our work will be wasted unless you can rouse up public opinion and compel the new government to take up the bill and pass it into law." Stead accordingly undertook a personal investigation at considerable risk, and published a series of articles in the *Pall Mall Gazette* under the title "The Maiden Tribute of Modern Babylon." These articles caused an instant sensation all over the world; and the government of the day was obliged to revive, strengthen, and pass the bill into law. No one has ever better demonstrated the power of the press than this crusading journalist who forced a government to bow to popular indignation. Of course, Stead made enemies over the affair, and through false evidence was prosecuted over a technicality and sentenced to a short period in prison. The foreman of the jury wept as he explained that on the evidence there was no alternative, but the jury added the unprecedented rider that they "wished to put on record their high appreciation of the services [Stead] had rendered the nation by securing the passage of a much needed law for the protection of young girls." Stead could have exposed the evidence against him but he chose to accept the experience of imprisonment, although a whole nation agitated for remission of sentence.

Against all this excitement as a heroic public figure, Stead had his own private life. In 1873 he had married Emma Lucy Wilson, and they had a family of six children. Presently it became common knowledge among Stead's friends and associates that he had strange psychic gifts.

In 1893 he founded *Borderland,* a quarterly journal devoted entirely to psychical subjects, launched with the good will of famous psychical researchers and distinguished men of science. In the first number he disclosed his own astonishing powers. He wrote, quite casually, from his acceptance of the paranormal as an everyday fact:

> However incredible it may appear, I can, and do constantly, receive messages from my assistant editor, Miss X. [*i.e.,* Miss Goodrich Freer], as accurately and as constantly as I receive telegrams from those with whom I do business, without the employment of any wires or any instrument. Whenever I wish to know where she is, whether she can keep an appointment, or how she is progressing with her work, I simply ask the question, and my hand automatically writes

out the answer. . . . Distance does not affect the messages, they are received equally when she is asleep or awake. . . . I can communicate with many of my friends in the same way.

Stead had first become aware of strangely imperative premonitions about future events from about 1880 onward. In the present book he describes his psychic warning that he would leave the *Northern Echo,* and that he would assume full control of the *Pall Mall Gazette.* In 1892 he experimented with automatic writing and, although at first highly skeptical, he suddenly found himself producing clear, rational communications from a former colleague, Miss Julia Ames—who had died in December, 1891. Through Stead's hand, "Julia" inscribed practical advice and predictions for the future, foretelling events with uncanny accuracy in a style exactly characteristic of her personality during her lifetime. As a result of these communications, Stead founded a psychic bureau to demonstrate the reality of survival after death, and to assist a spiritual revival. In 1908 "Julia" prophesied: "About the Bureau, that is all right. You will get the money you need for the establishment of the Bureau on a proper basis." Just as foretold, the money came a few months later, when William Randolph Hearst engaged Stead as special correspondent to the *New York American.* Julia's Bureau lasted for three years and brought comfort and spiritual awareness to some six hundred persons.

Stead always disclaimed any personal "courage" in propagandizing for spiritualism. With characteristically genuine humility he once said: "I deserve no praise in the matter. You know the thing is very simple. Either the thing is true or it is not. If it is true the brave man is the man who goes against it, the brave man is the man who goes against truth."

With all Stead's amazing psychic powers, it is astonishing that he did not foresee the manner of his own death, because the signs were clearly there if his attention had been directed to them. But he was too busy working for other people, and for the ideals which he held, to give much thought to himself.

He had frequently used the simile of a man drowning at sea, and in the Christmas, 1892, number of the *Review of Reviews* he wrote a striking fictional story about a ship called the *Majestic,* which received a psychic message from the survivor of another ship which had struck an iceberg in the Atlantic. The captain of the *Majestic* in the story, however, was a real person—Captain Smith, who afterward commanded the famous *Titanic* in which W. T. Stead and more than 1,600 other passengers perished after a collision with an iceberg in the Atlantic, April, 1912, just over twenty years after this prophetic story. . . .

In a tribute to Stead's unique combination of journalism, politics, and mysticism, his old journal, the *Pall Mall Gazette,* commented (September 25, 1913):

> For the best part of forty years Stead interpreted his Age with a clear and restless eloquence which had no superior and hardly a rival in his own profession of journalism. Statesmen and autocrats came under his spell and suffered him to prompt them when they would hardly brook advice from their appointed Ministers. This deference . . . would have made him the most consummate egotist of our time had it not been for his sense of a superhuman mission. It kept him a visionary to the end. . . .

The present book was originally published in two separate volumes—*Real Ghost Stories* and *More Ghost Stories*—as Christmas and New Year numbers of *Review of Reviews,* 1891-92. This revised edition in one volume, first published in 1897, is the best edition. A new edition was published in 1921, rearranged and abridged by Stead's daughter Estelle W. Stead, but it omitted almost half the contents of the present work.

The new title for this reprint is felt to be more in keeping with modern views on paranormal phenomena. It was also anticipated by Estelle Stead in her own version. In an introductory note she wrote:

> I demurred long as to whether I should change the title. The word "Ghost" has to a large extent in modern times lost its true meaning to the majority. . . . "Stories from the Borderland," "Psychic Experiences," were among the titles which suggested themselves to me. . . .

The present title of Stead's pioneer casebook revives the memory of his great psychic quarterly *Borderland,* in which he published so many additional case histories. His "CAUTION TO THE READER" has been retained. It may sound old-fashioned in an age where violence, murder, and horror are commonplaces in every newspaper, but it is still pertinent to remind those who wish to investigate the occult that a sincere and reverent attitude will avoid the very real dangers of pride, vanity, morbidity, or even madness, which still exist. As Stead himself wrote: "Demoniac possession, or if you prefer to call it mental aberration, occasioned by the apparent control of evil spirits, is a horribly real thing, as I can testify of my own observation. Ghosts and ghostly phenomena are not things to be played with. If you cannot or will not examine the subject seriously, you had a thousand times better leave it alone."

With the publication of the Society for Psychical Research's *Census of Hallucinations* in 1894, the case for the reality of apparitions of the kind already reported by W. T. Stead received strong support. The cautious term "hallucinations" is perhaps unfortunate, even though scientifically correct. The key question was:

Have you ever, when believing yourself to be completely awake, had a vivid impression of seeing or being touched by a living being or inanimate object, or of hearing a voice, which impression, so far as you could describe, was not due to any external physical cause?

Between April, 1889, and May, 1892, 17,000 persons were asked this question. No fewer than 2,272 individuals answered "Yes." After the committee had eliminated certain affirmative replies which it considered not precisely within the scope of the question, the number eventually considered acceptable was 1,684 out of the total of 17,000. That means, roughly speaking, that something like one person in ten had either heard a voice, or seen an apparition, or been touched by something invisible.

Most of these experiences were visual. Of those relating to human phantasms, 520 were unrecognized, 536 were those of the living, and 232 were of the dead. There were 16 angels or religious figures, 33 grotesque or horrible apparitions, and 27 phantasms of animals.

In conjunction with those massive related works, *Phantasms of the Living* by Gurney, Myers, and Podmore, and *Human Personality and Its Survival of Bodily Death* by F. W. H. Myers (both reissued by University Books Inc.), the *Census* completed the most comprehensive investigation of the whole subject-area which Stead had started with the present book. Nothing on such a grand scale has been attempted since, dealing with what is now known as "spontaneous phenomena," although modern techniques for collection and assessment of data have improved considerably. Nowadays the emphasis is more on ESP (extrasensory perception) effects in a clinical setting.

Stead was no impartially detached investigator. He was peculiarly involved with the phenomena he reported, since his own psychic faculties left no doubt for him that these things were real. And that they were related to one's responsibilities and ethics as a human being. This meant more to him than scientific validation.

In a lecture to the Spiritualists' National Union Convention, July 4, 1909, he stated: "The great mission of Spiritualism is to make men spiritual."

His whole life was a noble example of how an idealist and spiritualist may also be a realistic man of everyday affairs, with a keen perception of such mundane matters as politics. As the pioneer publicist of psychical phenomena and spiritualism, he blazed a trail which others have since followed. It will be remembered that the millionaire newspaper king Lord Rothermere employed Dr. Nandor Fodor, that talented writer and investigator of borderland phenomena. The great newspapers, particularly in Britain, still regularly take up sympathetic inquiry into the psychic field, and the proprietors are often believers in the reality of such phenomena.

Today the learned study of parapsychology is infinitely more respectable than in the nineteenth century, but unhappily much of the jargon and theory is as remote from the old-fashioned ghost story as the technology of space travel. Yet a great many ordinary persons continue to "see ghosts"; and, however one analyzes or interprets such experiences, no bare scientific assessment can really convey the uncanniness of the experience itself, or the intensity of meaning which it usually holds for the person concerned.

Even in a grossly materialistic and skeptical age, that borderland between dreaming and waking, between ghosts, demons, angels, and the living, still sometimes wears very thin when one least expects it. And when it does, it somehow heightens one's awareness that there is something in those basic tenets of all religions, which have held that the soul is distinct from the body, and that it survives death. That our brief lives have a purpose beyond immediately tangible gains and losses, and that our noblest strivings are not in vain.

This was the conviction which encouraged W. T. Stead to devote his life to a study of Borderland and its phenomena, as something more than a scientifically verifiable fact—rather something by which a man may shape his life and fulfill his immortal destiny.

Stead did more than anyone else in his day to popularize psychical research and spiritualism as serious topics for the man in the street. This important reissue honors the memory of a very great man who was a pioneer in these fields.

London, England   Leslie Shepard
1970

A PREFATORY WORD

MANY people will object—some have already objected—to the subject of this book. It is an offence to some to take a ghost too seriously; with others it is a still greater offence not to take ghosts seriously enough. One set of objections can be paired off against the other; neither objection has very solid foundation. The time has surely come when the fair claim of ghosts to the impartial attention and careful observation of mankind should no longer be ignored. In earlier times people believed in them so much that they cut their acquaintance; in later times people believe in them so little that they will not even admit their existence. Thus these mysterious visitants have hitherto failed to enter into that friendly relation with mankind which many of them seem sincerely to desire. But what with the superstitious credulity of the one age and the equally superstitious unbelief of another, it is necessary to begin from the beginning and to convince a sceptical world that apparitions really appear. In order to do this it is necessary to insist that your ghost should no longer be ignored as a phenomenon of Nature. He has a right to be examined and observed, studied and defined, which is equal to that of any other natural phenomenon. It is true that he is a rather difficult phenomenon; his comings and goings are rather intermittent and fitful, his substance is too shadowy to be handled, and he has avoided hitherto equally the obtrusive inquisitiveness of the microscope and telescope. A phenomenon which you can neither handle nor weigh, analyse nor dissect, is naturally regarded as intractable and troublesome; nevertheless, however intractable and troublesome he may be to reduce to any of the existing scientific categories, we have no right to allow his idiosyncrasies to deprive him of his innate right to be regarded as a phenomenon. As such he will be treated in the following pages, with all the respect due to Phenomena whose reality is attested by a sufficient number of witnesses. There will be no attempt in this

book to build up a theory of apparitions, or to define the
true inwardness of a ghost. There will be as many explanations as there are minds of the significance of the extraordinary narratives which I have collated from correspondence
and from accessible records. Leaving it to my readers to
discuss the rival hypotheses, I will stick to the humbler mission
of recording facts, from which they can form their own judgment.

The ordinary temper of the ordinary man in dealing with
ghosts is supremely unscientific, but it is less objectionable
than that of the pseudo-scientist. The Inquisitor who forbade
free inquiry into matters of religion because of human de-
pravity, was the natural precursor of the Scientist who forbids
the exercise of the reason on the subject of ghosts, on account
of inherited tendencies to attribute such phenomena to causes
outside the established order of nature. What difference there
is, is altogether in favour of the Inquisitor, who at least had
what he regarded as a divinely constituted authority, competent and willing to pronounce final decision upon any subject
that might trouble the human mind. Science has no such
tribunal, and when she forbids others to observe and to reflect
she is no better than a blind fetish.

Eclipses in old days used to drive whole nations half mad
with fright. To this day the black disc of the moon no sooner
begins to eat into the shining surface of the sun than millions
of savage men feel " creepy," and begin to tremble at the
thought of the approaching end of the world. But in civilised
lands even the most ignorant regard an eclipse with imper-
turbable composure. Eclipses are scientific phenomena
observed and understood. It is our object to reduce ghosts to
the same level, or rather to establish the claim of ghosts to be
regarded as belonging as much to the order of Nature as the
eclipse. At present they are disfranchised of their natural
birthright, and those who treat them with this injustice need
not wonder if they take their revenge in " creeps."

The third class of objection takes the ground that there is
something irreligious and contrary to Christianity in the chroni-
cling of such phenomena. It is fortunate that Mary Magdalene and the early disciples did not hold that theory. So far
from its being irreligious to ascertain facts, there is a subtle
impiety in the refusal to face phenomena, whether natural or
supernatural. Either these things exist or they do not. If
they do not exist, then obviously there can be no harm in a
searching examination of the delusion which possessed the

mind of almost every worthy in the Old Testament, and which was constantly affirmed by the authors of the New. If, on the other hand, they do exist, and are perceptible under certain conditions to our senses, it will be difficult to affirm the impiety of endeavouring to ascertain what is their nature, and what light they are able to throw upon the kingdom of the Unseen. We have no right to shut our eyes to facts and close our ears to evidence merely because Moses forbade the Hebrews to allow witches to live, or because some of the phenomena carry with them suggestions that do not altogether harmonise with the conventional orthodox theories of future life. The whole question that lies at bottom is whether this world is divine or diabolic. Those who believe it divine are bound by that belief to regard every phenomenon as a window through which man may gain fresh glimpses of the wonder and the glory of the Infinite. In this region, as in all others, faith and fear go ill together.

It is impossible for any impartial man to read the narratives of which the present book is composed without feeling that we have at least one hint or suggestion of quite incalculable possibilities in telepathy or thought transference. If there be, as many of these stories seem to suggest, a latent capacity in the human mind to communicate with other minds, entirely regardless of the conditions of time and space, it is undeniable that this would be a fact of the very first magnitude. It is quite possible that the telegraph may be to telepathy what the stage coach is to the steam engine. Neither can we afford to overlook the fact that these phenomena have in these latter days signally vindicated their power over the minds of men. Some of the acutest minds of our time have learned to recognise in them scientific demonstration of the existence of the fact that personal individuality survives death.

If it can be proved that it is occasionally possible for persons at the uttermost ends of the world to communicate instantaneously with each other, and even in some cases to make a vivid picture of themselves stand before the eyes of those to whom they speak, no prejudice as to the unhealthy nature of the inquiry should be allowed to stand in the way of the examination of such a fact with a view to ascertaining whether or not this latent capacity of the human mind can be utilised for the benefit of mankind. Wild as this suggestion may seem to-day, it is less fantastic than our grandfathers a hundred years ago would have deemed a statement that at the end of the nineteenth century portraits would be taken by the sun, that audible conversation would be carried on instantaneously across a distance of a thousand miles, that a ray of light could be made the agent for transmitting the human voice across an abyss which no wire had ever spanned, and that by a simple mechanical arrangement, which a man can carry in his hand, it would be possible to reproduce the words, voice, and accent of the dead. The photograph, the telegraph, the telephone, and the phonograph were all more or less latent in what seemed to our ancestors the kite-flying folly of Benjamin Franklin. Who knows but that in Telepathy we may have the faint foreshadowing of another latent force, which may yet be destined to cast into the shade even the marvels of electrical science !

At the end of this century, as at the end of last, there seems to be a growing interest in all the occult phenomena to which this work is devoted. It is in evidence on every hand. The topic is in the air, and will be discussed and is being discussed, whether we take notice of it or not. That it has its dangers those who have studied it most closely are most aware, but these dangers will exist in any case, and if those who ought to guide are silent, these perils will be encountered without the safeguards which experience would dictate and prudence suggest. It seems to me that it would be difficult to do better service in this direction than to strengthen the hands of those who have for many years past been trying to rationalise the consideration of the Science of Ghosts.

It is idle to say that this should be left for experts. We live in a democratic age and we democratise everything. It is too late in the day to propose to place the whole of this department under the care of any Brahmin caste ; the subject is one which every common man and woman can understand. It is one which comes home to every human being, for it adds a new interest to life, and vivifies the sombre but all-pervading problem of death.

Nevertheless, as the net result of my very cursory survey and amateur experimenting, it will be seen that I have come to a very decided opinion that for the majority—the immense majority of men and women—the subject had better be left alone so far as the direct intentional production of phenomena is concerned. This applies to all spiritualist séances, hypnotist experiments, and dabbling in magic. Those who meddle in such matters from idle curiosity run serious risks. To put it mildly, they may become the subjects of hallucinations indistinguishable from the delusions of the insane, or they may lose all control over their actions and become, as in cases of post-hypnotic suggestion, the absolute slaves of another and evil will. At the same time, while deprecating the deliberate inducing of these phenomena on the part of Tom, Dick, and Harry, there can be no objection to the scientific study of any and every subject that can engage the human mind. It is no argument against the laboratory of the chemist that children occasionally hurt themselves in making hydrogen out of zinc nails and sulphuric acid, nor do we suppress the manufacture of explosives because every year amateur pyrotechnists burn their fingers. If in these occult studies the scientific investigator can hope to discover the secret of telepathic communication, the art of transporting ourselves invisibly and instantly to the end of the earth, or of seeing clairvoyantly everything that has been done since the world began, it would be a crime against the progress of the race to place any bar upon such inquiries and experiments. But they are distinctly for the few who have leisure, culture, and the intellectual faculties indispensable for the profitable conduct of such investigations.

What then becomes of our favourite formula, the democratisation of knowledge? It remains where it was. The democratisation of railways does not mean that every man, woman, and child is to be allowed to drive the engine. It does mean that they have all to have free access to the train if they take their tickets. So the democratisation of the Science of Ghosts does not mean that every one is to set up a séance in his own house, or practise black magic in his own back parlour. What it means is that, instead of the subject being scouted and tabooed and ridiculed, and all information hidden from the common people, it shall be openly discussed, freely handled, and the results of investigation made known to every one. There is nothing in the world as healthy as light. It is because the light has not been let in upon this realm that the atmosphere is so mephitic. " Light, more light ! " must be in this, as in all other realms of nature, the constant cry of the searcher for truth.

But it is not merely in the communication of ascertained knowledge to the masses of the people that the democratiser of the Science of Ghosts seeks to carry on his work. He appeals to the ordinary man not to set about the invocation of spirits, but merely to pay observant attention to ghosts and all ghostly subjects. The phenomena which are not induced, but spontaneous, are of constant but irregular occurrence. At present people are more or less ashamed to admit they have seen them. They seldom or never record their experiences at the time, and hence legal evidence is lacking, which causes the enemy to blaspheme. What is wanted on the part of the masses is a recognition of the fact that certain phenomena occur which, if diligently noted and carefully studied, may help us to fresh mastery over nature, and to as yet unconceived triumphs over time and space.

CAUTION TO THE READER

Before reading the contents of this book,—

PLEASE NOTE.

1.—*That the narratives printed in these pages had better not be read by any one of tender years, of morbid excitability, or of excessively nervous temperament.*

2.—*That the latest students of the subject concur in the solemn warning addressed in the Sacred Writings to those who have dealings with familiar spirits, or who expose themselves to the horrible consequences of possession.*

3.—*That as the latent possibilities of our complex personality are so imperfectly understood, all experimenting in hypnotism, spiritualism, etc., excepting in the most careful and reverent spirit, by the most level-headed persons, had much better be avoided.*

This Caution is printed here at the suggestion of *Catholics, Theosophists,* and *Spiritualists,* who declare themselves to be profoundly convinced of its *necessity.*

CONTENTS

xxiii

CONTENTS

PART II

HAUNTED HOUSES

PART I

THE GHOST THAT DWELLS IN EACH OF US

"REAL GHOST STORIES!—How can there be real ghost stories when there are no real ghosts?"
But are there no real ghosts? You may not have seen one, but it does not follow that therefore they do not exist. How many of us have seen the microbe that kills? There are at least as many persons who testify they have seen apparitions as there are men of science who have examined the microbe. You and I, who have seen neither, must perforce take the testimony of others. The evidence for the microbe may be conclusive, the evidence as to apparitions may be worthless; but in both cases it is a case of testimony, not of personal experience.

The first thing to be done, therefore, is to collect testimony, and by way of generally widening the mind and shaking down the walls of prejudice which lead so many to refuse to admit the clearest possible evidence as to facts which have not occurred within their personal experience, I preface the report of my "Census of Hallucinations" or personal experiences of the so-called supernatural by a preliminary chapter on the perplexing subject of "Personality." This is the question that lies at the root of all the controversy as to ghosts. Before disputing about whether or not there are ghosts outside of us, let us face the preliminary question, whether we have not each of us a veritable ghost within our own skin?

THE GHOST THAT DWELLS IN EACH OF US.

THRILLING as are some of the stories of the apparitions of the living and the dead, they are less sensational than the suggestion recently made by hypnotists and psychical researchers of England and France, that each of us has a ghost inside him. They say that we are all haunted by a Spiritual Presence, of whose existence we are only fitfully and sometimes never

conscious, but which nevertheless inhabits the innermost
recesses of our personality.   The theory of these researchers
is that besides the body and the mind, meaning by the mind
the Conscious Personality, there is also within our material
frame the soul or Unconscious Personality, the nature of which
is shrouded in unfathomable mystery.   The latest word of
advanced science has thus landed us back to the apostolic
assertion that man is composed of body, soul, and spirit ; and
there are some who see in the scientific doctrine of the Unconscious Personality a welcome confirmation from an unexpected
quarter of the existence of the soul.

The fairy tales of science are innumerable, and, like the
fairy tales of old romance, they are not lacking in the grim,
the tragic, and even the horrible.   Of recent years nothing
has so fascinated the imagination even of the least imaginative
of men as the theory of disease which transforms every drop
of blood in our bodies into the lists in which phagocyte and
microbe wage the mortal strife on which our health depends.
Every white corpuscle that swims in our veins is now declared
to be the armed Knight of Life for ever on the look-out for
the microbe Fiend of Death.   Day and night, sleeping and
waking, the white knights of life are constantly on the alert,
for on their vigilance hangs our existence.   Sometimes, however, the invading microbes come in, not in companies but in
platoons, innumerable as Xerxes' Persians, and then "e'en
Roderick's best are backward borne," and we die.   For our
life is the prize of the combat in these novel lists which science
has revealed to our view through the microscope, and health
is but the token of the triumphant victory of the phagocyte
over the microbe.

But far more enthralling is the suggestion which psychical
science has made as to the existence of a combat not less
grave in the very inmost centre of our own mental or spiritual
existence.   The strife between the infinitely minute bacilli
that swarm in our blood has only the interest which attaches
to the conflict of inarticulate and apparently unconscious
animalculæ.   But the strife to which recent researches into
the nature and constitution of our mental processes call
attention concerns our conscious selves.   It suggests almost
inconceivable possibilities as to our own nature, and leaves us
appalled on the brink of a new world of being of which until
recently most of us were unaware.

There are no papers of such absorbing interest in the whole
of the " Proceedings of the Society for Psychical Research " as

those which deal with the question of the Personality of Man. "I," what am I? What is our Ego? Is this Conscious Personality which receives impressions through the five senses, and through them alone, is it the only dweller in this mortal tabernacle? May there not be other personalities, or at least one other that is not conscious, when we are awake, and alert, and about, but which comes into semi-consciousness when we sleep, and can be developed into complete consciousness when the other personality is thrown into a state of hypnotic trance? In other words, am I one personality or two? Is my nature dual? As I have two hemispheres in my brain, have I two minds or two souls?

The question will, no doubt, appear fantastic in its absurdity to those who hear it asked for the first time ; but those who are at all familiar with the mysterious but undisputed phenomena of hypnotism will realize how naturally this question arises, and how difficult it is to answer it otherwise than in the affirmative. Every one knows Mr. Louis Stevenson's wonderful story of " Dr. Jekyll and Mr. Hyde." The dual nature of man, the warfare between this body of sin and death, and the spiritual aspirations of the soul, forms part of the common stock of our orthodox belief. But the facts which recent researches have brought to light seem to point not to the old theological doctrine of the conflict between good and evil in one soul, but to the existence in each of us of at least two distinct selfs, two personalities, standing to each other somewhat in the relation of man and wife, according to the old ideal when the man is everything and the woman is almost entirely suppressed.

Every one is familiar with the phenomenon of occasional loss of memory. Men are constantly losing consciousness, from disease, violence, or violent emotion, and emerging again into active life with a gap in their memory. Nay, every night we become unconscious in sleep, and rarely, if ever, remember anything that we think of during slumber. Sometimes in rare cases there is a distinct memory of all that passes in the sleeping and the waking states, and we have read of one young man whose sleeping consciousness was so continuous that he led, to all intents and purposes, two lives. When he slept he resumed his dream existence at the point when he waked, just as we resume our consciousness at the point when we fall asleep. It was just as real to him as the life which he lived when awake. It was actual, progressive, continuous, but entirely different, holding no relation whatever to his waking life. Of his two existences he preferred that which was spent in sleep, as more vivid, more varied, and more pleasurable. This was no doubt an extreme and very unusual case. But it is not impossible to conceive the possibility of a continuous series of connected dreams, which would result in giving us a realizing sense of leading two existences. That we fail to realize this now is due to the fact that our memory is practically inert or non-existent during sleep. The part of our mind which dreams seldom registers its impressions in regions to which on waking our conscious personality has access.

The conception of a dual or even a multiple personality is worked out in a series of papers by Mr. F W. H. Myers, to which I refer all those who wish to make a serious study of this novel and startling hypothesis. But I may at least attempt to explain the theory, and to give some outline of the evidence on which it is based.

If I were free to use the simplest illustration without any pretence at scientific exactitude, I should say that the new theory supposes that there are inside each of us not one personality but two, and that these two correspond to the husband and wife. There is the Conscious Personality, which stands for the husband. It is vigorous, alert, active, positive, monopolising all the means of communication and production. So intense is its consciousness that it ignores the very existence of its partner, excepting as a mere appendage and convenience to itself. Then there is the Unconscious Personality, which corresponds to the wife who keeps cupboard and storehouse, and the old stocking which treasures up the accumulated wealth of impressions acquired by the Conscious Personality, but who is never able to assert any right to anything, or to the use of sense or limb except when her lord and master is asleep or entranced. When the Conscious Personality has acquired any habit or faculty so completely that it becomes instinctive, it is handed on to the Unconscious Personality to keep and use, the Conscious Ego giving it no longer any attention. Deprived, like the wife in countries where the subjection of woman is the universal law, of all right to an independent existence, or to the use of the senses, or of the limbs, the Unconscious Personality has discovered ways and means of communicating other than through the recognised organs of sense. How vast and powerful are those hidden organs of the Unconscious Personality we can only dimly see. It is through them that Divine revelation is vouchsafed to man. The visions of the mystic, the prophecies of the seer, the inspiration of the sibyl, all come through this Unconscious Soul. It is through this dumb and suppressed Ego that we communicate by telepathy,—that thought is transferred without using the five senses. This under-soul is in touch with the over-soul, which, in Emerson's noble phrase, "abolishes time and space." "This influence of the senses has," he says, "in most men, overpowered their mind to that degree that the walls of time and space have come to look real and insurmountable; and to speak with levity of these limits is in the world the sign of insanity. Yet time and space are but inverse measures of the force of the soul." It is this Unconscious Personality which sees the *Strathmore* foundering in mid-ocean, which hears a whisper spoken hundreds of miles off upon the battlefield, and which witnesses, as if it happened before the eyes, a tragedy occurring at the Antipodes. In proportion as the active, domineering Conscious Personality extinguishes his submissive unconscious partner, materialism flourishes, and man becomes blind to the Divinity that underlies all things. Hence in all religions the first step is to silence the noisy, bustling master of our earthly tabernacle, who, having monopolised the five senses, will listen to no voice which it cannot hear, and to allow the silent mistress to be open-souled to God. Hence the stress which all spiritual religions have laid upon contemplation, upon prayer and fasting. Whether it is an Indian Yogi, or a Trappist Monk, or one of our own Quakers, it is all the same. In the words of the Revivalist hymn, "We must lay our deadly doing down," and in receptive silence wait for the inspiration from on high. The Conscious Personality has usurped the visible world; but the Invisible, with its immeasurable expanse, is the domain of the Sub-conscious. Hence we read in the Scriptures of losing life that we may find it; for things of time and sense are temporal, but the things which are not seen are eternal.

It is extraordinary how close is the analogy when we come to work it out. The impressions stored up by the Conscious Personality and entrusted to the care of the Unconscious are often, much to our disgust, not forthcoming when wanted. It is as if we had given a memorandum to our wife and we could not discover where she had put it. But night comes; our Conscious Self sleeps, our Unconscious Housewife wakes, and turning over her stores produces the missing impression; and when our other self wakes it finds the mislaid memorandum, so to speak, ready to its hand. Sometimes, as in the case of somnambulism, the Sub-conscious Personality stealthily endeavours to use the body and limbs, from all direct control over which it is shut out as absolutely as the inmate of a Hindu zenana is forbidden to mount the charger of her warrior spouse. But it is only when the Conscious Personality is thrown into a state of hypnotic trance that the Unconscious Personality is emancipated from the marital despotism of her partner. Then for the first time she is allowed to help herself to the faculties and senses usually monopolised by the Conscious Self. But like the timid and submissive inmate of the zenana suddenly delivered from the thraldom of her lifelong partner, she immediately falls under the control of another. The Conscious Personality of another person exercises over her the same supreme authority that her own Conscious Personality did formerly; just as some assert of women that if they were to receive the franchise they would become the mere tools of the priests. There is nothing of sex in the ordinary material sense about the two personalities. But their union is so close as to suggest that the intrusion of the hypnotist is equivalent to an intrigue with a married woman. The Subconscious Personality is no longer faithful exclusively to its natural partner; it is under the control of the Conscious Personality of another; and in the latter case the dictator seems to be irresistibly over-riding for a time all the efforts of the Conscious Personality to recover its authority in its own domain.

What proof, it will be asked impatiently, is there for the splitting of our personality? The question is a just one, and I proceed to answer it.

There are often to be found in the records of lunatic asylums strange instances of a dual personality, in which there appear to be two minds in one body, as there are sometimes two yolks in one egg.

The French psychologists who write in the *Revue des Deux Mondes*, furnish us from time to time with very extraordinary illustrations of the dual consciousness. Only last month M. Jules Janet records the following experiment which, although simplicity itself, gives us a very vivid glimpse of a most appalling complex problem :—

"An hysterical subject with an insensitive limb is put to sleep, and is told, 'After you wake you will raise your finger when you mean Yes, and you will put it down when you mean No, in answer to the questions which I shall ask you.' The subject is then wakened, and M. Janet pricks the insensitive limb in several places. He asks, 'Do you feel anything?'

The conscious awakened person replies with the lips, ' No,' but at the same time, in accordance with the signal that has been agreed upon during the state of hypnotisation, the finger is raised to signify ' Yes.' It has been found that the finger will even indicate exactly the number of times that the apparently insensitive limb has been wounded."

The Double-souled Irishman. Dr. Robinson, of Lewisham, who has bestowed much attention on this subject, sends me the following delightful story about an Irishman who seems to have incarnated the Irish nationality in his own unhappy person:—

"An old colleague of mine at the Darlington Hospital told me that he once had an Irish lunatic under his care who imagined that his body was the dwelling-place of two individuals, one of whom was a Catholic, with Nationalist—not to say Fenian—proclivities, and the other was a Protestant and an Orangeman. The host of these incompatibles said he made it a fixed rule that the Protestant should occupy the right side of his body and the Catholic the left, 'so that he would not be annoyed wid them quarrelling in his inside." The sympathies of the host were with the green and against the orange, and he tried to weaken the latter by starving him, and for months would only chew his food on the left side of his mouth. The lunatic was not very troublesome, as a rule, but the attendants generally had to straight-waistcoat him on certain critical days—such as St. Patrick's Day and the anniversary of the battle of the Boyne ; because the Orange fist would punch the Fenian head unmercifully, and occasionally he and the Fenian leagued together against the Orangeman and banged him against the wall. This lunatic, when questioned, said he did his best to keep the peace between his troublesome guests, but that sometimes they got out of hand."

Ansel Bourne and A. J. Brown. A similar case, although not so violent or chronic in its manifestation, is recorded in Vol. VII. (Part xix.) of the Psychical Research Society's Proceedings, as having occurred on Rhode Island about four years ago. An excellent citizen, and a very religious lay preacher, of the name of Ansel Bourne, was the subject :—

"On January 17th, 1887, he went from his home in Coventry, R.I., to Providence, in order to get money to pay for a farm which he had arranged to buy, leaving his horse at Greene Station, in a stable, expecting to return the same afternoon from the city. He drew out of bank 551 dollars, and paid several small bills, after which he went to his nephew's store,

121, Broad Street, and then started to go to his sister's house on Westminster Street. This was the last that was known of his doings at that time. He did not appear at his sister's house, and did not return to Greene."

Nothing was heard of him until March the 14th, when a telegram came from a doctor in Norristown, Philadelphia, stating that he had just been discovered there. He was entirely unconscious of having been absent from home, or of the lapse of time between January 17th and March 14th. He was brought home by his relatives, who by diligent inquiry were able to make out that Mr. Ansel Bourne, five weeks after leaving Rhode Island, opened a shop in Norristown, and stocked it with toys and confectionery which he purchased in Philadelphia. He called himself A. J. Brown, and lived and did business, and went to meeting, like any ordinary mortal, giving no one any suspicion that he was any other than A. J. Brown.

"On the morning of Monday, March 14th, about five o'clock, he heard, he says, an explosion like the report of a gun or a pistol, and, waking, he noticed that there was a ridge in his bed not like the bed he had been accustomed to sleep in. He noticed the electric light opposite his windows. He rose and pulled away the curtains and looked out on the street. He felt very weak, and thought that he had been drugged. His next sensation was that of fear, knowing that he was in a place where he had no business to be. He feared arrest as a burglar, or possibly injury. He says this is the only time in his life he ever feared a policeman.

"The last thing he could remember before waking was seeing the Adams express wagons at the corner of Dorrance and Broad Streets, in Providence, on his way from the store of his nephew in Broad Street to his sister's residence in Westminster Street, on January 17th."

The memory of Ansel Bourne retained absolutely nothing of the doings of A. J. Brown, whose life he had lived for nearly two months. Last year Professor William James hypnotised him, and no sooner was he put into the trance and was told to remember what happened January 17th, 1887, than he became A. J. Brown again, and gave a clear and connected narrative of all his doings in the Brown state. He did not remember ever having met Ansel Bourne. Everything, however, in his past life, he said, was "mixed up." He only remembered that he was confused, wanted to get somewhere and have rest. He did not remember how he left Norristown.

His mind was confused, and since then it was a blank. He had no memory whatever of his name or of his second marriage and the place of his birth. He remembered, however, the date of his birth, and of his first wife's death, and his trade. But between January 17th, 1887, and March 14th he was not himself but another, and that other one Albert J. Brown, who ceased to exist consciously on March 14th, but who promptly returned four years afterwards, when Ansel Bourne was hypnotised, and showed that he remembered perfectly all that happened to him between these two dates. The confusion of his two memories in his earlier life is puzzling, but it in no way impairs the value of this illustration of the existence of two independent memories—two selfs, so to speak, within a single skin.

The phenomenon is not uncommon, especially with epileptic patients. Every mad-doctor knows cases in which there are what may be described as alternating consciousnesses with alternating memories. But the experiments of the French hypnotists carry us much further. In their hands this Subconscious Personality is capable of development, of tuition, and of emancipation. In this little suspected region lies a great resource. For when the Conscious Personality is hopeless, diseased, or demoralised the Unconscious Personality can be employed to renovate and restore the patient, and then when its work is done it can become unconscious once more and practically cease to exist.

Louis V. and his two Souls. There is at present a patient in France whose case is so extraordinary that I cannot do better than transcribe the report of it here, especially because it tends to show not only that we have two personalities, but that each may use by preference a separate lobe of the brain. The Conscious Personality occupies the left and controls the right hand, the Unconscious the right side of the head and controls the left hand. It also brings to light a very curious, not to say appalling, fact, viz. the immense moral difference there may be between the Conscious and the Unconscious Personalities. In the American case Bourne was a character practically identical with Brown. In this French case the character of each self is entirely different. What makes the case still more interesting is that, besides the two personalities which we all seem to possess, this patient had an arrested personality, which was only fourteen years old when the age of his body was over forty. Here is the story, however, make of it what you will.

"Louis V. began life (in 1863) as the neglected child of a turbulent mother. He was sent to a reformatory at ten years of age, and there showed himself, as he has always done when his organization had given him a chance, quiet, well-behaved, and obedient. Then at fourteen years old he had a great fright from a viper—a fright which threw him off his balance, and started the series of psychical oscillations on which he has been tossed ever since. At first the symptoms were only physical, epilepsy and hysterical paralysis of the legs; and at the asylum of Bonneval, whither he was next sent, he worked at tailoring steadily for a couple of months. Then suddenly he had a hystero-epileptic attack—fifty hours of convulsions and ecstasy—and when he awoke from it he was no longer paralysed, no longer acquainted with tailoring, and no longer virtuous. His memory was set back, so to say, to the moment of the viper's appearance, and he could remember nothing since. His character had become violent, greedy, quarrelsome, and his tastes were radically changed. For instance, though he had before the attack been a total abstainer, he now not only drank his own wine, but stole the wine of the other patients. He escaped from Bonneval, and after a few turbulent years, tracked by his occasional relapses into hospital or madhouse, he turned up once more at the Rochefort asylum in the character of a private of marines, convicted of theft, but considered to be of unsound mind. And at Rochefort and La Rochelle, by great good fortune, he fell into the hands of three physicians—Professors Bourru and Burot, and Dr. Mabille—able and willing to continue and extend the observations which Dr. Camuset at Bonneval, and Dr. Jules Voisin at Bicêtre, had already made on this most precious of *mauvais sujets* at earlier points in his chequered career.

"He is now no longer at Rochefort, and Dr. Burot informs me that his health has much improved, and that his peculiarities have in great part disappeared. I must, however, for clearness sake, use the present tense in briefly describing his condition at the time when the long series of experiments were made.

"The state into which he has gravitated is a very unpleasing one. There is paralysis and insensibility of the right side, and, as is often the case in right hemiplegia, the speech is indistinct and difficult. Nevertheless he is constantly haranguing any one who will listen to him, abusing his physicians, or preaching—with a monkey-like impudence rather than with reasoned clearness—radicalism in politics and atheism in religion. He makes bad jokes, and if any one pleases him he endeavours to caress him. He remembers recent events during his residence at Rochefort asylum, but only two scraps of his life before that date, namely, his vicious period at Bonneval and a part of his stay at Bicêtre.

" Except this strange fragmentary memory, there is nothing very unusual in this condition, and in many asylums no experiments on it would have been attempted. Fortunately the physicians at Rochefort were familiar with the efficacy of the contact of metals in provoking transfer of hysterical hemiplegia from one side to the other. They tried various metals in turn on Louis V. Lead, silver, and zinc had no effect. Copper produced a slight return of sensibility in the paralysed arm, but steel applied to the right arm transferred the whole insensibility to the left side of the body.

" Inexplicable as such a phenomenon is, it is sufficiently common, as French physicians hold, in hysterical cases to excite little surprise. What puzzled the doctors was the change of character which accompanied the change of sensibility. When Louis V. issued from the crisis of transfer, with its minute of anxious expression and panting breath, he might fairly be called a new man. The restless insolence, the savage impulsiveness, have wholly disappeared. The patient is now gentle, respectful, and modest, can speak clearly now, but he only speaks when he is spoken to. If he is asked his views on religion and politics, he prefers to leave such matters to wiser heads than his own. It might seem that morally and mentally the patient's cure had been complete.

" But now ask what he thinks of Rochefort; how he liked his regiment of marines. He will blankly answer that he knows nothing of Rochefort, and was never a soldier in his life. ' Where are you then, and what is the date of to-day?' 'I am at Bicêtre; it is January 2nd, 1884, and I hope to see M. Voisin, as I did yesterday.'

" It is found, in fact, that he has now the memory of two short periods of life (different from those which he remembers when his right side is paralysed), periods during which, so far as now can be ascertained, his character was of this same decorous type, and his paralysis was on his left side.

" These two conditions are what are called his first and his second, out of a series of six or more through which he can be made to pass. For brevity's sake I will further describe his fifth state only.

" If he is placed in an electric bath, or if a magnet is placed on his head, it looks at first sight as though a complete physical cure had been effected. All paralysis, all defect of sensibility, has disappeared. His movements are light and active, his expression gentle and timid, but ask him where he is, and you will find that he has gone back to a boy of fourteen, that he is at St. Urbain, his first reformatory, and that his memory embraces his years of childhood, and stops short on the very day on which he had the fright from the viper. If he is pressed to recollect the incident of the viper, a violent epileptiform crisis puts a sudden end to this phase of his personality." (Vol. IV. pp. 497, 498, 499, "Proceedings of the Society for Psychical Research.")

This carries us a good deal further. Here we have not only two distinct personalities, but two distinct characters, if not three, in one body. According to the side which is paralysed, the man is a savage reprobate or a decent modest citizen. The man seems born again when the steel touches his right side. Yet all that has happened has been that the Subconscious Personality has superseded his Conscious Personality in the control of Louis V.

Lucie and Adrienne   The next case, although not marked by the same violent contrast, is quite as remarkable, because it illustrates the extent to which the Sub-conscious Self can be utilised in curing the Conscious Personality.

" The subject was a girl of nineteen, called Lucie, who was highly hysterical, having daily attacks of several hours' duration. She was also devoid of the sense of pain or the sense of contact, so that she 'lost her legs in bed,' as she put it.

"On her fifth hypnotisation, however, Lucie underwent a kind of catalepsy, after which she returned to the somnambulic state ; but that state was deeper than before. She no longer made any sign whether of assent or refusal when she received the hypnotic commands, but she executed them infallibly, whether they were to take effect immediately, or after waking.

" In Lucie's case this went further, and the suggested actions became absolutely a portion of the trance-life. She executed them without apparently knowing what she was doing. If, for instance, in her waking state she was told (in the tone which in her hypnotic state signified command) to get up and walk about, she walked about, but to judge from her conversation she supposed herself to be still sitting quiet. She would weep violently when commanded, but while she wept she continued to talk as gaily and unconcernedly as if the tears had been turned on by a stop-cock.

"Any suggestion uttered by M. Janet in a brusque tone of command reached the Unconscious Self alone; and other remarks reached the subject—awake or somnambulic—in the ordinary way. The next step was to test the intelligence of this hidden ' slave of the lamp,' if I may so term it—this subconscious and indifferent executor of all that was bidden. How far was its attention alert? How far was it capable of reasoning and judgment? M. Janet began with a simple experiment. ' When I shall have clapped my hands together twelve times,' he said to the entranced subject before awakening her, 'you will go to sleep again.' There was no sign that the sleeper understood or heard; and when she was awakened the events of the trance was a blank to her as usual. She began talking to other persons. M. Janet, at some little distance, clapped his hands feebly together five times. Seeing that she did not seem to be attending to him, he went up to her and said, ' Did you hear what I did just now?' 'No; what?' ' Do you hear this?' and he clapped his hands once more. ' Yes, you clapped your hands.' 'How often?" 'Once.' M. Janet again withdrew and clapped his hands six times gently, with pauses between the claps. Lucie paid no apparent attention, but when the sixth clap of this second series —making the twelfth altogether—was reached, she fell instantly into the trance again. It seemed, then, that the "slave of the lamp" had counted the claps through all, and had obeyed the order much as a clock strikes after a certain number of swings of the pendulum, however often you stop it between hour and hour.

"Thus far, the knowledge gained as to the unconscious element in Lucie was not direct, but inferential. The nature of the command which it could execute showed it to be capable of attention and memory; but there was no way of learning its own conception of itself, if such existed, or of determining its relation to other phenomena of Lucie's trance. And here it was that automatic writing was successfully invoked; here we have, as I may say, the first fruits in France of the new attention directed to this seldom-trodden field. M. Janet began by the following simple command: ' When I clap my hands you will write Bonjour.' This was done in the usual scrawling script of automatism, and Lucie, though fully awake, was not aware that she had written anything at all.

"M. Janet simply ordered the entranced girl to write answers to all questions of his after her waking. The command thus given had a persistent effect, and while the awakened Lucie continued to chatter as usual with other persons, her Unconscious Self wrote brief and scrawling responses to M. Janet's questions. This was the moment at which, in many cases, a new and invading separate personality is assumed.

"A singular conversation gave to this limited creation, this statutory intelligence, an identity sufficient for practical convenience. 'Do you hear me?' asked Professor Janet. Answer (by writing), 'No.' 'But in order to answer one must hear.' 'Certainly.' 'Then how do you manage?' 'I don't know.' 'There must be somebody that hears me.' 'Yes.' 'Who is it?' 'Not Lucie.' 'Oh, some one else? Shall we call her Blanche?' 'Yes, Blanche.' Blanche, however, had to be changed. Another name had to be chosen. 'What name will you have?' 'No name.' 'You must, it will be more convenient.' 'Well, then, Adrienne.' Never, perhaps, has a personality had less spontaneity about it.

"Yet Adrienne was in some respects deeper down than Lucie. She could get at the genesis of certain psychical manifestations of which Lucie experienced only the results. A striking instance of this was afforded by the phenomena of the hystero-epileptic attacks to which this patient was subject.

"Lucie's special terror, which recurred in wild exclamation in her hysterical fits, was in some way connected with hidden men. She could not, however, recollect the incident to which her cries referred ; she only knew that she had had a severe fright at seven years old, and an illness in consequence. Now, during these "crises" Lucie (except, presumably, in the periods of unconsciousness which form a pretty constant element in such attacks) could hear what Prof. Janet said to her. Adrienne, on the contrary, was hard to get at ; could no longer obey orders, and if she wrote, wrote only ' J'ai peur, j'ai peur."

"M. Janet, however, waited until the attack was over, and then questioned Adrienne as to the true meaning of the agitated scene. Adrienne was able to describe to him the terrifying incident in her childish life which had originated the confused hallucinations which recurred during the attack. She could not explain the recrudescence of the hallucinations ; but she knew what Lucie saw, and why she saw it; nay, indeed, it was Adrienne, rather than Lucie, to whom the hallucination was directly visible.

"Lucie, it will be remembered, was a hysterical patient very seriously amiss. One conspicuous symptom was an almost absolute defect of sensibility, whether to pain, to heat, or to contact, which persisted both when she was awake and entranced. There was, as already mentioned, an entire defect of the muscular sense also, so that when her eyes were shut she did not know the position of her limbs. Nevertheless it was remarked as an anomaly that when she was thrown into a cataleptic state, not only did the movements impressed upon her continue to be made, but the corresponding or complimentary movements, the corresponding facial expression, followed just as they usually follow in such experiments. Thus, if M. Janet clenched her fist in the cataleptic state, her arm began to deal blows, and her face assumed a look of anger. The suggestion which was given through the so-called muscular sense had operated in a subject to whom the muscular sense, as tested in other ways, seemed to be wholly lacking. As soon as Adrienne could be communicated with, it was possible to get somewhat nearer to a solution of this puzzle. Lucie was thrown into catalepsy ; then M. Janet clenched her left hand (she began at once to strike out), put a pencil in her right, and said, ' Adrienne, what are you doing ? ' The left hand continued to strike, and the face to bear the look of rage, while the right hand wrote, 'I am furious.' 'With whom ? ' ' With F.' ' Why ? ' ' I don't know, but I am very angry. M. Janet then unclenched the subject's left hand, and put it gently to her lips. It began to ' blow kisses,' and the face smiled. ' Adrienne, are you still angry ? ' ' No, that's over.' ' And now ? ' ' Oh, I am happy ! ' ' And Lucie ? ' ' She knows nothing ; she is asleep."

" In Lucie's case, indeed, these odd manifestations were—as the pure experimentalist might say—only too sanative, only too rapidly tending to normality. M. Janet accompanied his psychological inquiries with therapeutic suggestion, telling Adrienne not only to go to sleep when he clapped his hands, or to answer his questions in writing, but to cease having headaches, to cease having convulsive attacks, to recover normal sensibility, and so on. Adrienne obeyed, and even as she obeyed the rational command, her own Undine-like identity vanished away. The day came when M. Janet called on Adrienne, and Lucie laughed and asked him who he was talking to. Lucie was now a healthy young woman, but Adrienne, who had risen out of the unconscious, had sunk into the unconscious again—must I say ?—for evermore.

" Few lives so brief have taught so many lessons. For us who are busied with automatic writing the lesson is clear. We have here demonstrably what we can find in other cases

only inferentially, an intelligence manifesting itself continu-
ously by written answers, of purport quite outside the normal
subject's conscious mind, while yet that intelligence was but a
part, a fraction, an aspect, of the normal subject's own identity.

"And we must remember that Adrienne—while she was, if
I may say so, the Unconscious Self reduced to its simplest
expression—did, nevertheless, manifest certain differences from
Lucie, which, if slightly exaggerated, might have been very perplexing. Her handwriting was slightly different, though only
in the loose and scrawling character so frequent in automatic
script. Again, Adrienne remembered certain incidents in
Lucie's childhood which Lucie had wholly forgotten. Once
more—and this last suggestion points to positive rather than to
negative conclusions—Adrienne possessed a faculty, the muscular sense, of which Lucie was devoid. I am anxious that this
point especially should be firmly grasped, for I wish the reader's
mind to be perfectly open as regards the relative faculties of
the Conscious and the Unconscious Self. It is plain that we
must be on the watch for completion, for evolution, as well as
for partition, for dissolution, of the corporate being."

Felida X. and her Sub-merged Soul. Side by side with this case we have another in
which the Conscious Personality, instead of being
cured, has been superseded by the Sub-conscious.
It was as if instead of "Adrienne" being submerged by Lucie,
"Adrienne" became Lucie and dethroned her former master.
The woman in question, Félida X., has been transformed.

"In her case the somnambulic life has become the normal
life; the 'second state,' which appeared at first only in short,
dream-like accesses, has gradually replaced the 'first state,'
which now recurs but for a few hours at long intervals.
Félida's second state is altogether superior to the first—physically superior, since the nervous pains which had troubled
her from childhood had disappeared; and morally superior,
inasmuch as her morose, self-centred disposition is exchanged
for a cheerful activity which enables her to attend to her
children and to her shop much more effectively than when she
was in the *état bête*, as she now calls what was once the only
personality that she knew. In this case, then, which is now
of nearly thirty years' standing, the spontaneous readjustment
of nervous activities—the second state, no memory of which
remains in the first state—has resulted in an improvement
profounder than could have been anticipated from any moral
or medical treatment that we know. The case shows us how
often the word 'normal' means nothing more than 'what

happens to exist.' For Félida's normal state was in fact her morbid state; and the new condition which seemed at first a mere hysterical abnormality, has brought her to a life of bodily and mental sanity, which makes her fully the equal of average women of her class." (Vol. IV. p. 503.)

Madame B. and her three Souls. Marvellous as these cases appear, they are thrown entirely into the shade by the case of Madame B., in which the two personalities not only exist side by side, but in the case of the Sub-conscious self knowingly co-exist, while over or beneath both there is a third personality which is aware of both the other two, and apparently superior to both. The possibilities which this case opens up are bewildering indeed. But it is better to state the case first and discuss it afterwards. Madame B., who is still under Prof. Richet's observation, is one of the favourite subjects of the French hypnotiser. She can be put to sleep at almost any distance, and when hypnotised completely changes her character. There are two well-defined personalities in her, and a third of a more mysterious nature than either of the two first. The normal waking state of the woman is called Léonie I., the hypnotic state Léonie II. The third occult Unconscious Personality of the lowest depth is called Léonie III.

"'This poor peasant,' says Professor Janet, 'is in her normal state a serious and somewhat melancholy woman, calm and slow, very gentle and extremely timid. No one would suspect the existence of the person whom she includes within her. Hardly is she entranced when she is metamorphosed; her face is no longer the same; her eyes, indeed, remain closed, but the acuteness of the other senses compensates for the loss of sight. She becomes gay, noisy, and restless to an insupportable degree; she continues good-natured, but she has acquired a singular tendency to irony and bitter jests. . . . In this state she does not recognise her identity with her waking self. "That good woman is not I," she says; "she is too stupid!"'"

"Madame B. has been so often hypnotised, and during so many years (for she was hypnotised by other physicians as long ago as 1860), that Léonie II. has by this time acquired a considerable stock of memories which Madame B. does not share. Léonie II., therefore, counts as properly belonging to her own history and not to Madame B.'s all the events which have taken place while Madame B.'s normal self was hypnotised into unconsciousness. It was not always easy at first to understand this partition of past experiences.

"'Madame B. in the normal state,' says Professor Janet, 'has a husband and children. Léonie II., speaking in the somnambulistic trance, attributes the husband to the "other" (Madame B.), but attributes the children to herself. . . . At last I learnt that her former mesmerisers, as bold in their practice as certain hypnotisers of to-day, had induced somnambulism at the time of her accouchements. Léonie II., therefore, was quite right in attributing the children to herself; the rule of partition was unbroken, and the somnambulism was characterised by a duplication of the subject's existence'" (p. 391).

Still more extraordinary are Léonie II.'s attempts to make use of Léonie I.'s limbs without her knowledge or against her will. She will write postscripts to Léonie I.'s letters, of the nature of which poor Léonie I. is unconscious.

"It seems, however, that when once set up this new personality can occasionally assume the initiative, and can say what it wants to say without any prompting. This is curiously illustrated by what may be termed a conjoint epistle addressed to Professor Janet by Madame B. and her secondary self, Léonie II. 'She had left Havre more than two months when I received from her a very curious letter. On the first page was a short note written in a serious and respectful style. She was unwell, she said—worse on some days than on others— and she signed her true name, Madame B. But over the page began another letter in quite a different style, and which I may quote as a curiosity :—" My dear good sir,—I must tell you that B. really makes me suffer very much ; she cannot sleep, she spits blood, she hurts me. I am going to demolish her, she bores me. I am ill also. This is from your devoted Leontine" (the name first given to Léonie II.). When Madame B. returned to Havre I naturally questioned her concerning this curious missive. She remembered the first letter very distinctly, but she had not the slightest recollection of the second. I at first thought there must have been an attack of spontaneous somnambulism between the moment when she finished the first letter and the moment when she closed the envelope. But afterwards these unconscious, spontaneous letters became common, and I was better able to study the mode of their production. I was fortunately able to watch Madame B. on one occasion while she went through this curious performance. She was seated at a table, and held in the left hand the piece of knitting at which she had been working. Her face was calm, her eyes looked into space with a certain fixity, but she was not cataleptic, for she was humming a rustic tune ; her right hand wrote quickly, and, as it were, surreptitiously. I removed the paper without her noticing me, and then spoke to her; she turned round wide-awake but was surprised to see me, for in her state of distraction she had not noticed my approach. Of the letter which she was writing she knew nothing whatever.

"Léonie II.'s independent action is not entirely confined to writing letters. She observed (apparently) that when her primary self, Léonie I., discovered these letters she (Léonie I.) tore them up. So Léonie II. hit upon a plan of placing them in a photographic album into which Léonie I. could not look without falling into catalepsy (on account of an association of ideas with Dr. Gibert, whose portrait had been in the album). In order to accomplish an act like this Léonie II. has to wait for a moment when Léonie I. is distracted, or, as we say, absent-minded. If she can catch her in this state Léonie II. can direct Léonie I.'s walks, for instance, or start on a long railway journey without baggage, in order to get to Havre as quickly as possible."

In the whole realm of imaginative literature, is there anything to compare to this actual fact of three selves in one body, each struggling to get possession of it? Léonie I., or the Conscious Personality, is in possession normally, but is constantly being ousted by Léonie II., or the Sub-conscious Personality. It is the old, old case of the wife trying to wear the breeches. But there is a fresh terror beyond. For behind both Léonie I. and Léonie II. stands the mysterious Léonie III.

"'The spontaneous acts of the Unconscious Self,' says M. Janet, here meaning by *l'inconscient* the entity to which he has given the name of Léonie III., 'may also assume a very reasonable form—a form which, were it better understood, might perhaps serve to explain certain cases of insanity. Mme. B., during her somnambulism (*i.e.* Léonie II.) had had a sort of hysterical crisis ; she was restless and noisy and I could not quiet her. Suddenly she stopped and said to me with terror. "Oh, who is talking to me like that? It frightens me.' "No one is talking to you." "Yes ! there on the left ! " And she got up and tried to open a wardrobe on her left hand, to see if some one was hidden there. "What is that you hear?" I asked. "I hear on the left a voice which repeats, ' Enough, enough, be quiet, you are a nuisance.' " Assuredly the voice which thus spoke was a reasonable one, for Léonie II. was insupportable ; but I had suggested nothing of the kind, and had no idea of inspiring a hallucination of hearing. Another day Léonie II. was quite calm, but obstinately refused to answer a question which I asked. Again she heard with terror the same voice to the left, saying, " Come, be sensible, you must answer." Thus the Unconscious sometimes gave her excellent advice.'

" And in effect, as soon as Léonie III. was summoned into communication, she accepted the responsibility of this counsel. ' What was it that happened ? ' asked M. Janet, ' when Léonie II. was so frightened ? ' ' Oh ! nothing. It was I who told her to keep quiet ; I saw she was annoying you ; I don't know why she was so frightened.'

" Note the significance of this incident. Here we have got at the root of a hallucination. We have not merely inferential but direct evidence that the imaginary voice which terrified Léonie II. proceeded from a profounder stratum of consciousness in the same individual. In what way, by the aid of what nervous mechanism, was the startling monition conveyed ?

" Just as Mme. B. was sent, by means of passes, into a state of lethargy, from which she emerged as Léonie II., so Léonie II., in her turn, was reduced by renewed passes to a state of lethargy from which she emerged no longer as Léonie II. but as Léonie III. This second waking is slow and gradual, but the personality which emerges is, in one important point, superior to either Léonie I. or Léonie II. Although one among the subject's phases, this phase possesses the memory of every phase. Léonie III., like Léonie II., knows the normal life of Léonie I., but distinguishes herself from Léonie I., in whom, it must be said, these subjacent personalities appear to take little interest. But Léonie III. also remembers the life of Léonie II.—condemns her as noisy and frivolous, and is anxious not to be confounded with her either. ' Vous voyez bien que je ne suis pas cette bavarde, cette folle ; nous ne nous ressemblons pas du tout.' "

We ask, in amazement, how many more personalities may there not be hidden in the human frame ? Here is simple Madame B., who is not one person but three—first her commonplace self ; secondly, the clever, chattering Léonie II., who is bored by B., and who therefore wants to demolish her ; and thirdly, the lordly Léonie III., who issues commands that strike terror into Léonie II., and disdains to be identified with either of the partners in Madame B.'s body.

It is evident, if the hypnotists are right, that the human body is more like a tenement house than a single cell, and that the inmates love each other no more than the ordinary occupants of tenemented property. But how many are there of us within each skin who can say ?

Some Suggested Theories. Of theories to account for these strange phenomena there are enough and to spare. I do not for a moment venture to claim for the man-and-wife illustration the slightest scientific value. It is only a figure of speech which brings out very clearly one aspect of the problem of personality. The theory that there are two independent personalities within the human skin is condemned by all orthodox psychologists. There is one personality manifesting itself, usually consciously, but occasionally unconsciously, and the different method of manifestation differs so widely as to give the inpression that there could not be the same personality behind both. A man who is ambidextrous will sign his name differently with his right or left hand, but it is the same signature. Mr. Myers thinks that the Secondary Personality or Subliminal Consciousness is merely a phase of the essential Unity of the Ego. Some time ago he expressed himself on this subject as follows :—

" I hold that hypnotism (itself a word covering a vast variety of different states) may be regarded as constituting one special case which falls under a far wider category—the category, namely, of developments of a Secondary Personality. I hold that we each of us contain the potentialities of many different arrangements of the elements of our personality, each arrangement being distinguishable from the rest by differences in the chain of memories which pertain to it. The arrangement with which we habitually identify ourselves—what we call the normal or primary self—consists, in my view, of elements selected for us in the struggle for existence with special reference to the maintenance of ordinary physical needs, and is not necessarily superior in any other respect to the latent personalities which lie alongside of it—the fresh combinations of our personal elements which may be evoked by accident or design, in a variety to which we at present can assign no limit. I consider that dreams, with natural somnambulism, automatic writing, with so-called mediumistic trance, as well as certain intoxications, epilepsies, hysterias, and recurrent insanities, afford examples of the development of what I have called secondary mnemonic chains ; fresh personalities, more or less complete, alongside the normal state. And I would add that

hypnotism is only the name given to a group of empirical
methods of inducing these fresh personalities."

A doctor in philosophy, to whom I submitted these pages,
writes me as follows :—" There can be no doubt that every
man lives a sub-conscious as well as a conscious life.   One side
of him is closed against examination by himself (*i.e.* unconscious); the other is conscious of itself.   The former carries
on processes of separation, combination, and distribution, of
the thought-stuff handed over to it, corresponding almost
exactly to the processes carried on by the stomach, which, as
compared with those of eating, etc., go on in the dark automatically.   But you might as well ascribe the aches and
revolutions of the stomach to a second stomach, as ordinarily
these sub-conscious, mental processes to an old female inside
blindfolded except occasionally, or here and there a queer
sleep-walker."

Another doctor, not of philosophy but of medicine, who has
devoted special attention to the phenomenon of sleep, suggests
a new illustration which is graphic and suggestive.   He
writes :—

" With regard to dual or multiple consciousness, my own
feeling has always been that the *individuals* stand one behind
the other in the chambers of the mind, or else, as it were, in
concentric circles.   You may compare it to the Jewish tabernacle.   First, there is the court of the Gentiles, where Ego No.
1 chaffers about trifles with the outer world.   While he is so
doing Ego No. 2 watches him from the court of the Levites,
but does not go forth on small occasions.   When we ' open
out' to a friend the Levite comes forth, and is in turn watched
by the priest from the inner court.   Let our emotions be
stirred in sincere converse and out strides the priest, and takes
precedence of the other two, they falling obediently and
submissively behind him.   But the priest is still watched by
the high priest from the tabernacle itself, and only on great
and solemn occasions does he make himself manifest by action.
When he does, the other three yield to his authority, and
then we say the man 'speaks with his whole soul' and 'from
the bottom of his heart.'   But even now the Shekinah is upon
the mercy-seat within the Holy of holies, and the high priest
knows it."

The latest word of the French psychologists is thus stated
by M. Foüillée :—

" Contemporary psychology deprives us of the illusion of a
definitely limited, impenetrable, and absolutely autonomous I.

The conception of individual consciousness must be of an idea rather than of a substance. Though separate *in* the universe, we are not separate *from* the universe. 'Continuity and reciprocity of action exist everywhere. This is the great law and the great mystery. There is no such thing as an isolated and veritably monad being, any more than there is such a thing as an indivisible point, except in the abstractions of geometry.' "

Whatever may be the true theory, it is evident that there is enough mystery about personality to make us very difficult about dogmatising, especially as to what is possible and what is not.

Whether we have one mind or two let us, at least, keep it (or them) open.

CHAPTER I

THE THOUGHT BODY, OR THE DOUBLE

"And as Peter knocked at the door of the gate, a damsel came to hearken, named Rhoda. And when she knew Peter's voice, she ran in and told how Peter stood before the gate. And they said unto her, Thou art mad. But she constantly affirmed that it was even so. Then said they, It is his angel (or double)."—ACTS xii. 13-15.

I BEGAN to write this in the autumn of 1891 in a small country-house among the Surrey hills, whither I had retreated in order to find undisturbed leisure in which to arrange my ideas and array my facts. It was a pleasant place enough, perched on the brow of a heath-covered slope that dipped down to a ravine, at the head of which stands Professor Tyndall's house with its famous screen. Hardly a mile away northward lies the Devil's Punch Bowl, with its memorial stone erected in abhorrence of the detestable murder perpetrated on its rim by ruffians whose corpses slowly rotted as they swung on the gibbet overhead; far to the south spreads the glorious amphitheatre of hills which constitute the Highlands of the South. The Portsmouth road, along which for hundreds of years rolled to and fro the tide of martial life between London and the great Sea Gate of the Realm, lies near by, silent and almost disused. Mr. Balfour's land, on the brow of Hindhead, is enclosed but not yet built upon, although a whole archipelago of cottages and villas is springing up amid the heather as the ground slopes towards Selborne— White's Selborne—that can dimly be descried to the westward beyond Liphook Common. Memories there are, enough and to spare, of the famous days of old, and of the not less famous men of our own time; but the ghosts have fled. "There used to be a ghost in the mill," said my driver, "and another in a comparatively new house over in Lord Tennyson's direction, but we hear nothing about them now." "Not even at the Murder Stone of the Devil's Punch Bowl?" "Not even at the Murder Stone. I have driven past it at all hours, and never saw anything—but the stone, of course."

24

Yet a more suitable spot for a ghost could hardly be conceived than the rim of the Devil's Punch Bowl, where the sailor was murdered, and where afterwards his murderers were hanged. I visited it late at night, when the young moon was beginning to struggle through the cloudy sky, and looked down into the ravine which Cobbett declared was the most horrid place God ever made; but no sign of ghostly visitant could be caught among the bracken, no sound of the dead voices was audible in the air. It is the way with ghosts—they seldom appear where they might be looked for. It is the unexpected in the world of shadows, as in the workaday world, which always happens.

Of this I had soon a very curious illustration. For, although there were no ghosts in the Devil's Punch Bowl by the Murder Stone, I found that there had been a ghost in the trim new little villa in which I was quartered! It didn't appear to me—at least, it has not done so as yet. But it appeared to some friends of mine whose statement is explicit enough. Here was a find indeed. I spent most of my boyhood within a mile of the famous haunted house or mill at Willington, but I had never slept before in a place which ghosts used as a trysting-place. I asked my hostess about it. She replied, "Yes, it is quite true; but, although you may not believe it, I am the ghost." "You? How?" "Yes," she replied, quite seriously; "it is quite true what your friends have told you. They did see what you would correctly describe as an apparition. That is to say, they saw a more or less shadowy figure, which they at once identified, and which then gradually faded away. It was an apparition in the true sense of the word. It entered the room without using the door or window, it was visibly manifested before them, and then it vanished. All that is quite true. But it is also true that the ghost, as you call it, was my ghost." "Your ghost, but ——" "I am not dead, you are going to say. Precisely. But surely you must be well aware of the fact that the ghosts of the living are much better authenticated than ghosts of the dead."

My hostess was the daughter of a well-known London solicitor, who, after spending her early youth in dancing and riding and other diversions of young ladies in society who have the advantage of a house in Park Lane, suddenly became possessed by a strange, almost savage, fascination for the occult lore of the ancient East. Abandoning the frivolities of Mayfair, she went to Girton, where she plunged into the study of Sanscrit. After leaving Girton, she applied herself to the study of the occult side of Theosophy. Then she married a black magician in the platonic fashion common to Occultists, early Christians, and Russian Nihilists, and since then she has prosecuted her studies into the invisible world with ever-increasing interest.

The Thought Body. "I see you are incredulous," she replied ; "but, if you like, I will some time afford you an opportunity of proving that I am simply speaking the truth. Tell me, will you speak to me if I appear to you in my thought body ? " "Certainly," I replied, "unless I am struck dumb. Nothing would please me better. But, of course, I have never seen a ghost, and no one can say how any utterly unaccustomed experience may effect him." "Unfortunately," she replied, "that is too often the case. All those to whom I have hitherto appeared have been so scared they could not speak." "But, my dear friend, do you actually mean to say that you have the faculty of——" "Going about in my Thought Body? Most certainly. It is not a very uncommon faculty, but it is one which needs cultivation and development." "But what is a Thought Body ? " My hostess smiled : "It is difficult to explain truths on the plane of thought to those who are immersed body and soul in matter. I can only tell you that every person has, in addition to this natural body of flesh, bones, and blood, a Thought Body, the exact counterpart in every respect of this material frame. It is contained within the material body, as air is contained in the lungs and in the blood. It is of finer matter than the gross fabric of our outward body. It is capable of motion with the rapidity of thought. The laws of space and time do not exist for the mind, and the Thought Envelope of which we are speaking moves with the swiftness of the mind."

"Then when your thought body appears ? "

"My mind goes with it. I see, I hear, and my consciousness is with my Thought Envelope. But I want to have a proper interview while on my thought journeys. That is why I ask you if you would try to speak to me if I appear."

"But," I objected, "do you really mean that you hope to appear before me, in my office, as immaterial as gas, as visible as light, and yet to speak, to touch ? "

"That is just what I mean," she replied, laughing, "that and nothing less. I was in your office the other morning at six o'clock, but no one was there. I have not got this curious power as yet under complete control. But when once we are able to direct it at will, imagine what possibilities it unfolds ! "

" But," said I, " if you can be seen and touched, you ought to be photographed !"

" I wish to be photographed, but no one can say as yet whether such thought bodies can be photographed. When next I make the experiment I want you to try. It would be very useful."

Useful indeed ! It does not require very vivid imagination to see that if you can come and go to the uttermost parts of the world in your thought shape, such Thought Bodies will be indispensable henceforth on every enterprising newspaper. It would be a great saving on telegraphy. When my ideal paper comes along, I mentally vowed I would have my hostess as first member of my staff. But of course it had got to be proved, and that not only once but a dozen times, before any reliance could be placed on it.

" I often come down here," said my hostess cheerfully, " after breakfast. I just lie down in my bedroom in town, and in a moment I find myself here at Hindhead. Sometimes I am seen, sometimes I am not. But I am here ; seen or unseen, I see. It is a curious gift, and one which I am studying hard to develop and to control."

" And what about clothes ? " I asked. " Oh," replied my hostess airily, " I go in whatever clothes I like. There are astral counterparts to all our garments. It by no means follows that I appear in the same dress as that which is worn by my material body. I remember, when I appeared to your friend, I wore the astral counterpart of a white silk shawl, which was at the time folded away in the wardrobe."

At this point, however, in order to anticipate the inevitable observation that my hostess was insane, I think I had better introduce the declarations of my two friends, who are quite clear and explicit as to their recollection of what they saw.

The Evidence of the White Shawl. My witnesses are mother and daughter. The daughter I have seen and interviewed ; the mother I could not see, but took a statement down from her husband, who subsequently submitted it in proof to her for correction. I print the daughter's statement first.

" About eighteen months ago (in May, 1890) I was staying at the house of my friend in M—— Mansions. Mrs. M. had gone to her country house at Hindhead for a fortnight and was not expected back for a week. I was sitting in the kitchen reading Edna Lyall's 'Donovan.' About half-past nine o'clock I distinctly heard Mrs. M. walk up and down the passage which ran from the front door past the open door of the room in which I was sitting. I was not thinking of Mrs. M. and did not at the time realize that she was not in the flat, when suddenly I heard her voice and saw her standing at the open door. I saw her quite distinctly, and saw that she was dressed in the dress in which I had usually seen her in an evening, without bonnet or hat, her hair being plaited low down close to the back of her head. The dress, I said, was the same, but there were two differences which I noticed at once. In her usual dress, the silk front was grey ; this time the grey colour had given place to a curious amber, and over her shoulders she wore a shawl of white Indian silk. I noticed it particularly, because the roses embroidered on it at its ends did not correspond with each other. All this I saw as I looked up and heard her say, ' T——, give me that book.' I answered, half mechanically, ' Yes, Mrs. M.,' but felt somewhat startled. I had hardly spoken when Mrs. M. turned, opened the door leading into the main building, and went out. I instantly got up and followed her to the door. It was closed. I opened it and looked out, but could see nobody. It was not until then that I fully realized that there was something uncanny in what I had seen. I was very frightened, and after having satisfied myself that Mrs. M. was not in the flat, I fastened the door, put out the lights, and went to bed, burying my head under the bedclothes. The post next day brought a letter from Mrs. M. saying that she was coming by eleven o'clock. I was too frightened to stay inethe house, and I went to my father and told him what I had seyn. He told me to go back and hear what Mrs. M. had to sa about the matter. When Mrs. M. arrived I told her what I had seen on the preceding evening. She laughed, and said, ' Oh'! I was here then, was I ? I did not expect to come here. With that exception I have seen no apparition whatever, or had any hallucination of any kind, neither have I seen the apparition of Mrs. M. again."

After hearing this statement I asked Mrs. M. what she meant by the remark she had made on hearing Miss C.'s explanation of what she had witnessed. My hostess replied, " That night when I passed into the trance state, and lay down on the couch in the sitting-room at Hindhead, I did so with the desire of visiting my husband, who was in his retreat at Wimbledon. That, I should say, was between nine and half-past. After I came out of the trance I was conscious that I had been somewhere, but I did not know where. I started from Hindhead for Wimbledon, but landed at M—— Mansions, where, no doubt, I was more at home." "Then you had no memory of where you had been?" "Not the least." "And what about the shawl?" "The shawl was one that Miss C. had never seen. I had not worn it for two years, and the fact that she saw it and described it, is conclusive evidence against the subjective character of the vision. The originals of all the phantom clothes were at M—— Mansions at the time Miss C. saw me wearing them. I was not wearing the shawl. At the time when she saw it on my Thought Body it was folded up and put away in a wardrobe in an adjoining room. She had never seen it." I asked Miss C. what was the appearance of Mrs. M. She replied, "She just looked as she does always, only much more beautiful." "How do you account," said I to my hostess, "for the change in colour of the silk front from grey to amber?" She replied, "It was a freak."

Haunted by a Thought Body. I then asked Mr. C., the father of the last witness, what had occurred in his wife's experience. He said, "Here is a statement which my wife made to me, and which you can rely upon as correct. 'I was staying at Hindhead, in the lodge connected with the house in which you are staying. I was in some trouble, and Mrs. M. had been somewhat anxious about me. I had gone to sleep, but was suddenly aroused by the consciousness that some one was bending over me. When I opened my eyes I saw in shimmering outline a figure which I recognised at once as that of Mrs. M. She was bending over me, and her great lustrous eyes seemed to pierce my very soul. For a time I lay still, as if paralysed, being unable either to speak or to move, but at last gaining courage with time I ventured to strike a match. As soon as I did so the figure of Mrs. M. disappeared. Feeling reassured and persuaded that I had been deluded by my senses, I at last put out the light and composed myself to sleep. To my horror, no sooner was the room dark than I saw the spectral, shimmering form of Mrs. M. moving about the room, and always turning towards me those wonderful, piercing eyes. I again struck a match, and again the apparition vanished from the room. By this time I was in a mortal terror, and it was some time before I ventured to put out the light again, when a third time I saw the familiar presence which had evidently never left the room but simply been invisible in the light. In the dark it shone by its own radiance. I was taken seriously ill with a violent palpitation of the heart, and kept my light burning. I felt so utterly upset that I could not remain any longer in the place and insisted next morning on going home. I did not touch the phantom, I simply saw it—saw it three times, and its haunting persistency rendered it quite impossible for me to mistake it for any mere nightmare.'"

Neither Mrs. nor Miss C. have had any other hallucinations, and Mrs. C. is strongly sceptical. She does not deny the accuracy of the above statement, but scouts the theory of a Thought Body, or of any supernatural or occult explanation. On hearing Mrs. C.'s evidence I asked my hostess whether she was conscious of haunting her guest in this way. "I knew nothing about it," she replied ; "all that I know was that I had been much troubled about her and was anxious to help her. I went into a very heavy, deep sleep ; but until next morning, when I heard of it from Mrs. C. I had no idea that my double had left my room." I said, "This power is rather gruesome, for you might take to haunting me." "I do not think so, unless there was something to be gained which could not be otherwise secured, some benefit to be conferred upon you." "That is to say, if I were in trouble or dangerously ill, and you were anxious about me, your double might come and attend my sick-bed." "That is quite possible," she said imperturbably. "Well," said I, "when are you coming to be photographed?" "Not for many months yet," she replied, with a laugh. "For the Thought Body to leave its corporeal tenement it needs a considerable concentration of thought, and an absence of all disturbing conditions or absorbing preoccupations at the time. I see no reason why I should not be photographed when the circumstances are propitious. I shall be very glad to furnish you with that evidence of the reality of the Thought Body, but such things cannot be fixed up to order."

This, indeed, was a ghost to some purpose—a ghost free from all the weird associations of death and the grave—a healthy, utilisable ghost, and a ghost, above all, which wanted to be photographed. It seemed too good to be true. Yet how strange it was! Here we have just been discussing whether or not we have each of us two souls, and, behold ! my good hostess tells me quite calmly that it is beyond all doubt that we have two bodies.

I asked Mrs. Besant whether she thought my *Mrs. Besant's* hostess was romancing, and whether my friends *Theory.* had not been the victim of some illusion. "Oh, no," said Mrs. Besant cheerfully. "There is nothing improbable about it. Very possibly she has this faculty. It is not so uncommon as you think. But its exercise is rather dangerous, and I hope she is well instructed." "How?" I asked. "Oh," Mrs. Besant replied, "it is all right if she knows what she is about, but it is just as dangerous to go waltzing about on the astral plane as it is for a girl to go skylarking down a dark slum when roughs are about. Elementals, with the desire to live, greedily appropriating the vitality and the passions of men, are not the pleasantest companions. Nor can other astrals of the dead, who have met with sudden or violent ends, and whose passions are unslaked, be regarded as desirable acquaintances. If she knows what she is about, well and good. But otherwise she is like a child playing with dynamite."

"But what is an astral body?"

Mrs. Besant replied, "There are several astrals, each with its own characteristics. The lowest astral body taken in itself is without conscience, will, or intelligence. It exists as a mere shadowy phantasm only as long as the material body lasts." "Then the mummies in the Museum?" "No doubt a clairvoyant could see their astrals keeping their silent watch by the dead. As the body decays so the astral fades away." "But that implies the possibility of a decaying ghost?" "Certainly. An old friend of mine, a lady who bears a well-known name, was once haunted for months by an astral. She was a strong-minded girl, and she didn't worry. But it was rather ghastly when the astral began to decay. As the corpse decomposed the astral shrank, until at last, to her great relief, it entirely disappeared."

Mrs. Besant mentioned the name of the lady, who is well known to many of my readers, and one of the last to be suspected of such haunting.

Three other Aerial Wanderers. A short time after hearing from my hostess this incredible account of her aerial journeyings, I received first hand from three other ladies, statements that they had also enjoyed this faculty of bodily duplication. All four ladies are between twenty and forty years of age. Three of them are married. The first says she has almost complete control over her movements, but for the most part her phantasmal envelope is invisible to those whom she visits.

This, it may be said, is mere conscious clairvoyance, in which the faculty of sight was accompanied by the consciousness of bodily presence, although it is invisible to other eyes.

It is, besides, purely subjective and therefore beside the mark.
Still, it is interesting as embodying the impressions of a mind,
presumably sane, as to the experiences through which it has
consciously passed.   On the same ground I may refer to the
experience of Miss X., the second lady referred to, who, when
lying, as it was believed, at the point of death, declares that
she was quite conscious of coming out of her body and looking
at it as it lay in the bed.   In all the cases I have yet mentioned
the departure of the phantasmal body is accompanied by a state
of trance on the part of the material body.   There is not dual
consciousness, but only a dual body, the consciousness being
confined to the immaterial body.

It is otherwise with the experience of the fourth wanderer
in my text.   Mrs. Wedgwood, the daughter-in-law of Mr.
Hensleigh Wedgwood, the well-known philologist, who was
Charles Darwin's cousin, declares that she had once a very
extraordinary experience.   She was lying on a couch in an
upper room one wintry morning at Shorncliffe, when she felt
her Thought Body leave her and, passing through the window,
alight on the snowy ground.   She was distinctly conscious
both in her material body and in its immaterial counterpart.
She lay on the couch watching the movements of the second
self, which at the same moment felt the snow cold under its
feet.   The second self met a labourer and spoke to him.   He
replied as if somewhat scared.   The second self walked down
the road and entered an officer's hut, which was standing
empty.   She noted the number of guns.   There were a score
or more of all kinds in all manner of places ; remarked upon
the quaint looking-glass ; took a mental inventory of the
furniture ; and then, coming out as she went in, she regained
her material body, which all the while lay perfectly conscious
on the couch.   Then, when the two selves were reunited, she
went down to breakfast and described where she had been.
" Bless me," said an officer, who was one of the party, " if you
have not been in Major ——'s hut.   You have described it
exactly, especially the guns, which he has a perfect mania for
collecting."

Here the immaterial body was not only visible but audible,
and that not merely to the casual passer-by, but also to the
material body which had for the moment parted with one of
its vital constituents without losing consciousness.

It must, of course, be admitted that, with the exception of
the statement by my two friends as to the apparition of Mrs.
M.'s immaterial body, none of the other statements can pre-

tend to the slightest evidential value. They may be worth as much as the confessions of the witches who swore they were dancing with Satan while their husbands held their material bodies clasped in their arms; but any explanation of subjective hallucination or of downright lying would be preferred by the majority of people to the acceptance of the simple accuracy of these statements. The phenomenon of the aerial flight is, however, not unfamiliar to those who are interested in this subject.

The evidence of the Psychical Research Society. I confess, as I revise these pages, to a feeling of shame that Mrs. M.'s statement should have seemed to me so utterly incredible. My suprise and incredulity simply proved that I had never read the great text-book on the subject, "The Phantasms of the Living," by Messrs. Gurney, Myers, and Podmore, in which the phenomenon is shown to be comparatively frequent. "M.A.," of Oxon, in his most interesting and suggestive weekly paper *Light*, began a synopsis of the evidence as to the reality of the Thought Body. The Psychical Research Society have about a hundred recorded instances of the apparition of the Thought Body. I will only quote here two or three of the more remarkable cases mentioned in these imposing volumes.

The Thought Body of a Stockbroker. The best case, however, of the projection of the Thought Body at will is that described, under the initials of "S. H. B.," in the first volume of the "Phantasms," pp. 104–109. Mr. B. is a member of the Stock Exchange, who is well known to many intimate friends of mine as a man of high character. The narrative, which is verified by the Psychical Research Society, places beyond doubt the existence of powers in certain individuals which open up an almost illimitable field of mystery and speculation. Mr. B.'s story, in brief, is this :—

"One Sunday night in November, 1881, I was in Kildare Gardens, when I willed very strongly that I would visit in spirit two lady friends, the Misses V., who were living three miles off in Hogarth Road. I willed that I should do this at one o'clock in the morning, and having willed it I went to sleep. Next Thursday, when I first met my friends, the elder lady told me she woke up and saw my apparition advancing to her bedside. She screamed and woke her sister, who also saw me." (A signed statement by both sisters accompanies this narrative. They fix the time at one o'clock, and say that Mr. B. wore evening dress.)

"On December 1st, 1882, I was at Southall. At half-past

nine I sat down to endeavour to fix my mind so strongly upon
the interior of a house at Kew, where Miss V. and her sister
lived, that I seemed to be actually in the house. I was conscious, but I was in a kind of mesmeric sleep. When I went
to bed that night I willed to be in the front bedroom of that
house at Kew at twelve, and make my presence felt by the
inmates. Next day I went to Kew. Miss V.'s married sister
told me, without any prompting from me, that she had seen
me in the passage going from one room to another at half-past
nine o'clock, and that at twelve, when she was wide awake,
she saw me come into the front bedroom where she slept and
take her hair, which is very long, into my hand. She said I
then took her hand and gazed into the palm intently. She
said, ' You need not look at the lines, for I never had any
trouble.' She then woke her sister. When Mrs. L. told me
this I took out the entry I had made the previous night and
read it to her. Mrs. L. is quite sure she was not dreaming.
She had only seen me once before, two years previously, at a
fancy ball.

"On March 22nd, 1884, I wrote to Mr. Gurney, of the
Psychical Research Society, telling him I was going to make
my presence felt by Miss V., at 44, Norland Square, at midnight. Ten days afterwards I saw Miss V., when she volun-
tarily told me that on Saturday at midnight she distinctly saw
me, when she was quite widely awake. I came towards her
and stroked her hair. She adds in her written statement,
' The appearance in my room was most vivid and quite unmistakable.' I was then at Ealing."

Here there is the thrice-repeated projection at will of the
Thought Body through space so as to make it both visible to,
and tangible by, friends. But the Conscious Personality
which willed the visit has not yet unlocked the memory of his
unconscious partner, and Mr. B., although able to go and see
and touch, could bring back no memory of his aerial flight.
All that he knew was that he willed and then he slept. The
fact that he appeared is attested not by his consciousness, but
by the evidence of those who saw him.

A Visitor from Burmah. Here is a report of the apparition of a Thought
Body, the material original of which was at the
time in Burmah. The case is important, because
the Thought Body was not recognised at the time, showing
that it could not have been a subjective revival of the memory
of a face. It is sent me by a gentleman in South Kensington,
who wishes to be mentioned only by his initials, R. S. S.

W 1555158

"Towards the close of 1888 my son, who had obtained an appointment in the Indian Civil Service, left England for Burmah.

"A few days after his arrival in Rangoon he was sent up the country to join the District Commissioner of a district still at that period much harassed by Dacoits.

"After this two mails passed by without news of him, and as, up to this period, his letters had reached us with unfailing regularity, we had a natural feeling of anxiety for his safety. As the day for the arrival of the third mail drew near I became quite unreasonably apprehensive of bad news, and in this state of mind I retired one evening to bed, and lay awake till long past the middle of the night, when suddenly, close to my bedside, appeared very distinctly the figure of a young man. The face had a worn and rather sad expression; but in the few seconds during which it was visible the impression was borne in upon me that the vision was intended to be reassuring.

"I cannot explain why I did not at once associate this form with my son, but it was so unlike the hale, fresh-looking youth we had parted from only four or five months previously that I supposed it must be his chief, whom I knew to be his senior by some five years only.

"I retailed this incident to my son by the next mail, and was perplexed when I got his reply to hear that his chief was a man with a beard and moustache, whereas the apparition was devoid of either. A little later came a portrait of himself recently taken. It was the subject of my vision, of which the traits had remained, and still remain, in every detail, perfectly distinct in my recollection."

Thought visits seen and remembered. Here is an account of a visit paid at will, which is reported at first hand in the "Proceedings of the Psychical Research Society." The narrator, Mr. John Moule, tells how he determined to make an experiment of the kind now under discussion :—

"I chose for this purpose a young lady, a Miss Drasey, and stated that some day I intended to visit her, wherever the place might be, although the place might be unknown to me ; and told her if anything particular should occur to note the time, and when she called at my house again to state if anything had occurred. One day, about two months after (I not having seen her in the interval), I was by myself in my chemical factory, Redman Row, Mile End, London, all alone, and I determined to try the experiment, the lady being in Dalston, about three miles off. I stood, raised my hands, and willed to act on the lady. I soon felt that I had expended energy. I immediately sat down in a chair and went to sleep. I then saw in a dream my friend coming down the kitchen stairs where I dreamt I was. She saw me, and exclaimed suddenly, 'Oh! Mr. Moule,' and fainted away. This I dreamt and then awoke. I thought very little about it, supposing I had had an ordinary dream ; but about three weeks after she came to my house and related to my wife the singular occurrence of her seeing me sitting in the kitchen where she then was, and she fainted away and nearly dropped some dishes she had in her hands. All this I saw exactly in my dream, so that I described the kitchen furniture and where I sat as perfectly as if I had been there, though I had never been in the house. I gave many details, and she said, 'It is just as if you had been there.' " (Vol. III. pp. 420, 421.)

Mr. W. A. S., to quote another case, in April, 1871, at two o'clock in the afternoon, was sitting in a house in Pall Mall. He saw a lady glide in backwards at the door of the room, as if she had been slid in on a slide, each part of her dress keeping its proper place without disturbance. She glided in until the whole of her could be seen, except the tip of her nose, her lips, and the tip of her chin, which were hidden by the edge of the door. She was an old acquaintance of his, whom he had not seen for twenty or twenty-five years. He observed her closely until his brother entered the house, and coming into the room passed completely through the phantasm, which shortly afterwards faded away. Another person in the room could not see it. Some years afterwards he learned that she had died the same year, six months afterwards, from a painful cancer of the face. It was curious that the phantasm never showed him the front of its face, which was always hid by the door. (Vol. II. p. 517.)

One of the cases mentioned in Vol. I. p. 226 of the " Proceedings of the Psychical Society," that of the Rev. Mr. Newnham, will probably induce many lovers to reproduce that phantasmal experience. I mention it, but do not dwell upon it. It opens up a vista of possibilities, which taken in connection with certain well-known phenomena treated by De Foe, in his " Natural History of the Devil," might carry us further than we should care to go.

Dr. F. R. Lees's Double. Another case in which the double appeared was that of Dr. F. R. Lees, the well-known temperance controversialist. On communicating with the Doctor, the following is his reply :—

"The little story or incident of which you have heard, occurred above thirty years ago, and may be related in very few words. Whether it was coincidence, or transference of vivid thought, I leave to the judgment of others.

"I had left Leeds for the Isle of Jersey (though my dear wife was only just recovering from a nervous fever), to fulfil an important engagement. On a Good Friday, myself and a party of friends in several carriages drove round a large portion of the island, coming back to St. Heliers from Boulay Bay, taking tea about seven o'clock at Captain ——'s villa. The party broke up about ten o'clock, and the weather being fine and warm, I walked to the house of a banker who entertained me. Naturally my evening thoughts reverted to my home, and after reading a few verses in my Testament, I walked about the room until nearly eleven, thinking of my wife, and breathing the prayer, 'God bless you.'

"I might not have recalled all the circumstances, save for the letter I received by the next post from her, with the query put in : 'Tell me what you were *doing within a few minutes of eleven o'clock* on Friday evening? I will tell you in my next why I ask ; for something happened to me.' In the middle of the week the letter came, and these words in it :—' I had just awoke from a slight repose, when I saw you in your night-dress bend over me, and utter the words, " God bless you ! " I seemed also to feel your breath as you kissed me. I felt no alarm, but comforted, went off into a gentle sleep, and have been better ever since.' I replied that this was an exact representation of my mind and words."

Here there was apparently the instantaneous reproduction in Leeds of the image, and not only of the image, but of the words spoken in Jersey, a hundred miles away. The theory that the phantasmal body is occasionally detachable from the material frame accounts for this in a fashion, and that is more than can be said for any other hypothesis that has yet been stated. In neither of these cases did an early death follow the apparition of the dual body.

A Mother's Double seen by her Daughter. I have received from a valued correspondent, Mrs. Mary A. M. Marks, a statement of her experience on the occasion when she saw the wraith of her mother, which I reproduce here.

The circumstance I am about to relate took place when I was just ten years old. My father, the late Professor Hoppus, of University College, London, lived in Camden Street, Camden Town. As in most houses of the same date, the drawing-

rooms were on the first floor, and communicated by folding
doors, each having, of course, a door on the landing. My
mother had been ill for three years ; the back drawing-room
was her bedroom. She was not confined to bed, but spent
most of the day on a sofa in the front drawing-room. Somewhere about 10 o'clock in the morning—as I remember, though
winter, it was rather bright—I was coming downstairs from
my own room on the second floor. I wanted some one to tie
my pinafore, and I was looking for my nurse. As I came
down, I saw that the door (on the landing) of the front room
was shut, but the door of the bedroom was wide open. I
knew therefore that my mother was probably already gone into
the front room, and I expected to find my nurse making the
bed. But when I reached the landing, and could see into the
back room, I saw my mother standing near the farther wall—
at most not more than five yards from me—close to the hot-
water pipes of the Arnott stove, which my father had had put up
for her comfort. I distinctly saw her tall figure, wrapped in
the blue-and-white striped dressing-gown she usually wore in
the daytime. In those days people wore nightcaps—hers was
on her head ; her face was turned away from me and towards
the wall. The folding doors were closed. I did not expect
to find my mother there at that hour, but the figure was as
distinct and seeming solid as reality, and I have never been
able to explain to myself the feeling which withheld me from
going up to her, and asking her to tie my pinafore. I did not
go in ; I opened the door of the front room and looked in.
As I somehow expected, I saw my mother there, asleep on the
sofa, in her blue-and-white gown.

"My father, who had a great horror of children being
frightened by ghost stories, had told me that garments, etc.,
had sometimes given rise to these stories, by real or fancied
resemblances to a human form. In spite of his attempts to
shield me from such knowledge, I had read a little about
'Second Sight,' and I determined to see whether anything of
this kind could have deceived me. I accordingly went at
once into the bedroom. The figure was no longer there, and
I could find nothing—not so much as a towel—near the spot
where scarcely a minute before I had seen my mother standing—except those dark-bronze pipes, which would not have
come much above her knee as she stood, and which no trick
of vision could have transformed into a tall white-and-blue
figure. My nurse was not there. I do not think I felt
frightened, but I remember now the dull pang with which I

thought—when I found it impossible to account for the appearance—'Then my mother will not get well.' She, however, did not die for six months. I told no one of what I had seen for many years—not until after I grew up. I have never had any other experience of the same kind."

Aimless Doubles. The following curious experience is sent me by a commercial traveller, who gives his name and address in support of his testimony. Writing from Nottingham, he says :—

"On Tuesday, the 6th October, I had a very singular experience. I am a commercial traveller, and represent a firm of cigar manufacturers. I left my hotel about four o'clock on the above date to call upon a customer, a Mr. Southam, Myton Gate, Hull. I met this gentleman in the street, nearly opposite his office ; he shook hands, and said, ' How are you ? I am waiting to see a friend ; I don't think I shall want any cigars this journey, but look in before eight o'clock.' I called at 7.30, and spoke to the clerk in the office. He said, ' Mr. Southam has made out your cheque, and there is also a small order.' I said, ' Thanks, I should have liked to have seen him ; he made an appointment this afternoon for about eight.' Clerk says, ' Where ? ' I said, ' Just outside.' He said, ' That is impossible, as both Mr. and Mrs. Southam have been confined to their room for a fortnight and never been out.' I said, ' How strange. I said to Mr. S——, "You look different to your usual ; what's the matter with you ?" Mr. S—— said, ' Don't you see I am in my *deshabille* ?' The clerk remarked, ' You must have seen his second self, for he has not been up to-day.' I came away feeling very strange.

"J. P. BROOKS.
"Sydney Villa, Ratcliffe Road, Bridgeford."

Mrs. Eliz. G. L——, of H—— House, sends me the following report of her experience of the double. She writes :—

"The only time I ever saw an apparition was on the evening of the last day of May, 1860. The impression then made is yet most vivid, and the day seldom recurs without my thinking of what happened then.

"It was a little after seven o'clock, the time for my husband's return from business. I was passing through the hall into the dining-room, where tea was laid, when (the front door being open) I saw my husband coming up the garden path, which was in a direct line with the hall. It was broad daylight, and nothing obstructed my view of him, and he was not more than nine or ten yards from me. Instead of going to him, I turned back, and said to the servant in the kitchen, 'Take tea in immediately, your master is come.' I then went into the dining-room, expecting him to be there. To my great surprise the room was empty, and there was no one in the garden. As my father was very ill in the next house but one to ours, I concluded that Mr. L—— had suddenly determined to turn back and enquire how he was before having tea. In half an hour he came into the room to me, and I asked how my father was, when, to my astonishment, he told me that he had not called, but had come home direct from the town. I said, ' *You were in the garden half an hour ago*, I saw you as distinctly as I see you *now* ; if you were not there *then*, you are not here *now*,' and I grasped his arm as I spoke to convince myself that it was really he. I thought that my husband was teasing me by his repeated denials, and that he would at last confess he was really there ; and it was only when he assured me in the most positive and serious manner that he was a mile away at the time I saw him in the garden, that I could believe him. I have never been able to account for the appearance. There was no one I could possibly have mistaken for Mr. L——. I was in good health at the time, and had no illness for long afterwards. My mother is still living, and she can corroborate my statement, and bear witness to the deep impression the occurrence made upon me. I *saw* my husband as plainly as I have ever seen him since during the many years we have lived together."

Mr. Robert Kidd, of Gray Street, Broughty
Two Dundee
Doubles. Ferry, who has filled many offices in Dundee, having been twenty-five years a police commissioner and five years a magistrate there, sends me the following report of two cases of the double :—

"A few years ago I had a shop on the High Street of Dundee—one door and one window, a cellar underneath, the entrance to which was at one corner of the shop. There was no way of getting in or out of the cellar but by that stair in the corner. It was lighted from the street by glass, but to protect that there was an iron grating, which was fixed down. Well, I had an old man, a servant, named Robert Chester. I sent him a message one forenoon about 12 o'clock ; he was in no hurry returning. I remarked to my daughter, who was book-keeper, whose desk was just by the trap-door, that he was stopping long. Just as I spoke he passed the window, came in at the door, carrying a large dish under his arm, went right past me, past my daughter, who looked at him, and went down into the cellar. After a few minutes, as I heard no noise, I remarked what he could be about, and went down to see. There was no Robert there. I cannot tell what my sensations were when I realized this ; there was no possibility of his getting out, and we both of us saw and heard him go down. Well, in about twenty minutes he re-passed the window, crossed the floor, and went downstairs, exactly as in the first time. There was no hallucination on our part. My daughter is a clever, highly-gifted woman ; I am seventy-eight years of age, and have seen a great deal of the world, a great reader, etc., etc., and not easily deceived or apt to be led away by fancy, and I can declare that his first appearance to us was a reality as much as the second. We concluded, and so did all his relations, that it portended his death, but he is still alive, over eighty years of age. I give this just as it occurred, without any varnish or exaggeration whatever. The other I firmly believe, as I knew the parties well, and that every means were used to prove its truthfulness.

" Mr. Alexander Drummond was a painter, who had a big business and a large staff of men. His clerk was Walter Souter, his brother-in-law. His business was to be at the shop (in Northgate, Dundee) sharp at six o'clock in the morning, to take an account of where the men were going, quantity of material, etc. In this he was assisted by Miss Drummond. One morning he did not turn up at the hour, but at twenty past six he came in at the door and appeared very much excited ; but instead of stepping to the desk, where Mr. and Miss Drummond were awaiting him, he went right through the front shop and out at a side door. This in sight of Mr. and Miss D——, and also in sight of a whole squad of workmen. Well, exactly in another twenty minutes he came in, also very much excited, and explained that it was twenty minutes past six when he awakened, and that he had run all the way from his house (he lived a mile from the place of business). He was a very exemplary, punctual man, and when Mr. Drummond asked him where he went to when he came first, he was dumbfounded, and could not comprehend what was meant. To test his truthfulness, Mr. D—— went out to his wife that afternoon, when she told him the same story : that it was twenty past six o'clock when he awoke, and that he was very much excited about it, as it was the first time he had slept in. This story I believe as firmly as in my own case, as it was much talked about at the time, and I have just told it as it was told to me by all the parties. Of course I am a

total stranger to you, and you may require to know something
about me before believing my somewhat singular stories. I
am well known about here, have filled many offices in Dundee,
and have been twenty-five years a police commissioner, and
five years a magistrate in this place, am very well known to the
Right Honourable C. Ritchie, and also to our county member,
Mr. Barclay. If this little story throws any light upon our
wondrous being I shall be glad."

A Manchester Parallel. The following narrative, supplied by Mr. R. P.
Roberts, 10, Exchange Street, Manchester, appears
in the " Proceedings of the Psychical Research
Society." It is a fitting pendant to Mr. Kidd's story :—

" The shop stood at the corner of Castle Street and Rating
Row, Beaumaris, and I lived in the latter street. One day
I went home to dinner at the usual hour. When I had
partly finished I looked at the clock. To my astonishment it
appeared that the time by the clock was 12.30. I gave an
unusual start. I certainly thought that it was most extraordinary. I had only half-finished my dinner, and it was time
for me to be at the shop. I felt dubious, so in a few seconds
had another look, when to my agreeable surprise I found that
I had been mistaken. It was only just turned 12.15. I could
never explain how it was I made the mistake. The error gave
me such a shock for a few minutes as if something had
happened, and I had to make an effort to shake off the sensation. I finished my dinner, and returned to business at 12.30.
On entering the shop I was accosted by Mrs. Owen, my
employer's wife, who used to assist in the business. She
asked me rather sternly where I had been since my return
from dinner. I replied that I had come straight from dinner.
A long discussion followed, which brought out the following
facts. About a quarter of an hour previous to my actual
entering the shop (i.e. about 12.15), I was seen by Mr. and
Mrs. Owen and a well-known customer, Mrs. Jones, to walk
into the shop, go behind the counter, and place my hat upon
the peg. As I was going behind the counter, Mrs. Owen
remarked, with the intention that I should hear, ' that I had
arrived now that I was not wanted.' This remark was
prompted by the fact that a few minutes previous a customer
was in the shop in want of an article which belonged to the
stock under my charge, and which could not be found in my
absence. As soon as this customer left I was seen to enter
the shop. It was observed by Mr. and Mrs. Owen and Mrs.
Jones that I did not appear to notice the remark made. In

fact, I looked quite absent-minded and vague. Immediately after putting my hat on the peg I returned to the same spot, put my hat on again, and walked out of the shop, still looking in a mysterious manner, which incensed one of the parties, I think Mrs. Owen, to say that my behaviour was very odd, and she wondered where I was off to.

"I, of course, contradicted these statements, and endeavoured to prove that I could not have eaten my dinner and returned in a quarter of an hour. This, however, availed nothing, and during our discussion the above-mentioned Mrs. Jones came into the shop again, and was appealed to at once by Mr. and Mrs. Owen. She corroborated every word of their account, and added that she saw me coming down Rating Row when within a few yards of the shop; that she was only a step or two behind me, and entered the shop in time to hear Mrs. Owen's remarks about my coming too late. These three persons gave their statement of the affair quite independently of each other. There was no other person near my age in the Owens' establishment, and there could be no reasonable doubt that my form had been seen by them and by Mrs. Jones. They would not believe my story until my aunt, who had dined with me, said positively that I had not left the table before my time was up. You will, no doubt, notice the coincidence. At the moment when I felt, with a startling sensation, that I ought to be at the shop, and when Mr. and Mrs. Owen were extremely anxious that I should be there, I appeared to them looking, as they said, 'as if in a dream or in a state of somnambulism.'" ("Proceedings of the Psychical Research Society," Vol. I. p. 135–6.)

A very visible Double. A correspondent, writing from a Yorkshire village, sends me the following account of an apparition of a Thought Body in circumstances when there was nothing more serious than a yearning desire on the part of a person whose phantasm appeared to occupy his old bed. My correspondent, Mr. J. G——, says that he took it down from the lips of one of the most truthful men he ever knew, and a sensible person to boot. This person is still living, and I am told he has confirmed Mr. G——'s story, which is as follows :—

"Sixty years ago I was a farm servant at a place in Pembrokeshire (I can give the name, but don't wish it to be published). I was about fifteen years old. I, along with three other men-servants, slept in a granary in the yard. Our bedchamber was reached by means of ten broad stone steps. It was soon after Allhallows time, when all farm servants change places in that part of the country. A good and faithful foreman, who had been years on the farm, had this time desired a change, and had engaged to service some fifteen miles off, a change which he afterwards much regretted.

"One night I woke up in my bed some time during the small hours of the morning, and obedient to the call of nature, I got up, opened the door, and stood on the upper step of the stairs. It was a beautiful moonlight night. I surveyed the yard and the fields about. To my surprise, but without the least apprehension, I noticed a man coming down a field, jump over a low wall, and walk straight towards me. He stepped the three first steps one by one, then he took two or three steps at a stride. I knew the man well and recognised him perfectly. I knew all the clothes he wore, particularly a light waistcoat which he put on on great occasions. As he drew near me I receded to the doorway, and as he lifted up his two hands, as in the act of opening the door, which was open already, I fled in screaming, and passing my own bed jumped in between two older men in the next bed. And neither time nor the sympathy of my comrades could pacify me for hours.

"I told my tale, which, after searching and seeing nobody, they disbelieved and put down to my timidity.

"Next morning, however, just as we were coming out from breakfast, in the presence of all of us the discharged foreman was seen coming down the same field, jumping the wall, walk toward the sleeping chamber, ascend the steps, lifting up his two hands to open the door in the self-same manner in every particular as I had described, and went straight to the same bed as I got into.

"I asked him, 'Were you here last night, John?'

"'No, my boy,' was the answer; 'my body was not here but my mind was. I have run away from that horrid place, travelled most of the night, and every step I took my mind was fixed on this old bed, where my weary bones might be at rest.'"

I can supply names and all particulars, but do not wish them to be published.

Seeing your own Thought Body. In his "Footfalls," Mr. Owen records a still more remarkable case of the duplication of the body. A gentleman in Ohio, in 1833, had built a new house, seventy or eighty yards distant from his old residence on the other side of a small ravine. One afternoon, about five o'clock, his wife saw his eldest daughter, Rhoda, aged sixteen, holding the youngest, Lucy, aged four, in her arm, sitting in a rocking-chair just within the kitchen door of the new residence. She called the attention of another sister to what she saw, and was startled to hear that Rhoda and Lucy were upstairs in the old house. They were at once sent for, and on coming downstairs they saw, to their amazement, their exact doubles sitting on the doorstep of the new house. All the family collected—twelve in all—and they all saw the phantasmal Rhoda and Lucy, the real Rhoda and Lucy standing beside them. " The figures seated at the hall door, and the two children now actually in their midst, were absolutely identical in appearance, even to each minute particular of dress." After watching them for five minutes, the father started to cross the ravine and solve the mystery. Hardly had he descended the ravine when the phantasmal Rhoda rose from the rocky chair, with the child in her arms, and lay down on the threshold. There she remained a moment or two, and then apparently sank into the earth. When the father reached the house no trace could be found of any human being. Both died within a year.

A correspondent of my own, a dressmaker in the North of England, sends me the following circumstantial account of how she saw her own double without any mischief following :—

" I have a sewing-machine, with a desk at one side and carved legs supporting the desk part; on the opposite side the machine part is. The lid of the machine rests on the desk part when open, so that it forms a high back. I had this machine across the corner of a room, so that the desk part formed a triangle with the corner of the room. I sat at the machine with my face towards the corner. To my left was the window, to my right the fire; at each side of my chair the doors of the machine walled me in as I sat working the treadles. Down each side of the machine are imitations of drawers. The wood is a beautiful walnut. I was sewing a long piece of material, which passed from left to right. It was dinner-time, so I looked down to see how much more I had to do. It was almost finished, but there, in the space near the window, between the wall and the machine, was a full-sized figure of myself from the waist upwards. The image was lower than myself, but clear enough, with brown hair and eyes. How earnestly the eyes regarded me; how thoughtfully! I laughed and nodded at the image, but still it gazed earnestly at me. At its neck was a bright red bow, coming unpinned. Its white linen collar was turned up at the right-hand corner. When I got down to dinner I told my brother George I had seen Pepper's Ghost, and it was a distinct image of myself, clear enough, and yet I could see the wall and the side of the machine through the image, and George said, ' Had it a red bow and white collar on ? ' ' Oh, yes,' I said. ' It was just like me, only nicer, and when I laughed and nodded, it looked grave.' 'Very likely,' said George. "It would think you very silly. And was its bow coming unpinned?' ' Yes,' I replied ; 'and the right point of its collar was turned up.' He reached me a hand-mirror, and I saw that my bow was coming unpinned and the right point of my collar was turned up. So it could not have been a reflection, or it would not have been the right point but the left of my collar that was turned up."

The Wraith as a Portent. In the North country it is of popular belief that to see the ghost of a living man portends his approaching decease. The Rev. Henry Kendall, of Darlington, from whose diary (unpublished) I have the liberty to quote, notes the following illustration of this belief, under date August 16th, 1870 :—

" Mrs. W. mentioned a curious incident that happened in Darlington : how Mrs. Percy, upholsterer, and known to several of us, was walking along the street one day when her husband was living, and she saw him walking a little way before her ; then he left the causeway and turned in at a public-house. When she spoke to him of this, he said he had not been near the place, and she was so little satisfied with his statement that she called in at the ' public,' and asked them if her husband had been there, but they told her ' No.' In a very short period after this happened he died."

The phenomenon of a dual body haunted the imagination of poor Shelley. Shortly before his death he believed he had seen his wraith :—

" ' On the 23rd of June,' says one of his biographers, ' he was heard screaming at midnight in the saloon. The Williamses ran in and found him staring on vacancy. He had had a vision of a cloaked figure which came to his bedside and beckoned him to follow. He did so, and when they had reached the sitting-room, the figure lifted the hood of his cloak and disclosed Shelley's own features, and saying, "Siete soddisfatto ? " vanished. This vision is accounted for on the ground that Shelley had been reading a drama attributed to Calderon, named "El Embozado o El Encapotado," in which a mysterious personage who had been haunting and thwarting the hero all his life, and is at last about to give him satisfaction in a duel, finally unmasks and proves to be the hero's own wraith. He also asks, " Art thou satisfied ? " and the haunted man dies of horror.'

"On the 2oth of June some friends distinctly saw Shelley walk into a little wood near Lerici, when in fact he was in a wholly different direction. This was related by Byron to Mr. Cowell."

It is difficult to frame any theory that will account for this double apparition, except, of course, the hypothesis of down-right lying on the part of the witnesses. But the hypothesis of the duplication of the body in this extraordinary fashion is one which cannot be accepted until the immaterial body is photographed under test conditions at the same time that the material body is under safe custody in another place. Of course, it is well to bear in mind that to all those who profess to know anything of occult lore, and also to those who have the gift of clairvoyance, there is nothing new or strange in the doctrine of the immaterial body. Many clairvoyants declare that they constantly see the apparitions of the living mingling with the apparitions of the dead. They are easily distinguish-able. The ghost of a living person is said to be opaque, where-as the ghost of one from whom life has departed is diaphanous as gossamer.

All this, of course, only causes the unbeliever to blaspheme. It is to him every whit as monstrous as the old stories of the witches riding on broomsticks. But the question is not to be settled by blasphemy on one side or credulity on the other. There is something behind these phantasmal apparitions ; there is a real substratum of truth, if we could but get at it. There seems to be some faculty latent in the human mind, by which it can in some cases impress upon the eye and ear of a person at almost any distance the image and the voice. We may call it telepathy or what we please. It is a marvellous power, the mere hint of which indefinitely expands the horizon of the imagination. The telephone is but a mere child's toy compared with the gift to transmit not only the sound of the voice but the actual visible image of the speaker for hundreds of miles without any conductor known to man.

The Hypnotic Key. Hypnotism is the key which will enable us to unlock most of these mysteries, and so far as hypnotism has spoken it does not tend to encour-age the belief that the immaterial body has any substance other than the hallucination of the person who sees it. Various cases are reported by hypnotist practitioners which suggest that there is an almost illimitable capacity of the human mind to see visions and to hear voices. One very remarkable case was that of a girl who was told at midsummer by the hypnotist, when in the hypnotic state, that he would come to see her on New Year's Day. When she awoke from the trance she knew nothing about the conversation. One hundred and seventy-one days passed without any reference to it. But on the 172nd day, being New Year's Day, she positively declared that the doctor had entered her room, greeted her, and then departed. Curiously enough, as showing the purely subjective character of the vision, the doctor appeared to her in the depth of winter wearing the light summer apparel he had on when he made the appointment in July. In this case there can be no question as to the apparition being purely subjective. The doctor did not make any attempt to visit her in his immaterial body, but she saw him and heard him as if he were there.

The late Mr. Gurney conducted some experiments with a hypnotic subject which seem to confirm the opinion that the phantasmal body is a merely subjective hallucination, although, of course, this would not explain how information had been actually imparted to the phantasmal visitant by the person who saw, or imagined they saw, his wraith. Mr. Gurney's cases are, however, very interesting, if only as indicating the absolute certainty which a hypnotised patient can be made to feel as to the objectivity of sights and sounds :—

"S. hypnotised Zillah, and told her that she would see him standing in the room at three o'clock next afternoon, and that she would hear him call her twice by name. She was told that he would not stop many seconds. On waking, as on the former occasion, she had no notion of the ideas impressed upon her.

"Next day, however, she came upstairs about five minutes past three, looking ghastly and startled. She said, 'I have seen a ghost.' I assumed intense amazement, and she said she was in the kitchen cleaning some silver, and suddenly she heard her name called sharply twice over, 'Zillah!' in Mr. Smith's voice. She said, 'And I dropped the spoon I was rubbing, and turned and saw Mr. S., without his hat, standing at the foot of the kitchen stairs. I saw him as plain as I see you,' she said, and looked very wild and vacant.

"The next experiment took place on Wednesday evening, July 13th, 1887, when S., told her, when hypnotised, that the next afternoon, at three o'clock, she would see me (Mr. Gurney) come into the room to her. She was further told that I would keep my hat on and say, ' Good-morning,' and that I would further remark, ' It is very warm,' and would then turn round and walk out.

"Next day this is what Zillah reported. She said, ' I was in the kitchen washing up, and had just looked at the clock, and was startled to see how late it was (five minutes to three) when I heard footsteps coming down the stairs—rather a quick, light step—and I thought it was Mr. Sleep' (the dentist whose rooms are in the house), ' but as I turned round, with a dish mop in one hand and a plate in the other, I saw some one with a hat on who had to stoop as he came down the last step, and there was Mr. Gurney. He was dressed just as I saw him last night, black coat and grey trousers, his hat on, and a roll of paper like manuscript in his hand, and he said, " Oh ! good-afternoon." And then he glanced all round the kitchen, and he glanced at me with an awful look, as if he was going to murder me, and said, " Warm afternoon, isn't it ? " and then " Good-afternoon," or, " Good-day," I am not sure which, and then turned and went up the stairs again ; and after standing thunderstruck a minute, I ran to the foot of the stairs and saw just like a boot disappearing on the top step.' She said, ' I think I must be going crazy. Why should I always see something at three o'clock each day after the seance?'" (Vol. V. pp. 11–13.)

Whatever hypothesis we select to explain these mysteries, they do not become less marvellous. Even if we grant that it is mere telepathy, or mind affecting mind at a distance without the use of the recognised organs of sense or of any of the ordinary conducting mediums, what an enormous extension it gives to the ordinary conception of the limits of the human mind ! To be able instantaneously to paint upon the retina of a friend's eye the life-like image of ourselves, to make our voice sound in his ears at a distance of many miles, and to com- municate to his mind information which he had never before heard of, all this is, it may be admitted, as tremendous a draft upon the credulity of mankind as the favourite Theosophical formula of the astral body. Yet who is there who, in face of the facts and experiences recorded above, will venture to deny that one or other of these hypotheses alone can account for the phenomena under consideration ?

Inconveni- ences of Doubling. It is obvious that when once the possibility of the Double is admitted, many mysteries could be cleared up, although it is also true that a great many inconveniences would immediately follow; as the Attorney-General for the Cape observed to me in discussing the matter, the establishment of the reality of the double would invalidate every plea of *alibi*. If a man can really be in two places at one time, there is an end to the plea which is most frequently resorted to by the accused to prove their innocence. There are other inconveniences, which are alluded to in the following letter from a lady correspondent, who believes that she has the faculty in frequent, although uncertain and unconscious, use :—

"'I saw you yesterday, and you cut me.' Such was the remark I frequently heard from my friends : in the broad daylight they saw me in street or tram, etc. Once a personal friend followed me into church on Christmas Day in a city at least 100 miles from where I really was. Another time I sat two pews in front of a friend at a cathedral service. When I denied having been there, she said, 'It's no good talking : I saw you, and you didn't want to wait for me.' 'But,' I said, 'you have my word that I was not there.' 'Yes,' she said, 'but I have my sight, and I saw you.' Of course, I naturally thought it was some one like me, and said, perhaps rather sarcastically, 'Would it be very strange if any one else bore some resemblance to me?' 'No,' said my friend, 'it would not; but some one else doesn't wear your clothes.' On one occasion I remember three people saw me where I certainly was not physically present the same day ; all knew me personally. I often bought books of a man who kept a second-hand bookstall. One day he told me that he had a somewhat rare edition of a book I wanted, but that it was at the shop. I said, 'I'll come across to-morrow for it if I make up my mind to give the price.' The next day I was prevented from going, and went the day after, to hear it was sold. 'Why didn't you keep it?' I asked. 'I thought you did not want it when you came yesterday and did not buy it.' 'But I didn't come yesterday.' 'Why, excuse me, you did, and took the book up and laid it down again while I was serving Mr. M., and you went away before I could ask you about it ; Mr. M. remarked that it was strange you did not answer him when he spoke.' When I asked the gentleman referred to, he confirmed the story. Mrs. B. also saw me lower down the same street that morning.

"Still it never struck me that it was anything strange; I was only rather curious to see the woman who was so like me. I saw her in an unexpected manner. Going into my room one night, I happened to glance down at my bed, and saw a form there. I thought it strange, yet was not startled. I bent over it, and recognised my own features distinctly. I was in perfect health at the time, and no disaster followed."

Queen Elizabeth's Double. In a volume just published by Macmillan & Co., entitled "Legendary Fictions of the Irish Celt," I find the following references to the Double :—

"If this phantom be seen in the morning it betokens good fortune and long life to its prototype ; if in the evening a near death awaits him. This superstition was known and felt in England even in the reign of Elizabeth. We quote passage from Miss Strickland's account of her last illness :—

" 'As her mortal illness drew towards a close, the superstitious fears of her simple ladies were excited almost to mania, even to conjuring up a spectral apparition of the Queen while she was yet alive. Lady Guildford, who was then in waiting on the Queen, leaving her in an almost breathless sleep in her privy chamber, went out to take a little air, and met her Majesty, as she thought, three or four chambers off. Alarmed at the thought of being discovered in the act of leaving the Royal patient alone, she hurried forward in some trepidation in order to excuse herself, when the apparition vanished away. She returned terrified to the chamber, but there lay the Queen still in the same lethargic slumber in which she left her.' "

CHAPTER II

CLAIRVOYANCE—THE VISION OF THE OUT OF SIGHT

" Moreover, the spirit lifted me up and brought me unto the East gate, and, behold, at the door of the gate five-and-twenty men, among whom I saw," etc. —EZEKIEL xi. 1.

WHEN I was staying the other day at Orchardlea, in Windsor Forest, I did most of my writing in a spacious window on the first floor looking out over the garden. It opened French fashion, and thereby occasioned a curious optical illusion, which may perhaps help to shed some light upon the phenomena now under consideration. For when the sun was high in the sky and the French window was set at a certain angle, the whole of the flowers, figures, etc., on my right hand appeared reflected upon the lawn on the left hand as vividly as if they actually existed in duplicate. So real was the illusion that for some hours I was under the impression that a broad yellow gravel path actually stretched across the lawn on my left. It was only when a little dog ran along the spectral path and suddenly vanished into thin air that I discovered the illusion. Nothing could be more complete, more life-like. The real persons who walked up the gravel to the house walked across the spectral gravel, apparently in duplicate. Both could be seen at one and the same time. I instantly thought that they could be photographed, so as to show the duplication produced by the illusion. Unfortunately, although the spectral path was distinctly visible through the glass to the eye, no impression whatever was left on the sensitive plate. My friend writes :—

" I have tried the phantom path, and I am sorry to say it is too phantom to make any impression on the plate. All that you get is the blaze of light from the glass window, some very faint trees, and no path at all. Possibly, with a June sun, it might have been different; but I doubt it, as one is told never to put the camera facing a window. It is having to take through the glass window which is fatal."

This set me thinking. It was a simple optical illusion, no

doubt, similar to that which enabled Pepper to produce his ghosts at the Polytechnic. But what was the agency which enabled me to see the figures and flowers, and trees and gravel, all transferred, as by the cunning act of some magician, from the right to the left? Simply a swinging pane of perfectly transparent glass. To those who have neither studied the laws of optics nor seen the phenomenon in question, it must seem impossible that a pellucid window-pane could transfer so faithfully that which happened at one end of the garden to the other as to cause it to be mistaken for reality. Yet there was the phenomenon before my eyes. The dog ran double—the real dog to the right, the spectral dog to the left— and no one could tell at first sight " t'other from which." Now, may it not be that this supplies a suggestion as to the cause of the phenomenon of clairvoyance ? Is it not possible that there may exist in Nature some as yet undiscovered analogue to the swinging window-pane which may enable us to see before our eyes here and now events which are transpiring at the other end of the world? In the mysterious, sub-conscious world in which the clairvoyant lives, may there not be some subtle, sympathetic lens, fashioned out of strong affection or some other relation, which may enable some of us to see that which is quite invisible to the ordinary eye?

A Natural Camera Obscura. The usual explanation of these things is that the vision is the revival of some forgotten impressions on the brain. But in neither of the foregoing cases will that explanation suffice, for in neither case had the person who saw ever been in the place of which they had a vision. One desperate resource, the convenient theory of pre-existence, is useless here. The fact seems to be that there is a kind of invisible camera obscura in Nature, which at odd times gives us glimpses of things happening or existing far beyond the range of our ordinary vision. The other day when in Edinburgh I climbed up to the Camera Obscura that stands near the castle, and admired the simple device by which, in a darkened room upon a white, paper-covered table, the whole panorama of Edinburgh life was displayed before me. There were the "recruities" drilling on the Castle Esplanade ; there were the passers-by hurrying along High Street ; there were the birds on the housetops, and the landscape of chimneys and steeples, all revealed as if in the crystal of a wizard's cave. The coloured shadows chased each other across the paper, leaving no trace behind. Five hundred years ago the owner of that camera would have been burned as a wizard; now he makes a comfortable living out of the three-pennypieces of inquisitive visitors. Is it possible to account for the phenomena of clairvoyance other than by the supposition that there exists somewhere in Nature a gigantic camera obscura which reflects everything, and to which clairvoyants habitually, and other mortals occasionally, have access?

Seen and Heard at 150 Miles Range. The preceding incidents simply record a prevision of places subsequently visited. The following are instances in which not only places, but occurrences, were seen as in a camera by persons at a distance varying from 150 to several thousand miles. Space seems to have no existence for the clairvoyant. They are quoted from the published "Proceedings of the Psychical Research Society":—

"On September 9th, 1848, at the siege of Mooltan, Major-General R——, C.B., then adjutant of his regiment, was most severely and dangerously wounded; and supposing himself to be dying, asked one of the officers with him to take the ring off his finger and send it to his wife, who at the time was fully 150 miles distant, at Ferozepore.

"'On the night of September 9th, 1848,' writes his wife, 'I was lying on my bed between sleeping and waking, when I distinctly saw my husband being carried off the field, seriously wounded, and heard his voice saying, "Take this ring off my finger and send it to my wife." All the next day I could not get the sight or the voice out of my mind. In due time I heard of General R—— having been severely wounded in the assault of Mooltan. He survived, however, and is still living. It was not for some time after the siege that I heard from General L——, the officer who helped to carry General R—— off the field, that the request as to the ring was actually made to him, just as I heard it at Ferozepore at that very time.'" (Vol. I. p. 30).

A Royal Deathbed in France seen in Scotland. The above case is remarkable because the voice was transmitted as well as the spectacle. In the next story the ear heard nothing, but the scene itself was very remarkable. A correspondent of the Psychical Research Society writes:—

"I was staying with my mother's cousin, Mrs. Elizabeth Broughton, wife of Mr. Edward Broughton, Edinburgh, and daughter of the late Colonel Blanckley, in the year 1844, and she told me the following strange story:—

"She awoke one night and roused her husband, telling him that something dreadful had happened in France. He begged her to go to sleep again and not to trouble him. She assured him that she was not asleep when she saw what she insisted on then telling him—what she saw, in fact. First, a carriage accident—which she did not actually see, but what she saw was the result—a broken carriage, a crowd collected, a figure gently raised and carried into the nearest house, then a figure lying on a bed, which she then recognised as the Duke of Orleans. Gradually friends collecting round the bed — among them several members of the French royal family—the queen, then the king, all silently, tearfully watching the evidently dying duke. One man (she could see his back, but did not know who he was) was a doctor. He stood bending over the duke, feeling his pulse, his watch in the other hand. And then all passed away ; she saw no more. As soon as it was daylight she wrote down in her journal all that she had seen. From that journal she read this to me. It was before the days of electric telegraph, and two or more days passed before the *Times* announced 'The Death of the Duke of Orleans.' Visiting Paris a short time afterwards, she saw and recognised the place of the accident and received the explanation of her impression. The doctor who attended the dying duke was an old friend of hers, and as he watched by the bed his mind had been constantly occupied with her and her family." (Vol. II. p. 160.)

The doctor's sympathy may have been the key to the secret camera of Nature, but it in no wise "explains" how a lady in Edinburgh could see what went on inside a house in Paris so clearly as to know what had happened two days before the intelligence reached the *Times*.

Dr. Horace Bushnell's Story. Dr. Horace Bushnell, in his " Nature and the Supernatural," tells a story, on the authority of Captain Yonnt, which differs from the foregoing in having a definite purpose, which, fortunately, was attained. Captain Yonnt, a patriarch in the Napa valley of California, told Dr. Bushnell that six or seven years before their conversation he had seen a vision which saved several lives. Here is his story :—

"At my request he gave me his story. About six or seven years previous, in a mid-winter's night, he had a dream, in which he saw what appeared to be a company of emigrants arrested by the snows of the mountains and perishing rapidly by cold and hunger. He noted the very cast of the scenery, marked by a huge, perpendicular front of white rock cliff ; he saw the men cutting off what appeared to be tree-tops rising out of deep gulfs of snow ; he distinguished the very features of the persons and the look of their particular distress. He awoke profoundly impressed by the distinctness and apparent reality of the dream. He at length fell asleep, and dreamed exactly the same dream over again. In the morning he could not expel it from his mind. Falling in shortly after with an old hunter comrade, he told his story, and was only the more deeply impressed by his recognising without hesitation the scenery of the dream. This comrade came over the Sierra, by the Carson Valley Pass, and declared that a spot in the Pass answered exactly his description. By this the unsophistical patriarch was decided. He immediately collected a company of men, with mules and blankets and all necessary provisions. The neighbours were laughing meantime at his credulity. ' No matter,' he said, ' I am able to do this, and I will ; for I verily believe that the fact is according to my dream.' The men were sent into the mountains one hundred and fifty miles distant, directly to the Carson Valley Pass. And there they found the company exactly in the condition of the dream, and brought in the remnant alive." ("Nature and the Supernatural," p. 14.)

The wife of a Dean of the Episcopal Church in one of the Southern States of America was visiting at my house while I was busy collecting materials for this work. Asking her the usual question as to whether she had ever experienced anything of the phenomena usually called supernatural, apparently because it is not the habitual experience of every twenty-four hours, she ridiculed the idea. Ghosts? not she. She was a severely practical, matter-of-fact person, who used her natural senses, and had nothing to do with spirits. But was she quite sure ; had nothing ever occurred to her which she could not explain? Then she hesitated and said, " Well, yes ; but there is nothing supernatural about it. I was staying away down in Virginia, some hundred miles from home, when one morning, about eleven o'clock, I felt an over-powering sleepiness. I never sleep in the daytime, and that drowsiness was, I think, almost my only experience of that kind. I was so sleepy I went to my room and lay down. In my sleep I saw quite distinctly my home at Richmond in flames. The fire had broken out in one wing of the house, which I saw with dismay was where I kept all my best dresses. The people were all about trying to check the flames, but it was of no use. My husband was there, walking about before the burning house, carrying a portrait in

The Vision of a Fire.

his hand. Everything was quite clear and distinct, exactly as if I had actually been present and seen everything. After a time I woke up, and, going downstairs, told my friends the strange dream I had had. They laughed at me, and made such game of my vision that I did my best to think no more about it. I was travelling about, a day or two passed, and when Sunday came I found myself in a church where some relatives were worshipping. When I entered the pew they looked rather strange, and as soon as the service was over I asked them what was the matter. 'Don't be alarmed,' they said, 'there is nothing serious.' They then handed me a post-card from my husband which simply said, 'House burned out; covered by insurance.' The date was the day on which my dream occurred. I hastened home, and then I learned that everything had happened exactly as I had seen it. The fire had broken out in the wing which I had seen blazing. My clothes were all burnt, and the oddest thing about it was that my husband, having rescued a favourite picture from the burning building, had carried it about among the crowd for some time before he could find a place in which to put it safely." Swedenborg, it will be remembered, also had a clairvoyant vision of a fire at a great distance.

The Loss of the "Strathmore." A classic instance of the exercise of this faculty is the story of the wreck of the *Strathmore*. In brief the story is as follows :—The father of a son who had sailed in the *Strathmore*, an emigrant ship outward bound from the Clyde, saw one night the ship foundering amid the waves, and saw that his son, with some others, had escaped safely to a desert island near which the wreck had taken place. He was so much impressed by this vision that he wrote to the owner of the *Strathmore*, telling him what he had seen. His information was scouted ; but after awhile the *Strathmore* was overdue and the owner got uneasy. Day followed day, and still no tidings of the missing ship. Then, like Pharaoh's butler, the owner remembered his sins one day and hunted up the letter describing the vision. It supplied at least a theory to account for the vessel's disappearance. All outward-bound ships were requested to look out for any survivors on the island indicated in the vision. These orders being obeyed, the survivors of the *Strathmore* were found exactly where the father had seen them. In itself this is suffi-cient to confound all accepted hypotheses. Taken in con-nection with other instances of a similar nature, what can be said of it excepting that it almost necessitates the supposition of the existence of the invisible camera obscura which the Theosophists describe as the astral light?

The exceeding triviality of the incident often destroys the possibility of belief in the ordinary superstition that it was a direct Divine revelation. This may be plausible in cases of the *Strathmore*, where the intelligence was communicated of the loss of an English ship, but no one can seriously hold it when the only information to be communicated was a stumble on the stairs.

Considering the enormous advantages which such an astral camera would place in the hands of the detective police, I was not surprised to be told that the officers of the Criminal Investigation Department in London and Chicago occasionally consult clairvoyants as to the place where stolen goods are to be found, or where the missing criminals may be lurking.

An Irish out-rage seen in a Dream. One of the best stories of clairvoyance as a means of throwing light on crime is thus told by a correspondent of the Psychical Research Society:—

"One morning in December, 1836, he had the following dream, or, he would prefer to call it, revelation. He found himself suddenly at the gate of Major N. M.'s avenue, many miles from his home. Close to him was a group of persons, one of whom was a woman with a basket on her arm, the rest men, four of whom were tenants of his own, while the others were unknown to him. Some of the strangers seemed to be murderously assaulting H. W., one of his tenants, and he interfered. 'I struck violently at the man on my left, and then with greater violence at the man's face on my right. Finding, to my surprise, that I had not knocked down either, I struck again and again with all the violence of a man frenzied at the sight of my poor friend's murder. To my great amazement I saw my arms, although visible to my eye, were without substance, and the bodies of the men I struck at and my own came close together after each blow through the shadowy arms I struck with. My blows were delivered with more extreme violence than I ever think I exerted, but I became painfully convinced of my incompetency. I have no consciousness of what happened after this feeling of unsubstantiality came upon me.' Next morning A. experienced the stiffness and soreness of violent bodily exercise, and was informed by his wife that in the course of the night he had much alarmed her by striking out again and again with his arms in a terrific manner, 'as if fighting for his life.' He, in turn, informed her of his dream, and begged her to remember the names of those actors in it who were known to him. On the morning of the following day (Wednesday) A. received a letter from his agent, who resided in the town close to the scene of the dream, informing him that his tenant had been found on Tuesday morning at Major N. M.'s gate, speechless and apparently dying from a fracture of the skull, and that there was no trace of the murderers. That night A. started for the town, and arrived there on Thursday morning. On his way to a meeting of magistrates he met the senior magistrate of that part of the country, and requested him to give orders for the arrest of the three men whom, besides H. W., he had recognised in his dream, and to have them examined separately. This was at once done. The three men gave identical accounts of the occurrence, and all named the woman who was with them. She was then arrested, and gave precisely similar testimony. They said that between eleven and twelve on the Monday night they had been walking homewards altogether along the road, when they were overtaken by three strangers, two of whom savagely assaulted H. W., while the other prevented his friends from interfering. H. W. did not die, but was never the same man afterwards; he subsequently emigrated." (Vol. I. p. 142.)

The advantage which would accrue from the universal establishment of this instantaneous vision would not be unmixed. That it is occasionally very useful is obvious.

Mr. Burt's Dream. When I was in Newcastle I availed myself of the opportunity to call upon Mr. Burt, M.P., who has left his old house in Lovaine Crescent, and now lives in one of the new streets nearer the Moor. On questioning him as to whether he had ever seen a ghost, he replied in the negative, but remarked that he had had one experience which had made a deep impression upon his mind, which partook more of the nature of clairvoyance than the apparition of a phantom. "I suppose it was a dream," said Mr. Burt. "The dream or vision, or whatever else you call it, made a deep impression upon my mind. You remember Mr. Crawford, the Durham miners' agent, was ill for a long time before his death. Just before his death he rallied, and we all hoped he was going to get better. I had heard nothing to the contrary, when one morning early I had a very vivid dream. I dreamed that I was standing by the beside of my old friend. I passed my hand over his brow, and he spoke to me with great tenderness, with much greater tenderness than he had ever spoken before. He said he was going to die, and that he was comforted by the long and close friendship that had existed between us. I was much touched by the feeling with which he spoke, and felt awed as if I were in the presence of death. When I woke up the impression was still strong in my mind, and I could not resist the feeling that Crawford was dying. In a few hours I received a telegram stating that he was dead. This is more remarkable because I fully expected he was going to get better, and at the moment of my dream he seems to have died. I cannot give any explanation of how it came about. It is a mystery to me, and likely to remain so."

This astral camera, to which "future things unfolded lie," also retains the imperishable image of all past events. Mr. Browning's great uncle's studs brought vividly to the mind of the clairvoyant a smell of blood, and recalled all the particulars of the crime of which they had been silent witnesses. Any article or relic may serve as a key to unlock the chamber of this hidden camera.

A Clairvoyant Vision of a Murder. The most remarkable experiment in clairvoyant detection that I have ever come across is told by Dr. Backman, of Kalmar, in a recent number of the "Psychical Research Society's Proceedings." It is as follows:—

In the month of October, 1888, the neighbourhood of Kalmar was shocked by a horrible murder committed in the parish of Wissefjerda, which was about fifty kilometres from Kalmar as the crow flies. What happened was that a farmer named P. J. Gustafsson had been killed by a shot when driving, having been forced to stop by stones having been placed on the road. The murder had been committed in the evening, and a certain tramp was suspected, because Gustafsson, in his capacity of under bailiff, had arrested him, and he had then undergone several years' penal servitude.

This was all that I or the public knew about the case on November 1st of the same year. The place where the murder was committed and the persons implicated in it were quite unknown to me and the clairvoyant.

On the same day, November 1st, having some reason to believe that such a trial would be at least partially successful, I experimented with a clairvoyant, Miss Agda Olsen, to try if it was possible to get some information in this way about such an event.

The judge of the neighbourhood, who had promised to be present, was unfortunately prevented from coming. The clairvoyant was hypnotised in my wife's presence, and was then ordered " to look for the place where the murder had been committed and see the whole scene, follow the murderer in his flight, and describe him and his home and the motive for the murder.' Miss Olsen then spoke as follows, in great agitation, sometimes using violent gestures. I took notes of her exact words and reproduce them here fully.

"'It is between two villages—I see a road—in a wood— now it is coming—the gun—now he is coming along, driving —the horse is afraid of the stones—hold the horse! hold the horse! now! now he is killing him—he was kneeling when he fired—blood! blood!—now he is running in the wood— seize him!—he is running in an opposite direction to the horse in many circuits—not on any footpaths. He wears a cap and grey clothes—light—has long coarse brown hair, which has not been cut for a long time—grey-blue eyes— treacherous looks—great dark brown beard—he is accustomed to work on the land. I believe he has cut his right hand. He has a scar or a streak between his thumb and forefinger. He is suspicious and a coward.

"'The murderer's home is a red wooden house, standing a little way back from the road. On the ground-floor is a room which leads into the kitchen, and from that again into the passage. There is also a larger room which does not communicate with the kitchen. The church of Wissefjerda is situated obliquely to your right when you are standing in the passage.

"'His motive was enmity; it seems as if he had bought something—taken something—a paper. He went away from home at daybreak, and the murder was committed in the evening.'

"Miss Olsen was then awakened, and, like all my subjects, she remembered perfectly what she had been seeing, which had made a very profound impression on her; she added several things which I did not write down.

"On November 6th (Monday) I met Miss Olsen, and she told me in great agitation that she had met the murderer from Wissefjerda in the street. He was accompanied by a younger person and followed by two policemen, and was walking from the police office to the gaol. I at once expressed my doubts of her being right, partly because country people are generally arrested by the country police, partly because they are always taken directly to gaol. But when she insisted on it, and maintained that it was the person she had seen when asleep, I went to the police office.

"I inquired if any one had been arrested on suspicion of the crime in question, and a police-constable answered that such was the case, and that, as they had been taken to the town on Sunday, they had been kept in the police-station over night, and after that had been obliged to go on foot to gaol, accompanied by two constables. The police-constable, T. A. Ljung, states that Dr. Backman described quite accurately the appearance of the house, its furniture, how the rooms were situated, where the suspected man lived, and gave a very correct account of Niklas Jonnasson's personal appearance. The doctor also asked me if I had observed that Jonnasson had a scar on his right hand. I had not then observed it, but since then I have ascertained that it really is so, and Jonnasson says that he got it from an abscess.

" The trial was a long one, and showed that Gustafsson had agreed to buy for Jonnasson, but in his own name, the latter's farm, which was sold by auction on account of Jonnasson's debts. This is what is called a thief's bargain. Gustafsson bought the farm, but kept it for himself. The statements of the accused men were very vague ; the father had prepared an *alibi* with much care, but it failed on account for just the length of time that was probably enough to commit the murder in. The son tried to prove an *alibi* by means of two witnesses, but these confessed that they had given false evidence, which he had bribed them to do when they were in prison with him on account of another matter.

" But though the evidence against the defendants was very strong, it was not considered that there was sufficient legal evidence, and, there being no jury in Sweden, they were left to the verdict of posterity " (pp. 213–216).

Clairvoyance and the Double. Clairvoyance is closely related to the phenomenon of the Double, for the clairvoyant seems to have either the faculty of transporting herself to distant places, or of bringing the places within range of her sight. Here is a narrative sent me by Mr. Masey, Fellow of the Geological Society, writing to me from 8, Gloucester Road, Kew, which illustrates the connection between clairvoyance and the Double :—

" Mrs. Mary Masey, who resided on Redcliffe Hill, Bristol, at the beginning of this century, was a member of the Society of Friends, and was held in high esteem for piety.

" A memorable incident in her life was that one night she dreamt that a Mr. John Henderson, a noted man of the same community, had gone to Oxford, and that he had died there. In the course of the next day, Mr. Henderson called to take leave of her, saying he was going to Oxford to study a subject concerning which he could not obtain the information he wanted in Bristol. Mrs. Masey said to him, 'John Henderson, thou wilt die there.' Some time afterwards, Mrs. Masey woke her husband one night, saying, 'Remember, John Henderson died at Oxford at two o'clock this morning, and it is now three.' Her husband, Philip Masey, made light of it; but she told him that while asleep she had been transported to Oxford, where she had never been before, and that she had entered a room there, in which she saw Mr. John Henderson in bed, the landlady supporting his head, and the landlord with several other persons standing around. While gazing at him some one gave him medicine, and the patient, turning round, perceived her, and exclaimed, 'Oh, Mrs. Masey, I am going to die; I am so glad you are come, for I want to tell you that my father is going to be very ill, and you must go and see him.' He then proceeded to describe a room in his father's house, and a bureau in it, 'in which is a box containing a remedy; give it him, and he will recover.' Her impression and recollection of all the persons in the room at Oxford was most vivid, and she even described the appearance of the house on the opposite side of the street. The only person she appeared not to have seen in the room was a clergyman who was present. The husband of Mrs. Masey accompanied Mr. Henderson's father to the funeral, and on their journey from Bristol to Oxford by coach (the period being before railways and telegraphs existed), Mr. Philip Masey related to him the particulars of his son's death, as described by his wife, which, on arrival, they found to have been exactly as told by Mrs. Masey.

"Mrs. Masey was so much concerned about the death of Mr. Henderson, jun., that she forgot all about the direction she had given her respecting the approaching illness of his father, but some time afterwards she was sent for by the father, who was very ill. She then remembered the directions given her by the son on his death-bed at Oxford. She immediately proceeded to the residence of Mr. Henderson, and on arrival at the house she found the room, the bureau, the box, and the medicine exactly as had been foretold to her. She administered the remedy as directed, and had the pleasure of witnessing the beneficial effect by the complete recovery of Mr. Henderson from a serious illness."

Here we have almost every variety of psychic experience. First of all there is second sight pure and simple; second, there is the aerial journey of the Double, with the memory of everything that had been seen and heard at the scene which it had witnessed; third, there is communication of information which at that moment was not known to the precipient; fourth, we have another prediction; and finally, we have a complete verification and fulfilment of everything that was witnessed. It is idle to attempt to prove the accuracy of statements made concerning one who has been dead nearly a hundred years, but the story, although possessing no evidential value, is interesting as an almost unique specimen of the comprehensive and complicated prophetic ghost and clairvoyant story.

Clairvoyance is a gift, and a comparatively rare gift. It is a gift which requires to be much more carefully studied and scientifically examined than it has been hitherto. It is a by-path to many secrets. It may hold in it the clue to the acquisition of great faculties, hitherto regarded as forbidden to mere mortals.

It is difficult for those who are not clairvoyant to understand what those who are clairvoyant describe, often with the most extraordinary precision and detail. Unfortunately for myself I am not a clairvoyant, but on one occasion I had an experience which enabled me to understand something of clairvoyant vision. I had been working late at night, and had gone to bed at about two o'clock in the morning somewhat tired, having spent several hours in preparing "Real Ghost Stories" for the press. I got into bed, but was not able to go to sleep, as usual, as soon as my head touched the pillow. I suppose my mind had been too much excited by hard work right up to the moment of going to bed for me readily to go to sleep. I shut my eyes and waited for sleep to come; instead of sleep, however, there came to me a succession of curiously vivid clairvoyant pictures. There was no light in the room, and it was perfectly dark; I had my eyes shut also. But, notwithstanding the darkness, I suddenly was conscious of looking at a scene of singular beauty. It was as if I saw a living miniature about the size of a magic-lantern slide. At this moment I can recall the scene as if I saw it again. It was a seaside piece. The moon was shining upon the water, which rippled slowly on to the beach. Right before me a long mole ran out into the water. On either side of the mole irregular rocks stood up above the sea-level. On the shore stood several houses, square and rude, which resembled nothing that I had ever seen in house architecture. No one was stirring, but the moon was there, and the sea and the

My own Experience.

gleam of the moonlight on the rippling waters was just as if I had been looking out upon the actual scene. It was so beautiful that I remember thinking that if it continued I should be so interested in looking at it that I should never go to sleep. I was wide awake, and at the same time that I saw the scene I distinctly heard the dripping of the rain outside the window. Then suddenly, without any apparent object or reason, the scene changed. The moonlit sea vanished, and in its place I was looking right into the interior of a reading-room. It seemed as if it had been used as a schoolroom in the daytime and was employed as a reading-room in the evening. I remember seeing one reader, who had a curious resemblance to Tim Harrington, although it was not he, hold up a magazine or book in his hand and laugh. It was not a picture—it was there. The scene was just as if you were looking through an opera-glass; you saw the play of the muscles, the gleaming of the eye, every movement of the unknown persons in the unnamed place into which you were gazing. I saw all that without opening my eyes, nor did my eyes have anything to do with it. You see such things as these, as it were, with another sense, which is more inside your head than in your eyes. This was a very poor and paltry experience, but it enabled me to understand better how it was that clairvoyants see than any amount of disquisition. The pictures were *apropos* of nothing ; they had been suggested by nothing I had been reading or talking of, they simply came as if I had been able to look through a glass at what was occurring somewhere else in the world. I had my peep and then it passed, nor have I had a recurrence of a similar experience.

Crystal-gazing is somewhat akin to clairvoyance.
Crystal-
gazing. There are some people who cannot look into an ordinary globular bottle without seeing pictures form themselves, without any effort or will on their part, in the crystal globe. This is an experience which I have never been able to enjoy. But I have seen crystal-gazing going on at a table at which I have been sitting on one or two occasions with rather remarkable results. The experiences of Miss X. in crystal-gazing have been told at length and in detail in the " Proceedings of the Psychical Research Society." On looking into the crystal on two occasions as a test, to see if she could see me when she was several miles off, she saw, not me, but a different friend of mine on each occasion, whom she had never seen, but whom she immediately identified on seeing them afterwards at my office. On one of the evenings on which we

experimented in the vain attempt to photograph a Double,
I dined with Madame C. and her friend at a neighbouring
restaurant. As she glanced at the water-bottle Madame C.
saw a picture beginning to form, and, looking at it from
curiosity, described with considerable detail an elderly gentleman whom she had never seen before, and whom I did not in
the least recognise from her description at the moment. Three
hours afterwards, when the séance was over, Madame C.
entered the room and recognised Mr. Elliott, of Messrs. Elliott
& Fry, as the gentleman whom she had seen and described in
the water-bottle at the restaurant. On another occasion the
picture was less agreeable : it was an old man lying dead in a
bed with some one weeping at his feet ; but what it was or
what it related to no one knew.

Crystal-gazing seems to be the least dangerous and most
simple of all methods of experimenting. You simply look into
a crystal globe the size of a five-shilling piece, or a water-bottle
which is full of clear water, and is placed so that too much
light does not fall upon it, and then simply look at it. You
make no incantations and engage in no mumbo-jumbo business ; you simply look at it for two or three minutes, taking
care not to tire yourself, winking as much as you please, but
fixing your thought upon whoever it is you wish to see. Then,
if you have the faculty, the glass will cloud over with a milky
mist, and in the centre the image is gradually precipitated in
just the same way as a photograph forms on the sensitive
plate. At least, the description given by crystal-gazers as to
the way in which the picture appears reminded me of nothing
so much as what I saw when I stood inside the largest camera
in the world, in which the Ordnance Survey photographs its
maps at Southampton.

CHAPTER III

PREMONITIONS AND SECOND SIGHT.

" But there are many such things in Nature, though we have not the right key to them. We all walk in mysteries. We are surrounded by an atmosphere of which we do not know what is stirring in it, or how it is connected with our own spirit. So much is certain—that in particular cases we can put out the feelers of our soul beyond its bodily limits, and that a presentiment, nay, an actual insight into, the immediate future is accorded to it."—Goethe's "Conversations with Eckermann."

IF clairvoyance partakes of the nature of the camera obscura, by which persons can see at a distance that which is going on beyond the direct range of their vision, it is less easy to suggest an analogy to explain the phenomena of premonition or second sight. Although I have never seen a ghost—for none of my hallucinations are scenic—I may fairly claim to have a place in this census on the ground of the extraordinary premonitions I have had at various times of coming events. The second sight of the Highlander is always scenic; he does not hear so much as he sees. If death is foreshadowed, the circumstances preceding and following the event pass as in dramatic scene before the eyes of the seer. It is much as if the seers had access to a camera obscura which enabled them not only to see that which was occurring at the same moment in various parts of the world, but in its magic mirror could reflect events which have not yet been as if they were already existent. The phenomena of premonition, combined with the faculties of clairvoyance by which the percipient is able to reproduce the past, make a great breach in our conceptions of both time and space. To the Deity, in the familiar line of the hymn, "future things unfolded lie"; but from time to time future things, sometimes most trivial, sometimes most important, are unfolded to the eye of mortal man. Why or how one does not know. All that he can say is that the vision came and went in obedience to some power over which he had no conscious control. The faculty of foreseeing, which in its higher forms constitutes no small part of a prophet's power, is said to exist among certain families, and to vary according to the locality in which they are living.   Men who have second sight in Skye are said to lose it on the mainland.   But residence in Skye itself is not sufficient to give the Englishman the faculty once said to be possessed by its natives.   In England it is rare, and when it exists it is often mixed up with curious and somewhat bewildering superstitions, signs and omens portending death and disaster, which can hardly be regarded as being more than seventh cousins of the true faculty.

The Burden of Second Sight. The gift of second sight is by no means an unmixed boon.   Dr. Baumgarten tells me that the Westphalians in Prussia possess the same gift which in Scotland is said to be indigenous to the islanders of Skye.   The Westphalian peasantry, so far from regarding it as a privilege, are delighted when an opportunity is afforded them of transferring the unwelcome faculty to some stranger who is willing to bear the burden of seership.   Von Goerris, whom Napoleon jestingly called the fifth power in Europe on account of the indomitable manner in which he used the Press in order to rouse Prussia against French dominance, collected an immense number of cases which are to be found, together with many other matters, in his book "Mystic," the three volumes of which have never been translated into the English language, and are not likely to be, owing to the abstruseness of the subject and the crabbedness of the German.   Some Westphalians appear to be literally haunted by their uncanny faculty of seeing into the future.   It is bad enough to face death when it comes, without having anticipatory coffins coming into sight all round you.   The Westphalian usually sees his coffin seven days before he dies; nor is it only his own coffin that is revealed to him, he has a faculty of seeing the coffins of his neighbours with a clearness which makes it somewhat disagreeable for him to be in a crowd, especially when an epidemic is about.   Their second sight is nearly always a vision of disaster; they do not, as a rule, foresee pleasant things.   The method by which the gift of second sight is transferred from one to another Dr. Baumgarten did not explain.

I can make no claim to the proud prerogative of the seer, but upon several occasions I have had some extraordinary premonitions of what was about to happen.   I can give no explanation as to how they came, all that I know is they arrived, and when they arrived I recognised them beyond all possibility of mistake.   I have had three or four very striking and vivid premonitions in my life which have been fulfilled to the letter. I have others which await fulfilment. Of the latter, I will not speak here—although I have them duly recorded—for were I to do so I should be accused of being party to bringing about the fulfilment of my own predictions. Those which have already been fulfilled, although of no general importance to any one else, were of considerable importance to me, as will be seen by the brief outline concerning three of them.

Leaving Darlington Fore-seen. The first occasion on which I had an absolutely unmistakable intimation of the change about to occur in my own circumstances was in 1880, the year in which I left the editorship of the *Northern Echo* to become the assistant of Mr. John Morley on the *Pall Mall Gazette*,

On New Year's Day, 1880, it was forcibly impressed upon my mind that I was to leave Darlington in the course of that year. I remember on the 1st of January meeting a journalistic confrère on my way from Darlington station to the *Northern Echo* office. After wishing him a Happy New Year, I said, "This is the last New Year's Day I shall ever spend in Darlington; I shall leave the *Northern Echo* this year." My friend looked at me in some amazement, and said, "And where are you going to?" "To London," I replied, "because it is the only place which could tempt me from my present position, which is very comfortable, and where I have perfect freedom to say my say." "But," said my friend, somewhat dubiously, "what paper are you going to?" "I have no idea in the world," I said; "neither do I know a single London paper which would offer me a position on their staff of any kind, let alone one on which I would have any liberty of utterance. I see no prospect of any opening anywhere. But I know for certain that before the year is out I shall be on the staff of a London paper." "Come," said my friend, "this is superstition, and with a wife and family I hope you will do nothing rashly." "You need not fear as to that," I said; "I shall not seek any position elsewhere, it will have to come to me if I have to go to it. I am not going to throw myself out of a berth until I know where my next place is to be. Humanly speaking, I see no chance of my leaving Darlington, yet I have no more doubt than of my own existence that I shall be gone by this time next year." We parted. The General Election soon came upon us, and when the time came for renewing my engagement on the *Northern Echo*, I had no option but to renew my contract and bind myself to remain at Darlington until July, 1880. Although I signed the contract, when the day arrived on which I had either to give notice or renew my engagement, I could not shake from me the conviction that I was destined to leave Darlington at least six months before my engagement expired. At that time the *Pall Mall Gazette* was edited by Mr. Greenwood, and was, of all the papers in the land, the most antipathetic to the principles upon which I had conducted the *Northern Echo*. The possibility of my becoming assistant editor to the editor of the *Pall Mall Gazette* seemed at that time about as remote as that of the Moderator of the Free Church of Scotland receiving a cardinal's hat from the Pope of Rome. Nevertheless, no sooner had Mr. Gladstone been seated in power than Mr. George Smith handed over the *Pall Mall Gazette* to his son-in-law, Mr. Henry Yates Thompson. Mr. Greenwood departed to found and edit the *St. James' Gazette*, and Mr. Morley became editor. Even then I never dreamed of going to the *Pall Mall*. Two other North-country editors and I, thinking that Mr. Morley was left in rather a difficulty by the secession of several of the *Pall Mall* staff, agreed to send up occasional contributions solely for the purpose of enabling Mr. Morley to get through the temporary difficulty in which he was placed by being suddenly summoned to edit a daily paper under such circumstances. Midsummer had hardly passed before Mr. Thompson came down to Darlington and offered me the assistant editorship. The proprietor of the *Northern Echo* kindly waived his right to my services in deference to the request of Mr. Morley. As a result I left the *Northern Echo* in September, 1880, and my presentiment was fulfilled. At the time when it was first impressed upon my mind, no living being probably anticipated the possibility of such a change occurring in the *Pall Mall Gazette* as would render it possible for me to become assistant editor, so that the presentiment could in no way have been due to any possible calculation of chances on my part.

The Editor-ship of the "Pall Mall Gazette." The second presentiment to which I shall refer was also connected with the *Pall Mall Gazette*, and was equally clear and without any suggestion from outward circumstances. It was in October, 1883. My wife and I were spending a brief holiday in the Isle of Wight, and I remember that the great troopers, which had just brought back Lord Wolseley's army from the first Egyptian campaign, were lying in the Solent when we crossed. One morning about noon we were walking in the drizzling rain round St. Catherine's Point. It was a miserable day, the ground slippery and the footpath here and there rather difficult to follow. Just as we were at about the ugliest part of our climb I felt distinctly, as it were, a voice within myself saying, You will have to look sharp and make ready, because by a certain date (which as near as I can recollect was the 16th of March next year) you will have sole charge of the *Pall Mall Gazette.* I was just a little startled and rather awed because, as Mr. Morley was then in full command and there was no expectation on his part of abandoning his post, the inference which I immediately drew was that he was going to die. So firmly was this impressed upon my mind that for two hours I did not like to speak about it to my wife. We took shelter for a time from the rain, but afterwards, on going home, I spoke on the subject which filled me with sadness, not without reluctance, and said to my wife, " Something has happened to me which has made a great impression upon my mind. When we were beside St. Catherine's Lighthouse I got into my head that Mr. Morley was going to die." "Nonsense," she said, "what made you think that?" "Only this," said I, "that I received an intimation as clear and unmistakable as that which I had when I was going to leave Darlington, that I had to look sharp and prepare for taking the sole charge of the *Pall Mall Gazette* on March 16th next. That is all, and I do not see how that is likely to happen unless Mr. Morley is going to die." "Nonsense," said my wife, "he is not going to die ; he is going to get into Parliament, that is what is going to happen." "Well," said I, "that may be. Whether he dies or whether he gets into Parliament, the one thing certain to me is that I shall have sole charge of the *Pall Mall Gazette* next year, and I am so convinced of that that when we return to London I shall make all my plans on the basis of that certainty." And so I did. I do not hedge and hesitate at burning my boats. As soon as I arrived at the *Pall Mall Gazette* office, I announced to Mr. Thompson, to Mr. Morley, and to Mr. Milner, who was then on the staff, that Mr. Morley was going to be in Parliament before March next year, for I need hardly say that I never mentioned my first sinister intimation. I told Mr. Morley and the others exactly what had happened, namely, that I had received notice to be ready to take sole charge of the *Pall Mall Gazette* by March 16th next. They shrugged their shoulders, and Mr. Morley scouted the idea. He said he had almost given up the idea of entering Parliament, all preceding negotiations had fallen through, and he had come to the conclusion that he would stick to the

Pall Mall. I said that he might come to what conclusion he liked, the fact remained that he was going to go. I remember having a talk at the time with Mr. Milner about it. I remarked that the worst of people having premonitions is that they carefully hide up their prophecies until after the event, and then no one believed in them. "This time no one shall have the least doubt as to the fact that I have had my premonition well in advance of the fact. It is now October. I have told everybody whom it concerns whom I know. If it happens not to come to pass I will never have faith in my premonitions any more, and you may chaff me as much as you please as to the superstition. But if it turns up trumps, then please remember that I have played doubles or quits and won." Nobody at the office paid much attention to my vision, and a couple of months later Mr. Morley came to consult me as to some slight change which he proposed to make in the terms of his engagement which he was renewing for another year. As this change affected me slightly he came, with that courtesy and consideration which he always displayed in his dealings with his staff, to ask whether I should have any objection to this alteration. As he was beginning to explain what this alteration would be I interrupted him. "Excuse me, Mr. Morley," said I, "when will this new arrangement come into effect?" "In May, I think," was the reply. "Then," said I, "you do not need to discuss it with me. I shall have sole charge of the *Pall Mall Gazette* before that time. You will not be here then, you will be in Parliament." "But," said Mr. Morley, "that is only your idea. What I want to know is whether you agree to the changes which I propose to make and which will somewhat affect your work in the office?" "But," I replied, "it is no use talking about that matter to me. You will not be here, and I shall be carrying on the *Pall Mall Gazette*; then what is the use of talking about it." Then Mr. Morley lifted his chin slightly in the air, and looking at me with somewhat natural disdain, he asked, "And, pray, do you mean to tell me that I have not to make a business arrangement because you have had a vision?" "Not at all," said I; "you, of course, will make what business arrangements you please,—I cannot expect you to govern your conduct by my vision;—but as I shall have charge of the paper it is no use discussing the question with me. You can make what arrangements you please so far as I am concerned. They are so much waste paper. I ask you nothing about the arrangement, because I know it will never come into effect so far as relates to my work on the paper." Finding that I was impracticable, Mr. Morley left and concluded his arrangement without consultation. One month later Mr. Ashton Dilke sickened with his fatal illness, and Mr. Morley was elected on February 24th, 1884, as Liberal candidate for Newcastle-on-Tyne. I remember that when the news came to Northumberland Street, the first remark which Mr. Thompson made was, " Well, Stead's presentiment is coming right after all." I remember all through that contest, when the issue was for some time somewhat in doubt, feeling quite certain that if Mr. Morley did not get in he would die, or he would find some other constituency. I had no vision as to the success of his candidature at Newcastle. The one thing certain was that I was to have charge of the paper, and that he was to be out of it. When he was elected the question came as to what should be done ? The control of the paper passed almost entirely into my hands at once, and Mr. Morley would have left altogether on the day mentioned in my vision, had not Mr. Thompson kindly interfered to secure me a holiday before saddling me with the sole responsibility. Mr. Morley, therefore, remained till midsummer ; but his connection with the paper was very slight, parliamentary duties, as he understood them, being incompatible with close day-to-day editing of an evening paper. Here, again, it could not possibly have been said that my premonition had any share in bringing about its realisation. It was not known by Mr. Ashton Dilke's most intimate friends in October that he would not be able to face another session. I did not even know that he was ill, and my vision, so far from being based on any calculation of Mr. Morley's chances of securing a seat in Parliament, was quite independent of all electoral changes. My vision, my message, my premonition, or whatever you please to call it, was strictly limited to one point, Mr. Morley only coming into it indirectly. I was to have charge of certain duties which necessitated his disappearance from Northumberland Street. Note also that my message did not say that I was to be *editor* of the *Pall Mall Gazette* on Mr. Morley's departure, nor was I ever in strict title editor of that paper. I edited it, but Mr. Yates Thompson was nominally editor-in-chief, nor did I ever admit that I was editor until I was in the dock at the Old Bailey, when it would have been cowardly to have seemed to evade the responsibility of a position which I practically occupied, although, as a matter of fact, the post was never really conferred upon me.

The third instance which I will quote is even
My Im-
prisonment. more remarkable, and entirely precluded any
possibility of my premonition having any influence
whatever in bring about its realization. During what is known
as the Armstrong trial it became evident from the judge's
ruling that a conviction must necessarily follow. I was
accused of having conspired to take Eliza Armstrong from her
parents without their consent. My defence was that her
mother had sold the child through a neighbour for immoral
purposes. I never alleged that the father had consented, and
the judge ruled with unmistakable emphasis that her mother's
consent, even if proved, was not sufficient. Here I may
interpolate a remark to the effect that if Mrs. Armstrong had
been asked to produce her marriage lines the sheet anchor of
the prosecution would have given way, for long after the trial
it was discovered that from a point of law Mr. Armstrong had
no legal rights over Eliza, as she was born out of wedlock.
The council in the case, however, said we had no right to
suggest this, however much we suspected it, unless we were
prepared with evidence to justify the suggestion. As at that
time we could not find the register of marriage at Somerset
House the question was not put, and we were condemned
largely on the false assumption that her father had legal rights
as custodian of his daughter. And this, as it happened, was
not the case. This, however, by the way. When the trial
was drawing to a close, conviction being certain, the question
was naturally discussed as to what the sentence would be.
Many of my friends, including those actively engaged in the
trial on both sides, were strongly of opinion that under the
circumstances it was certain I should only be bound over in
my own recognisance to come up for judgment when called for.
The circumstances were almost unprecedented ; the judge, and
the Attorney-General, who prosecuted, had in the strongest
manner asserted that they recognised the excellence of the
motives which had led me to take the course which had landed
me in the dock. The Attorney-General himself was perfectly
aware that his Government could never have passed the Criminal Law Amendment Act—would never even have attempted
to do so—but for what I had done. The jury had found me
guilty, but strongly recommended me to mercy on the ground,
as they said, that I had been deceived by my agent. The
conviction was very general that no sentence of imprisonment
would be inflicted. I was never a moment in doubt. I knew
I was going to gaol from the moment Rebecca Jarrett broke

down in the witness-box. This may be said to be nothing extraordinary; but what was extraordinary was that I had the most absolute conviction that I was going to gaol for two months. I was told by those who considered themselves in a position to speak with authority that I was perfectly safe, that I should not be imprisoned, and that I should make preparations to go abroad for a holiday as soon as the trial was over. To all such representations I always replied by asserting with the most implicit confidence that I was certain to go to gaol, and that my sentence would be two months. When, however, on November 10th, 1885, I stood in the dock to receive sentence, and received from the judge a sentence of three months, I was very considerably taken aback. I remember distinctly that I had to remember where I was in order to restrain the almost irresistible impulse to interrupt the judge and say, "I beg your pardon, my lord, you have made a mistake, the sentence ought to have been *two* months." But mark what followed. When I had been duly confined in Coldbath-on-the-Fields Prison, I looked at the little card which is fastened on the door of every cell giving the name of the prisoner, his offence, and the duration of his sentence. I found to my great relief that my presentiment had not been wrong after all. I had, it is true, been sentenced to three months' imprisonment, but the sentence was dated from the first day of the sessions. Our trial had been a very long one, and there had been other cases before it. The consequence was that the judge's sentence was as near two months as he possibly could have passed. My actual sojourn in gaol was two months and seven days. Had he sentenced me to two months' imprisonment I should only have been in gaol one month and seven days.

These three presentiments were quite unmistakable, and were not in the least to be confounded with the ordinary uneasy forebodings which come and go like clouds in a summer sky. Of the premonitions which still remain unfulfilled I will say nothing, excepting that they govern my action, and more or less colour the whole of my life. No person can have had three or four premonitions such as those which I have described without feeling that such premonitions are the only certainties of the future. They will be fulfilled, no matter how incredible they may appear; and amid the endless shifting circumstances of our life, these fixed points, towards which we are inevitably tending, help to give steadiness to a career, and a feeling of security to which the majority of men are strangers.

Goethe, in his Autobiography, records the fact
Goethe's Grandfather. that his maternal grandfather had a premonition of his election to the aldermanic dignity, not unlike that which I had about my promotion to the *Pall Mall*. Goethe writes :—

"We knew well enough that he was often informed, in remarkable dreams, of things which were to happen. For example, he assured his wife, at a time when he was still one of the youngest magistrates, that at the very next vacancy he should be appointed to a seat on the board of aldermen. And when, very soon after, one of the aldermen was struck with a fatal stroke of apoplexy, he ordered that on the day when the choice was to be made by lot the house should be arranged and everything prepared to receive the guests coming to congratulate him on his elevation; and, sure enough, it was for him that was drawn the golden ball which decides the choice of aldermen in Frankfort. The dream which foreshadowed to him this event he confided to his wife as follows : He found himself in session with his colleagues, and everything was going on as usual, when an alderman, the same who afterwards died, descended from his seat, came to my grandfather, politely begged him to take his place, and then left the chamber. Something similar happened on the provost's death. It was usual in such cases to make great haste to fill the vacancy, seeing that there was always ground to fear that the Emperor, who used to nominate the provost, would some day or other reassert his ancient privilege. On this particular occasion the sheriff received orders at midnight to call an extra session for the next morning. When in his rounds the officer reached my grandfather's house, he begged for another bit of candle to replace that which had just burned down in his lantern. 'Give him a whole candle,' said my grandfather to the woman; 'it is for me he is taking all this trouble.' The event justified his words. He was actually chosen provost. And it is worthy of notice that the person who drew in his stead, having the third and last chance, the two silver balls were drawn first, and thus the golden one remained for him at the bottom of the bag." (Quoted by Owen, in " Footfalls on the Boundary of Another World.")

My good friend, Captain Wiggins, one of the
Captain Wiggins' Warning. most Elizabethan of English mariners, is full of stories of visions which have occurred to him. Unfortunately at the moment of writing he is on his way to Brazil, so that I cannot obtain first-hand evidence as to some of the

things with which he used to surprise his friends. One dream, however, which made a vivid impression on him may be cited, as it saved his canvas, if not his life. He was in the Mediterranean in a sailing vessel with a tranquil sea and a cloudless sky, with all sail set, when he dreamed he saw a white squall come up and strike the ship with a fury which portended its destruction. So vivid was the impression that he ran on deck, and, to the amazement of his officers and crew, ordered every inch of canvas to be furled. Believing that Captain Wiggins had suddenly gone mad, they nevertheless set about executing his orders. They had hardly finished their task when a white squall struck the ship with a fury which would have torn the canvas to ribbons, if indeed it had not capsized the vessel.

An Unavailing Warning. Dreams which give timely notice of coming accidents are, unfortunately, quite as often useless as they are efficacious for the protection of those to whom they are sent. Mr. Kendall, from whose psychical diary I have often quoted, sends me the following story of a dream which occurred, but which failed to save the dreamer's leg, although he struggled against it, and did his best to avert his evil fate :—

"Taking tea at a friend's house in the road where I live, I met with the Rev. Mr. Johnson, superintendent of the South Shields Circuit among the Primitive Methodists. He spoke with great confidence of the authenticity of a remarkable dream which he related. He used to reside at Shipley, near Bradford. His class-leader there had lost a leg, and he had heard direct from himself the circumstances under which the loss took place and the dream that accompanied. This class-leader was a blacksmith at a manufacturing mill which was driven by a water-wheel. He knew the wheel to be out of repair, when one night he dreamed that at the close of the day's work the manager detained him to repair it, that his foot slipped and became entangled between the two wheels, and was injured and afterwards amputated. In consequence he told his wife the dream in the morning, and made up his mind to be out of the way that evening, if he was wanted to repair the wheel. During the day the manager announced that the wheel must be repaired when the workpeople left that evening, but the blacksmith determined to make himself scarce before the hour arrived. He fled to a wood in the vicinity, and thought to hide himself there in its recesses. He came to a spot where some timber lay which belonged to the mill, and detected a lad stealing some pieces of wood from the heap.

He pursued him in crder to rescue the stolen property, became excited, and forgot all about his resolution. He found himself ere he was aware of it back at the mill just as the workpeople were being dismissed. He could not escape, and as he was principal smith he had to go upon the wheel, but he resolved to be very careful. In spite of his care, however, his foot slipped and got entangled between the two wheels just as he had dreamed. It was crushed so badly that he had to be carried to the Bradford Infirmary, where the leg was amputated above the knee. The premonitory dream was thus fulfilled throughout."

"I know it will come true." A much more painful story and far more detailed is contained in the fifth volume of the "Proceedings of the Psychical Research Society," on the authority of C. F. Fleet, of 26, Grosvenor Road, Gainsborough. He swears to the authenticity of the facts. The detailed story is full of the tragic fascination which attaches to the struggle of a brave man, repeatedly warned of his coming death, struggling in vain to avert the event which was to prove fatal, and ultimately perishing within the sight of those to whom he had revealed the vision. The story in brief is as follows : Mr. Fleet was third mate on the sailing ship *Persian Empire*, which left Adelaide for London in 1868. One of the crew, Cleary by name, dreamed before starting that on Christmas morning, as the *Persian Empire* was passing Cape Horn in a heavy gale, he was ordered, with the rest of his watch, to secure a boat hanging in davits over the side. He and another got into the boat, when a fearful sea broke over the ship, washing them both out of the boat into the sea, where they were both drowned. The dream made such an impression upon him that he was most reluctant to join the ship, but he overcame his scruples and sailed. On Christmas Eve, when they were nearing Cape Horn, Cleary had a repetition of his dream, exact in all particulars. He uttered a terrible cry, and kept muttering, " I know it will come true." On Christmas Day, exactly as he had foreseen, Cleary and the rest of the watch were ordered to secure a boat hanging in the davits. Cleary flatly refused. He said he refused because he knew he would be drowned, that all the circumstances of his dream had come true up to that moment, and if he went into that boat he would die. He was taken below to the captain, and his refusal to discharge duty was entered in the log. Then the chief officer, Douglas, took the pen to sign his name. Cleary suddenly looked at him and exclaimed, " I will go to my duty, for now I know the other man in my dream." He told Douglas, as they were on deck, of his dream. They got into the boat, and when they were all making tight a heavy sea struck the vessel with such force that the crew would have been washed overboard had they not clung to the mast. The boat was turned over, and Douglas and Cleary were flung into the sea. They swam for a little time, and then went down. It was just three months after he had dreamed of it before leaving Adelaide.

Here we have inexorable destiny fulfilling itself in spite of the struggles of its destined victim. It reminds me of a well-known Oriental story, which tells how a friend who was with Solomon saw the Angel of Death looking at him very intently. On learning from Solomon whom the strange visitor was, he felt very uncomfortable under his gaze, and asked Solomon to transport him on his magic carpet to Damascus. No sooner said than done. Then said the Angel of Death to Solomon, " The reason why I looked so intently at your friend was because I had orders to take him at Damascus, and, behold, I found him at Jerusalem. Now, therefore, that he has transported himself thither I shall be able to obey my orders."

Of the premonitions of history there are many, Some His- too familiar to need more than a passing allusion torical Cases. here. The leading case is, of course, the dream of Pilate's wife, which, if it had been attended to, might have averted the crucifixion. But there again foreknowledge was impotent against fate. Calphurnia, Cæsar's wife, in like manner strove in vain to avert the doom of her lord. There is no story more trite than that which tells of the apparition which warned Brutus that Cæsar would make Philippi his trysting-place. In these cases the dreams occurred to those closely associated with the doomed. One of the best known of dream presentiments in English history occurred to a person who had no connection with the victim. The assassination of Mr. Perceval in the Lobby of the House of Commons was foreseen in the minutest detail by John Williams, a Cornish mine manager, eight or nine days before the assassination took place. Three times over he dreamed that he saw a small man, dressed in a blue coat and white waistcoat, enter the Lobby of the House of Commons, when immediately another person, dressed in a snuff-coloured coat, took a pistol from under his coat and shot the little man in his left breast. On asking who the sufferer was he was informed that it was Mr. Perceval, Chancellor of the Exchequer. He was so much impressed by the dream that he consulted his friends as to whether he should not go up to London and warn Mr. Perceval. Unfortunately they dissuaded him, and on May 13th the news arrived that Mr. Perceval had been killed on the 11th. Some time afterwards, when he saw a picture of the scene of the assassination, it reproduced all the details of the thrice-dreamed vision. There does not seem to have been any connection between Mr. Williams and Mr. Perceval, nor does there seem to have been any reason why it should have been revealed to him rather than to any one else.

The Inner Light of the Quakers.   The Quakers, whether it is because they allow their Unconscious Personality to have more say in their lives than others who do not practise quietism as a religion, or whether it be from any other cause, it is difficult to say, seem to have more than their fair share of premonitions. Every one remembers how George Fox saw a "waft" of death go out against Oliver Cromwell when he met him riding at Hampton Court the day before he was prostrated with his fatal illness. Fox was full of visions. He foresaw the expulsion of the "Rump," the restoration of Charles II., and the Fire of London. Stephen Grellet is another notable Friend who was constantly foreseeing things. He not only foresaw things himself, but his faculty seemed to bring him into contact with others who foresaw things ; and in his Life there is an excellent instance of a premonitory dream, told by Countess Tontschkoff three months before Napoleon's Invasion. The countess, whose husband was a general in the Russian army, dreamed that her father came to the room, having her only son by the hand, and, in a tone of great sadness, said, "All thy comforts are gone ; thy husband has fallen at Borodino."

As her husband at that time was sleeping beside her she dismissed the matter as a mere dream. But when it was repeated a second and a third time, she awoke her husband and asked him where Borodino was. She told him her dream, and they searched through the maps with the greatest care, but could not discover any such place. Three months later Napoleon entered Russia, and fought the bloody battle which opened the way to Moscow near the river Borodino, from which an obscure village takes its name. Her father announced her husband's death, having her son by the hand, in the exact terms that she had heard him say in her dream three months before. She instantly recognised the inn in which she was then staying as the place that she had seen in her dream.

Wanted a Dream Diary. This array of facts, which are well accredited, would seem to show that in the book of Job Elihu was not far wrong when he said, "In slumberings upon the bed God openeth the ears of men and sealeth their instruction." Or, to quote from an author who uses more modern dialect, it justifies Abercromby's remark that "the subject of dreaming appears to be worthy of careful investigation, and there is much reason to believe that an extensive collection of authentic facts, carefully analysed, would unfold principles of very great interest in reference to the philosophy of the mental powers." ("Intellectual Powers," p. 224.)

Of premonitions, especially of premonitions in dreams, it is easy to have too much. The best antidote for an excessive surfeit for such things is to note them down when they occur. When you have noted down 100 dreams, and find that one has come true, you may effectively destroy the superstitious dread that is apt to be engendered by stories such as the foregoing. It would be one excellent result of the publication of this volume if all those who are scared about dreams and forebodings would take the trouble to keep a dream diary, noting the dream and the fulfilment or falsification following. By these means they can not only confound sceptics, who accuse them of prophesying after the event, but what is much more important, they can most speedily rid themselves of the preposterous delusion that all dreams alike, whether they issue from the ivory gate or the gate of horn, are equally to be held in reverence. A quantitative estimate of the value of dreams is one of those things for which psychical science still sighs in vain.

The subject of this chapter is one of strange fascination. Premonitions are distinct from dreams, although many times they are communicated in sleep. Whether in the sleeping or waking stage there are times when mortal men gain, as it were, chance glimpses behind the veil which conceals the future. Sometimes this premonition takes the shape of a deep indwelling consciousness, based not on reason or on observation, that for us awaits some great work to be done, which we know but dimly, but which is, nevertheless, the one reality of life.

> " Souls destined to o'erleap the vulgar lot,
> And mould the world unto the scheme of God,
> Have a foreconsciousness of their high doom,
> As men are known to shiver at the heart
> When the cold shadow of some coming ill
> Creeps slowly o'er their spirits unawares.
> Hath good less power of prophecy than ill ? "

It was this that sustained Moses in exile in the wilderness, and Cromwell, when, in the darkest hour of his country's fortunes, he resolved to face the dungeon and the scaffold rather than seek liberty and peace across the Atlantic.

But the spirit of prophecy, "this inward feeling of the glorious end," which has been the sustaining element in most heroic lives, is but the highest form of a foreseeing gift which seems to be distributed haphazard among all sorts and conditions of men, and which quite as frequently foresees small things as great. Nothing is more extraordinary and, indeed, more perplexing than the odd freaks of the vaticinating spirit. Its exercise is often so fantastic and purposeless that it is not suprising practical men lose patience with it altogether.

Mr. Blackham's Prediction. Among many odd premonitions brought under my notice since the publication of "Real Ghost Stories," one of the oddest was that told me by Mr. Blackham, the respected and energetic founder of the movement known as the Pleasant Sunday Afternoons. Mr. Blackham, more than twenty years ago, was going along a road with his sister when they met a young man. Instantly Mr. Blackham turned to his sister, and said : " I see that you will marry that young man, you will become as fat as a landlady, and you will have thirteen children." All of which was fulfilled to the letter. Here the chances against the fulfilment of the threefold prediction were enormous. Mr. Blackham did not even know at the time whether his sister and the young man they met were on terms of friendship, much less affection, and he could not possibly have guessed the future rotundity of his sister's body or the abnormal size of her family. He simply seemed to see the fact, and seeing it, mentioned it on the spot, as his sister, who is still living, can testify. The thirteen children are also *en evidence.*

Purpose there seems to be none in those things, any more than there is purpose in the glimpse you obtain of a landscape through a gap in a wall, past which you are driving at full speed.

Miss X.'s Dogcart. Some people have this gift of seeing in advance very much developed. There is, for instance, Miss X——, of the Psychical Research Society, whose exploits in seeing a dogcart and its passengers half an hour before they really arrived, has taken its place as the classical illustration of this fantastic faculty of intermittent foresight. As the story is so well authenticated, and has become a leading case in the discussion, I reprint the passage in which it occurs from the "Proceedings of the Psychical Research Society."

The narrative is by a friend of the recipient :—

"About eight years ago (April, 1882), X. and I were staying in a country house, in a neighbourhood quite strange to us both. One morning, soon after our arrival, we drove with a party of four or five others in a waggonette to the neighbouring town, and, on our return, as we came in sight of the house, X. remarked to our hostess, 'You have very early visitors; who are your friends?'

"(I was sitting, says Miss X., either beside or immediately behind our host, who was driving, and what at first attracted my attention was the sight, as I believe, of fresh wheel marks.)

"We all turned to find the cause of the question, but could see no one, and as we were still in view of the front door on which Miss X.'s eyes were fixed, we asked her what she could possibly be dreaming of. She then described to us, the more minutely that we all joined in absolute denial of the existence of anything at all, the appearance of a dog-cart standing at the door of the house with a white horse and two men, one of whom had got down and was talking to a terrier; she even commented upon the dress of one of the gentlemen, who was wearing an ulster, she said, a detail which we certainly should not have supposed it possible for her to recognise at such a distance from the spot. As we drove up the drive X. drew attention to the fresh wheel marks, but here also we were all unable to see as she did, and when we arrived at the house and found no sign of cart and visitors, and on inquiry learned that no one had been near in our absence, we naturally treated the whole story as a mistake, caused by X.'s somewhat short sight.

"Shortly after she and I were in an upstairs room in the front of the house, when the sound of wheels was heard, and I went to the window to see what it might be. 'There's your dog-cart, after all!' I exclaimed; for there before the door was the identical dog-cart as X. had described it, correct in every detail, one of the gentlemen—having got down to ring the bell—being at the moment engaged in playing with a small fox-terrier. The visitors were strangers to our friends— officers from the barracks near, who had driven over with an invitation to a ball.

"C. having read over D.'s account, had added, 'This is substantially the same account as I heard from one of the party in the carriage.' Mr. Myers adds, 'I heard C., an old family servant, tell the story independently with the same details.'

"Both D. and I were surprised at her accurate knowledge of the story, which she had not learnt from us, but from another.lady present on the occasion." ("Proceedings of the Psychical Research Society," Vol. VI. p. 374.)

Seeing seven years Ahead. Here is a curious but apparently purposeless premonitory dream, sent me by the head mistress of a Board school in the north of England. It is the narrative of a dream which occurred to her aunt, from whose mouth she took down the story :—

"In 1855 I was 'keeping school' at H. H., lodging with my aunt.

"I was much troubled at that time by the approaching marriage of my sister; for we had been close companions, and I knew that marriage would involve separation.

"One night, a week before her wedding, I dreamed that my sister was already married, and living in London, and that I had gone up on a visit to her. I went to the door of a house with two steps up to it, and inquired if Mrs. L—— lived there.

"'Yes,' said the woman who answered the door, 'Mrs. L—— lives here, but she is not at home. Follow me and I'll show you where she is. I followed my guide through several streets, until we reached the foot of a flight of stone steps leading into a large building. 'My sister is not here,' I said with energy; 'this is a workhouse.'

"'No,' said the woman, 'it is not a workhouse, and your sister is here.'

"To a porter standing within the portico she said, 'Show this person the ward where Mrs. L. is.' He conducted me up another broad flight of steps, along a long corridor, with numbered doors at each side of it. The door at the end of the corridor facing us was numbered 101. In this room I was told I should find Mrs. L.

"In the bed immediately within the door was a young woman.

"'That's not my sister,' I said, and was taken to the farthest corner of the ward. I got on to the bed indicated, and saw the face of my sister.

"Crying 'Oh, my Polly, my Polly ; what have they brought you here for?' I awoke. My aunt, who heard the words, evidently thought I was going silly over my sister's marriage.

"A week later, having gone home to be present at the

wedding, I told my sister what I had dreamt. She said it was only a dream, but it had made her feel very unhappy.

"In 1862 I went to London for the first time (to the Exhibition), and my sister showed me the house in which she had lived, which was the same as I saw in my dream. She had previously told me that the rest of my dream had come true in every particular. For the year after her marriage, being ill, she was advised by her medical attendant to go (as a paying patient) into Guy's Hospital for the best treatment. She told me that my description of the place (as dreamed) was accurate in every particular, even to the number of the door of her ward, the young woman who lay just inside the door, and the position of her own bed at the far end of the ward."

This was purposeless enough, as apparently purposeless as the fall of a meteor from the sky. People were willing to admit that meteors might fall if they were hurled, like Jove's thunderbolts, to execute vengeance on the evil doer; but to fall *à propos de rien*—that was another matter. Still science does not refuse to believe in meteors, merely because their advent on this earth's crust is not linked on in any definite manner to the affairs of mortal men. Neither is it sensible to refuse to recognise the facts of foreseeing, because the thing foreseen was not worth seeing when it occurred, let alone seeing it before it happened.

The Rev. Alexander Stewart, LL.D., F.S.A.,
A life saved
by a Dream. etc., Nether Lochaber, sends me the following instance of a profitable premonition :—

"It was in the winter of 1853 that my brother-in-law, Mr. Kenneth Morrison, came on a visit to us here at the Manse of Nether Lochaber. Mr. Morrison was at that time chief officer of the steamship *City of Manchester*, of the Inman line, one of the ocean 'greyhounds' of her day, sailing between Liverpool and Philadelphia.

"In my service here, at the time of Mr. Morrison's visit, was a native of Lochaber, Angus MacMaster by name, an active, intelligent man, of about thirty years of age, a most useful man, a capital shot, an expert angler, and one of the best violinists in the West Highlands. No great wonder, therefore, that Morrison took a liking for Angus, and that the end of it was that Morrison invited Angus to join him on board the *City of Manchester*, where, it was arranged, he should act as one of the steerage stewards, and, at the same time, as Mr. Morrison's valet. To this Angus very willingly agreed, and so it was that when Mr. Morrison's leave of absence expired, he and Angus joined the *City of Manchester* at Liverpool.

"Within a twelvemonth afterwards, Mr. Morrison wrote to say that he was about to be promoted to the command of the new Inman Steamship *City of Glasgow*—at that time, of her class and kind, the finest ship afloat—and that having got a few weeks' holiday, he was coming down to visit his friends in Lochaber, bringing Angus MacMaster along with him, for he had proved so good and faithful a servant that he was resolved not to part with him.

"Sooner than was expected, and when his leave had only extended to some twenty days, Captain Morrison was summoned to Liverpool to take charge of his ship, which had already booked her full complement of passengers, and taken in most of her cargo, and only required some little putting to rights, which had better be done under her commander's supervision, before she sailed on her maiden trip to Philadelphia. 'I must be off the day after to-morrow,' said Morrison, as he handed the letter to me across the table. 'Please send for Angus,' he continued, 'I wish him to come at once, that we may be ready to start by Wednesday morning.' This was at the breakfast table on a Monday morning ; and that same evening Angus, summoned by a special messenger from the glen in which he was staying with his friends, arrived at the Manse, but in so grave and cheerless a mood that I noticed it at once, and wondered what could be the matter with him. Taking him into a private room, I said, 'Angus, Captain Morrison leaves the day after to-morrow. You had better get his things packed at once. And, by the way, what a lucky fellow you are ! If you did so well on the *City of Manchester*, you will in a year or two make quite a fortune in the *City of Glasgow*.' To my astonishment Angus replied, 'I am not going in the *City of Glasgow*—at least, not on this voyage—and I wish you could persuade Captain Morrison—the best and kindest master ever man had—not to go either.' 'Not going? What in the world do you mean, Angus ?' was my very natural exclamation of surprise. 'Well, sir,' said Angus (the reader will please understand that our talk was in Gaelic). 'Well, sir,' said Angus, 'You must not be angry with me if I tell you that on the last three nights my father, who has been dead nine years, as you know, has appeared to me and warned me not to go on this voyage, for that it will prove disastrous. Whether in dream or waking vision of the night, I cannot say; but I saw him, sir, as distinctly as I now see you; clothed exactly as I remember him in life; and he stood by my bedside, and with up-lifted hand and warning finger, and with a most solemn and earnest expression of countenance, he said, "Angus, my beloved son, don't go on this voyage. It will not be a prosperous one." On three nights running has my father appeared to me in this form, and with the same words of warning; and although much against my will, I have made up my mind that in the face of such warning, thrice repeated, it would be wrong in me to go on this voyage. It does not become me to do it, but I wish you, sir, would tell Captain Morrison what I have now told you; and persuade him if possible to make the best excuse he can, and on no account to go on this voyage in the *City of Glasgow.*' I said all I could, of course, and when Captain Morrison was told of it, he, too, said all he could to shake Angus from his resolution; but all in vain. And so it was that Morrison left without him; poor Angus actually weeping as he bade his master good-bye.

"Early in March of that year, the *City of Glasgow,* with a valuable cargo and upwards of five hundred passengers on board, sailed under Morrison's command for Philadelphia; and all that was good and prosperous was confidently predicted of the voyage of so fine a ship under charge of so capable a commander. When sufficient time had expired, and there was still no word of the ship's arrival at Philadelphia, Angus came to enquire if we had heard anything about her. I could only reply that there was as yet no word of her, but that the owners, in reply to my inquiries, were confident of her safety—their theory being that something had gone wrong with her engines, and that she was probably proceeding under sail. 'Pray God it may be so!' said Angus, with the tears in his eyes; and then in his own emphatic language—*ach s'eagal leam, aon chuid dhuibhse na dhomhsa nach tig fios na forfhais oiree gu brath*—(but great is my fear that neither to you, sir, nor to me shall word of her safety, or message from her at all ever arrive). And it was even so: from the day she left the Mersey until this day no word of the *City of Glasgow* has ever been heard. It was the opinion of those best able to offer a probable conjecture at the time, that she must have come into contact with an iceberg, and instantly gone down with all on board.

"I may add that Angus was a Catholic, and that Father Macdonald, his priest, told me shortly afterwards that Angus, before my messenger calling him to the Manse could have reached him, had communicated the thrice-repeated dream or vision to him in confession, and precisely in the same terms he used in describing it to me. When no hope of the safety of the *City of Glasgow* could any longer be entertained, Angus emigrated to Australia, whence after the lapse of several years, he wrote me to say that he was well and doing well. Whether he is still in life, or gone over to the majority, I do not know."

This, however, is exceptional.

A Highlander's Dream of his Drowning. Another story, which was sent me by my old friend the housekeeper of the Hon. Auberon Hubert's Highland retreat on the shores of Loch Awe, is an awful tale of destiny, the premonition of which only renders it more tragic.

"They were all sitting round the fire one winter night each relating his best storys. They had all told a story of the most wonderfull things he had heard or seen in the Ghost line, but Martin Barraw from Uist who sat silently lestening to all

Come, Martin, said the man of the house are you not going to tell a story I am sure you know many

Well yes said Martin. I know some and there is one strange one, running in my mind all this night, that I have never told to anyone yet, but I think I must tell it tonight.

Oh yes do Martin cried all present

Well said Martin you all I am sure remember the night of the fatal boat accident at Portroch ferry, when Murdoch McLane, big David the Gamekeeper, and Donald McRae, the ferryman were drownd and I was the only one saved of the four

Yes we do that Martin, remember it well, said the good man, that was the night the Taybrige was blowen down, it was a Sunday night the 28th of Decr/79.

Yes you are right that was the very night. Well you know Murdoch and I were Salmon watching down the other side of the Loch that winter. Well one night about the middle of November we were sitting by the side of Altanlarich, it would be about midnight, we had sat for some time without speaking I thought Murdoch was asleep and I was very nearly so to when suddenly Murdoch sprung to his feet with a jump that brought me to mine in a second

Goodness what is wrong with you said I looking round in every direction to see what startled him but could see nothing.

O dear dear what a horrid dream I have had said he　**A**

dream said I. My I thought you had seen a ghost or something by the spring you gave

Well you would spring to if you could and you drowning.
Then he told me that he thought it was the 28th of Dec. and
there was such a storm he had never seen anything like it, in
his life before, We were crossing the loch at the ferry said
he. We had the big white boat and four oars on her. Big
David the keeper Donald the ferryman you and I. And man
but it was awful. the boat right up on end at times every
wave washing over us and filling the boat more and more,
and no way of bailing her, because no one could let go his
oar, you and I were on the weather side, and Big David and
Donald on the other, they of course had the worst of it, we
got on untell we were near the other side, the waves were
getting bigger and the boat getting heavier, we were going to
run for the creek, when she was struck by a huge wave that
filled her up to the seats and sent David & Donald on their
backs, they lost their oars, and the nixt wave came right over
her and down she went. The other two never were seen, you
and I came up and tryed to swim to the shore, you got near
enough to catch a rope that was throwen you, but I could not
get through the tremendous waves and was Just going down
when I awoke with such a start.

My what a frightful dream said I. I should not like to
have such a dream although I do not believe in dreams or
Ghosts or these things it was the rain falling on your face
did it

Well maybe it was said he but all the same I could see he
was thinking a good deal about it all night, although I tryed
to laugh him out of it. Well time passed untell about the
beining of Dec. there was heavy rain Murdoch went home to
see his wife and family as all the rivers were flooded and there
was no need of watching. He was on his way back to his
work on the evening of the nixt day, when he got to the ferry,
it was raining blowing like to blow the breeks of a Hieland
man as they say, Dear me Murdoch, said Donald the ferryman
you surely don't mean to go out to-night.

It is very stormy said Murdoch if you would be so kind as
come over for me at six oclock in the morning I would go
home again I must be down passed the Governor's before he
gets up you know.

Oh I'll do that for you Murdoch said Donald. So Murdoch
went home again that night. and nixt morning by six o'clock
he was at the ferry again. Well done, Donald. You are a

man of your word said he. As he seen what he thought was
Donald on the peir waiting him with his boat along side,—the
morning was calm and fair though pretty dark, he thought it
strange Donald did not answer him, but hurrying down the
peir was about to step into the boat, when he felt someone
strike him a violent blow on the ear with the open hand.
looking sharply round he was astonished to find no one near,
but as he thought as he turned round he had seen a dark
shadow disappear in the distance.

God be with us, said he turning to Donald what was that.
he was horror struck to see a most hideous Object in what he
had taken to be Donald. glaring at him with eyes of fire.
God have mercy on my soul. said he, as he turned to run, but
he had no sooner done so then he was seized by a Grasp of
iron and pressed down towards the boat, then began a struggle
for life. he wrestled and struggled with all his strength and you
know he was a very strong man, but he could do nothing in
the iron Grasp of his foe, and that foe a mere shadow, he
was surely and steadly forced towards the boat, he was being
forced over the side of the peir and into the boat through
which he could see the waves rolling quite clearly, it was a
mere shadow also

Oh God help me he cried from the depth of his heart as he
gave himself up for lost. Suddenty as from some unseen
power the grasp that held him ceased and Murdoch fell back
upon the peir unconscious.

How long he lay he could not say, but it was Donald
throwing water in his face that brought him round, they went
into the Hotel where the people were Just getting up, and he
got a glass of Brandy to steady his nerves, and after a short
time they started and Murdoch got back to his work some-
time during the day, where he told me the whole affair.

Poor Murdoch was much changed after that, for the few
day that he lived. you could easily see the thing was pressing
upon his mind a good deal.

I need not tell you of the boat accident you all know that
well enough already, how Murdoch's dream became true even
to the very letter. Mr. Ross the Minister was preaching in
the little church up here we went to put him across the Loch
and it was while comming back that we were caught in the
storm and the boat was swamped. Big David and Donald
never were seen Murdoch and I tryed to swim to the shore
but he only got a short way when he also sank and was
drowned I got near enough to catch a rope that they threw

out to me and they pulled me in although I was just about dead two "

There are many cases of this unavailing warning. Mr. T. A. Hamilton, of Ryedale Terrace, Maxwelltown, Dumfries, writes :—

" Thirty years ago I had the misfortune to lose my right eye under peculiar circumstances, and the night previous to the day on which it happened my sister dreamt that such had happened under precisely the same circumstances to which it did, and related her dream to the household before it had occurred. The distance between the scene of the accident and the house in which she slept was eight miles.

How a Betting Man was Converted. One of the most interesting cases of premonitions occurring in a dream is that which I have received from the Rev. Mr. Champness, who is very well known in the Wesleyan denomination, and whose reputation for sterling philanthropy and fervent evangelical Christianity is much wider than his denomination. Here is the story, as Mr. Champness sends it me :—

" When reading the Ghost Number of the *Review of Reviews*, especially that which relates to doubles in dreams, I was reminded of something which happened to myself. Some years ago, when working as an Evangelist, it was arranged that I should conduct a Mission in a town which I had never visited before, and where, so far as I remember, I did not know a single person, though I ought to say I was very much interested in what I had heard about the place, and had been led to think with some anxiety about the Mission. It would appear that on the Saturday night preceding the Mission a man in the town dreamed that he was standing opposite the chapel where the Mission was to be held, and that while he was standing there watching the people leave the chapel, a minister, whom he had never seen before, came up to him and spoke to him with great earnestness about religious matters. He was so much impressed by the dream that he awoke his wife, and told her how excited he was. On the Sunday morning he went to the chapel, and greatly to his astonishment, when I came into the pulpit he saw that it was the man whom he had seen in his dream. I need not say that he was very much impressed, and took notice of everything that the preacher said and did. When he got home he reminded his wife of the dream he had had, and said, ' The man I saw in my dream is the preacher this morning, and preaches again to-night.' This interested his wife so much that she went to chapel with him in the evening. He attended on Monday and Tuesday evenings. On the Tuesday evening after the service he waited outside the chapel. To his great surprise, when I came out of the chapel I walked straight up to him, and spoke to him energetically, just as he had seen on the Saturday night. The whole thing was gone over again in reality, just as it had been done in the vision. On the Wednesday evening he was there again, and I remonstrated with those who had not yielded to the claims of Jesus Christ. I pushed them very hard, and was led to say, without premeditation, 'What hinders you? Why do you not yield yourself to Christ? Have you something on a horse?' Strange to say, there was a race to be run next day, and he had backed the favourite, and stood to win 8 to 1. As he said afterwards, 'I could not lug a racehorse to the penitent form.' After the service, he went straight to the man with whom he had made the bet, and said, 'That bet's off,' which the man was very glad, as he expected to lose the bet. Sure enough, when the race was run the one that had been backed did win, but he had given up any intention of winning money in that way, and that night decided to become a Christian. He has since then died, and I have good hope of seeing him in the country where we may perhaps understand these things better than we do now."

The same kind of dream, foreshadowing something to happen in connection with public worship, is sent me by an old lady in Yorkshire, who vouches for its accuracy :—

"When young, and staying in the town of W., I was much troubled for a long time by spiritual doubts, so much so that sleep became an impossibility.

"One morning, while lying awake with closed eyes, between two and three o'clock, I became conscious of a bright light in the room. Opening my eyes, I saw at the foot of my bed a very beautiful woman, shrouded from head to foot in a veil of light, a lovely smile on her face.

"She held in her hand a Bible, and fixing her shining eyes on me, said, in soft, silvery, angelic tones :—

"'Because of thine unbelief hast thou brought darkness into thy soul. Hope thou in God, for thou shalt yet praise Him !'

"I closed my eyes for awe, and when I ventured to look up the vision had disappeared.

"The spiritual darkness continued.

"Three weeks afterwards, at the same hour as before, as I

lay awake, the same beautiful vision appeared again, and the same angel voice said :—

"'Take to thyself the shield of faith, the sword of the spirit, and the helmet of salvation.' Then, after a moment's pause, it repeated, very impressively,—

> " 'But above all lay hold
> On faith's victorious shield.'

"I closed my eyes as before, and the vision had fled when I re-opened them.

"The week following, on the Sabbath, I stood at the house door, strangely undecided as to what place of worship to go to that morning, although I had all my life attended the services of the Wesleyan Methodists.

"My companion, now dead, noticing my unusual indecision, recommended a chapel near at hand, which was a favourite with her; but I could not feel that that was the right place. Passing along the street, hesitating and undecided still, we came to the door of a church which I never attended. A sudden impulse drew me into it. Singularly enough the clergyman gave out as his text the very passage repeated by the angel at her second visit; and at the conclusion of the sermon, the hymn was sung containing the quoted couplet :—

> " 'But above all lay hold
> On faith's victorious shield.' "

How the Vision comes. A lady in Yorkshire, who seems to be more capable of analysing her sensations than most persons, sends me the following account of her gift :—

"I can give one or two instances in which I think I can say I have possessed this faculty. I may premise that it is entirely above and beyond my own control, and that I cannot command it at will, also that I have only been able to exercise it in connection with my own affairs. For some time before the power awakens (if I may so speak) I feel very restless, nervous, and irritable, then the future event flashes into my mind with the vividness of lightning, and gradually fades away again, leaving me in the depths of low spirits, which continue for several days. The events unfolded to me are always in the future, some are yet awaiting fulfilment. I will give two which came to pass in a comparatively short time :—

"In the year 1883 my husband was engaged in a law suit, about the success of which he was particularly anxious. The trial was to begin on Monday, and as we lived near the assize town he was to leave for it that morning. I had been feeling very anxious about it also, and went to church the Sunday before much troubled in mind. Suddenly, during the singing of the psalms, I saw the whole matter arrange itself, and heard the verdict given in my husband's favour. I told him this when we reached home, and though he laughed at me for my credulity, still I believe my words comforted him. He went away next morning, and in due course got his verdict.

"We were settled in a house in the Midlands, when by a remarkable chain of circumstances, a small place in the north of England was offered us to buy. The price asked, however, was far too high for us to entertain any idea of it, and we wrote to decline it. Nevertheless I said to my husband, 'I know we shall go there, and that So-and-So will offer you some agency business which you will accept.'

"'Pooh! Pooh!' he said, 'that is not at all likely. All So-and-So's arrangements are made.'

"But notwithstanding, in six months time we had bought the house, and in about two years the agency business had been offered to my husband."

CHAPTER IV

GHOSTS OF THE LIVING ON BUSINESS

" ' A strange coincidence,' to use a phrase
By which such things are settled nowadays."—BYRON.

IT is said that every family has a skeleton in its cupboard. It would be equally true to say that every family has a ghost in its records. Sometimes it is a ghost of the living, sometimes of the dead ; but there are few who, if they inquire among their relatives, will not find one or more instances of apparitions, which, however small their evidential credentials, are implicitly accepted as genuine by those who witnessed them. In taking the Census of Hallucinations I made inquiry of an old schoolfellow of mine, who, after I came to Wimbledon, was minister of the Congregational Church in that suburb. He subsequently removed to Portsmouth, where I found him with his father one morning, on the occasion of the laying of the foundation-stone of the new Sunday School. On mentioning the subject of the Census of Ghosts, the Rev. Mr. Talbot, senior, mentioned a very remarkable apparition which, unlike most apparitions, appeared in time to save the life of its owner.

How a Double saved a Life. The Rev. Mr. Talbot, who is now, as he has been for fifteen years, at Wooburn, Bucks, the father of my late pastor. He gave me the following account of the apparition :—"My mother had an extraordinary power of foreseeing and also of seeing visions. Of her premonitions and dreams I could give you many instances ; but as that is not the point at present, I will give you the narrative of her other faculty, that of seeing spiritual or phantasmal forms which were not visible to others. We were sitting at tea one evening when my mother suddenly exclaimed, ' Dear me, Mrs. Lister is coming up the path, with her handkerchief to her eyes as if crying, on her way to the door. What can have brought her out at this time ? There seems to be something the matter with her head. I will go to the door and let her in.' So saying, my mother arose and went to the front door, where she firmly expected to find Mrs. Lister. None of the rest of us had seen Mrs. Lister come up the path, but as our attention might have been occupied in another direction we did not think anything of it. To my mother's astonishment, when she reached the door Mrs. Lister was not visible. She came back into the room much disturbed. 'There is something the matter with Mrs. Lister,' she said. 'I am certain there is. Yoke the horse and we will drive over at once to the Lister's house—which stood about one mile from our place—and see what is the matter. My father, knowing from of old that mother had reason for what she said, yoked the horse and drove off with my mother as rapidly as possible to Lister's house. When they arrived there they knocked at the door; there was no answer. Opening the door they found no one downstairs. My mother then went to Mrs. Lister's bedroom and found the unfortunate lady, apparently breathing her last, lying in a pool of blood. Her husband, in a fit of insanity, had severely beaten her and left her for dead, and then went and drowned himself in a pond. My father immediately went off for a doctor, who was able to stitch up Mrs. Lister's worst wounds and arrest the bleeding. In the end Mrs. Lister recovered, owing her life entirely to the fortunate circumstance that at the moment of losing consciousness she had apparently been able to project a visual phantasm of herself before the window of our tea-room. She was a friend of my mother's, and no doubt in her dire extremity had longed for her company. This longing in Mrs. Lister, in some way unknown to us, probably produced the appearance which startled my mother and led to her prompt appearance on the scene of the tragedy."

This story was told me by Mr. Talbot, who was then a boy, seated at the table at which his mother witnessed the apparition, and was regarded by him as absolutely true. Evidence in support of it now will be somewhat difficult to get, as almost all the witnesses have passed over to the majority, but I have no reason to doubt the truth of the story.

The story of Mrs. Lister's double appearing to **More Doubles seeking Help.** Mrs. Talbot when in imminent peril of death, however it may be scouted by the sceptics, is at least entirely in accord with many other narratives of the kind.

A member of the Psychical Research Society in Southport sends me the following account of an apparition of a severely wounded man, which bears considerable resemblance to Mr. Talbot's, although its evidential value is nothing like so good.

Its importance rests solely in the fact that the apparition appeared as the result, not of death, but of a very serious injury which might have had fatal consequences :—

"A Scotch waitress in my employ, whilst laying the cloth for dinner one day, was startled by perceiving her father's face looking at her through the window. She rushed out of the room and opened the front door, expecting to see him. Greatly surprised at finding no trace of him, after carefully searching the front garden, and looking up and down the road, she came in, and sitting down in the hall nearly fainted with fright. On inquiring for particulars she told me she had distinctly seen her father's face, with a distressed expression upon it, looking earnestly at her. She seemed much troubled, and felt sure something was wrong. A few days after this vision a letter came, saying that her father (a Scotch gamekeeper) had been thrown from a dog-cart and nearly killed. She left my employ to go and nurse him."

Here is another story that is sent me by a correspondent in Belsize Park Gardens, who vouches for the *bonâ fides* of the lady on whose authority he tells the tale :—

"50, BELSIZE PARK GARDENS, LONDON, N.W.,
"*October* 17*th*, 1891.

"Some years ago, a lady named L. B. was staying with relations at Beckenham, her husband being away at a shooting party in Essex. On a certain afternoon, when she had, as she says, no especial reason for her husband being recalled to her mind, she was somewhat surprised, on looking out of her bedroom window, to see him, as she imagined, entering the front garden gate. Wondering what could have been the cause of the unexpected arrival, she exclaimed to her sister-in-law, 'Why, there's Tom !' and went downstairs thinking to meet him entering the house. He was nowhere to be seen. Not long afterwards there arrived the news that her husband had been shot accidentally and considerably injured. Directly they met she related to him her curious vision, and on comparing notes it was discovered that it had certainly taken place more or less at the same hour as the accident, the husband declaring that as he fainted away his wife was most distinctly present in his thoughts. There was, unfortunately, no means of exactly fixing the hour, but there was no doubt at the time that the two occurrences—viz. the hallucination and the accident—must have anyhow taken place within a short time of one another, if not simultaneously."

Here we have an incident not unlike that which occurred to

Mrs. Talbot—the unexpected apparition of the phantasm or dual body of one who at the moment was in imminent danger of death. Tales of this class are somewhat rare, but when they do occur they indicate conclusively that there is no connection between the apparition of the wraith and the disease of the person to whom it belongs.

The next narrative should rather have come **Two Doubles** under the head of premonitions, but as the pre-**summon a** **Priest to their** monition in this case was accompanied by an **Deathbeds.** apparition, I include it in the present chapter. It is, in its way, even more remarkable than the story of my schoolfellow. It is more recent, it is prophetic, and the apparitions of two living men appeared together to predict the day of their death. The narrative rests on the excellent authority of the Rev. Father Fleming, the hard-working Catholic priest of Slindon, in Sussex. I heard it from one of his parishioners who is a friend of mine, and on applying to Father Fleming he was kind enough to write out the following account of his strange experience, for the truth of every word of which he is prepared to vouch. In all the wide range of spectral literature I know no story that is quite like this :—

"I was spending my usual vacation in Dublin in the year 1868, I may add very pleasantly, since I was staying at the house of an old friend of my father's, and whilst there was treated with the attention which is claimed by an honoured guest, and with as much kindness and heartiness as if I were a member of his family. I was perfectly comfortable, perfectly at home. As to my professional engagements, I was free for the whole time of my holiday, and could not in any manner admit a scruple or doubt as to the manner in which my work was done in my absence, for a fully qualified and earnest clergyman was supplying for me. Perhaps this preamble is necessary to show that my mind was at rest, and that nothing in the ordinary course of events would have recalled me so suddenly and abruptly to the scene of my labours at Woolwich. I had about a week of my unexpired leave of absence yet to run when what I am about to relate occurred to me. No comment or explanation is offered. It is simply a narrative.

"I had retired to rest at night, my mind perfectly at rest, and slept, as young men do in robust health, until about four o'clock in the morning. It appeared to me about that hour that I was conscious of a knock at the door. Thinking it to be the man-servant, who was accustomed to call me in the morning, I at once said, 'Come in.' To my surprise there appeared at the foot of the bed two figures, one a man of medium height, fair and well fleshed, the other tall, dark, and spare, both dressed as artisans belonging to Woolwich Arsenal. On asking them what they wanted, the shorter man replied, 'My name is C——s. I belong to Woolwich. I died on —— of ——, and you must attend me.'

"Probably the novelty of the situation and feelings attendant upon it, prevented me from noticing that he had used the past tense. The reply which I received to my question from the other man was like in form, 'My name is M——ll, I belong to Woolwich, I died on —— of ——, and you must attend me.' I then remarked that the past tense had been used, and cried out, 'Stop! You said "died," and the day you mentioned has not come yet!' at which they both smiled, and added, 'We know this very well; it was done to fix your attention, but'—and they seemed to say very earnestly and in a marked manner—'you must attend us!' at which they disappeared, leaving me awe-stricken, surprised and thoroughly aroused from sleep. Whether what I narrate was seen during sleep, or when wholly awake, I do not pretend to say. It appeared to me that I was perfectly awake and perfectly conscious. Of this I had no doubt at the time, and I can scarcely summon up a doubt as to what I heard and saw whilst I am telling it. As I had lighted my lamp, I rose, dressed, and, seating myself at a table in the room, read and thought, and, I need hardly say, from time to time prayed, fervently, until day came. When I was called in the morning, I sent a message to the lady of the house to say that I should not go to the University Chapel to say Mass that morning, and should be present at the usual family breakfast at nine.

"On entering the dining-room my hostess very kindly inquired after my health, naturally surmising that I had omitted Mass from illness, or at least want of rest and consequent indisposition. I merely answered that I had not slept well, and that there was something weighing heavily upon my mind which obliged me to return at once to Woolwich. After the usual regrets and leave-takings, I started by the mid-day boat for England. As the first date mentioned by my visitors gave me time, I travelled by easy stages, and spent more than two days on the road, although I could not remain in Dublin after I had received what appeared to me then, and appears to me still, as a solemn warning.

"On my arrival at Woolwich, as may be easily imagined, my

brother clergy were very puzzled at my sudden and unlooked-for return, and concluded that I had lost my reckoning, thinking that I had to resume my duties a week earlier than I was expected to do. The other assistant priest was waiting for my return to start on his vacation—and he did so the very evening of my return. Scarcely, however, had he left the town when the first of my visitors sent in a request for me to go at once to attend him. You may, perhaps, imagine my feelings at that moment. I am sure you cannot realize them as I do even now after the lapse of so many years. Well, I lost no time. I had, in truth, been prepared, except hat and umbrella, from the first hour after my return. I went to consult the books in which all the sick-calls were entered and to speak to our aged, respected sacristan who kept them. He remarked at once, 'You do not know this man, father ; his children come to our school, but he is, or has always been, considered as a Protestant.' Expressing my surprise, less at the fact than at his statement, I hurried to the bedside of the sufferer. After the first few words of introduction were over he said, 'I sent for you, father, on Friday morning early, and they told me that you were away from home, but that you were expected back in a few days, and I said I would wait.' I found the sick man had been stricken down by inflammation of the lungs, and that the doctor gave no hope of his recovery, yet that he would probably linger some days. I applied myself very earnestly indeed to prepare the poor man for death. Again the next day, and every day until he departed this life, did I visit him, and spent not minutes, but hours, by his bedside.

"A few days after the first summons came the second. The man had previously been a stranger to me, but I recognised him by his name and appearance. As I sat by his bedside he told me, as the former had already done, that he had sent for me, had been told that I was absent, and had declared that he would wait for me. Thus far their cases were alike. In each case there was a great wrong to be undone, a conscience to be set right that had erred and erred deeply—and not merely that, it is probable, from the circumstances of their lives, that it was necessary that their spiritual adviser should have been solemnly warned. They made their peace with God, and I have seldom assisted at a deathbed and felt greater consolation than I did in each and both of these. Even now, after the lapse of many years, I cannot help feeling that I received a very solemn warning in Dublin, and am not far wrong in calling it, the Shadow of Death.

"T. O. FLEMING."

The familiar story told by Mr. Dale Owen, but somewhat discredited by the severe scrutineers of the Psychical Research Society, of the rescue of the crew of a derelict ship by the timely visit of the Double, who wrote, "Steer nor'.-west" on the slate in the cabin of another ship, is the best of its kind.

A Dying Double demands its Portraits! Perhaps the most remarkable and most authentic ghost of 1891 is the ghost which appeared at Newcastle, for the purpose of demanding its photographs! The story was first told me by the late secretary of the Bradford Association of Helpers, Mr. Snowden Ward. I subsequently obtained it first hand from the man who saw the ghost. Running from the central railway station at Newcastle, a broad, busy thoroughfare connects Neville Street with Grainger Street. On one side stands St. John's Church, on the other the Savings Bank, and a little past the Savings Bank, proceeding from the station, stand the shops and offices of Grainger Street. It is a comparatively new street, and is quite one of the last places in the world where one would expect to find visitants of a ghostly nature. Nevertheless, it was in one of the places of business in this busy and bustling thoroughfare that the ghost in question appeared, for that it did appear there can be no manner of doubt. Even if all the other cases published in this Christmas Number were discarded as lacking in evidential value, this would of itself suffice to establish the fact that apparitions appear, for the circumstances are such as to preclude the adoption of any of the usual hypotheses to account for the apparition. I called upon Mr. Dickinson at 43, Grainger Street, on October 14th, examined his premises, was shown the entry in his book, and cross-examined himself and Miss Simon, the lady clerk, who figures in the subsequent narrative. It will probably be best to reprint the statement, which originally appeared in the *Practical Photographer*, merely filling in names and supplementing it here and there with a little more detail :—

"On Saturday, the 3rd of January this year," said Mr. Dickinson, "I arrived at my place of business, 43, Grainger Street, Newcastle, a few minutes before 8 a.m. The outer door is protected by an iron gate in which is a smaller lock-up gate, through which I passed into the premises. Having opened the office and turned the gas on at meter, and lit the gas fire, I stood at the office counter for a few minutes waiting for the lad who takes down the iron gate at the front door."

Mr. Dickinson told me that the reason he was down so

early was because the lad who usually brought the keys was ill, and he had come earlier than usual on that account. The place is lit with electric light. Mr. Dickinson does not remember turning on the light, although, as it was only eight o'clock on the third of January, he must have done so in order to read the entry in the book. The accompanying photograph shows the general outlines of the office. Mr. Dickinson stood in front of the window behind the counter shown in the photograph.

Before the lad came, however, a gentleman called to inquire if his photographs were finished.

He was a stranger to him. He came into the room and came up to the counter in the ordinary way. He was wearing a hat and overcoat, and there was nothing unusual about his appearance excepting that he did not seem very well. He said to me, "Are my photographs ready?" I said, "Who are you? We are not opened yet." He said his name was Thompson. I asked him if he had the receipt (which usually accompanies any inquiry), and he replied that he had no receipt, but his photograph was taken on December 6th, and that the prints were promised to be sent to him before this call.

I then asked him whether it was a cash order or a subscription one. The reason for asking this is because we have two books in which orders are entered. He said he had paid for them at the time; his name would therefore be in the cash orders. Having got the date and his name, I referred to my book, and found the order as he stated. I read out to him the name and address, to which he replied, "That is right."

Here is an exact copy of the entry in the order book :—

7976.   *Sat., Dec. 6th,* '90.
              Mr. J. S. THOMPSON,
                   154, William Street,
                        Hebburn Quay.
        6 cabinets.   7s. pd.

The above was written in pencil ; on the margin was written in ink, "Dec. 16," which, Mr. Dickinson explained, is the date on which the negative came to the office, named and numbered, and ready to go to the printers.

Below this again was written in ink.

5th.—3 Cabinets gratis, neg. broken, letter sent asking to re-sit.

In my book I found a date given, on which the negative

was ready to be put into the printer's hands; and the date being seventeen days previous, I had no hesitation in saying, "Well, if you call later on you will get some;" and I called his attention to the fact that it was very early, and explained to him that the employées would not be at work until nine o'clock, and if he could call after that time he would be certain to get some of his photographs. He said, "I have been travelling all night, and cannot call again."

Some short time before I had been at a hydropathic establishment in Yorkshire, and had travelled home at night. When he said he had been travelling all night, I remembered my own journey, and I thought perhaps he has been to some hydropathic establishment to benefit his health; and, finding that he was getting no better, he had come back, perhaps to die, for he looked wretchedly ill. He spoke wearily and rather impatiently, when he said he could not call again.

With that, he turned abruptly and went out. Anxious to retain his good-will, I shouted after him, "Can I post what may be done?" but I got no answer. I turned once more to the book, looked at the number, and on a slip of paper wrote *No. 7976, Thompson, Post.* (This I wrote with pen and ink, and have the paper yet.)

Mr. Dickinson said he had handed over this piece of paper to a representative of the Psychical Research Society who had lost it. It was, however, a mere memorandum written on the back of a traveller's card.

At nine o'clock, when Miss Simon (clerk and reception room attendant, a bright, intelligent young lady) came, I handed the slip of paper to her, and asked her to have it attended to, telling her that the man had called for them, and seemed much disappointed that he had not received them before. Miss Simon, with considerable surprise, exclaimed, "Why, an old man called about these photographs yesterday (Friday), and I told him they could not be ready this week owing to the bad weather, and that we were nearly three weeks behind with our work." I suggested that it was quite time Mr. Thompson's were ready, and inquired who was printing the order. I was told that it was not in print, and, pointing to a pile of negatives, Miss Simon said, "Thompson's is amongst that lot, and they have been waiting quite a fortnight."

I asked to be shown the negative, and about half an hour later Miss S. called me, saying, "This is Thompson's negative."

I took it in my hands and looked at it carefully, remarking, "Yes, that is it; that is the chap who called this morning."

Mr. Dickinson said he had no difficulty in recognising it, although the man wore a hat and top coat when he called, whereas in the portrait, as shown in the accompnying picture, which is taken from the original negative, the sitter wore neither hat nor top coat.

Miss Simon again referred to the fact that she had told the man who had called on the previous day that none were done, or could be done that week.

"Well," I said, "put this to one side, and I will see to it myself on Monday, and endeavour to hurry it forward."

On the Monday (January 5th) I was in one of the printing rooms, and about 10.30 a.m., having one or two printing frames empty, I thought of Thompson's negative, and accordingly went down to the office and asked Miss S. for it. "Oh, yes," she replied, "and here are a few more equally urgent; you may take them as well." I said, "That cannot be, as I have only two or three frames at liberty" (she had about twenty negatives in her hand, holding them out to me); "give me Thompson's first, and let me get my mind at rest about it." To which she answered, "His is amongst this lot, I will have to pick it out." (Each negative was in a paper bag.)

I offered to help her, and she commenced at one end of the batch and I at the other; and before we got halfway through I came across one which I knew was very urgent, and turned away to look up the date of taking it when crash! went part of the negatives on the floor. This accident seemed so serious that I was almost afraid to pick up the fallen negatives, but on doing so, one by one, I was greatly relieved to find *only one* was broken; but, judge of my horror, to find that that one was Thompson's!

I muttered something (not loud, but deep), and would fain have relieved my feelings, but the presence of ladies restrained me (this accident being witnessed also by my head printer, Miss L.).

I could not honestly blame Miss Simon for this—each thought the other was holding the lot, and between us we let them drop.

The negative was broken in two, right across the forehead of figure. I put the pieces carefully away, and taking out a memo. form, wrote to Mr. Thompson, asking him to kindly give another sitting, and offering to recoup him for his trouble and loss of time. This letter was posted five minutes after the negative was broken, and the affair was forgotten by me for the time.

However, on Friday, January 9th, I was in the printing-room upstairs, when I was signalled by the whistle which communicates with the office, and Miss Simon asked if I could go down, as the gentleman had called about the negative. I asked " What negative ? " " Well," she replied, " the one we broke."

" Mr. Thompson's," I answered. " I am very busy and cannot come down, but you know the terms I offered him ; send him up to be taken at once."

" But he is *dead !* " said Miss Simon.

" Dead !" I exclaimed, and without another word I hastened down the stairs to my office. Here I saw an elderly gentleman, who seemed in great trouble.

" Surely," said I to him, " you don't mean to say that this man is dead ? "

" It is only too true," he replied.

" Well, it must have been dreadfully sudden," I said sympathetically, " because I saw him only last Saturday."

The old gentleman shook his head sadly, and said, " You are mistaken, for he died last Saturday."

" Nay," I returned, " I am not mistaken, for I recognised him by the negative."

However, the father (for such was his relationship to my sitter) persisted in saying I was mistaken, and that it was he who called on the Friday and not his son, and, he said, " I saw that young lady (pointing to Miss Simon), and she told me the photographs would not be ready that week."

" 'That is quite right," said Miss Simon, " but Mr. Dickinson also saw a gentleman on the Saturday morning, and when I showed Mr. Dickinson the negative, he said, ' Yes, that's the man who called.' I told Mr. Dickinson *then* of your having called on the Friday."

Still Mr. Thompson, sen., seemed to think that we were wrong, and the many questions and cross-questions I put to him only served to confirm him in his opinion that I had got mixed ; but this he said—no one was authorised to call, nor had they any friend or relative who would know of the portraits being ordered, neither was there any one likely to impersonate the man who had sat for his portrait.

I had no further interview with the old gentleman until a week later, when he was much calmer in his appearance and conversation, and at this interview he told me that his son died on Saturday, January 3rd, at about 2.30 p.m.; he also stated that at the time I saw him (the sitter) he was unconscious, and remained so up to the time of his death. I have not had any explanation of this mysterious visit up to present date, February 26th, 1891.

It is curious to me that I have no recollection of hearing the man come upstairs, or of him going down. In appearance he was pale and careworn, and looked as though he had been very ill. This thought occurred to me when he said he had been travelling all night.

JAMES DICKINSON."

43, GRAINGER STREET, NEWCASTLE."

Miss Simon, in further conversation with me, stated that when the father called on Friday night and asked for the photographs he came late, at least after the electric light was lit. He seemed disappointed, but made no further remark when he was told they were not ready. Mr. Dickinson stated that in conversation with the father afterwards, he told him that his son, on the Friday, had been delirious and had cried out for his photographs so frequently that they had tried to get them, and that was why he had called on Friday night. Hebburn is on the south side of the Tyne, about four miles from Newcastle. The father was absolutely certain that it was physically impossible for his son to have left the house. He did not leave it. They knew the end was approaching, and he and his wife were in constant attendance at the death-bed. He also stated that it was impossible, from the position of the bedroom, for him to have left the house, even if he had been able to get out of bed without their hearing him. As a matter of fact, he did not get out of bed, and at the moment when his Double was talking to Mr. Dickinson in Grainger Street, he was lying unconscious at Hebburn.

It is impossible to explain this on the theory that Mr. Dickinson visualised the impression left upon his mind by Mr. Thompson, for Mr. Dickinson had never seen Mr. Thompson in his life. Neither could he have given apparent objectivity to a photograph which he might possibly have seen, although Mr. Dickinson asserts that he had never seen the photograph until it was brought him on the Saturday morning. If he had done so by any chance he would not have fitted his man with a top-coat and hat. It cannot therefore be regarded as a subjective hallucination; besides, the evidence afforded by the looking up of the book, the making an entry of what occurred, and the conversation which took place, in which the visitor mentioned facts which were not present in Mr. Dickinson's own mind, but which he verified there and then by looking up his books, bring it as near certainty as it is possible to arrive in a case such as this. Whoever the visitor was, it was not a subjective hallucination on the part of Mr. Dickinson. It is equally impossible to believe that it was the actual Mr. Thompson, because he was at that moment within six hours of death, and the evidence of his father is that his son at that moment was physically incapable of getting out of bed, and that he was actually lying unconscious before their eyes at Hebburn at the moment when his apparition was talking to Mr. Dickinson at Newcastle. The only other hypothesis that can be brought forward is that some one personated Thompson. Against this we have the fact that Mr. Dickinson, who had never seen Thompson, recognised him immediately as soon as he saw the negative of his portrait. Further, if any one had come from Hebburn on behalf of Thompson, he would not have asserted that he was Thompson himself, knowing, as he would, that he was speaking to a photographer, who, if the photographs had been ready, would at once have compared the photographs with the person standing before him, when the attempted personation would at once have been detected. Besides, no one was likely to have been so anxious about the photographs as to come up to Newcastle an hour before the studio opened in order to get them. We may turn it which way we please, there is no hypothesis which will fit the facts except the assumption that there is such a thing as a Thought Body, capable of locomotion and speech, which can transfer itself wherever it pleases, clothing itself with whatever clothes it desires to wear, which are phantasmal like itself. Short of that hypothesis, I do not see any explanation possible; and yet, if we admit that hypothesis, what an immense vista of possibilities is opened up to our view!

CHAPTER V.

GHOSTS KEEPING PROMISE.

"There is something in that ancient superstition
Which, erring as it is, our fancy loves."—SCOTT.

MANY of the apparitions that are reported are of phantasms that appear in fulfilment of a promise made to survivors during life. Of this class I came, in the course of my census, upon a very remarkable case.

Among my acquaintances is an Irish lady, the widow of an official who held a responsible position in the Dublin Post Office. She is Celt to her backbone, with all the qualities of her race. After her husband's death she contracted an unfortunate marriage—which really was no marriage legally—with an engineer of remarkable character and no small native talent. He, however, did not add to his other qualities the saving virtues of principle and honesty. Owing to these defects my friend woke up one fine morning to find that her new husband had been married previously, and that his wife was still living. On making this discovery she left her partner and came to London, where I met her. She is a woman of very strong character, and of some considerable, although irregular, ability. She has many superstitions, and her dreams were something wonderful to hear. After she had been in London two years her bigamist lover found out where she was, and leaving his home in Italy followed her to London. There was no doubt as to the sincerity of his attachment to the woman whom he had betrayed, and the scenes which took place between them were painful, and at one time threatened to have a very tragic ending. Fortunately, although she never ceased to cherish a very passionate affection for her lover, she refused to resume her old relations with him, and after many stormy scenes he departed for Italy, loading her with reproaches. Some months after his departure she came to me and told me she was afraid something had happened to him. She had heard him calling her outside her window, and shortly afterwards saw him quite distinctly in her room. She was

108

much upset about it. I pooh-poohed the story, and put it down to a hallucination caused by the revival of the stormy and painful scenes of the parting. Shortly afterwards she received news from Italy that her late husband, if we may so call him, had died about the same time she heard him calling her by her maiden name under her window in East London.

I only learnt when the above was passing through the press that the unfortunate man, whose phantasm appeared to my friend, died suddenly either by his own hand or by accident. On leaving London he drank on steadily, hardly being sober for a single day. After a prolonged period of intoxication he went out of the house, and was subsequently found dead, either having thrown himself, or fallen over, a considerable height, at the foot of which he was found dead.

I asked Mrs. G. F. to write out for me, as clearly as she could remember it after the lapse of two years, exactly what she saw and heard. Here is her report :—

The Promise. " In the end of the summer of 1886 it happened one morning that Irwin and myself were awake at 5.30 a.m., and as we could not go asleep again, we lay talking of our future possible happiness and present troubles. We were at the time sleeping in Room No. 46, Hotel Washington, overlooking the Bay of Naples. We agreed that nothing would force us to separate in this life—neither poverty nor persecution from his family, nor any other thing on earth. (I believed myself his wife then.) We each agreed that we would die together rather than separate. We spoke a great deal that morning about our views of what was or was not likely to be the condition of souls after death, and whether it was likely that spirits could communicate, by any transmitted feeling or apparition, the fact that they had died to their surviving friends. Finally, we made a solemn promise to each other that whichever of us died first would appear to the other after death, if such was permitted. Well, after the fact of his being already married came to light, we parted. I left him, and he followed me to London on December '87. During his stay here I once asked if he had ever thought of or forgotten since about our agreement as to who should die first appealing to the other ; and he said, ' Oh, Georgie, you do not need to remind me; my spirit is a part of yours, and can never be separated nor dissolved even through all eternity ; *no, not even* though you treat me as you do ; even though you became the wife of another you cannot divorce our spirits. And whenever my spirit leaves this earth I will appear to you.' Well, in the beginning of August '88 he

left England for Naples; his last words were that I would
never again see him; I should *see* him, but not alive, for he
would put an end to his life and heart-break. After that he
never wrote to me; still I did not altogether think he would
kill himself. On the 22nd or 23rd of the following November
('88), I posted a note to him at Sarno post-office. No reply
came, and I thought it might be he was not at Sarno, or was
sick, or travelling, so did not call at post-office, and so never
dreamed of his being dead.

Its Fulfilment: "Time went on, and nothing occurred till November 27th (or I should say 28th, for it occurred
at 12.30, or between 12 and 1 a.m., I forget the exact time).
It was just at that period when I used to sit up night
after night till 1, 2, and 3 o'clock a.m. at home doing the
class books; on this occasion I was sitting close to the fire,
with the table beside me, sorting cuttings. Looking up from
papers my eyes chanced to fall on the door, which stood about
a foot and a half open, and right inside, but not so far in but
that his clothes touched the edge of the door, stood Irwin; he
was dressed as I last had seen him—overcoat, tall hat, and his
arms were down by his sides in his natural, usual way. He
stood in his exact own perfectly upright attitude, and held his
head and face up in a sort of dignified way, which he used
generally to adopt on all occasions of importance or during a
controversy or dispute. He had his face turned towards me,
but his body, or breast rather, faced towards another direction,
just as if at the same as the door. His face looked at me with
a terribly meaning expression, very pale, and as if pained by
being deprived of the power of speech or of local movements.
I got a shocking fright, for I thought at first sight he was living,
and had got in unknown to me to surprise me. I felt my
heart jump with fright, and I said, 'Oh!' but before I had
hardly finished the exclamation, his figure was fading away,
and, horrible to relate, it faded in such a way that the flesh
seemed to fade out of the clothes, or at all events the hat
and coat were longer visible than the whole man. I turned
white and cold, felt an awful dread; I was too much afraid to
go near enough to shut the door when he had vanished. I
was so shaken and confused, and half paralysed, I felt I could
not even cry out; but like as if something had a grip on my
spirit, I feared to stir, and sat up all night, fearing to take my
eyes off the door, not daring to go and shut it. Later on I
got an umbrella and walked tremblingly, and pushed the door
close without fastening it. I feared to touch it with my hand.

I felt such a relief when I saw daylight and heard the landlady moving about. Now, though I was frightened, I did not for a moment think he was dead, nor did it enter my mind then about our agreement. I tried to shake off the nervousness, and quite thought it must be something in my sight caused by imagination, and nerves being overdone by sitting up so late for so many nights together. Still, I thought it dreadfully strange, it was *so real*.

A Ghost's Cough.   " Well, about three days passed, and then I was startled by hearing his voice outside my window, as plain as a voice could be, calling, ' Georgie ! Are you there, Georgie ? ' I felt certain it was really him come back to England. I could not mistake his voice. I felt quite flurried, and ran out to the hall door, but no one in sight. I went back in, and felt rather upset and disappointed, for I would have been glad if it was him back again, and began to wish he really would turn up. I then thought to myself, ' Well, that was so queer. Oh, it *must* be Irwin, and perhaps he is just hiding in some hall door to see if I *will* go out and let him in, or what I will do.' So out I went again. This time I put my hat on, and ran along and peeped into hall doors where he might be hiding, but with no result. Later on that night I could have sworn I heard him cough twice right at the window, as if he did it to attract attention. Out I went again. No result. Well, to make a long story short, from that night till about nine weeks after that voice called to me, and coughed, and coughed, sometimes every night for a week, then three nights a week, then miss a night and call on two nights, miss three or four days, and keep calling me the whole night long, on and off, up till 12 midnight or later. One time it would be, ' Georgie ! It's *me !* Ah, Georgie !' Or, ' Georgie, are you in ? Will you *speak* to *Irwin ?* ' Then a long pause, and at the end of, say, ten minutes, a most strange, unearthly *sigh*, or a cough—a perfectly intentional, forced cough, other times nothing but, ' Ah, Georgie !' On one night there was a dreadful fog. He called me so plain, I got up and said, ' Oh, really ! that man MUST be here ; he must be lodging somewhere near, as sure as life ; if he is not outside I must be going mad in my mind or imagination.' I went and stood outside the hall door steps in the thick black fog. No lights could be seen that night. I called out, ' Irwin ! Irwin ! here, come on, I *know* you're there, trying to humbug me, I *saw* you in *town ;* come on in, and don't be making a fool of yourself.'

" Well, I declare to you, a voice that seemed *within three yards* of me, replied out of the fog, 'It's *only Irwin,*' and a most awful, and great, and supernatural sort of sigh faded away in the distance.   I went in, feeling quite unhinged and nervous, and could not sleep.   After that night it was chiefly sighs and coughing, and it was kept up until one day, at the end of about nine weeks, my letter was returned marked, 'Signor O'Neill e morto,' together with a letter from the Consul to say he had died on November 28, 1888, *the day he appeared to me on.*"

On enquiring as to dates and verification, Mrs. F.
The Question replied :—
of Dates.

"I don't know the *hour* of his death, but if you write to Mr. Turner, Vice-Consul, Naples, he can get it for you.   He appeared to me at the hour I say; of course there is a difference of time between here and Naples.   The strange part is that once I was informed of his death by human means (the letter), his spirit seemed to be satisfied, for no voice ever came again after; it was as if he wanted to inform and make me know he had died, and as if he *knew* I had not been informed by human agency.   I was so struck with the apparition of November 28th, that I made a note of the date at the time so as to tell him of it when next I wrote.   My letter reached Sarno the day or day after he died.   There is no possible doubt about the voice being his, for he had a peculiar and uncommon voice, one such as I never heard any exactly like, or like at all in any other person.   And in life he used to call me through the window as he passed, so I would know who it was knocked at the door, and open it.   When he said, '*Ah !*' after death, it was so awfully sad and long drawn out, and as if expressing that now all was over and our separation and his being dead was all so very, very pitiful and unutterable ; the sigh was so real, so almost *solid*, and discernible and unmistakable, till at the end it seemed to have such a supernatural, strange, awful dying-away sound, a sort of fading, retreating into distance sound, that gave the impression that it was not *quite all* spirit, but that the spirit had some sort of visible and half-material being or condition.   This was especially so the night of the fog, when the voice seemed nearer to me as I stood there, and as if it was able to come or stay nearer to me because there *was* a fog to hide its materialism. On the other occasions it seemed to keep at the same distance off on each occasion and about four times further than on that night, and always sounded as if at an elevation of about 10 ft, or 11 ft. from the ground, except the night of the fog, when it came down on a *level* with me as well as nearer.

"GEORGINA F."

The promise to appear was given and kept in the case of the apparition seen by Lord Brougham.

Lord Brougham's Testimony. When we come to the question of the apparition pure and simple, one of the best-known leading cases is that recorded by Lord Brougham, who was certainly one of the hardest-headed persons that ever lived, a Lord Chancellor, trained from his youth up to weigh evidence. The story is given as follows in the first volume of "Lord Brougham's Memoirs " :—

"A most remarkable thing happened to me, so remarkable that I must tell the story from the beginning. After I left the High School I went with G——, my most intimate friend, to attend the classes in the University. There was no divinity class, but we frequently in our walks discussed many grave subjects—among others, the immortality of the soul and a future state. This question, and the possibility of the dead appearing to the living, were subjects of much speculation, and we actually committed the folly of drawing up an agreement, written with our blood, to the effect that whichever of us died the first should appear to the other, and thus solve any doubts we had entertained of the 'life after death.' After we had finished our classes at the college, G—— went to India, having got an appointment there in the Civil Service. He seldom wrote to me, and after the lapse of a few years I had nearly forgotten his existence. . . . One day I had taken, as I have said, a warm bath ; and, while lying in it and enjoying the comfort of the heat, I turned my head round, looking towards the chair on which I had deposited my clothes, as I was about to get out of the bath. On the chair sat G——, looking calmly at me. How I got out of the bath I know not ; but on recovering my senses I found myself sprawling on the floor. The apparition, or whatever it was that had taken the likeness of G——, had disappeared. This vision had produced such a shock that I had no inclination to talk about it, or to speak about it even to Stewart, but the impression it made upon me was too vivid to be easily forgotten, and so strongly was I affected by it that I have here written down the whole history, with the date, December 19th, and all the particulars, as they are now fresh before me. No doubt I had fallen asleep, and that the appearance presented so distinctly before my eyes was a dream I cannot for a moment doubt ; yet for years I had had no communication with G——, nor had there been anything to recall him to my recollection. Nothing had taken place concerning our Swedish travels connected with G——, or with India, or with anything relating to him, or to any member of his family. I recollected quickly enough our old discussion, and the bargain we had made. I could not discharge from my mind the impression that G —— must have died, and that his appearance to me was to be received by me as a proof of a future state. This was on December 19th, 1799."

In October, 1862, Lord Brougham added as a postscript:— "I have just been copying out from my journal the account of this strange dream. 'Certissima mortis imago!' And now to finish the story begun about sixty years since. Soon after my return to Edinburgh there arrived a letter from India announcing G——'s death, and stating that he died on December 19th."

A Vow Fulfilled. Very many of the apparitions of this description appear in connection with a promise made during lifetime to do so. A lady correspondent sends me the following narrative, which she declares she had from the sister of a student at the Royal Academy who was personally known to her. He told the story first to his mother, who is dead, so that all chance of verifying the story is impossible. It may be quoted, however, as a pendant to Lord Brougham's vision, and is much more remarkable than his, inasmuch as the phantom was seen by several persons at the same time :—

"I think it was about the year 1856, as nearly as I can remember, that a party of young men, students of the Royal Academy, and some of them members also, used to meet in a certain room in London, so many evenings in the week, to smoke and chat, one of them the son of a colonel in the army long since dead. This only son kept yet a remnant, if no more, of the faith of his childhood, cherished in him by his widowed mother with jealous care, as he detailed to her from time to time fragments of the nightly discussions against the immortality of the soul.

"On one particular evening the conversation drifted into theological matters—this young Academician taking up the positive side, and asserting his belief in a hereafter of weal or woe for all *human* life.

"Two or three of the others endeavoured to 'put him down,' but he, maintaining his position quietly, provoked a suggestion, half in earnest and half in jest, from one of their number, that 'the first among them who should die, should appear to the rest of their assembly afterwards in that room at the usual hour of meeting.' The suggestion was received with jests and laughter by some, and with graver faces by others—but at last each man solemnly entered into a pledge that if he were the first to die amongst them, he would, if permitted, return for a few brief seconds to this earth and appear to the rest to certify to the truth.

"Before very long one young man's place was empty. No mention being made of the vow that they had taken, probably time enough had elapsed for it to have been more or less, for the present, forgotten.

"The meetings continued. One evening when they were sitting smoking round the fire, one of the party uttered an exclamation, causing the rest to look up. Following the direction of his gaze, each man saw distinctly for himself a *shadowy* figure, in the likeness of the only absent one of their number, distinctly facing them on the other side of the room. The eyes looked earnestly, with a yearning, sad expression in them, slowly upon each member there assembled, and then vanished as a rainbow fades out of existence from the evening sky. For a few seconds no one spoke, then the most confirmed unbeliever among them tried to explain it all away, but his words fell flat, and no one echoed his sentiments ; and then the widow's son spoke. 'Poor —— is dead,' he said, 'and has appeared to us according to his vow.' Then followed a comparison of their sensations during the visitation, and all agreed in stating that they felt a cold chill similar to the entrance of a winter fog at door or window of a room which has been warm, and when the appearance had faded from their view the cold breath also passed away. *I think*, but will not be positive on *this*, the son of the widow lady died long after this event, but how long or how short a time I never heard ; but the facts of the above story were told me by the sister of this young man. I also knew their mother well. She was of a gentle, placid disposition, by no means excitable or likely to credit any superstitious tales. Her son returned home on that memorable evening looking very white and subdued, and, sinking into a chair, he told her he should never doubt again the truths that she had taught him, and a little reluctantly he told her the above, bit by bit, as it were, as she drew it from him."

Quite recently—in fact, in the June of 1891— "The Gate that Clanged." the Rev. H. Chapman published in the *Ushaw College Magazine* a story, without giving genuine names, of an apparition which had sufficient truth about it to convert the writer to the Catholic faith. Mr. Chapman

says that in telling the story persons and places are changed
and details added, but the backbone of it is genuine in other
particulars.   The story, briefly told, is as follows :—Mr. Chapman was at school in England ; he spent his holidays with his
uncle, who was in the habit of receiving visitors from various
friends, including, among others, a Catholic priest, whom he
calls Reuben Crockford.   Father Crockford had the peculiarity
of clanging the garden gate.   It was a tiresome gate to open
and shut, and they always knew when Father Crockford came
because he always gave the gate a vicious little kick with his
heel after he had entered, so that it sent it with some force
against the latch, making it rebound, and then closing again
with another clang.   This mode of gate-shutting was peculiar
to Father Crockford, who always did it and was never mistaken.
One time there was a discussion of the resurrection of the
dead at his uncle's house.   His uncle said the resurrection
occurred too long a time ago—one wanted present evidence.
"Now, if you came back from the dead and told me the
Catholic religion is true, that would be evidence," he said.
Father Crockford replied, "If I die first, and God permit me,
I will come back and tell you, for I would do anything to see
you converted to the faith."   Three years after that conversation Mr. Chapman was again spending his holidays with his
uncle.   One morning his uncle came down late to breakfast
and announced that he had been dreaming all night that
Father Crockford was coming that day.   He ordered his room
to be put ready, and he put off dinner a quarter of an hour in
order to allow him more time to arrive.   Mr. Chapman was
reading a book in the study when his uncle went down to the
gate to meet Father Crockford.   Suddenly he heard a double
clang, the clang of the gate that Father Crockford alone ever
gave, and the invariable precursor of his visits.   Thinking his
uncle's presentiment had come true, he laid down his book
and looked out of the window to catch the first glimpse of his
visitor.   As he did so he looked at his watch ; it was just ten
minutes past five.   He saw the good priest emerge from the
bushes ; he was walking rather quickly, and carried his black
bag, which he always brought with him.   His uncle also saw
him, called welcome to him, and shouted to him to stop until
he came to him.   He did not do so, but went up to the front
door and looked in at the window.   Mr. Chapman nodded
and smiled but the priest took no notice of his salutation.
The dog howled and fled away.   Then he felt a curious cold
wind at the roots of his hair, and he noticed that the priest's

eyes looked somewhat as if they were gazing into eternity, and that his face was deathly pale. Again the dog gave a low howl, and the sound of a deep sigh at his ear made Mr. Chapman spring from his seat in an agony of terror. His uncle then came in and ordered the dinner bell to be rung, exclaiming in high glee, " I knew I was right. He has come." The dinner was served, but the priest did not come down ; the bell was rung again, and as he still did not come, they sent up to his room, when to their blank amazement they found that no one was there and the door was locked on the outside. The house was searched from cellar to garret, but he could not be found. Next morning his uncle handed Mr. Chapman a letter from the presbytery which informed him that the Rev. Reuben Crockford had died the previous day. The letter ran as follows :—

" He intended to have paid you a visit yesterday, and had got as far as the railway station when, being seized with sudden failure at the heart, he fell fainting on the platform and was carried in a dying state into the waiting-room. One of his brother priests was hastily summoned, who administered to him the consolation of our holy religion, and he also had the best available medical assistance. Unhappily, all efforts were useless, and he calmly expired at ten minutes past five, his last words being, ' John, there is a life to come.' "

"What do you think of that?" said his uncle. "I think," said Mr. Chapman, " that the Catholic religion is true. Father Crockford told you he would come and tell you if it were true." Mr. Chapman joined the Catholic Church, and is now a priest, on account of the vision of the good priest whom he describes under the pseudonym of the Rev. Reuben Crockford.

CHAPTER VI

APPARITIONS AT OR BEFORE DEATH

"There is no people, rude or unlearned, among whom apparitions of the dead are not related and believed. This opinion, which prevails as far as human nature is diffused, could only become universal by its truth; those that never heard of one another could not have agreed upon a tale which nothing but experience would make credible."—Johnson's " Rasselas."

THE number of apparitions recorded at or about the moment of death is so great that even when they are divided into three it is difficult to deal with them. They crop up on all sides.

When I made my last visit to Edinburgh, I stayed at the house of Mr. M——, a well-known jeweller in Princes Street. Mrs. M—— informed me that before her marriage she was informed of the death of her younger brother by an apparition. She saw him laid out as on a bier, with his face pale and dead, the body covered with a white shroud. He was a great athlete and an adventurous youth. He at that time was in India. For some time no confirmation of the uneasy forebodings occasioned by the vision occurred, but one morning when the minister approached the house to break ill news, they knew at once that their brother was dead. It was too true. He had ventured for a foolhardy wager to swim out under a waterfall, and had been drowned.

During my stay in Edinburgh I visited the workhouse and got into conversation with the master. I learned that he also had had an experience of the same kind. He was officer on board a man-of-war on the China station. Steaming between Singapore and Hong Kong he saw the apparition of a relative on deck, and reported the same to the lieutenant the next morning. That officer recommended him to make a note of the date, which he did. On his arrival at Yokohama he received intelligence that the relative had died that same day on which he had seen the apparition.

A Sailor Boy's Return In my own family I have known of one case of a similar nature. My grand-aunt, a Northumbrian matron, sturdy and practical, and full of common sense and not given to hallucinations, was awakened one night by the presence of her son, whom she saw standing by her bed-side. He had started a few days before on his first voyage as an apprentice on board an Australian merchantman. She was intensely surprised to see him at her bedside, and turning to her husband she cried, " Christopher, wake up ; here is John come back ! " When Christopher rubbed open his drowsy eyes and looked for his son he was no longer to be seen. " But I saw him," said my grand-aunt. " I saw him quite clearly. He must have come back, and is playing some prank." There-upon the two got up, lit candles, and began a thorough search of the house. They found no one and were much disturbed, but comforted themselves with the thought that, finding them asleep, he had gone to some friend's or neighbour's until morn-ing. In the morning, however, every inquiry failed to bring to light any trace of their boy. Of course it might have been a dream, but the old lady was so certain that she had seen her boy that the day and hour of his appearance were noted. No news was heard of his ship, which made the voyage safely, and they waited with some anxiety for the mail from Australia, which in those days was much longer in transit than it is now. When, however, the letter arrived, with the Australian post-mark on it, it brought the news that on the night on which the boy had appeared at Blyth, in Northumberland, he had fallen from the rigging of the ship in the English Channel and had never been seen again.

A Captain's Apparition This autumn Mr. Worthington, of 324, Scots-wood Road, Newcastle, furnished me the following account of the apparition of a sea captain's death :—

"Some years ago, my uncle, Captain Thos. Worthington, was away at sea. His wife was at the time living in Sunder-land, and one afternoon she came on a visit to Newcastle. After meeting my mother the two called to see another rela-tive—a Mrs. Hails, the caretaker of West Clayton Street Congregational Chapel, who was (and is still) living in a cottage behind, and which overlooks the chapel. Just before reaching Mrs. Hails's door my aunt said to mother, ' Why, there is our Tom ! ' pointing to the schoolroom. Mother, in surprise, says, ' Where ? ' ' Why, there ! Look ! he is in the school.' By this time Mrs. H. met them, and aunt re-peated to her what she saw, but Mrs. H. only laughed, and

said, 'Nonsense ! because here are the keys of the place, and
I am sure there is nobody there.' However, my aunt would
not be dissuaded, and to convince her Mrs. H. opened the
gate leading down the stairs, then opened the schoolroom door,
and entered the schoolroom, lit a candle (it being rather dusk,
being towards the back end of the year), but could see no one.
A note was made of the date and hour ; and strange to say, in
a few days, as soon as words could reach her, my aunt received
a letter from the person in charge of the ship in which my
uncle had sailed, informing her that her husband had fallen
overboard, and was drowned, on that very day and hour on
which my aunt had noticed the phantom which none but herself could see."

Some Stories   There are several stories of a similar kind re-
from the Sea. corded by the Psychical Research Society.   A
curious one is a narrative (sent by Engineer Dunlop, of
Bangkok, Siam) of an apparition seen "when the ship was
under all plain sail off the pitch of Cape Horn," when the
seaman who had started aloft to bend the fore-top-gallant,
flung his arms round the top-gallant shrouds and held on without moving, till he was lowered on deck in the bight of a
bowline.   For as he "kept looking to the windward at the
squall, suddenly in the midst of it he saw his sweetheart,
dressed in white flowing robes, who came flying down towards
him before the wind," and who, as it afterwards proved, had
died in England at that very same time.

Another seafaring story is communicated to a correspondent
by Lord Charles Beresford, and by him sent to the Psychical
Research Society :—

"It was in the spring of 1864, whilst on board H.M.S.
Racoon, between Gibraltar and Marseilles, that I went into my
office on the main deck to get a pipe ; and as I opened the
door I saw my father lying in his coffin as plainly as I could.
It gave me an awful jerk, and I immediately told some of the
fellows who were smoking just outside, the usual place between
the guns, and I also told dear old Onslow, our chaplain.   A
few days after, we arrived at Marseilles, and I heard of my
father's death, and he had been buried that very day and at
the time, half-past twelve in the day.   I may add that at the
time it was a bright, sunny day, and I had not been fretting
about my father, as the latest news I had of him was that,
although very ill, he was better.   My dear old father and I
were great chums, more so than is usual between a man of
seventy-two and a boy of twenty, our respective ages then."

A Death
Scene Wit-
nessed 3,000
Miles off.Whatever may be the cause, there are more stories of this kind told about sailors and soldiers than about all other classes of the community. Of the sailor stories, one of the best, concerning the apparition at the moment of death, with the clairvoyant accompaniment, is sent me by a Master of Arts in the North of Scotland, who has made it the subject of a carefully written and very interesting story, for the accuracy of which my correspondent vouches, as occurring many years ago to the person on whose authority the story is told. He is still living, and persists in the absolute accuracy of his most extraordinary narrative. It will be seen that there is not only in this case the phantasm of the unfortunate man who died, but also a vivid reproduction of the scene in which he perished, so that the person who saw it recognised, many weeks after, a total stranger as the person who was present at the hour of his death.

"Thirteen years ago," said Captain S——, "I was on board the C——, homeward bound with cotton from Calcutta to Liverpool. On Tuesday, the 25th August, 1868, when in lat. 33° 4' S., long. 31° 27' E., the sky darkened, and it was evident a storm was about to burst upon us; the crew were sent aloft to furl the sails, and before we had completed the task a great gust of wind seized the half-slackened maintopsail, and sent it fluttering into fragments. At the same moment the ship reeled nearly on her beam ends, and, above the howling of the gale, we heard a sudden cry of despair. I was horrified to see an apprentice, J—— P——, sent whirling headlong from the masthead into the sea. Even yet I can see the look of agony stamped on his upturned face, and I can hear the very tones of his heartrending cry, 'Oh! Lucy, Lucy,' as he disappeared for ever in the darkness below.

"After the storm abated, the captain made a careful note of the exact time of the occurrence, the position of the ship, and the other particulars. He seemed struck at my mention of the exclamation I had overheard, falling from the poor fellow's lips as he clutched in vain at the yielding air.

"'Ah,' he said, 'that must have been his sister, Lucy V., to whom he was greatly attached.'

"I then produced his cap, which I had managed to seize as it fell, and which the captain locked up with the rest of his effects, remarking, as he did so, that no doubt his people would prize it as a last keepsake of their son.

"The rest of the voyage passed without incident, and as

soon as the ship arrived at Liverpool I made my way to the train which was to take me to Manchester.

"I was walking idly along the platform when I saw the face of an old gentleman, who, with a young lady on his arm, was elbowing his way through the crowd. His resemblance to our lost mate was so striking that I stood and looked at him. The young lady's eyes happened suddenly to meet mine. Instantly she gave a violent start, uttered a low scream, and exclaiming, 'Oh, look, there's the face of my dream!' stared at me as if fascinated. Her companion gently rallied her, and half led, half carried her, to the nearest waiting-room. As he passed he begged me to come with them, and handed me his card.

"When we were alone the old gentleman explained that the sight of my face had reminded his daughter of a very peculiar and unpleasant dream, to which she still persisted in attaching importance. He said, 'At the present moment, indeed, we are on our way to discover if the owners of my son's ship have received any news of its arrival.'

"I said, 'I am an apprentice of the C——, and have but lately left her lying in the harbour.'

"'Then,' the young lady cried, 'I *must* be right. It *must* be true. 'Twas that man's face I saw gazing at him as he fell. I saw Joe's ship in the midst of a fearful storm, and him clinging to the slippery shrouds. A bright flash seemed to pass before my eyes, and I saw him falling backwards into the sea. I saw *your* face in the momentary gleam, and I woke perfectly terrified to hear the sound of my own name—"O Lucy! Lucy!"—whispered in my ears.'

"The expression of my face must have conveyed but too well the meaning of my silence.

"'My God,' cried Mr. ——, 'is it true, then? Is he dead?'

"I stammered—'Too true, sir. Yes, every word of it! I was beside him at the moment, and even tried to save him.'

"From the statement subsequently given to the captain, it appeared that the sister had retired as usual before eleven o'clock. About midnight they were roused by a loud scream, and, on hurrying to her room, found her sitting up under the influence of extreme terror, declaring that she had actually seen her brother falling from the mast-head into the sea, and heard him whisper her name.

"On comparing notes, we found that the dream took place the very day and, allowing for the difference in longitude, even the very hour when the accident occurred!"

This story did not reach me in time for exhaustive verification, but it is one which ought to be capable of being proved up to the hilt; for there is first the captain, who was apprentice, on whose authority the story at present exclusively rests. His story ought to be capable of confirmation by the lady to whom the vision appeared, the log-book of the ship from which the apprentice was drowned, while the captain and her companion at the station would be of first importance in establishing its truth. Should this be forthcoming, and the story verified as told by my Brecon correspondent, nothing in any other of the stories in this number can be regarded as antecedently incredible. This is not merely the sight of what occurred at a distance of 3,000 miles, but the hearing of the death cry which was raised in the midst of the howling of a tropical storm in mid-ocean. Compared with this, other narratives are but as an anticlimax; but even after this story, one told by Mrs. Green, of Newry, in 1885, is worthy of notice.

An Australian Tragedy seen in Ireland. Although there is no transmission of sound, nor any of the dramatic developments which took place in the previous story, there was the instantaneous transmission of the scene of an accident from Australia to Ireland. Mrs. Green writes :—

" I saw two respectably dressed females driving along in a vehicle like a mineral-water cart. Their horse stopped at a water to drink, but, as there was no footing, he lost his balance, and in trying to recover it he fell right in. With the shock the women stood up and shouted for help, and their hats rose off their heads, and as all was going on I turned away crying and saying, ' Was there no one at all to help them ? ' Upon which I awoke, and my husband asked me what was the matter. I related the above dream to him, and he asked me if I knew them. I said I did not, and thought I had never seen them. The impression of the dream and the trouble it brought was over me all day. I remarked to my son that it was the anniversary of his birthday and my own also—the 10th of the first month—and this is why I remember the day.

" The following third month I got a letter and a newspaper from my brother in Australia, named Allen, letting me know the sad trouble which had befallen him in the loss by drowning of one of his daughters and her companion. You will see by the description given in the paper how the events corresponded with my dream. My niece was born in Australia, and I never saw her. Please return the paper at your convenience. Considering that our night is their day, I must have been in sympathy with the sufferers at the time of the accident, on the 10th of the first month, 1878."

The following extract from the *Inglewood Advertiser* shows that she actually saw what happened :—

" A dreadful accident occurred in the neighbourhood of Wedderburn on Wednesday last, resulting in the death of two women, named Lehey and Allen. It appears that the deceased were driving into Wedderburn in a spring cart from the direction of Kinypanial, when they attempted to water their horse on the dam of the boundary of Torpichen station. The dam was ten or twelve feet deep in one spot, and into this hole they must have inadvertently driven, for Mr. W. McKechnie, manager of Torpichen Station, upon going to the dam some hours afterwards, discovered the cart and horse under the water, and two women's hats floating on the water. . . . The dam was searched, and the bodies of the two women, clasped in each other's arms, recovered." (Vol. v., p. 420).

The foregoing narratives contain the double element of the phantasm of the person at the moment of death, together with the clairvoyant vision of the scene in which the accident occurred. We now come to the second class, not less remarkable, namely, those in which the phantasm not only appears but speaks.

The most remarkable of all those which are re-
Major Poole's Ghost corded by the Psychical Research Society is that
Reports his Death which tells how Major Poole, who was killed in the battle of Lang's Neck in the Transvaal, reported his own death in London to his friend Colonel H. many hours before the telegraphic despatches brought news that the battle had been fought. The story is so complete in itself, and so remarkable in every respect, that I quote the whole of the evidence as it stands in the Report of the Society. Colonel H. writes :—

"February 13*th*, 1886.

" I am not a believer in ghosts, spirit manifestations, or esoteric Buddhism. It has been my lot—a lot sought by myself over and over again, and never falling to me by chance—to sleep in well-known or rather well-believed-to-be haunted rooms. I have endeavoured to encounter ghosts, spirits of beings (if you like) from another world, but, like other good things that one seeks for in life, without success. When I least expected it, however, I experienced a visitation so remarkable in its phenomena, so realistic in its nature, so supported by actual facts, that I was constrained, at the request of my friends, to put my experience into writing."

The narrator then described how, nearly twenty-three years before, he had formed a friendship with two brother subalterns, J. P. and J. S., and how his intercourse with J. P. had been continued at intervals up to the time of the Transvaal war, when J. P. was ordered out upon the staff. J. S. was already upon the scene of action. Both had now attained major's rank; the narrator himself had left the service some years previously.

In the morning that J. P. was leaving London to embark for the Cape, he invited the narrator to breakfast with him at the club, and they finally parted at the club door.

"'Good-bye, old fellow,' I said; 'we shall meet again, I hope.'

"'Yes,' he said, 'we shall meet again.'

"I can see him now as he stood smart and erect, with his bright black eyes looking intently into mine. A wave of his hand as the hansom whirled off, and he was gone.

"The Transvaal war was at its height. One night, after reading for some time in the library of the club, I had gone to my rooms late. It must have been nearly one o'clock before I turned into bed. I had slept, perhaps, some three hours or so, when I woke with a start. The grey dawn was stealing in through the windows, and the light fell sharply and distinctly on the military chest of drawers that stood at the further end of the room, and which I had carried about with me everywhere during my service. Standing by my bed, between me and the chest of drawers, I saw a figure which, in spite of the unwonted dress—unwonted, at least, to me—and of a full black beard, I at once recognised as that of my old brother officer. He had on the usual kharki coat worn by officers on active service in Eastern climates, a brown leather strap which might have been the strap of his field service glass crossed his breast. A brown leather girdle, with sword attached on left side, and revolver case on the right, passed round his waist. On his head he wore the ordinary white pith helmet of the service. I noted all these particulars in the moment that I started from sleep, and sat up in bed looking at him. His face was pale, but his black bright eyes shone as keenly as when, a year and a half before, they had looked at me, as he stood with one foot on the hansom, bidding me adieu.

"Fully impressed for the brief moment that we were stationed together at C—— in Ireland or somewhere, and thinking I was in my barrack-room, I said, 'Hallo! P., am I late for Parade?' P. looked at me steadily, and replied, 'I'm shot.'

"'Shot!' I exclaimed. 'Good God! how and where?'

"'Through the lungs,' replied P., and as he spoke his right hand moved slowly up the breast, until the fingers rested upon the right lung.

"'What were you doing?' I asked.

"'The General sent me forward,' he answered, and the right hand left the breast to move slowly to the front, pointing over my head to the window, and at the same moment the figure melted away. I rubbed my eyes to make sure I was not dreaming, and sprang out of bed. It was then 4.10 p.m. by the clock on my mantelpiece.

"I felt sure that my old friend was no more, and what I had seen was only his apparition. But yet how account for the voice, the ready and distinct answers? That I had seen a spirit, certainly something that was not flesh and blood, and that I had conversed with it, were alike indisputable facts. But how to reconcile these apparent impossibilities? The thought disquieted me, and I longed for the hour when the club would open, and I could get a chance of learning from the papers any news from the seat of war in the Transvaal. The hours passed feverishly. I was first at the club that morning, and snatched greedily at the first newspaper. No news of the war whatever!

"I passed the day in a more or less unquiet mood, and talked over the whole circumstance with an old brother officer, Colonel W. He was as fully impressed with the apparition as I was. The following morning I was again a solitary member at the club, and seized with avidity the first paper that came to my hand. This time my anxiety was painfully set at rest, for my eyes fell at once on the brief lines that told of the battle of Lang's Neck, and on the list of killed, foremost among them all being poor J. P. I noted the time that the battle was fought, calculated it with the hour at which I had seen the figure, and found that it almost coincided. From this simple fact I could only surmise that the figure had appeared to me in London almost at the moment that the fatal bullet had done its work in the Transvaal.

"Two questions now arose in my mind. First, as to proof that poor P. happened to wear that particular uniform at the time of his death, and whether he wore a beard—which I myself had never seen him wear. Second, whether he had met his death in the manner indicated, viz. by a bullet through the right lung. The first facts I established beyond dispute about six months afterwards, through an officer who was at the battle of Lang's Neck and who had been invalided home. He confirmed every detail. The second fact was, strangely enough, confirmed by no less a person than J. S., more than a year after the occurrence, he having also left the Cape, the war being over. On asking J. S. if he had heard how poor P., our brother officer, was shot, he replied, "Just here," and his fingers travelled up his breast, exactly as the fingers of the figure had done, until they rested over the very spot over the right lung.

"I have set down the foregoing, without any attempt at embellishment, exactly as everything occurred."

We find from the *London Gazette* that the battle in which Major P. was killed began (according to General Elley's despatch) at 9.30 a.m. on January 28th, 1881. Major P. was probably killed between 11 and 12 a.m., which would be between 9 and 10 in London, the difference of time being a little under two hours. I drew Colonel H.'s attention to this point, and to the impossibility that the dawn should be beginning at 4.10 a.m. at that time of the year, and he sent the following reply :—

"February 20th, 1886.

"It may have been 7.10, and not 4.10. The impression, writing now after some years' interval, is that it was 4.10 a.m., but I may be wrong.

"All I know is that I calculated the time at the time, with the hour at which the battle was fought, and it was to all practical purposes the same time.

"It was a winter morning, and the blinds were down over the window. The morning light at 7 a.m. in a winter month, coming through the blinds, would not be much stronger than the morning light at 4 a.m. in a summer month under the same circumstances. Hence I may have been mistaken in the hour, or the clock might have stopped unknown to me at 4.10 a.m. that day, or even the day before."

The first account of the battle of Lang's Neck appeared in the *Times, Telegraph* and *Daily News* of Saturday, January 29th, 1881. "No list of casualties." The first announcement of Major Poole's death was in a telegraphic despatch from the Transvaal, dated January 28th, and received by the

Secretary of State for War in London on the 29th. "Killed:
—Major Poole, Royal Artillery," and it appeared in the
Observer of Sunday, January 30th, and in the three above
mentioned papers on the 31st (Monday).

The precise date of this vision is now irrecoverable; but
Mr. Gurney, who discussed the matter with Colonel H., concludes that the apparition probably occurred after the death,
and certainly occurred before the death was announced in
England. (Vol. V. pp. 412–415.)

Another Ghost report- ing Death. A similar story, although much less carefully told,
is the following, in which the phantasm speaks and
points to the place where the bullet struck him, in
this resembling the case of Major Poole:—

Mr. Ira Sayles, of Washington, D.C., geologist U.S. Geo-
graphical Survey, states that one day in the spring of 1857 his
dear neighbour and intimate friend, Mrs. Stewart (now dead),
told him that on the night previous she had woke her husband
(now dead) with a scream. "What is the matter?" he said.
"Why, don't you see Johnny there? He says to me, 'Mother,
they've shot me. The bullet entered right here;' and he
pointed to a hole right over his right eye." Mr. Stewart
replied, "I don't see anything—you've been dreaming."
"No, I have not been dreaming, I was as wide awake as I am
now." This Johnny was a son who had gone with a friend to
Kansas, "then in a state of belligerent excitement over the
status of the incipient State on the slavery and free-soil
issue."

The mother was consequently anxious about him, but the
young man wrote in a sanguine tone. A fortnight after the
vision Johnny's friend returned from Kansas, and told Mrs.
Stewart that on a certain day, at 4 p.m., a Missourian shot
Johnny, the ball entering his head just above the right eye.
Moreover, the day of the shooting proved to be the very day
on which Mrs. Stewart had her vision, at night, about six
hours after the shooting." (Vol. V. p. 129.)

"Let not the Sun go down upon thy Wrath." All of these preceding phantasms spoke, and
there are many such instances in which the phan-
tasm does speak. One of these comes to me from
South Africa from the experience of the mother of
a well-known writer. A missionary on leaving Africa called
to bid his neighbour farewell. For some reason or other he
had given Mrs. —— reason to think ill of him, and when he
came to wish her good-bye she absolutely refused to see him.
He pressed earnestly for the favour of a parting word, but she,

being somewhat irate, said loudly in her room, so that her words could be heard by the person to whom they referred, " I will not shake hands with him, that's flat ! " He went away, and all thought of him passed from her mind. Some years afterwards the family was aroused by a cry of alarm after they had gone to bed, and on hurrying to their mother's room they found her in a state of great excitement. When she was sufficiently calm to tell them what was the matter, she said that she had suddenly been aroused by the sense that some one was in the room. She awoke wide awake in a moment, and to her horror she saw the missionary enter the room, and advancing towards her, heard him exclaim quite audibly, " You will shake hands with me now, Mrs. ——." As he approached she shrieked, and the apparition vanished. Some months afterwards they received information from England, stating that the missionary had died that day.

A similar tale is told by Mr. Pearsall Smith :—

At a meeting of the American Psychical Research Society, Mr. R. Pearsall Smith said that among the illustrations of the claim that animals have a perception of these extraordinary alleged apparitions after death, might be mentioned one occurring to a neighbour of his own, a prominent barrister in Philadelphia. He had parted under painful circumstances of controversy with a friend, who had later gone to Italy for his health. Afterwards, while camping out on the wilds of the Adirondacks one day, his horse became excited and refused to advance when urged. While engaged in the contest with the horse, the barrister saw before him the apparition of his friend, with blood pouring from his mouth, and in an interval of the effusion he heard him say, " I have nothing against you." Soon afterwards he heard that his friend had died at that time during a discharge of blood from the lungs. Mr. Pearsall Smith was prevented from procuring a statement directly from the barrister by the fact that after relating it to his friends the recollection of the incident had become so painful to him that he refused to converse upon the subject. He added that it may easily be conceived that the barrister, under painful recollections of the parting of his friend, and with the knowledge of his ill-health, might picture his friend forgiving a supposed injury, and also his dying scene. The extraordinary features are the coincidence of time and manner between the vision and the death, with the added circumstances of the alarm of the horse previous to the apparition. (Proceedings Psychical Research Society, Vol. V. p. 454)

Mr. George King, of 12, Sunderland Terrace,
The Wreck of Westbourne Park, W., sends to the Psychical
"La Plata." Research Society the following account of his
brother's apparition :—

"My brother D., a few years my junior, was a handsome,
powerful young man, twenty-one years of age at the time of
his death, and he was an unusually vigorous swimmer.

"In November, 1874, the cable was finished and shipped on
board the *La Plata*, a magnificent steamship, carrying with
her every appliance that could be required to render the expedition safe. Next Wednesday evening, December 2nd, I
attended a conversazione, at King's College, given by Sir
W. Thompson, President of the Society of Telegraphic
Engineers.

"I was soon asleep, but how long I remained so I do not
know. So far as recollection goes, I had not been dreaming,
but suddenly I found myself in the midst of a brilliant
assembly, such as I had recently left at King's College.

"Suddenly my brother stepped out from behind them, and
advanced towards me. He was dressed in evening dress, like
all the rest, and was the very image of buoyant health. I
was much surprised to meet him, and going forward I said,
'Hullo! D., how are you here?' He shook me warmly by
the hand and replied, 'Did you not know that I have been
wrecked again?' At these words a deadly faintness came
over me. I seemed to swim away and sink to the ground.
After a momentary unconsciousness I awoke and found myself in bed.

"Later on I went to my office and began my work, but
presently one of the messengers, with a strange look in his
face, came to me and said : "Is it true, sir, that your brother
has been lost in the *La Plata*?" I started up and ran to the
marine office next door, and there the worst fears were confirmed.

"The last seen of my brother was that he was helping to
launch the lifeboat. The *La Plata* foundered at about noon
on Sunday, November 29th, and possibly D. perished there
and then. But he may have possibly survived for several
days. He was of a strong constitution and a powerful swimmer ; he had on an air belt, and was beside the life-raft when
the ship went down." (Vol. V. pp. 456–457).

Here is a story which reaches me from a former
A Miser and resident in North Shields :—
her Store.

"During the cholera epidemic in the North of

England about 1867–8, I remember an incident which had a great effect upon my boyish mind at the time. I lived in North Shields, and was the favourite of my great-grandmother, with whom I often stayed. The old lady was rather a recluse in her habits, and occupied two upper rooms in her daughter's house. She was known to have some paper money about her, which, however, she carefully concealed somewhere from all her relatives. At the same time it was known she had a particular partiality for one certain cupboard which she used as a wardrobe in her bedroom. I mention these particulars as possibly explaining what followed.

"At three o'clock one morning, while sleeping at my own home, I awoke to find the old lady standing at the foot of my bed, calling to me and beckoning to me to follow her. I sat up in bed, terrified at the sight, but, of course, manifested no desire to move. The old lady then became impatient, and saying she could not remain longer, begged of me to be sure and go to 'the cupboard,' this being her usual phrase when referring to the small wardrobe I have alluded to. On the old lady's departure, I was so frightened that I felt I dare not stay in the room, and yet, strange to say, I had sufficient courage to get out of bed in the dark and hurry off to my mother's bedroom, crossing a dark landing on the way. I awoke my mother and told her what had happened. She calmed me as much as possible and saw me off to bed again, but in the morning she was so much impressed with my story that she accompanied me on my way to school, and we called to see if anything was wrong with the old lady. Imagine our surprise on reaching the house to learn that she had been found dead in bed a short time before our visit. The body was cold, proving she had been dead some hours, the doctor declaring she had died of cholera. The inference formed was that she must have died about the hour she visited me. Suffice it to say, an inspection of 'the cupboard' revealed the fact that other hands had done duty there before ours had a chance, but with what result will never be known."

Are they Ghosts or Doubles? It is a moot question whether the phantom that is seen at death is the ghost of one who has expired or the double of a living person on the point of death. There is considerable probability that in most cases it is the double of the dying and not the ghost of the dead that is manifested to the living. The foregoing three cases all point in this direction. In each case the dying person was conscious and living after the double had appeared, although in all three cases death followed in the course of a few hours.

In the cases I am about to recount, the appearance of a phantasm very shortly preceded death. One of the most remarkable of its kind is the following, which is sent me by Mr. H. Brett, English and American Agent, 14, Sophia Street, Leipzig. Mr. Brett sends me the name of the solicitor, "the most unsentimental solicitor I ever met in the City of London," upon whose authority the story rests. It was told him some eight or nine years ago within ten days of the occurrence, and is, from every point of view, very remarkable :—

"Having professional relations together, I called
A Clear Case on him one day, and, after the matter was dis-
of a Double. posed of, he asked if I had ten minutes to spare ;
we were both busy men. I replied affirmatively, whereupon he told me he was puzzled to account for something that had happened, and related to me the following in the matter-of-fact-manner of a lawyer when engaged on a particularly dry case :—

"'You know that since my wife's death I live alone except for the old servant, who has been with us for many years. A favourite old black tom-cat transferred his affections to me after my wife died, and when I am at home reading—my sole dissipation—he sits either on my shoulder or on the arm of my chair. About ten days ago he occupied the former position, as I, after a meat-tea, was reading one of the funniest parts of "Pickwick." I had had nothing to disturb my mind, no troublesome case to wade through ; my thoughts were immersed in the book, and I felt as cheerful as possible. The servant had gone out shopping ; the house was perfectly quiet. Suddenly the cat, which had been dozing on my shoulder, jumped down and began rushing about the room with bristling hair, and at last made for the closed door. I thought of burglars, so, taking up the light, began a search. When I reached the kitchen I found a woman dressed in deep mourning seated on a chair and cowering over the fire. Surprised at having heard no one enter, and with no other thought in my mind than that she was a friend of my servant, I asked what she wanted. She turned round and rose, showing a very haggard and suffering face which I did not recognise at all. Looking all the while at me, she slowly backed to the wall and disappeared through it without a word. I was surprised but not startled. I had only drunk tea and eaten a

APPARITIONS

133

moderate meal. I was, furthermore, reading a book tending
to laughter and not to depression. On reaching my office
next morning, one of the clerks handed me a telegram, saying
that it came after my departure, and as he had forgotten my
private address, he could not forward it. Supposing it to be
a business matter, I opened it unconcernedly. It stated that
my favourite sister was dying, and urged my immediate
presence. I hurried off to her, having till then been ignorant of her illness. A niece opened the door to me and, in
reply to my question, said her mother was still alive, but very
nearly gone, adding, 'But oh, uncle, between half-past nine
and ten last night we thought she was gone; there were no
signs of breathing or of life, and then she rallied a little!' I
hastened upstairs and found my sister near her last, and so
altered from suffering that I should not have known her. It
was the very face I had seen in my kitchen, and at the very
time when she was thought to be dead. She recognised me,
but could not speak, and soon afterwards breathed her last.
Now, I have never given a thought to ghosts or apparitions.
How do you account for it?'"

One of the best authenticated cases of this kind
The Birkbeck Double. is what is known as the Birkbeck Ghost. It is
told as follows in the "Proceedings of the
Psychical Research Society":—

"In 1789, Mrs. Birkbeck, wife of William Birkbeck, banker,
of Settle, and a member of the Society of Friends, was taken
ill and died at Cockermouth, while returning from a journey
to Scotland, which she had undertaken alone—her husband
and three children, aged seven, five, and four years respectively, remaining at Settle. The friends at whose house the
death occurred made notes of every circumstance attending
Mrs. Birkbeck's last hours, so that the accuracy of the several
statements as to time as well as place was beyond the doubt-
fulness of man's memory, or of any even unconscious attempt
to bring them into agreement with each other. One morning
between seven and eight o'clock, the relation to whom the
care of the children had been entrusted, and who kept a
minute journal of all that concerned them, went into their bedroom as usual and found them all sitting up in bed in great
excitement and delight. 'Mamma has been here,' they cried,
and the little one said, 'She called "Come, Esther!"'
Nothing could make them doubt the fact, and it was carefully
noted down to entertain the mother when she came home.
That same morning, as their mother lay on her dying bed at

Cockermouth, she said, 'I should be ready to go if I could but see my children.' She then closed her eyes to reopen them, as they thought, no more. But after ten minutes of perfect stillness, she looked up brightly and said, 'I am ready now, I have been with my children,' and then at once peacefully passed away. When the notes taken at the two places were compared, the day, hour, and minutes were the same." (Vol. I. p. 122).

A Parallel to the Birkbeck Double. In Dr. Lees' "Glimpses of the Supernatural," there is a similar instance, which differs only from that of the Birkbeck Ghost in being more recent and the distance between the mother and the children greater, for she was dying in Egypt when she appeared to the children in England. The story is as follows :—

"A lady and her husband, who held a position of some distinction in India, were returning home (A.D. 1854) after an absence of four years, to join a family of young children, when the former was seized in Egypt with an illness of the most alarming character ; and, though carefully attended by an English Physician and nursed with the greatest care, grew so weak that little or no hope of her recovery existed. With that true kindness which is sometimes withheld by those about a dying bed, she was properly and painfully informed of her dangerous state, and bidden to prepare for the worst. Of a devout, pious, and reverential mind, she is reported to have made a careful preparation for her latter end, though no clergyman was at hand to administer the last sacrament or to afford spiritual consolation. The only point which seemed to disturb her mind, after the delirium of fever had passed away, was a deep-seated desire to see her absent children once more, which she frequently expressed to those attending upon her. Day after day, for more than a week, she gave utterance of her longings and prayers, remarking that she would die happily if only this one wish could be gratified. On the morning of the day of her departure hence, she fell into a long and heavy sleep, from which her attendants found it difficult to arouse her. During the whole period of it she lay perfectly tranquil. Soon after noon, however, she suddenly awoke, exclaiming, 'I have seen them all, I have seen them. God be praised, for Jesus Christ's sake !' and then slept again. Towards the evening, in perfect peace, and with many devout exclamations, she calmly yielded up her spirit to God who gave it. Her body was brought to England and buried in the family burying-place. The most remarkable part of this incident remains to be told. The children of the dying lady were being educated in Torquay under the supervision of a friend of the family. At the very time that their mother was asleep, they were confined to the house where they were by a severe storm of thunder and lightning. Two apartments on one floor, perfectly distinct, were then occupied by them as play and recreation rooms. All were thus gathered together. No one of the children was absent. They were amusing themselves with games of chance, books, and toys in company of the nursemaid, who had never seen their parents. All of a sudden their mother, as she usually appeared, entered the larger room of the two, pausing, looked for some minutes at each, and smiled, passed into the next room, and then vanished away. Three of the elder children recognised her at once, but were greatly disturbed and impressed at her appearance, silence, and manner. The younger and the nursemaid each and all saw a lady in white come into the smaller room, and then slowly glide by and fade away."

The date of this occurrence, September 10th, 1854, was carefully noted, and it was afterwards found that the two events above recorded happened almost contemporaneously. A record of the event was committed to paper, and transcribed on the fly-leaf of the Family Bible, from which the above account was taken and given to the editor of this book in the autumn of the year 1871, by a relation of the lady in question, who is well acquainted with the fact of her spectral appearance at Torquay, and has vouched for the truth of it in the most distinct and formal manner. The husband, who was reported to have been of a somewhat sceptical habit of mind, was deeply impressed by the occurrence. And though it is seldom re-ferred to now, it is known to have had a very deep and lasting religious effect on more than one person who was permitted directly to witness it. ("Glimpses of the Supernatural," pp. 64-66).

From Elsinore to Durham. The number of apparitions of sailors is very re-markable. Here is one taken from Mr. Kendall's diary, which is told by Mr. Alderman Fowler, of Durham. Mr. Fowler, who is one of the patriarchs of the North of England, tells the story as follows:—

"I was assistant at a shop in Durham, near my present place of business, when a singular circumstance happened to me which seemed to imply that the spirits of the departed have, at least at the time of their departure, the power to manifest them-selves to survivors. I had a brother whom I familiarly called

Mat, who was a sailor, and had gone on a voyage to the Baltic.
One Saturday afternoon I was attending to a customer, reckoning up an amount to be paid after serving the articles, when I
happened to look towards the window, and was surprised to
see my brother Mat outside. Our eyes met : I smiled and
nodded to him, and said, 'I'll be with you presently,' or
something of that sort. I told my master that my brother
Mat had come and was standing outside. I was immediately
released from my engagement with the customer and told that
I might go to my brother and also bring him to sleep with me
that night. When I went out into the street expecting to see
my brother Mat, he was nowhere to be seen. I spent all the
evening seeking for him at places where he might have called,
but without success. I was so disturbed at this that I went
off home to Shiney Row next morning to see if they knew
aught ; but he had not been there, nor had they heard any
news of him. But this was the astonishing coincidence which
I learned afterwards. Mat died in the hospital at Elsinore
about the time when I saw him standing in the street in
Durham. The date was October 21st, 1837."

Alderman Fowler, who is still living, has been five times
Mayor of Durham. His son, named from the sailor of the
vision, has been mayor this year (1891).

A story of very much the same character, describing the
vision of a lieutenant at the moment of death, is sent me by a
journalist at Bournemouth, but the circumstances are not such
as call for narration at length.

A Ghost with a Cut Across the Cheek. A story of a fisherman, much more recent, is
sent me by Mr. H. Walton, Dent, Sedburgh. In
this case the apparition not only notified its death,
but showed the existence of a cut on one of the cheeks, which
was found subsequently on the corpse :—

"In the month of April, 1881, I was located in Norfolk, and
my duties took me once a fortnight to a fishing village on
that coast, so I can guarantee the following facts :—It is
customary for the fishing smacks to go to Grimsby 'line fishing ' in the spring. The vessels started one afternoon on their
journey north. In the evening a heavy north-east wind blew,
and one of the boats mistook the white surf on the rocks for
the reflection of a lighthouse. In consequence the boat got
into shallow water, a heavy sea came, and swept two men from
the deck. One man grasped a rope and was saved ; the other, a
young man, failed to save himself, though an expert swimmer.
It was said that he was heard to shout about eleven o'clock.

Towards one o'clock the young man's mother, lying awake, saw his apparition come to the feet of the bed clad in white, and she screamed with fright and told her husband what she had seen, and that J. was drowned. He sought to calm her by saying she must have been dreaming. She asserted the contrary. Next day, when her daughter came in with the telegram of the sad event, before her daughter had time to speak, she cried out 'J. is drowned!' and became unconscious; she remained in this state for many hours. When she regained consciousness, she told them particularly and distinctly what she saw; and what is to the point is this remarkable thing : she said, 'If ever the body is found, it has a cut across the cheek,' specifying which cheek. The body was found some days after, and exactly as the mother had seen it was the cut on the cheek."

This, however, is nothing compared with the awful story of a sister who appeared to a brother in America nine years after death with a scratch on her cheek as red as if it had been made yesterday, the said scratch having been caused by the needle used in sewing the corpse's shroud. The brother knew nothing of this, for the mother had kept it to herself. He recognised his sister, but could not understand the scratch. When he mentioned it to his mother, she confessed what she had done nine years before.

The Latest Recorded Apparition. The latest ghost in our collection appeared on September 30th, 1891. The writer, who sends me his name and address, requests me not to publish it, inasmuch as he objects to be pestered to death by inquiries, and if it were known that he had seen a ghost in his present house he would be left without any servants. The story is as follows :—

"I am a 'Popish' priest stationed in a country district, lead a very quiet life, and am free from excitements of any kind. I enjoy excellent health, and, I am thankful to say, possess a sound mind in a sound body. I am by no means superstitious, and my friends describe me as a most unimpressionable man. On the afternoon of Wednesday, the 30th of September of this present year, I visited one of my sick people, a man who had been suffering from a chest disease for many years. I heard his confession, and having chatted with him for some time, left the house, promising to bring him Holy Communion the following morning. I walked briskly home, a distance of two miles or thereabouts, calling at one house on the way. I reached my cottage shortly before dusk, and while my servant was preparing my tea I amused myself by glancing over the paper which had arrived by the afternoon post. While I was folding over the sheet I happened to look across the room. I was simply astounded at what I saw. It seemed as if the opposite wall had disappeared. I distinctly saw poor John's (the sick man I had visited that afternoon) bed. There was the man himself, so it seemed to me, sitting up in the bed and looking straight at me. I saw him as distinctly as I now see this paper upon which I write. I was greatly astonished, but by no means frightened. I sat staring at the appearance for quite five seconds, and then it gradually disappeared in much the same fashion as a 'dissolving view,' the wall coming back again to sight as the other picture faded away. At first I thought that it had no objective reality, but was purely subjective. But then John and his illness were not at all in my mind. I was thinking about what I was reading. I had often visited this particular man, had seen many sick people, and had been present at the death of several ; besides, I did not think that John was, as yet, near death.

"The next morning, as I was entering the church, to say mass, I saw John's wife in the porch, crying, 'O, Father !' she cried out, 'my heart is broke, O Father ! John, my dear one, died last night, and so sudden ! You hadn't gone an hour scarce. He (John ——) sits up in the bed and he says : "Is the Father gone, Moll." "Why ?" says I, "didn't you say good-bye to he, Jack ?" "Ah, yes," says he, "but I wants he. I'm bad, Moll. I'm a dyin', he's to say mass for me, mind that ;" and with your name on his lips, father, he fell back— dead.' I ascertained that it was heart disease.

"I did not mention what I saw to the woman, nor have I mentioned it to a single soul, except to yourself. If it got known that I had seen a 'spirit' in my house it would be all over with my comfort. My housekeeper would pack off, and I should be left to make my own bed, scrub my own house down, and cook my own food. You must, therefore, accept my statement for what it is worth in your own estimation. I can only give you my bare word that it is quite true, that I have no wish to deceive, and that, as a priest of God's true Church, I should not so far forget my mission as to propagate a falsehood.

CHAPTER VII

GHOSTS ANNOUNCING THEIR OWN DEATH

" The stubborn, unlaid Ghost
That breaks its magic chains at curfew-time."—*Comus*.

IN this chapter I have given the narrative of occurrences at spiritualist séances a wide birth. But considering the immense array of evidence—evidence which has convinced Professor Crookes and Mr. A. R. Wallace—as to the reality of spiritualistic phenomena, it would be unscientific to exclude the evidence of spiritualists merely because they are spiritualists. I do not enter here upon the much-debated question of the phenomena witnessed at séances. I only quote their evidence as to apparitions announcing death after the persons are unmistakably dead. Miss Rowan Vincent is a lady living in London, who, although not a professional medium, is an enthusiastic spiritualist. She is at this moment engaged in painting, under what she regards as "spirit control," a large historical picture of the assassination of the Emperor Paul. As she says she never learnt painting, and did not even know that the Emperor Paul was assassinated, her equipments for the task are of the slenderest. Her own account is that her spirit guides directed her as to what brushes and paints to buy, control her in mixing the colours, and use her hand to wield the brush. One curious little detail she mentioned, that the list of paints given by the " spirits," and which she took to the colourman's, contained the names of colours long since disused or known only by another name. I mention this in order to afford the strongest possible justification-to the ordinary reader for distrusting Miss Rowan Vincent's evidence. Her story, however, is verified, notwithstanding its antecedent incredibility. Here is the remarkable narrative of an apparition, twelve hours after death, which Miss A. Rowan Vincent, of 31, Gower Place, Endsleigh Gardens, W.C., saw in April of last year :—

"On the night of Thursday, April 24th, 1890, I had retired to rest, when I found I had not turned the cat out of the room. I then rose to do so, and after closing the door, turned round to go to my bed, and was surprised to see, standing between myself and the bedstead, the form of a man, whom I recognised as a friend I had not seen for several years, although I had heard he was ill. As I looked, his form slowly faded away. I then took up a written alphabet which in my occult investigations I am accustomed to use, when at once these words were spelt out : ' My name is Charles C——. I died between twelve and half-past.' I looked at my watch ; it was then ten minutes to one o'clock. The next morning I told the friend in whose house I am living, Mrs. Brinkley, 31, Gower Place, W.C. I also told my medical man, who called during the day, Dr. Marsh, 56, Fitzroy Street, W. On the following Monday morning I received a letter from my old friend, Mrs. C., telling me her husband had died on Thursday, the 24th instant, between twelve and half-past in the day, so that he had been dead twelve hours when he appeared to me.

"The name of the ghost I have not given in full, but enclose it in confidence."

I wrote to the persons named, and here is their replies :—

"56, Fitzroy Street, W.,
"*Nov. 9th*, 1891.

"DEAR SIR,—The description and details of ghost story as given in the slip enclosed is quite correct. Miss Vincent gave me the account of the same April 25th, 1890. I have known her for some years, and I am convinced of her absolute truthfulness.

"C. C. MARSH."
"London, *Nov. 10th*, 1891.

"DEAR SIR,—I can vouch for the truth of the statement made by Miss Vincent as regards my husband. I was present at his death, and can only say he passed away on Thursday, April 24th, 1890, at twenty minutes past twelve p.m.

"Yours faithfully,
"E. F. C."

"31, Gower Place, Endsleigh Gardens.
"DEAR SIR,—I have much pleasure in confirming Miss Rowan Vincent's narrative. It is quite correct, all she states.
"Yours very truly,
"M. J. BRINKLEY."

This seems, therefore, to be a clear case of an apparition of the dead. The alphabet to which Miss Rowan Vincent refers is simply a printed A B C, which she uses by allowing the forefinger of the right hand to remain passive, when, according to her own account, it is rapidly removed from letter to letter, which form words and compose sentences. I have seen Miss Rowan Vincent, and questioned her as to why the deceased should have come to her, and as to the confirmation possible. Unfortunately, the note she made at the time was burnt in a fire that took place some time subsequently, but with that exception the evidence seems clear.

A Death announced at a Séance. Mr. Matthew M. Cameron, of Gowan Bank, Hamilton, sends the following account of a communication, made at a séance, of the death of a stranger by his ghost :—

"About ten years ago I was filling a situation in the town of Hawick. Previous to that I had engaged often in the amusement and recreation of table-turning, etc., so that I knew something of the *modus operandi*.

"In Hawick I had interested a couple of gentlemen, whose friendship I had made, in what are termed spiritualistic séances, and we had many evenings together around the table. One night in particular, in my lodgings, we commenced operations. In five minutes or so the table was heaving, cracking, and tilting. When we felt sure that full command of the table had been got, I began asking questions. The way we got answers was as follows :—One knock meant 'No,' while three meant 'Yes'; when we wanted names or words we went over the alphabet slowly, and the table tilted at the correct letter. We asked if any one was controlling the table. Three smart raps was the answer.

"'Would the person kindly give his or her name?'—'Yes.'

"Then we spelled it out—George Moffat.

"'Have you been long in the spirit world?'—'No.'

"'When did you leave earth life?"—No answer.

"'A month ago?'—'No.'

"'A week?'—'No.'

"'A day?"—'No.'

"At this we had to go over the alphabet to get the hours. Two hours was the number.

"'Where did you die?'—'Glasgow.'

"'Where were you born?'—Applying the alphabet, we got Innerleithen.

"'What did you do?'—At this we went over every possible trade and profession likely to be found in such a place as Innerleithen. This was to save the trouble of going over the alphabet, but all to no purpose. We registered No's to every query. At last we took to spelling it out, and we got, what certainly none of us were looking for, Elocutionist.

"Then it flashed upon one of us who he was, and that he was advertised to give an entertainment in the district in a few days.

"Our party broke up that night, each saying, 'We'll see.' Next morning I was at my place of business as usual, when about my first visitor was one of the friends who had been of the party the night previous.

"'Have you seen the papers?'—'No,' I answered.

"'Well, look here,' pointing to a paragraph. To my amazement it stated that Mr. George Moffat, the elocutionist, had suddenly died in Glasgow the night previous, at the certain hour of which we had received notice.

"This is my story, on which I make no comment. The two gentlemen, who, along with myself, were actors in the séance, do not know I am writing this, and therefore I cannot use their names, but I will enclose their names and addresses so that you may be able to communicate with them if you think fit. I think it best not to let them know, because they will be able to give an independent corroboration of the above statement."

Another Spiritualist's Story. Mr. Andrew Glendinning, of 11, St. Philip's Road, Dalston, furnishes me with the following narrative of a ghost which showed commendable anxiety that the news of its death should be broken kindly to its widow. Mr. Glendinning writes:—

"In September, 1870, Captain Buchan, of Port-Glasgow, was trading between China and Japan. He was 41 years of age, a gentleman of good education, intelligent, of refined manners and, being in excellent health, seemed likely to live long. He had no premonition of illness, for about that time he sent me a letter setting forth his plans for some months to come. On the evening of 30th September, 1870 (I give the date as best I can), a lady who is a clairvoyant said to me, 'Captain Buchan was here to-day; he is dead, and he wishes you to go and break the news to Mrs. Buchan.' I said, 'You are mistaken, the captain is alive and well.' I placed in her hands a letter, then recently received from the captain, and told her the letter might put her *en rapport* with him. She replied, 'Yes, he was alive when he wrote this, and he is alive still, but is what you call dead, and he desires you to call on Mrs. Buchan and break the news to her.' About three weeks afterwards the owners of the steamer received a telegram from the mate announcing the death of the captain. It was re-marked by me at the time that the date of death given in the telegram confirmed to that extent the statement made by the lady. A memorial stone in Port-Glasgow cemetery bears the following inscription :—

"ALEXANDER THOMSON BUCHAN,
Shipmaster,
Died at Amoy, China,
30th September, 1870.

Aged 41 years.

"In 1887 I asked Mrs. Buchan (now Mrs. McMurtrie) how long was it after her husband's death ere she received the intelligence. She replied she could not give the exact date, but that it was a few days after the bazaar in Port-Glasgow for the new Town Hall. The *Greenock Telegraph* gives the dates of the Bazaar as October 20th, 21st, and 22nd, 1870. The first telegram from the mate was to the owners of the steamer, and stated why he had been unable to send it sooner."

I have asked Mr. Alexander Rose, of 10, Hayburn Cres-cent, Patrick Hill, Glasgow, a native of Port-Glasgow, who knew Captain Buchan, to give some particulars of this ghost case. The following is his statement :—

"On October 1st, 1870, Mr. Andrew Glendinning informed me that, on the previous evening, a lady well known to us both, residing in Port-Glasgow, told him Captain Buchan was dead, that his wraith had appeared to her that day, and had desired her to request my friend, Mr. Glendinning, to let his widow know. On the following October 20th, 1870 (a Thurs-day), a bazaar was held in the New Town Hall, Port-Glasgow. Mrs. Buchan was one of the stall-holders. I visited the Hall with Mr. Glendinning. In the midst of the usual hilarity of a bazaar, Mr. Glendinning suddenly took hold of my arm, and said to me, 'There is Captain Buchan's wife, and she does not know she is a widow.' A few days afterwards a telegram was received announcing the captain's death. The place where the captain died was not in telegraphic communication with this country, and there was a delay of some days ere the mate could send a message. I also remember Mr. Glendinning telling me that he had doubted the lady's statement, and that he had placed in her hand a letter he had received from the captain, and that the lady then minutely described the death-scene. The captain, when walking with his first officer, suddenly put his hand to his heart, and said, 'My God!' and dropped dead. This was afterwards confirmed when letters arrived giving details—even to the date of death. Mr. Glendinning also informed me that when the lady was in an abnormal condition she asked for a map, and putting her finger on a spot in the China Seas, said the vessel will go down there in twenty-nine fathoms of water. We were interested in the prophecy, as we had entrusted the captain with a quantity of oils and paints to sell for us ; all the spare money I had at that time I put in the venture. Some time after Captain Buchan's death, when the vessel was lost, the Admiralty chart showed it to be in twenty-nine fathoms of water."

A Dead Man describes his Death. The following narrative, which was sent me by a Free Church minister in Dumbartonshire, reads, I admit, somewhat too much like a magazine article. Believing that it had been "written up," I returned the MS. to the writer with an intimation to that effect. He replied, somewhat indignantly, that the story was literally true :—

"The story is in all its essential parts absolutely true. The incident on which it is based took place in the village in which my early home was situated. I knew well the man who fell over the rocks. We were together at the same school, and we often played on the sands that stretched out before him as he lay in his helpless condition. I also knew the person who held the strange monologue with him after his death. I got the story as I have given it from his own lips.

"It is some years since the event happened ; but it caused a good deal of noise at the time, all the more so that Ewan was suspected of having murdered Ronald. It was only when it was proved that Ewan was in the habit of seeing visions, and that he was residing, at the time of Ronald's disappearance, in another part of the country, that he was acquitted.

"I could, if necessary, get many witnesses to authenticate the facts. Even within no great distance of your own office there are two who could verify its accuracy—a sister in one of the largest of the London Hospitals, and a master in an English School.

"I have entered into this matter at such length because you seem to throw doubt on the truth of my story. The circumstance that I am a clergyman, a member of the Royal Society, and of the Society of Antiquaries of Scotland, and that I have contributed to many of the learned and popular publications and journals, from the *Encyclopædia Britannica* downwards, ought in itself to be a sufficient guarantee."

Here, then, is his story, carefully revised by himself, so as to make it correspond as exactly as possible to the facts :—

"The wayside inn at Ballvona, in the far north, was picturesque and comfortable, and within easy reach was abundance of excellent fishing. I had a 'ghillie' who was as well versed in piscatorial lore as ancient Walton himself. Ronald MacIvor knew every pool in the river, and every nook in it where a salmon lay; and he was an equally unerring authority away among the lonely mountain lochs and streams. He was an intelligent, manly fellow, light of heart and foot, and just such a guide as makes a holiday bright and pleasant. Little did I dream, as I parted with him one evening, after a memorable day's sport, that I should never again hear his cheerful laugh, or listen to those weird Highland stories that so often lightened the tedium of the homeward journey.

" Ronald was engaged to be married to the miller's daughter —a rustic beauty residing in the adjacent hamlet. It was his custom to visit her at the close of each day. His course, for more than a mile, lay along the ledge of high rocks which sloped down to the sea. Though the way was dangerous to one unacquainted with it, he was familiar from childhood with every step of it. One night he started later than usual, and in order to shorten the distance he struck down towards the rocks, with the intention of getting to the base at a point further on, but in doing so he lost his foothold, and fell a distance of thirty feet.

"The following morning, after waiting for Ronald until mid day, I had to go alone to a favourite moorland stream, and did not return till late. Then it was that I found he had disappeared. Ominous fears and whispers were soon in full wing. But the general alarm did not move me. I had confidence in Ronald, and was certain that he would shortly turn up. This he did, though in a way far other than I had anticipated.

" In the gloom of the third evening, as Ewan Matheson—a thoughtful but absent-minded villager—was wending his way homewards, he saw Ronald coming in his direction from one of the neighbouring houses. Never doubting it was he, Ewan accosted him as they met; but the words that fell on his ears, so plaintive and supernatural, filled him with unutterable dread.

" 'I am gone, gone for ever,' said he. 'They seek me, but in life they shall never find me. It is not I you see; it is my spirit, my shadow. As we move on I will tell you how the great change came.'

" With that the two moved side by side, the living human personality and the strange unearthly spectre, and the following monologue — which the narrator afterwards declared held him with a grip and a fascination that were more than human — took place.

" 'Three nights ago, when on my way to the Old Mill, I took the short cut along the edge of the cliff; but, in attempting to strike down through the passage in the rocks, I put my foot on a tuft of wet grass, and slipped and fell. It was the work of an instant, but it seemed an age; and then there was a sharp, blinding sensation, and I knew no more till at midnight I awoke as from a troubled dream. There was a dull pain in my head, where the projecting rock came in contact with it; otherwise I was unhurt, for I fell on the loose, soft sand, within the sea margin. The moon was up, and in its broken light I managed to bind my pocket-handkerchief around the wound.

" 'I then lay down and tried to rest, but I could not rest. My brain was in a tempestuous whirl, and thought chased thought like the waves which rolled on in front. What was to become of me? Would I die before the morning? Or if I lived to see the day, was there any chance of my being found? I looked around in the vague hope that some one might be near; but the spot where I lay was lonely and unfrequented, and though I heard the distant barking of dogs, and the startled cry of a solitary sea bird, as it flew overhead, no human being was near. Far out in the bay I saw the light of a passing ship, and instinctively I endeavoured to cry, but my voice was drowned by the wind and the waves, and the light soon went out in the void. Then I knew there was no deliverance that night.

" 'Shortly afterwards I fell asleep; but my sleep was disturbed, and full of dreams. When I awoke the sun was rising behind the mountains, and crowning the hills and the dales with the glory of a new-born day. Yet the light for which I longed was more terrible than the darkness. There to the right stretched the beautiful sands on which we used, with free, joyous hearts, to play our boyish games. And there, further up, on the green slope, stood the village burying-ground, with its tall, white stones. But worse than all I saw, with horror, that the waves were within a few feet of me, and that the last tide had swept the place where I lay.

" 'Oh, the agony of it; to have life, full and buoyant, crushed out slowly inch by inch ! The waves were nearing, creeping on like serpents towards their prey. Could I only get out of their reach, I felt sure I should be found by the children on their way to school, or as they wandered at the play hour. While I thus reflected a wave came dashing over me, and stirred up what of energy there was still within me. I managed, though the pain was excruciating, to drag myself outside the sea level, and then for a time there was another troubled blank.

" 'When I next awoke I heard the voices of the children at play above me ; but I could neither speak nor cry. A parching in my throat stifled the words as they came, and they sounded to myself like painful whispers. And the children were so near I could recognize them by their voices—the children that could save me, did they but know !

" 'The sun had passed slowly to the west, and the dark shadows fell once more. I was faint and tired, and in utter weariness I lay back on the earth, with the sky overhead, and the stars looking down with infinite pity in their far-away eyes. I could not pray, for my soul seemed heavy as lead, and wild, rebellious thoughts filled my heart. And yet I was dying. Before me no green island rose out of the infinite blackness, no haven of peace to which I could flee and be at rest. Behind me, amid much that was obscure, there stood forth the memories and the deeds of the past. They became as living things, stamped each one with my own figure and character. They pressed on nearer and nearer. I tried to escape them, but I could not, any more than I could rise from the place where I lay. At last they came up behind me, and with cruel hands they thrust me out over the margin into the dark and boundless ocean of death. The earth and sea and sky are blotted out from my view, and the woe and the mystery of the Eternal penetrate every chamber of my being.'

"The spectral voice ceased ; and Ewan, looking round, saw what he had not noticed before, that the clothes and the body of his ghostly companion were burning from within outwards, and yet were not consumed. The sight, preceded by the weird story, was too much for him, and coming at the instant to a house, the door of which stood open, he rushed in and swooned. On recovering he told what he had seen and heard, but no one believed his tale. They said it was the creation of his own imagination, the mere phantasy of an overheated brain ; and so little heed did they give to it that they did not even seek to verify its truth or discover its falsehood by going to the spot where Ronald was said to have met his death.

"Next day was dark and lowering. The clouds chased each other in wild array, and the birds hovered low, with a wide circling flight. About mid-day the storm raged, and the white capped waves rolled mountain-high, and dashed in fury against the rocks of the north—the first barrier to break their course during an onward reach of more than three thousand miles. In nature, grand as it is, there is nothing grander than this war of the storm, the sea, and the beetling cliff.

"It was not, however, to admire the grandeur of the elemental strife that the inhabitants of Ballvona hastened to the shore. A vessel hove in sight with dismantled masts, and, unable to brave the heavy sea, had turned landwards, and was drifting for the bay. This was her only chance, but it was full of risk, for there was no depth of water, and beneath were treacherous banks of sand. On she came, with her living freight, at one time hidden altogether from view, then perched aloft; but at last there is a crash—she has grounded and heeled over on her side. Those on shore put out manfully to the rescue of the unfortunate crew, and soon all of them, not already swept overboard, were brought in safety to land.

"It was a sad day, and it cast a gloom over many a heart. But its saddest sight had yet to be revealed. As the villagers who had been viewing the shipwreck were returning, they discovered the dead body of Ronald MacIvor, stretched on the sand a few feet beyond the sea margin, with a gash in his forehead and a pocket-handkerchief used as a bandage for the wound.

"The rivers and the lochs of Ballvona are as full of fish as ever; but somehow I have not the same interest in them now that I had in the old days, when Ronald MacIvor was my unfailing guide and counsellor."

I print his communication, which is quite unique in the widely varied narratives which I have received, with all reserve. But for his voucher I should certainly have doubted the possibility of any statement so long and so detailed being made by a ghost. Ghosts are usually either monosyllabic or exceedingly reserved in their communications, whereas this ghost made quite a long harangue. However, the story is interesting, and in one point quite awful in its gruesome detail.

A Dead Man. Accompanied by a Saint. One of the best authenticated ghosts on record is that of Philip Weld, who appeared to his father after he had been drowned, accompanied by two persons, one of whom was never recognised and the third was subsequently discovered to be St. Stanislaus Kostka. Philip Weld had been drowned when at St. Edmund's College in Hertfordshire. The Principal went to Southampton next day to break the news to the boy's father. He met Mr. Weld walking towards Southampton. He immediately stopped the carriage, alighted, and was about to address him when Mr. Weld prevented him by saying :—

" 'You need not say one word, for I know that Philip is dead. Yesterday afternoon I was walking with my daughter, Catherine, and we suddenly saw him. He was standing on the path, on the opposite side, of the turnpike road, between two persons, one of whom was a youth dressed in a black robe. My daughter was the first to perceive them, and exclaimed, " Oh, papa ! did you ever see anything so like Philip as that is ? " " Like him," I answered, " why, it is him." Strange to say, my daughter thought nothing of the circumstance, beyond that we had seen an extraordinary likeness of her brother. We walked on towards these three figures. Philip was looking, with a smiling, happy expression of countenance, at the young man in a black robe, who was shorter than himself. Suddenly they seemed to me all to have vanished : I saw nothing but a countryman whom I had seen before through the three figures, which gave me the impression that they were spirits.'

" Mr. Weld went to the funeral of his son, and as he left the church after the sad ceremony looked round to see if any of the religious at all resembled the young man he had seen with Philip, but he could not trace the slightest likeness in any of them.

" Four months later, when visiting at Chipping, in Lancaster, suddenly Mr. Weld stopped before a picture which had no name. 'That is the person whom I saw with Philip ; I do not know whose likeness this print is, but I am *certain* that it was *that* person I saw with Philip.'

" The priest entered the room a few minutes afterwards, and was immediately questioned by Mr. Weld concerning the print.

" He answered that it was a print of St. Stanislaus Kostka, and supposed to be a very good likeness of the young saint.

" Mr. Weld was much moved at hearing this, for St. Stanislaus was a Jesuit who died when quite young, and Mr. Weld's father, having been a great benefactor of the Order, his family was supposed to be under the particular protection of the

Jesuit saints; also, Philip had been led of late, by various circumstances, to a particular devotion to St. Stanislaus.

"Moreover, St. Stanislaus is supposed to be the especial advocate of drowned men, as is mentioned in his life" (vol. ii. pp. 180-182).

The appearance of St. Stanislaus side by side with young Weld is quite inexplicable by any theory of telepathy or the astral *camera obscura*, or any other analogy which has ever been invented to suggest an explanation for such apparitions.

A Ghost in a Railway Station. One of the best and at the same time one of the simplest ghost stories I have heard from my friends was that which was told me by the manager of Mr. Burgess, who used to print the *Review of Reviews*. Mr. Archer is a brother Tynesider. When he was a youth he was employed as telegraphist at the Gateshead railway station. At the end of the platform stood, and possibly still stands, the dead house, which was an eerie and unpleasant object to young Archer, who was on night duty at the station, and when he left his office in the early hours of the morning he was always uneasy in passing the dead house, and was always exceedingly glad when he could find any one to accompany him while he was in the immediate vicinity. One morning, about two o'clock he came out upon the platform, and was walking in the direction of the dead house, feeling that he would have to go past it alone. To his great delight he saw standing on the platform, at a short distance in front of him, the familiar figure of a man in the employ of the railway company. Hoping to secure the company of the workman past the dead house, he stepped up to him, when, to his utter astonishment and no little dismay, the figure vanished into thin air. Feeling very uncomfortable, but not knowing what to make of it, he went to the signalman at Greenfield and told him he could not understand it; he had just seen —— standing on the platform, and when he went up to him he suddenly disappeared. The signalman looked rather astonished, and said, "You have seen ——? It is impossible; did you not know that he was killed yesterday, and his body is lying in the dead house at this moment?" It was now Mr. Archer's turn to be dismayed; he was perfectly certain he had seen the man, and yet the man was dead.

A Ghost in the Sunlight. Mr. Archer's vision was that of an unmistakably dead man, and so is the following, which I quote from the " Proceedings of the Psychical Research

Society." The story is told by the Rev. Gerard Louis, of St. Paul's Vicarage, Margate. He says :—

" It was a hot and bright afternoon in summer, and as if it were only yesterday, I remember perfectly well walking down the broad bright street in the bright afternoon. I had to pass the house of P——. I remarked, indeed, that all his window blinds were drawn carefully down, as if to screen his furniture, of which his wife was inordinately proud, from the despoiling rays of the afternoon sun. I smiled inwardly at the thought. I then left the road and stepped upon the side pavement, and looked over the area rails into the front court below. A young man dressed in dark clothes and without a hat, and apparently about twenty, was standing at the door beneath the front steps. On the instant, from his likeness to my friend P——, I seemed to recognise his son. We both stood and looked very hard at each other. Suddenly, however, he advanced to that part of the area which was immediately below where I was standing, fixed on me a wide, dilated, winkless sort of stare, and halted. The desire to speak was evidently legible on his face, though nothing audible escaped his lips. But his eyes spoke, every feature of his face spoke —spoke, as it were, in silent language, in which reproach and pain seemed to be equally intermingled. At first I was startled, then I began to feel angry. 'Why,' I said to myself, 'does he look at me in that manner?' At last, annoyance prevailed over surprise; I turned away with the half-muttered thought, ' He certainly knows me by sight as a friend of his father, and yet he has not the civility to salute me. I will call on the first opportunity and ask his reason for such behaviour.' I then pursued my way and thought no more of what had occurred.

" On Wednesday it was my turn to officiate at the local cemetery, and, to my surprise, I had to bury Mr. P——'s son. I lost no time in calling upon Mr. P—— and his wife. I found the latter at home, and what she had to say only made me more uncomfortable still. James Henry P—— died terribly in earnest, wishing in vain to the last that I would come, on the Thursday before the Sunday on which I had seen him. He had died, too, in the front room on a level with the area into which its window opened. He had also lain there until the Wednesday following awaiting burial. His corpse then was lying in that very room on the very Sunday, and at the very moment, too, that I had seen his living like-ness, as it were, in the area outside." (Pp. 93, 94, 95).

This ghost in the sunlight ought to have been photographed.

CHAPTER VIII

HOW PHANTOMS COME AND GO

The Precipitation of a Spectral Face. As a rule, witnesses of phantoms are so much flurried that they do not appear to be able to notice how the phantoms come or how they go. This, however, is not the case in two remarkable instances which I shall now proceed to relate. The first, which I found in Mr. Kendall's diary, relates to an old friend of mine, the Rev. Colin McKechnie, who occupied my father's pulpit many years ago, and whom I have known for years. Mr. McKechnie is a hard-headed Scotchman, and his account of how the face of his grandfather gradually formed itself on the kitchen ceiling and then as gradually faded away, is one of the most precise descriptions that I ever read of the coming and going of a phantasmal appearance :—

"I was about ten years of age at the time, and had for several years been living with my grandfather, who was an elder in the Kirk of Scotland, and in good circumstances. He was very much attached to me, and often expressed his intention of having me educated for the ministry of the Kirk. Suddenly, however, he was seized with an illness which in a couple of days proved mortal. At the time of his death, and without my having any apprehension of it, I happened to be at my father's house, about a mile off. I was leaning in a listless sort of way against the kitchen table, looking upwards at the ceiling, and thinking of nothing in particular, when my grandfather's face appeared, at first dim and indistinct, and then becoming more and more complete, until it seemed in every respect as full and perfect as I had ever seen it. It looked down upon me as though with a wonderful expression of tenderness and affection. Then it disappeared, not suddenly, but gradually, its features fading and becoming dim and indistinct until I saw nothing but the ceiling. I spoke at the time of what I saw to my mother, but she made no account of it, thinking probably that it was nothing more than a boyish vagary. In about fifteen or twenty minutes after seeing the vision a boy came running, breathless, to my father's with the news that my grandfather had just died.

" I have never been able to persuade myself that the vision was purely subjective. I have rather been inclined to thinking the explanation is to be sought in my grandfather's exceptionally strong love for me, impelling and enabling him to bring himself into connection with me at the moment of his decease in the way I have stated. It was at Paisley when the above occurred.

"To the best of my recollection this is a correct statement.

"COLIN CAMPBELL MCKECHNIE.

"Darlington, *Sept. 24th*, 1889."

"To the best of my recollection the boyish vision, if I may so call it, occurred in 1830 or 1831. The register of deaths kept in the Gaelic chapel of Paisley, if consulted, would enable one to fix the date. Grandfather lived in Sneddon Street, and his name was John McKechnie.

"(Signed) COLIN MCKECHNIE.

"*Oct. 3rd*, 1889."

Mr. McKechnie died in 1896. He had been in the ministry about fifty years; was editor of the *Primitive Methodist Quarterly Review*.

Another Floating Head. A lady at Brockley sends me an account of an apparition she witnessed, which she describes as minutely as Mr. McKechnie. It is, however, much more horrible :—

"One Saturday evening last summer, about eight, I was alone in the house, with the exception of my two little boys (of eight and nine years), who were at that moment in the bath. I left them for a minute, and, closing the bath-room door, walked along the short corridor to the head of the stairs, thinking of the article for which I was going down. I raised my eyes and saw to my great surprise a peculiar light about 6 feet from the stair in the corner, 5 in. or 6 in. above, and facing me. My first act was to look in every direction for a possible reflection, but in vain. There was no light in the house, the meter being turned off; the corner was a very light one, with a lofty ceiling. I looked again at the light, watching it intently, and in less time than it takes me to write it, I saw this light develop into a head and face of yellowish greenish light, with a mass of matted hair above it. The face was very wide and broad, larger than ours in all respects, very large eyes of green, which, not being distinctly outlined, appeared to merge into the yellow of the cheeks; no hair whatever on the lower part of the face, and nothing to be seen below. The expression of the face was diabolically malignant, and as it gazed straight at me my horror was intense as my wonder, but I was not nervous in the least; the thought darted through my mind that Gustave Doré had drawn his originals from such.

I felt that such an awful thing could only be Satanic, so keeping my gaze fixed on the thing I said to it, ' In the name of Christ, be gone,' and the fiendish thing faded from my sight, and has not troubled me since. I am not troubled with liver complaint, and never had a bilious attack in my life. I am also a member of a temperance association, and generally considered strong-minded."

The Development of a Phantasm. Another lady, resident in Gloucestershire, sends me, under the initials " Y. Z.," an account of a singular experience through which she passed fourteen years ago. It describes with greater minuteness than any other narrative I have seen of the kind the process of visualising, or the giving of an apparent objectivity to what there is no evidence to prove was other than a purely subjective hallucination. The following is a copy of the narrative written fourteen years ago immediately after the occurrence took place :—

It was an autumn afternoon, about six o'clock. I had returned from a stroll in the garden, and was in my own room, sitting on a straight-backed easy chair, leisurely dipping into Thackeray's " Vanity Fair," which I had brought upstairs to while away the half hour before tea. While turning over the pages in search of some favourite passage, I became aware of an abnormal and quite indescribable sensation. My chest and breathing seemed inwardly oppressed by some ponderous weight, while I became conscious of some presence behind me, exerting a powerful influence on the forces within. On trying to turn my head to see what this could be, I was powerless to do so, neither could I lift a hand or move in any way. I was not a little alarmed, and began immediately to reason. Was it a fainting fit coming on, epilepsy, paralysis, possibly even death ? No, the mind was too much alive, though physically I felt an absolutely passive instrument operated upon by some powerful external agent, as if the current of nerve force within seemed forcibly drawn together and focussed on a spot in front of me. I gazed motionless, as though through something intenser than ordinary eyesight, on what was no longer vacant space. There, an oval, misty light was forming ; elongatory, widening, yes, actually developing into a human face and form. Was this hallucination, or some vision of the unseen, coming in so unexpected fashion ? Before me had arisen a remarkable figure, never seen before in picture or life— dark-skinned, aged, with white beard, the expression intensely earnest, the features small, the bald head finely moulded, lofty over the forehead, the whole demeanour instinct with solemn grace. The hands, too, how unlike any hands I knew, yet how expressive! Dark as the face, hair, long in fingers and narrow in palms, the veins like sinews, standing out as they moved to and fro in eager gesture. He was speaking to me in deep tones, as if in urgent entreaty. What would I not give to hear words from such a figure! But no effort availed me to distinguish one articulate sound. I tried to speak, but could not. With desperate effort I shook out the words, 'Speak louder!' The face grew more intent, the voice louder and more emphatic. Was there something amiss in my own hearing, then, that I could distinguish no word amid these deeply emphasised tones? Slowly and deliberately the figure vanished, through the same stages of indistinctness, back to the globular lamp-like whiteness, till it faded to nothingness. Before it had quite faded away, the face only of a woman arose, indistinct and dim. The same emphatic hum, though in a subdued note, the same paralysis of voice and muscle, the same strange force, as it were overshadowing me. With the disappearance of this second and far less interesting figure, I recovered my power of movement, and rose.

"My first impulse was to look round for the origin of this strange force; my second, to rush to the looking-glass to make sure I was myself. There could be no delusion. There I was, paler than usual, the forehead bathed in perspiration. I sponged my face, and, greatly agitated, walked hurriedly to and fro. True, there had been nothing alarming in the apparition itself, but the sensation preceding had been vivid in the extreme. What was it? Was it night, or had I been in some strange sleep? Certainly not. Was I in my right mind? I believed so. Then if so, and the conditions being the same, would it be possible to bring back this strange phenomenon that I might know it had really existed, whether subjectively or objectively? Like an inspiration, I determined that if this experience had a basis in objective or subjective fact, it might certainly recur. I would sit down in the same position, try to feel calm, open a book, and remain as positively still and passive as I could. To my intense interest, and almost at once, the strange sense of some power operating on the nerve forces within, followed by the same loss of muscular power, the same wide awakeness of the reason, the same drawing out and concentrating of the energies on that spot in front, repeated itself, this time more deliberately, leaving me freer to take mental notes of what was happening. Again arose the same noble, earnest figure, gazing at me, the hands moving in

solemn accompaniment to the deep tones of voice. The same
painful effort on my part to hear, with no result. The vision
passed. Again the woman's face, insignificant and meaningless, succeeded it as before. She spoke, but in less emphatic
tones. It flashed upon me I *would* hear. After a frantic
effort, I caught two words—"land," "America"—with positively no clue to their meaning.

"I was wide awake when the apparition first appeared, and
in a highly excited state of mind on its reappearance."

A Portrait of a Spectre. I close this chapter by quoting the following
remarkable description of the gradual formation of
a spirit face at a private séance, the account of
which, with the names and addresses of those present, is sent
me by Mr. Charles Lillie, 249, High Holborn :—

"Permit me to record an event whereby four people out of a
party of seven saw what, for the sake of clearness, I may term
a ghostly visitant.

"The month was October, the house was in Bayswater, and
there were seven people present—Mrs. T., our hostess, a firm
believer in spiritualism—*i.e.* a belief in supernatural beings,
and their ministrations on earth ; Miss T., her daughter, a believer with reservation ; Miss Muriel T., a believer; and Miss
W., the governess, also a believer. The rest of the party included Geoffrey T., a young fellow of twenty, a thorough non-
believer; Captain W., a non-believer, one who had never
troubled his head about the matter at all ; and myself, open to
belief, but sceptical.

"From talking of ghosts, it easily came about that a séance
should be held, and for that purpose we adjourned to another
room, where, by Mrs. T.'s wish and stipulation, all the pre-
scribed formula devised by the spiritualists should be adhered
to. After the usual knockings and answers we asked if the
agencies for the sounds could be made visible, and received an
affirmative reply, desiring at the same time that the fire should
be quite extinguished, and that we should remain quietly in
our places and wait.

"These requests having been complied with, we waited. At
the end of twenty minutes or half an hour, Miss Thornton
complained of intense cold. The intermittent rapping on
the table ceased, and I saw what appeared to be a slightly
luminous 'something,' oval in shape, rise just behind and
above Miss Thornton's head. As I conjectured it might be
some optical illusion on my part, induced by continued
staring in the dark, I said nothing. The faintly luminous

cloud had become stationary, and was, or seemed to be, gradually contracting while still preserving its oval outline; Captain W. suddenly cried out he saw something that looked like a face. Mrs. T. could see nothing, failed to perceive anything. Young T. said he saw it, and added that 'it was growing plainer.'

"The curious part of the apparition was this, that not only did it look like a hollow-eyed and expressionless mask, but, artistically speaking, it was apparently 'lit by a top light,' that is, under the brow, the nose and the chin were black shadows, as they would be in nature, as there are in paintings or plastic heads, 'lit' as mentioned above. Whatever process the 'thing' was undergoing, it was true that it was growing distinctly plainer, and just before W. exclaimed, 'It is a woman's face,' I had seen two darkly sad eyes gleam from the shadow, and a sensitive mouth grow from the darkness that enshrouded them. The hair was parted in the middle in the old-fashioned way upon a broad, low brow, and round the head was a slightly perceptible scintillation of electrical light, steely-blue in colour. The face was a dull, luminous grey, neither waxen nor flesh-like, but vapoury, and did not look tangible.

"Neither Mrs. T., Miss W., or Miss T. (the latter perhaps naturally so) saw any face at all, but the remaining four saw it as I have here described. We tried to make it speak, but it had only inclined its head in reply to a second question, when Miss T. turned round in her chair, and then resuming her former position, said, 'I can see nothing; I am tired and frightened, mamma,' and I think she became a little hysterical. The face was fading away, and though Miss W. at once rose and went round to where Miss T. sat, the action did not disturb or retard the curious dimness that was creeping across the ghostly face. As it had come, so it was going. It gradually grew greyer, and the great shadows came beneath the brow where the eyes had been, and the darkness grew upon the mouth, the faint scintillation had gone, and there was only left remaining the same faint cloud that it had grown from, and that in its turn died away, and there was nothing left in the room but the darkness."

Many circumstances have come to my knowledge in the course of my investigations, however superficial and tentative they may have been, which make me look askance at any proposal to take part in a spiritualistic séance. In your own family circle, when you know the character and antecedents of

all present, it is possible that no unpleasant consequences may
follow experiments in table-rapping ; but a general séance
attended by persons some of whom may be evil livers, reeking
with vice and stained with crime, should be avoided as a pest-
house.

There is a great deal in a name, and scientists
Diabolical object to the use of the term possession.   They
Possession. prefer some other word to explain the abdication
or supersession of the conscious will of the individual by what
appears to the sufferer and his friends the direct intervention
of another and an evil intelligence.   At the same time, as the
New Testament has popularised the idea of diabolical possession, I shall use the term without in the least wishing to assert
that the phrase has any claim to scientific accuracy.   There
may not be any devils.   There may not be such a thing as
possession.   It may be only a form of mental disease, or it
may be attributed to hypnotic suggestion.   That must be left
to experts to determine.   What I have to do is to chronicle
the phenomena, not to explain them.   Call them hallucinations, hysteria, hypnotic suggestion, what you please ; they are
so closely connected with the phenomena of spiritualism that
it is impossible to ignore them.   I therefore give here the reports of two cases of alleged possession, both, oddly enough,
occurring in Wurtemberg about fifty years since.   The first was
sent me by a Dutch correspondent, and has not hitherto been
published in English ; the second I take from William Howitt's
account of Dr. Kerner's experiences in dealing with occult
phenomena.

Pfarrer Blumhardt prefixes to his narrative (which
The Möttlin- has never been printed) the following note :—
gen Case. "The following paper was, in August, 1884,
handed over (at their expressed wish) to the Wurtemberg Con-
sistory, as a confidential communication ; but some MS. copies
of it got into circulation without the knowledge of the under-
signed.   In order to supersede these copies, the paper (with
various corrections) was lithographed six years later ; but the
writer does not wish for a more extended circulation, and therefore requests every reader kindly to consider a wish only
expressed after mature deliberation."

The date of this note is July 31st, 1850.   The substance of
the narrative is as follows :—

"G. D., a single woman, in poor circumstances, born in
or about 1816, suffered between 1836 and 1838 from a serious
illness, which left her in weak health and with a contraction of

the muscles, so that one leg was shorter than the other, and one side higher. Previous to her illness, she had been in service with various families, where she had given entire satisfaction by her conduct, and she was also known to the clergyman of her village (Dr. Barth, Pf. Blumhardt's predecessor) as a sincerely religious woman. In 1840 she went to live with her two sisters and a brother, who was nearly blind, on the ground floor of a house in her native village of Möttlingen. Before long she began to perceive something uncanny about the place.

How It Began. " On the very first day, when saying grace before dinner, she had a sudden seizure, and fell to the ground unconscious. Strange noises were heard at night— a swishing, trailing sound (Geschlürfe), and one like heavy objects being rolled over or thrown about (Gepoller): these were not only heard by all four, but also caused uneasiness to the family on the upper floor of the house. G. herself saw figures and moving lights which were not visible to the others, and sometimes, at night, felt her hands seized and laid forcibly one over the other. From that time forward her manner became strange and even repellent ; but, as the poor family had few friends and acquaintances, it was not much noticed. In the autumn of 1841 her nightly visitations had become such a trouble to her, that she consulted Pf. Blumhardt, but only in such general terms that he was unable to make anything of the matter. During the following winter she had a sharp attack of erysipelas, during which he sometimes visited her, but was discouraged from doing so frequently by the inattention and apathy —not to say hostility—which she manifested.

A Haunted House. " By April, 1842, the noises, etc., had so increased as to be perceptible to the whole neighbourhood. G. frequently saw the figure of a woman who had died in the village two years before—always with a dead child in her arms. This figure always stood in the same spot, and kept repeating the words, ' I want rest !' or ' Give me a paper, and I will not come again.' One night a light was seen near the door, and, on examination, some money and a written paper were found under a loose board ; the paper, however, was so soiled with soot as to be illegible. About a fortnight later the noise was heard again, and a light was seen behind the stove. When search was made, various objects were discovered under the floor—money wrapped in paper, packets of some kind of powder, bones of birds, etc. Their presence was never explained, but they were supposed

to have been connected with some superstitious rites. At last
the clergyman induced G. to leave this house, and placed her
with a relative, where she was kindly cared for ; but it continued to be haunted, and the noises only ceased in 1844.
Before long they began to be heard in G.'s new abode ; and
she herself became subject to strange convulsive attacks, and
at last showed all the symptoms of 'possession.'

"I was already becoming more hopeful when I was told that
a noise like the tapping of fingers was heard all round G.,
and that at such times she was suddenly struck on the chest,
and sank backwards ; she was also said to see the same woman
who had appeared at her former lodgings. She declared the
latter to be a widow who had died two years previous, and
who, on her deathbed, had confessed grievous sins to me, and
had scarcely been able to find peace. I went to the house,
accompanied by witnesses, and soon heard the unearthly
sounds. She was lying in bed quite conscious, and without
pain.

Possessed by   "Suddenly, something seemed to enter into her,
a Witch's   and her whole body began to move. I said a few
Ghost.   words of prayer, mentioning the name of Jesus.
Immediately she rolled her eyes, threw out her hands, and spoke
in a voice that was at once recognised as that of a stranger—
not only on account of the sound, as of the expression and
choice of words. The voice cried, 'I cannot endure to hear
that name !' All shuddered. I had never heard anything of
the kind, and offered a silent prayer for wisdom and discretion.
At last I ventured to put a few questions, as this. 'Have you
no rest in the grave ?' 'No !' 'Why not ?' 'That is the
reward of my actions !' 'Did you not then confess all your
sins to me ?' (I asked her this, assuming that it was the
woman alluded to above.) 'No—I killed two children and
buried them in the fields.' 'Do you know of no hope ? Can
you not pray ?' 'No, I cannot.' 'Do you not know Jesus,
who forgives sins ?' 'I cannot endure to hear that name !'
'Are you alone ?' 'No !' 'Who is with you ?' The voice
replied, hesitating at first, 'The worst of all beings !' The
conversation went on a little longer ; the speaker accused herself of having practised magic, on which account she was now
the devil's bondswoman, and said that she had been cast out
seven times and would not go out again. I asked her if I
might pray for her (to which she only agreed after some hesitation), and told her that she must not and should not remain
in G——'s body. She seemed to entreat piteously, and then

to become defiant; but I commanded her, in a stern voice, to go out—not, however, in the name of Christ, which, for a long time, I did not dare to do. G. then struck her hands violently on the bed, and the possession seemed to be over.

Fourteen Devils Cast Out. "This scene was repeated many times, but the number of spirits increased, so that as many as fourteen were cast out of her at one time. Those present, including the mayor of the village, sometimes received knocks and blows, but Blumhardt never felt anything—indeed, he heard the demons say, repeatedly, that they were unable to touch him on account of his office. It would be tedious to follow the record of these scenes, which became more and more terrible. One night, when asleep, she felt a burning hand seize her neck. Her aunt, who was sleeping with her, immediately struck a light, and found that the place was blistered, as if from a bad burn. The doctor, calling on the following morning, saw the wound, and could offer no explanation, and it did not heal for weeks. By day and night she received blows from invisible hands, or felt her feet seized when descending the stairs or walking along the street, so as to make her fall. On the night of July 25th, 1842, after she had lain for some time like one dead, over a thousand demons appeared to leave her, passing out through the mouth. Blumhardt says they went out twelve, fourteen, or twenty-eight at a time, but does not explain how this was made clear. After this nothing occurred for some weeks; but worse was to follow. She was sorely plagued by demons, especially on Wednesday and Friday nights, and her health was being more and more undermined by her sufferings.

One Thousand and Sixty-seven Demons. "Blumhardt resisted the temptation to make use of any of the charms or 'sympathetic' remedies current among the peasantry, although he seems quite willing to believe in their efficacy, convinced that he would only be invoking the aid of Satan against himself, and confined himself to prayer. He found that he was always able to give relief in this way, but only after great suffering on the part of the patient, and the attacks were always renewed in his absence. He tried the effect of prayer without visiting the patient, and was successful. The demons, who on one occasion gave their number as 1,067, frequently made detailed communications, and sometimes spoke French and Italian or unknown languages — always through the mouth of G. After being cast out, they remained in the room for some time, visible to the patient, but to no one else. One, who seemed to be the principal, appeared to her in strangely rich garments of some ancient fashion, and always carried a large book. At length they were all cast out, some (according to their own assertions), having been delivered by prayer from the power of the devil (*i.e.* from the state of servitude in which he compelled them to work evil to the living), and assigned a place of rest till the Day of Judgment; others being in a state of utter despair. Among the first-named was the woman with the dead child: she was allowed at her entreaty to haunt the church, and was subsequently seen there by G. D., but by no one else. Blumhardt is of opinion that these people had, when living, brought themselves under the devil's power, either by wilful sin, or by trafficking in what is known as white magic (which, as a matter of fact, is still largely practised in out-of-the-way parts of rural Germany), *i.e.* charms, amulets, so-called 'sympathetic' cures, fortune-telling, finding of lost property, etc.

"By February 8th, 1843, the last demon was expelled. On that day, the patient lay for some hours unconscious, and afterwards related that she had appeared to be transported to a strange country (which, from the description given, appeared to be the West Indies), where she witnessed a terrible earthquake, and saw many of the spirits who had been tormenting her cast into the crater of a volcano — among them the one with the book, who had seemed to be the chief. A few days later arrived the news of the great earthquake of that date in the West Indies.

"Subsequently occurred a series of symptoms familiar to those who have read the accounts of the old witch trials—vomiting of sand, pieces of glass, nails, etc., even shoe-buckles, and, at a later date, live grasshoppers, a frog, and a snake. Pins, needles, and knitting-needles, were drawn out of various parts of the body. Pfarrer Blumhardt assures us that he frequently extracted them himself, and felt them gradually working to the surface. The worst case was the extraction (described in detail) of two nails—one a large bent one—from her head, accompanied by violent bleeding from the nose, ears, and eyes. This phenomenon he explains thus: "Supposing matter to consist—as some philosophers have supposed—of an aggregate of atoms, we might conceive it possible by supernatural (*i.e.*, demoniac) power, so to destroy cohesion, and reduce any given object to its compound atoms. It could then be administered in a person's food, or otherwise introduced into his body, and thus—the atoms having resumed their former shape—cause suffering and

A Vision of an Earthquake.

Physical Phenomena.

injury." G. asserted that she had sometimes noticed a strange taste in her food, and at others, had seen various persons standing by her bed at night, who either touched her or put something like bread into her mouth, whereupon she experienced unaccustomed sensations, as if some foreign substance had been introduced into her system. It seemed as if the spirits had determined, having been cast out of her, to destroy her life; but in this, in spite of many attempts, they could not succeed. Sometimes, quite unconsciously, she attempted to commit suicide, but was almost miraculously saved. Her complete recovery took place about Christmas, 1843, but was preceded by another terrible struggle, which affected her brother and sister (especially the latter) as well as herself. Both, however, were eventually restored.

Why? "It may seem hard to understand why a Christian woman, whose character and reputation were without reproach, should become a victim to such persecution as this. Pfarrar Blumhardt suggests, in answer, that she had when a child, unconsciously come in contact with the powers of darkness, through staying with a relative, who was reputed a witch and was undoubtedly a person of bad character; and who, moreover, openly expressed her intention of teaching her magic arts, so soon as she should be ten years old. This woman died when the child was eight, but it would seem as if the devil had looked upon her as a destined victim, and felt himself baulked of his prey. Pf. Blumhardt adds in conclusion that she was then (July, 1850), living in his house, not so much as a servant, as the trusted and valued friend of the whole family."

The Maid of Orlach. The following is a summary of William Howitt's account of this most remarkable of all Dr. Kerner's experiences :—

" In the small village of Orlach, in Wurtemburg, there lived a peasant named Grombach, a Lutheran Protestant, God-fearing man, much respected by his neighbours. In February, 1831, strange things began to happen in his cow-house. One of the cows was several times found fastened to a different part of the house than that to which it had been secured on the previous evening. Suddenly the three cows' tails would be plaited as if by a skilled weaver, this sometimes happening three or four times during the day. Though a strict watch was kept, no human agency could be traced. Grombach's daughter, Magdalene, when sitting in the cow-house, received a box on the ear which was so violent as to send her cap

flying against the wall. Similar occurrences happened throughout the year. On the 8th of February, 1832, while the cow-
house was being cleaned out, a fire was suddenly observed to
be burning within it. It was extinguished, but burst forth
again on the 9th, 10th, and 11th. As it was thought they
had been ignited by evilly-disposed persons, the police placed
watchers within the house day and night ; still the fires continued, but no cause could be found, although the cottage was
cleared of all its furniture. A few days later on, entering the
house, Magdalene heard the whimpering of a child, but could
find none.

The Ghost of a Guilty Nun. " At half-past eight on the same day she saw a
shadowy grey figure of a woman on a wall behind
the cow-house, who beckoned to her. An hour
later the figure again appeared to her and said : ' Remove the
house, remove the house. If it be not removed before the 5th
of March of next year a misfortune will befall you.' She said
the fires had been caused by an evil spirit, but that she had
protected them. Her father and brother were present, saw
Magdalene talking, but could not see the spirit. After this
the spirit appeared to her frequently. It told Magdalene, on
being questioned, that it was called Anna Maria, and had, 400
years before, been put into a convent against her will when
fourteen years old, and had been guilty of sin, which she
could not reveal. The ghost always spoke in a religious
manner, using texts and usually praying the 112th Psalm. She
appeared to be able to read the girl's thoughts before she expressed them. She frequently foretold events which were
about to occur.

The Black Spirit. "This continued from February till May, when
the spirit told Magdalene that she would not be
able to present herself for some time, that Magdalene would be persecuted by the Black Spirit, her evil companion, but that she must never answer him. From this time
she saw spirits in various shapes, such as frogs, a black cat,
dogs, and a black horse without a head, also men's voices
following with scornful laughter. Then the Black Spirit appeared to her in a dress like that of a monk. He usually
appeared in the hayfield and tempted her by all sorts of
questions to answer him. He also imitated the voices of her
neighbours ; but all in vain. One day he appeared to her no
fewer than three times, always laughing contemptuously.
About this time Magdalene discovered a bag of coins in the
cow-house. It was inexplicable how they had come there ; but

the Black Spirit appeared and told her he had given them to her for the box on the ear which he gave her in the cow-house.

The White Spirit. " The White Spirit, however, appeared in the evening, and said that the money must not be used but given to the poor, which it accordingly was. On July the 15th the Black Spirit appeared in the form of a bear and threatened her that if she would not answer him he would plague her. From this time the Black Spirit appeared in the shape of some hideous animal, promising her in turn money and then threatening her with torture. On August the 21st the Spirit appeared to her as an animal with its neck in the middle of its body ; she fell in a swoon, crying, ' The Black One ! ' She remained unconscious for several hours, and had similar attacks the succeeding day. She could answer to all questions put to her, but when she came out of the trance remembered nothing of them. On coming out of her trance she related that the Black Spirit had flown upon her and endeavoured to throttle her unless she would answer him. At that moment the White Spirit appeared and the Black One vanished. On the 23rd of August the White Spirit appeared to her and promised to protect her from harm, and said further that her sufferings would have an end on March 5th the next year. On other occasions the White Spirit told her that the Black Spirit would get entire possession of her body, but when she fell into this condition the White Spirit would take her soul to a place of safety. Magdalene's father now began to pull down the house and build a new one.

The Process of Possession. " From August 25th her struggles with the Black Spirit gradually became more violent, and he entered her body and spoke out of her mouth. She gave the following account of the process by which the demon took possession of her. In the midst of her work she would see a figure of a man clothed in a monk's frock, which seemed to be made from black mist, approach and say, when she refused to answer his questions : ' Now I will enter thy body in spite of thee.' Then she always felt him tread on her left side, seize her with five cold fingers at the back of the neck and then enter her body. She lost consciousness and individuality. Her voice was no longer her own, but that of the monk's. The speeches which she uttered when in this state were worthy of a demon. Magdalene lay during the whole time with her head sunk towards her left side, and her eyes firmly closed ; if the eyelids were raised the pupils would be discovered upwards. The left foot constantly moved up and down upon the ground throughout the attack, which frequently lasted four or five hours. The boards would be rubbed smooth by the friction of the bare foot, which remained as cold as ice. On her awaking she felt nothing the matter with her foot, and could walk miles, and she had no recollection of what occurred. Her right foot remained warm. In awakening a struggle seemed to take place between the right and the left side. The head would move itself from right to left until it fell on the right side, when the spirit departed. Usually she had a faint recollection of having been to church, which was attributed to the White Spirit's promised protection. If a Bible were held near the girl's body the Black Spirit would try to spit upon it, and hissed like a serpent. The doctors regarded her condition a natural sickness, but Dr. Kerner, who observed her in his own house for some weeks, was convinced that it was demoniac possession. When he made magnetic passes over Magdalene, the demon at once neutralised them by making counter passes with the girl's hands. Crowds of people flocked to Orlach to see and hear Magdalene when in her paroxysms.

"On March the 4th, at six in the morning, the *The Story of the Nun.* White Spirit appeared to her in dazzling brightness. She confessed to Magdalene that she had been seduced by a monk, the Black Spirit, who had been guilty of fearful crimes; had lived some years with him, and on partially betraying his wickedness had been murdered by him. The spirit then stretched out her hand towards the girl, who touched it with a handkerchief, which sparkled, and was found afterwards with a large hole for the palm of the hand and five smaller for the fingers and thumb of the spirit whose hand it had touched. The White Spirit bade her farewell, saying she was free from earthly things. While the spirit was speaking with Magdalene, a black dog seemed to spit fire against her, but did not touch her. Magdalene, who was in a part of the old house which was rapidly disappearing, was carried to a neighbouring farmer's, where the Black Spirit appeared to her and took possession of her body. He had a white tuft or tassel upon his head, and was not entirely black as heretofore. Magdalene tasted no food from Sunday night until Tuesday at noon, being incessantly possessed by the spirit. An immense multitude had gathered to witness the spectacle and questioned the demon, who answered correctly concerning places of interest in the neighbouring locality.

Deliverance. "At night the demon prayed, and was able to speak the words Jesus, Bible, Heaven, and the Church, which he had been unable to do before. He made a full confession of his crimes and said, 'My belief was that it was with men even as with the beast when it is slain; but it is quite different; there comes the reckoning after death.' He also said he must appear before the judgment seat a second time, when he left the girl. At half-past eleven in the morning the workmen came upon the last part of the wall of the house, which was of very ancient construction, and as soon as this was destroyed the demon departed from Magdalene. 'The transformation,' says an eye-witness, 'was astounding, from the disfigured demoniac countenance to a purely human, cheerful one; from the hollow, repellent voice of the evil spirit to its accustomed sounds, and from the partially paralysed, partially restless, possessed body to a beautiful, healthful young form. Magdalene was never again troubled with apparitions, and enjoyed perfect health. In removing the rubbish from the house a deep hole was discovered in which were found some brown bones, some of them those of children, probably the remains of the monk's wickedness, whose murders he had fully confessed."

CHAPTER IX

GHOSTS OF THE DEAD WITH A PRACTICAL OBJECT

"Shapes upon the dark without
From the dark within, a guess
At the spirit's deathlessness."—LOWELL.

THE character of ghosts has been seriously impeached of late by the committee of the Psychical Research Society. The time-honoured old ghost was a severely practical entity. He came to haunt the evil-doer, to reveal hidden crimes, to vindicate injured innocence, to reveal lost wills, and in various other ways to do work which flesh-and-blood mortals had failed to accomplish. But the report of the Psychical Society on the modern ghost contains as its fourth article, "There is a total absence of any apparent object or intelligent action on the part of ghosts." This is unjust, and I now proceed to adduce some evidence that may tend to rebut this unsparing impeachment, and as a beginning I will cite the story of my reporter, which I will take next in my Census of Hallucinations.

This story comes home to me because I have always had an uneasy kind of conviction that if all had their due this particular ghost would, occasionally at least, haunt me. It is a story of the ghost of a man who seems to have been unjustly hanged for a murder which he did not commit, and as I, quite innocently, helped indirectly to consummate this judicial murder, it would not have been surprising if the ghost had paid me a visit once in a way. But the deceased was not of a high order of intelligence during his life, and possibly enough was totally unaware that I had any responsibility, however remote, in his hanging.

The way in which I came into it was very simple. Several years ago I found myself confronted by a series of atrocious murders which were committed in horrible sequence by the Irish factions in England. It was a difficult matter to discover the murderers, and when they were discovered the strong repugnance of many excellent persons to the taking of human life led to such earnest and successful attempts to secure a commutation of sentence that a murderer's chance of the gallows was comparatively remote. When these murders increased and multiplied, I came to the conclusion that the petitions to the Home Secretary had gone too far. "Abolish capital punishment if you will, make a Court of Criminal Appeal if you like, but do not let us have the Home Secretary perpetually commuting judicial sentences on the more or less spasmodic representations of benevolent persons who are dominated by a passionate hatred of the death penalty." So I wrote with such vehemence as I had at command. I think I succeeded in somewhat damping down local zeal for sparing the lives of convicted murderers, and so became indirectly responsible to some small extent for the hanging against which the ghost of this man came back to protest. I may say that, although for the sake of the relatives of the man in question I must suppress all names and addresses, I am fully aware of all the circumstances of the case so far as they concern persons of flesh and blood. The evidence as to the ghostly visitant rests upon the statement, which I proceed to quote, of a thoroughly competent and absolutely trustworthy friend of mine, who is a reporter and newspaper correspondent in his district of many of the first dailies in the land. I have known him for years as a friend and colleague, and I know few men whose veracity is more unimpeachable and whose conscientiousness in observing and recording facts is more sensitive. I print his statement exactly as he wrote it out for me. He first told it me in the autumn of 1880, that is to say within little more than twelve months of the occurrence, and I shall never forget the impression which the narrative produced on my mind. There was something very pathetic in the thought of the poor ghost wandering round the scene of the crime for which he had been wrongfully executed, in order to proclaim that God judgeth not as man judges, and that he was innocent of the blood of the murdered man ; and I felt it all the more from a lurking suspicion that if I had not been so hard upon the people who got up petitions to the Home Secretary, he might have escaped the hanging, against which he made so solemn and persistent a protest.

"In the summer of 1879 a lady of my acquaint-
My Reporter's Story. ance, who had, as occasion served, paid some attention to the subject of spiritualism, as I was also known to have done, told me that she had been brought into contact with a medium in a distant town. She was desirous of further testing his powers, if arrangements could

be made for his calling at the town where she and I resided.
I replied that I should be very happy to put the gentleman up
for two or three days, as the lady could not do so.   I heard
nothing further of the matter until I received a letter from the
lady stating that the medium, whom I will denominate A.,
would call on me on such a day.   He duly arrived.   I found
him a pleasant and fairly intelligent young man, with whose
frankness and demeanour I and my family circle (which had
at that time been enlarged by two ladies, relatives of my wife)
were well pleased.   A. had not been in the house more than
half an hour when he said he clairvoyantly saw by the side of
one of the ladies a gentleman, deceased (a spirit), whom he
described, and who told him that he wished to speak to the
lady about Susan.   The lady in question recognised the description of the 'spirit' as that of her father, while Susan was
the name of her sister, of whom I had never heard, who had
been deceased for a long period.   Whilst sitting at supper in
the evening, A. described a former servant of my family who
had died ten years before, after having left us and got married.
He described the room in which she died, even to a peculiar
picture on the wall, by which hangs a tale which I cannot take
up your space to narrate, but which was a most striking
instance of clairvoyant powers.   He also remarked that the
said servant's spirit asked after her son, giving her son's name ;
said she exhibited before him a green dress which I had given
her before she was married from my house (perfectly true), and
many other minute and trustworthy tests, showing that some
peculiar abnormal power enabled him to read the circumstances
and surroundings of our past domestic life of many years before.
All this, I will premise, was given spontaneously.   Nobody
was 'pumped' or questioned to obtain a clue on which to base
these strange revelations of the past.   But I am reminded that
I must not be too diffuse, as these matters, however clear and
satisfactory they might have been to those who heard them,
pale in interest before the somewhat apparently sensational
but perfectly true and strange story which it was my purpose
in writing this notice to relate.

"During the time that A. was with me—three or
four days—as we were sitting one morning in the
breakfast room, there passed through a woman who
occasionally came to the house in the capacity of charwoman.
The woman did not linger at all in the room ; she merely
passed through to the kitchen in the rear of the house.
Almost immediately afterwards A. remarked, 'I felt a singular

The Apparition.

influence as that woman passed through, and was compelled to look up. There was a spirit of a man accompanying her who said in my hearing, " God judgeth not as man judgeth." And he (the spirit) further went on to say that he had suffered capital punishment for the crime of murder, but that, although mixed up with the party who dealt the blow which led to the death of the man who received it, he (the spirit) was not the one who struck the blow.' I was naturally interested in this statement, having been aware of all the circumstances of the murder alluded to, which had occurred a few years previously, and having felt great sympathy for the widow (the woman who passed through the breakfast room) and the family of the man who was hung, as they—and also he, as far as I had ever heard —were highly respectable and honest working-class people. Some time afterwards A. again said that the 'spirit' was still about there, and described him exactly as I had known him in life, repeating the previous statement that the 'spirit' declared that he was not guilty of the crime, not being the person who gave the death-blow, but admitting that he was morally guilty in leaguing himself with those who sought to accomplish the injury, or possibly death, of a person against whom they—a band of factious Irishmen—had some ill will.

The Murder. " I have said I was interested in A.'s statement. Ordinarily I should have simply passed the matter over as an exhibition of ordinary mediumship, or seership, or clairvoyance, no more striking in itself than that relating to the circumstances first detailed as affecting my family surroundings. When, however, the information was vouchsafed that the young Irishman who was hung was not guilty of the crime, there was brought to my mind a matter told me by a friend on whom I could implicitly rely, a year or two before. This gentleman, who held a responsible and somewhat public position, was not, I may remark, living in the town when the murder was committed, and one day in the course of conversation, asked me respecting it. I gave him an outline of the circumstances, which were fresh in my memory, and, being somewhat surprised at the interest he took in the matter, asked his reason. He replied that he was a particular friend—which I knew, though not himself a Catholic—of the leading Catholic priest in the town—a man, by the way, well known as most estimable, clear-headed, and intelligent, who comes of a good family, and now holds a somewhat exalted position in his Church—and that this priest had on one occasion told him that the man who was executed was not the real murderer.

Said my friend : ' He (the priest) spoke to me in the most decided and remarkably impressive way. He looked at me very pointedly, and remarked with great emphasis, " I *know* that the man who was executed for the crime never committed that murder."' My friend added, 'The impression made upon me was that the priest had had the confession of the real murderer.' In addition to this statement of the priest, I may remark that the criminal died asseverating his innocence to the last, and that his neighbours and friends—the Irish, who are, as is well known, very clannish, and ordinarily know more than they tell—never believed him guilty, or at least so they always said. Having attentively considered the evidence at the trial, I had believed the man to be guilty. At the same time I have had a good deal of experience as to the looseness of evidence in general, and the way in which persons can be deceived in a matter of identity ; in fact, one has been often deceived oneself. In the case in point the murder, or attack —possibly murder was not premeditated, only a minor exhibition of bad blood and violence—took place at night. That it was concerted there was no doubt. Two rather rough-looking young fellows—not, I think, out of their teens, and certainly not over-intelligent—were looking on at a street corner, on the opposite side of the road, by the aid of gaslight at the time. The murdered man was suddenly surrounded by half a dozen others, and the blow which felled him, and which ultimately was the cause of his death, was administered, they stated, by the young man who suffered for the capital crime. It must be considered that it was night, that there was a sort of scuffle with many men, and, therefore, that these two onlookers might possibly, under such circumstances, have been mistaken. I believe they honestly gave their evidence, but they were evidently ignorant, uncultivated, and of a somewhat low type—people of such a mould as one would not ordinarily care to entrust with the issues of life and death, even on their oath. Still, they were consistent and clear in their evidence. They supported each other, the jury convicted, the judge passed sentence, and the hangman did his work, on the strength of their testimony.

" But possibly I am digressing by making this **Shadowed by a Ghost.** explanation before I have told the whole of my story of A.'s mediumistic powers. I kept all these circumstances that I have mentioned from him, except that the charwoman's husband had suffered capital punishment, as he had stated, desiring to test his powers to the utmost, and obtain, if possible, further information from the 'spirit' of the so-called murderer as to the truth of the statement now so curiously made, and confirmed on the authority of the Roman Catholic priest, viz., that the wrong man had been hanged. Accordingly I remarked to A. that later on in the day we should be going into the town (I lived in the suburbs some way out), and that we should be passing the place where the murder was committed, when possibly the 'spirit' might tell him something more about the matter, and show him the spot where the crime took place. Some time afterwards we started for the town. When we left the house A. remarked, 'There he is following us,' alluding to the 'spirit.' When we had proceeded part of the way along the road, which was quite unknown to A., being a stranger, I made a *detour* for the purpose of making a business call, passing into a side street, A. following me. Just as, without a word on my part, we were turning out of the main road, Mr. A. said, 'The spirit is standing at the corner. He says we are not going the right way towards the place where the murder was committed, and which he has promised to point out to me.' I replied, 'Oh, we shall come out into the right road again by-and-by before we reach the spot.' We proceeded on about a quarter of a mile, and having done my business and struck the right road again, which differed, I may remark, from none of the other roads we had traversed, Mr. A. soon after declared, 'There is that man, the spirit, just on there, waiting for us.' As we continued our walk I purposely refrained from uttering a word or even from thinking as far as I could about the murder, so as to prevent any possibility of my companion obtaining any clue.

At the Scene of the Murder.
"As we were passing through the lowest parts of the town, Mr. A. suddenly exclaimed, 'He tells me that it was here the murder was committed. It was just there' (pointing to the place in the road where the murdered man fell). 'I see the hubbub and confusion rise before me as a picture, with the people round. He, however, again tells me that he did not strike the fatal blow. He does not excuse himself from being morally guilty, as being mixed up with those who accomplished the death of the man, but strongly maintains that he was not the murderer.' I will only add in relation to the last incident, that Mr. A. described the exact spot where the murder was committed, and the circumstances in connection therewith. How can this be accounted for? Mr. A. had never been in the town before; he had never lived within a couple of hundred miles of it; he did not know till within a day or two before that he would ever visit it; he

could not by any possibility have known that the poor woman
in my employ, coming casually into my house that morning,
was the widow of a man who was hanged. Then he had no
conceivable interest in deceiving me, nor was he concerned to
prosecute the matter any farther. But it might be objected
that A. had heard of the murder, which, of course, received considerable publicity at the time, and came fully primed with it.
But even supposing that he had got to know some of these
facts, how could he know that there was any particular value
attaching to the asseveration of the innocence of the man who
suffered capital punishment, when nobody believed it except
a few of the ignorant neighbours of the deceased man and the
Catholic priest, who had really kept the matter quiet, and who,
no doubt, had received the confession of the real murderer.
Then, again, how could he get to know the identity of the
widow coming unexpectedly into my house that morning.
Personally, I was as anxious as any one could be to prevent
any fraud on the part of the medium. The declarations he
made respecting it came to me as a surprise, and I purposely
did everything possible to test its genuineness, and satisfied
myself that it was all spontaneous and genuine."

It is a very curious story, and one which, so far as it goes,
helps to deliver the ghosts of to-day from the sweeping accusa-
tions brought against them of total lack of any apparent object
or of intelligent action.

A short time ago, when I was making up our
How a Ghost saved a Life. census, a journalistic friend of high standing and
reputation, whom I had met abroad, paid me a
visit. When I asked him if he had ever seen a ghost, he
replied, with unusual gravity, that a ghost had one time saved
his life, and that he never spoke lightly on the subject. His
story, which he told me with evident emotion and intense conviction, was remarkable, even if, as is probable, we should
regard the apparition as purely subjective :—

"It was many years ago," he said, "when I was younger,
and when the temptations of youth had not yet become memories
of the past. I was alone in a country hotel, and one night I
had decided to carry out a project which I still remember with
shame. At ten o'clock I retired to my room to wait till the
hotel was quiet, in order to carry out my design and enter an
adjoining room chamber. I lay in my bed watching the
moonlight which flooded the room, counting the moments till
all was still. After I had lain there for some time, I was
conscious of a presence in the room, and looking towards the

window I saw the familiar form of the woman whose death three years before had darkened my existence. I had loved her with my whole soul, as I had never loved any one before. She was my ideal of womanhood, my whole life had been entwined with hers, and her death was the cruellest blow ever dealt me by Fate. In the three years that had elapsed since her death I had striven to escape from the gnawing agony of the memory of my loss in scenes where she would least have sought me. Time, travel, dissipation had so dulled my pain that of late I had never thought of her, nor was I thinking of her when, suddenly, I saw her standing by the window. Her face was in the shadow, but there was no mistaking that queenly figure, those stately shoulders, and the familiar dress. She wore no hat or bonnet, but was as she had been when in her own drawing-room, thousands of miles away. She was standing in the moonlight, looking at me. Then she slowly moved towards me, and approached the bedside, fixing her gaze full on my face. Then, without saying a word, she vanished. I had lain, as it were, paralysed until she vanished, and I was once more alone. The passion of remorse obliterated in a moment the formerly imperious temptation. I no more thought of my design. It was as if the very thought of evil had been absolutely wiped out. I was overwhelmed with the thought of her, and abased. Remembering at what moment she had revisited me, I wept like a child, bitter, passionate tears of repentance, until from sheer exhaustion I fell asleep. I had no more doubt of the reality, the objective reality, of my visitor than I have of the objective reality of yourself or any one else whom I may meet in the street. This conviction was deepened when, on the following day, I learned to my surprise that if I had carried out my design and had entered the next room, I should have been knifed on the spot. In the chamber I had intended to enter was a reckless young bravo, who would have certainly had no more compunction in planting his stiletto in the heart of any unarmed intruder than you would of killing a rat. Between me, therefore, that night, and a bloody and shameful death, there was but an unlocked door and the watchful love of one who, in this simple but supernatural way, intervened to save me from myself and the doom that otherwise would have overtaken me."

Now even if we suppose that this phantasm was visualised subjectively by the unconscious personality, the faculty of the unconscious personality to give a mere subjective memory such vivid and real apparent objectivity just at the critical moment, is a very interesting and suggestive fact.

The Catholic Church abounds in ghost stories, in which the ghost has a practical object for revisiting the world. Father Keating told me last September that when he was at the College of the Propaganda at Rome, a Danish student died. He had been in the habit of writing out his confessions before he went to confessional. A short while after the student's death his confessor heard a knock at the door. He said, "Come in." The door opened, and the young Danish student entered the room. Although the priest knew he was dead, he was not frightened, and asked him what he wanted.

He said, "Will you look in my Latin dictionary? You will find there a paper on which I wrote down my last confession which I wished to make to you, but I was taken off before I saw you."

The priest asked him if he was happy.

"Yes," said he, "quite happy. That confession is the only thing that is troubling me. Will you get it?" The priest said he would, and the interview ended.

He then went to the dictionary, and there, between the pages, he found the written confession. He read it, and then destroyed it. The young student never afterwards appeared.

I hope to get confirmation of this from Rome, but as yet I have not received any reply to my inquiries, the person concerned being absent on his travels.

Father Keating also told me a story of a priest, whom he said he knew, who had entered the priesthood because of a ghost which appeared to him in an old country house. He followed this ghost to the room which it haunted. It pointed to a place in the floor and disappeared; they took up the floor, and found the sacred vessels which had been hidden there since the time of the Reformation, and which still contained some of the Host or sacred wafer. The vessels were removed and the ghost ceased to haunt. This story also needs verification, and until it is forthcoming it cannot be regarded as having any evidential value.

Another Catholic legend is the familiar story of the persistent haunting of the library at Slindon, Arundel, by the ghost of a Catholic priest. The story goes that he had forgotten to destroy the confession of a penitent. He had placed it between the leaves of the book he was reading. Sudden death deprived him of the opportunity of destroying the paper, and he was unable to rest in his grave until he found it and got some one to destroy it. Every night he revisited the library and hunted for the confession. At last a Catholic priest saw him and asked him what was the matter. He told him eagerly, and pointed out the book, in which the confession was found. He destroyed it at once, and the grateful spirit disappeared. Such is the local tradition, which, however, has never been verified so far as I can discover, but the same story is told of a library near Paris, where, oddly enough, Bishop Wilberforce is said to have been the liberating agent.

A Ghost that Wished to Pay its Debts. There is an odd story told by a Catholic priest in the " Proceedings of the Psychical Society," which seems to show that considerations of £ s. d. are not altogether forgotten on the other side of the grave. It is as follows :—

" In July, 1838, I left Edinburgh to take charge of the Perthshire missions. On my arrival in Perth I was called upon by a Presbyterian woman, Anne Simpson, who for more than a week had been in the utmost anxiety to see a priest. This woman stated that a woman lately dead (date not given), named Moloy, slightly known to Anne Simpson, had appeared to her during the night for several nights, urging her to go to the priest, who would pay a sum of money, three and tenpence, which the deceased owed to a person not specified.

" I made inquiries, and found that a woman of that name had died, who had acted as washerwoman and followed the regiment. Following up the inquiry, I found a grocer with whom she had dealt, and on asking him if a female named Moloy owed him anything, he turned up his books and told me that she did owe him three and tenpence. I paid the sum. Subsequently the Presbyterian woman came to me, saying that she was no more troubled."

Another that Wished to Clear its Character. The " Proceedings of the Psychical Society " contains several instances in which ghosts appear with an object. One of the most detailed and curious of these is the apparition of Robert Mackenzie. His employer tells it as follows :—

" In 1862 I settled in London, and have never been in Glasgow since. Robert Mackenzie and my workmen generally gradually lost their individuality in my recollection. I dreamt that I was seated at a desk engaged in a business conversation with an unknown gentleman, who stood on my right hand. Towards me in front advanced Robert Mackenzie, and feeling annoyed, I addressed him with some asperity, asking him if he did not see that I was engaged. He retired a short distance with exceeding reluctance, turned again to approach me, as if more desirous for an immediate colloquy, when I spoke to him still more sharply as to his want of manners. On this the person with whom I was conversing took his leave, and Mackenzie once more came forward. 'What is all this, Robert?' I asked somewhat angrily. 'Did you not see that I was engaged?' 'Yes, sir,' he replied, 'but I must speak with you at once.' 'What about?' I said. 'What is it that can be so important?' 'I wish to tell you, sir,' he said, 'that I am accused of doing a thing I did not do, and that I want you to know it, and to tell you so, and that you are to forgive me, because I am innocent.' Then, 'I did not do the thing they said I did.' I said, 'What?' getting the same answer. I then naturally asked, 'But how can I forgive you if you do not tell me what you are accused of?' I can never forget the emphatic manner of his answer in the Scotch dialect, ' Ye'll sune, sune ken " (You'll soon know). This question and answer were repeated at least twice. I am certain the answer was repeated thrice in the most fervid tone. On that I awoke and was in that state of bewilderment and surprise which such a remarkable dream might induce, and was wondering what it all meant, when my wife burst into my bedroom much excited, and holding an open letter in her hand, exclaimed, 'Oh, James, here's a terrible end to the workmen's ball : Robert Mackenzie has committed suicide !' With now a full conviction of the meaning of the vision, I at once quietly and firmly said, ' No, he has not committed suicide.' 'How can you possibly know that ?' 'Because he has just been here to tell me.'

"I have purposely not mentioned in its proper place, so as not to break the narrative, that on looking at Mackenzie I was struck by the peculiar appearance of his countenance. It was of an indescribable bluish-pale colour, and on his forehead appeared spots which seemed like blots of sweat. For this I could not account, but by the following post my manager informed me that he was wrong in writing to me of suicide. That, on Saturday night, Mackenzie was going home, had lifted a small black bottle containing aquafortis (which he used for staining the wood of bird-cages, made for amusement), believing this to be whisky, and poured out a wineglassful, had drunk it off at a gulp, dying on Sunday in great agony. Here, then, was the solution of his being innocent of what he was accused of—suicide—seeing that he had

inadvertently drunk aquafortis, a deadly poison. Still, pon-
dering upon the peculiar colour of his countenance, it struck
me to consult some authorities on the symptoms of poisoning
by aquafortis, and in Mr. J. H. Walsh's 'Domestic Medicine
and Surgery,' p. 172, I found these words, under symptoms
of poisoning by sulphuric acid : ' The skin covered with
a cold sweat, the countenance livid, and expressive of
dreadful suffering. . . . Aquafortis produces the same
effect as sulphuric, the only difference being that the external
stains, if any, are yellow instead of brown.' " (Vol. III. p.
97).

A Ghost Looking after its Widow. Another, in which the ghost of a husband visited
a friend who had failed to keep his word by seeing
after his widow, is thus told by Mr. C. Happerfield
himself :—

"When my old friend, John Harford, who had been a
Wesleyan lay preacher for half a century, lay dying, in June
of 1851, he sent for me, and when I went to his bedside, he
said, 'I am glad you have come, friend Happerfield ; I
cannot die easy until I am assured that my wife will be
looked after and cared for until she may be called to join me
in the other world. I have known you for many years, and
now want you to promise to look to her well-being during the
little time which she may remain after me.' I said, ' I will do
what I can, so let your mind be at rest.' He said, ' I can
trust you,' and then soon afterwards, on the 20th of the month,
fell asleep in the Lord. I administered his affairs, and when all
was settled there remained a balance in favour of the widow,
but not sufficient to keep her. I put her into a small cottage,
interested some friends in her case, and saw that she was
comfortable. After a little while Mrs. Harford's grandson came
and proposed to take the old lady to his house in Gloucestershire, where he held a situation as schoolmaster. The request
seemed reasonable. I consented, provided that she was quite
willing to go, and the young man took her accordingly. Time
passed on. We had no correspondence. I had done my duty
to my dying friend, and there the matter rested. But one night
as I lay in bed wakeful, towards morning, turning over business and other matters in my mind, I suddenly became conscious that some one was in my room. Then the curtain of
my bed was drawn aside, and there stood my departed friend,
gazing upon me with a sorrowful and troubled look. I felt no
fear, but surprise and astonishment kept me silent. He spoke
to me distinctly and audibly in his own familiar voice, and

said, 'Friend Happerfield, I have come to you because you
have not kept your promise to see to my wife. She is in
trouble and in want.' I assured him that I had done my duty
and was not aware that she was in any difficulty, and that I
would see about her first thing, and have her attended to. He
looked satisfied and vanished from my sight. I awoke my
wife, who was asleep at my side, and told her of what had
occurred. Sleep departed from us, and on arising, the first
thing I did was to write to the grandson. In reply, he informed me that he had been deprived of his situation through
persecution, and was in great straits, in so much that he had
decided on sending his grandmother to the union. Forthwith
I sent some money, and a request to have the old lady forwarded to me immediately. She came, and was again provided with a home, and her wants supplied. These are the
circumstances as they occurred. I am not a nervous man, nor
am I superstitious. At the time my old friend came to me I
was wide awake, collected, and calm. The above is very
correct, not overdrawn."

There is one instance recorded of a ghost that
came back in order to make two lovers happy.
It is as follows :—

A Match-
making
Ghost.

"A young couple were engaged. The father of the woman
withdrew his consent. The mother, on her death-bed, made
its renewal her last request. The father, instead of getting
over his sorrow, seemed more and more bowed down with
an increasing sense of horror. One day he told his married
daughter and her husband that his wife haunted him every
morning at four, the hour at which she died, always talking
of the young couple. They asked him what clothes the apparition wore, and he said, 'The last dress I gave, and a cap
of your making.' On her way home the married daughter told
her husband that it was when in that dress and cap her mother
had said to her, 'If I die before your father renews his consent, I shall haunt him till he does.' She was then in perfect
health. This was never told to the father, but he was urged
to renew his consent. For some months he could only escape
the visitations by having some one awake with him in the
room. From the day he consented again to the marriage his
wife's visits ceased." (Vol. III. p. 100.)

Here is a ghost that was impelled by love of
a wife to remind a daughter to do her duty :—

"Take care
of Mother."

"About two months before the death of my
dear father, which occurred on December 10th, 1887, one

night, about 12 or 1 a.m., when I was in bed in a perfectly waking condition, he came to my bedside and led me right through the cemetery at Kensal Green, stopping at the spot where his grave was afterwards made.

" Again, a day or two before his death, somewhere between December 4th and 10th (the day of his decease), when he was lying in an unconscious state in a room on the ground floor, and I was sleeping on the second floor, I was awoke suddenly by seeing a bright light in my bedroom—the whole room was flooded with a radiance quite indescribable—and my father was standing by my bedside, an etherealised, semi-transparent figure, but yet his voice and his aspect were normal. His voice seemed a far-off sound, and yet it was his same voice as in life. All he said was, ' Take care of mother.' He then disappeared, floating in the air, as it were, and the light also vanished.

" About a week afterwards, that is to say, between the 12th and the 17th of December, the same apparition came to me again, and repeated the same words. An aunt to whom I related these three experiences, suggested to me the possibility that something was troubling his spirit, and I then promised her that should my dear father visit me again I would answer him. This occurred a short time afterwards. On this, the fourth occasion, he repeated the same words, and I replied, ' Yes, father.' He then added, ' I am in perfect peace.'

" Apparently he was satisfied with this my assurance. Since that time I have neither heard nor seen him more." (Vol. V. p. 451.)

The next ghosts that I shall mention came for *Consolatory Ghosts.* a spiritual or religious purpose :—A correspondent.

"My father died suddenly. He had been seriously troubled with many doubts regarding various points of Christian faith. . . . I was lying in deepest anguish, beset not only with the grief of the sudden loss sustained, but with the wretched fear that my beloved father had died too suddenly to find peace with God regarding those miserable doubts that had so troubled him. As the night wore on, the pain of the heart and thought grew worse and worse, and at length I knelt in prayer, earnestly pleading that my distressful thoughts might be taken away, and an assurance of my father's peace be given me by God's most Holy Spirit. No immediate relief came, however, and it was early dawn when I rose from my knees, and felt that I must be patient and wait for the answer to my prayer.

"I was just about to slip quietly down into the bed, when

on the opposite side of it (that on which the nurse was sleeping) the room became suddenly full of beautiful light, in the midst of which stood my father, absolutely transfigured, clothed with brightness. He slowly moved towards the bed, raising his hands, as I thought, to clasp me in his arms, and I ejaculated, 'Father!' He replied, 'Blessed for ever, my child! For ever blessed!' I moved to climb over nurse and kiss him, reaching out my arms to him, but with a look of mingled sadness and love he appeared to float back with the light towards the wall and was gone! The vision occupied so short a time that, glancing involuntarily at the window again, I saw the morning dawn, and the little birds just as they had looked a few minutes before. I felt sure that God had vouchsafed me a wonderful vision, and was not in the least afraid, but, on the contrary, full of joy that brought floods of grateful tears, and completely removed all anguish except that of having lost my father from earth. I offer no explanation, and can only say most simply and truthfully that it all happened just as I have related it." (Vol. XI. p. 26.)

Mr. Angus Ross, 62, Calder Street, Govanhill, Glasgow, writes me as follows :—

"In a small village in the north of Scotland, where I was born, my mother was very much sought after as a sick nurse to the poor. One of our neighbours sickened and died; my mother was a good deal with her during her illness. Deceased and my mother lived for a long time on very friendly terms, and now that she was gone, and did not leave very clear evidence as to what her future state would be, my mother's mind was much perplexed about the matter.

"So a night or two after the death of her friend, as she was lying in bed perfectly awake, the dead woman came to her bedside in form as perfect as ever she had in life; my mother was overcome with fear at the sight, and could not utter a word, so after awhile she vanished away. During next day the matter scarcely left her mind, and next night at the same time and in like manner the visitation was made. My mother was unable to speak, and this seemed to give offence, for she looked angry-like, then vanished as before. Next day my mother resolved if the visit was repeated that she would ask her if she was happy. The opportunity of doing so was given her next night, but in her agitated state of mind she used the word 'weel' instead of happy. She replied, 'Yes, be praying;' this she repeated three times, and vanished and was seen no more."

A "Fetch."   I will conclude this chapter by the following brief note of one of the most circumstantial ghost stories of recent times. It is the only story I print that illustrates the beautiful belief that the spirit of the best beloved in life attends the death-bed to conduct the parting spirit into the other world :—

"About fourteen of the 5th Lancers were seated in their mess-room in the East Cavalry Barracks, Aldershot, one day in the autumn of 1876. They had just finished their dinner, a little after half-past eight o'clock, when a lady in full evening dress in white silk, and with a long bridal veil, walked past the window outside, the curtains being but partially drawn. Her movement was pretty rapid, but two officers at least who sat at the table saw her. She moved in the direction of Mr. Norton, who rang the bell and asked the mess sergeant if any one had been in the conservatory at the back of the room, as it was thought the apparition might be due to reflection. As the sergeant denied that any woman had entered the room, it was said that she must have been a ghost, as there was no ledge outside the window, which was about 40 feet from the ground. Her features were discussed. She was described by those who saw her as handsome, very dark, and with a very sad countenance. One officer present, on hearing the description, said, 'Why, that is little old ——'s wife, who died in India.' The officer whom he named was the regimental veterinary, who was supposed at that time to be home on leave. It turned out, however, that the veterinary had returned that afternoon, unknown to any of his brother officers, and although some weeks of his leave remained. He had walked up to his room, which was immediately above the butler's pantry. He rang for his servant, and complained of great fatigue, ordered brandy, and then sent his servant away. He continued drinking. A few days later, about half-past eight o'clock, the servant went up to his room and found him dying in bed. An officer present, Adjutant Fletcher, had to enter his room, and after taking an inventory of his effects, to lock it up as a caution against pilfering. The very first thing Dr. Atkinson, who attended him, saw was a cabinet portrait of the lady, in the same dress which they had seen a few days before. Witnesses of the apparition : Captain Norton, Surgeon Atkinson (who died last year), the regimental doctor, Lieutenant Fred Russell, *alias* 'Brer Rabbit' of the *Sporting Times*, since dead.

CHAPTER X

OUT OF DOOR GHOSTS

DURING my visit to Scotland in 1891 I had the honour of being entertained at a dinner, given at the City Liberal Club, by my helpers in Glasgow. There were fourteen of us altogether, Professor Lindsay being in the chair. After dinner I turned the conversation upon the subject of apparitions, and remarked that I did not think that a dozen persons ever met without one of their number having seen a ghost. "Now who is there," I asked, "who has seen a ghost here?" Sitting opposite me at the table was Mr. David Dick, auctioneer, of 98, Sauchiehall Street, a young married man, about thirty-five, a member of the Glasgow Ruskin Society, as well as one of the earliest members of our Association of Helpers. He said, "I do not believe in ghosts, but I have seen one." At first I thought he was joking, but in reply to my question he repeated his remark, "I do not believe in ghosts, I never did and do not now; but, nevertheless, I have seen one. I am not in the least superstitious," he continued. "I remember once, before my father died, receiving a practical lesson in the absurdity of most of the alarms which scare the nerves of the timid. My father came into the house from the garden with a feeling that some one had been following him, and when we looked out of the window there certainly was something uncanny beside the door. When we came out it disappeared, but on looking at it again from the window we saw it. At last, after nearly half an hour's diligent search and examination, we discovered that the apparent apparition was caused by the light of the moon shining through a small window in the porch. I remember, although it is nearly twenty years ago, my father saying that if every one would take as much pains as we had to investigate ghosts they would be found to have a similar natural explanation. I have always held to that; but, nevertheless, I have seen a ghost, and I find it utterly impossible to explain it on any so-called natural grounds." "But tell us about your ghost; when did you see it?" "I cannot remember the exact date. My memory is bad for dates ; I do not even remember the date of my birth or of my marriage. But it is about nine or ten years ago." "Was it the ghost of a living or of a dead person ? " "A ghost of a dead person.' "How long had it been dead ? " "Six years." "Where did you see it ? " "In Glasgow." "In the day or night ? " "At half-past three in the afternoon, in broad daylight." "But tell us how it occurred ? " "I had left the office in Sauchiehall Street at half past three in the afternoon. I was going on an errand to St. Vincent Street, and had my mind full of my business. I went along Sauchiehall Srreet and entered Ren-field Street, where the ghost joined me." "You knew it was a ghost ? " "Perfectly." "How did you know it was a ghost ? " "Because I recognised it at once." "Did it speak to you ? " "It did." "What did it say to you ? " "That I cannot tell you ; it spoke of a matter which was only known to myself." "You answered ? " "Yes, and continued to walk on, the ghost accompanying me exactly as if it had been an ordinary person. We walked down Renfield Street together, talking. There was nothing in the appearance of the ghost to impress any one who met it that it was not a living man. It wore a black coat and a flat felt hat which I had only seen worn once in the lifetime of the deceascd. The part of Renfield Street we traversed together is about 250 yards long, and one of the busiest streets in Glasgow. When I got to the corner of Vincent Street the ghost vanished. I did not see it come, and I did not see it go : I only knew it was not there." "Were you not frightened ? " "Not the least in the world." "Did you not ask it any questions ? " "No, none, I simply carried on the conversation which it had begun." "Did not its sudden disappearance disturb you ? " "Not at all ; it joined me without notice, and left me as simply. I did not see it dissolve, it simply was not there any longer." "And you knew the ghost ? " "Perfectly." "Who was it, may I ask ? " "It was the ghost of my father." "Were you thinking of your father ? " "Not at all." "And when he spoke to you, were you not surprised ? " "Not in the least." "Nor inquisitive ? " "No, it seemed so natural. I was chiefly thinking of the place I was going to. In fact, it was not until the next day that I began to realize how strange it was that I had been speaking familiarly to my father, six years after he had died, in a busy Glasgow street. But that it was so I have not the slightest doubt in the world. That I know. I have had no other experience of a similar nature. As I said, I do not believe in ghosts ; all that I know is that I did walk down Renfield Street with my father six years after his death."

Here was a pretty story, utterly at variance with almost all the traditional ghost stories, yet Mr. Dick stoutly maintains that whatever his ghost may have been, it was a ghost notwithstanding, and not a subjective hallucination in any sense. He saw it as plainly as any one in the street, and, so far as he could see, any one else must have seen it also. The ghost went off the pavement in order to prevent a collision just as if it had been in its ordinary body. The crucial question, of course, is whether the ghost communicated to Mr. Dick any fact which at the time was not within his knowledge, and had never been known to him. That we did not think of asking him at the time, but when I put the question directly to Mr. Dick, he answered :—

"The 'vision,' as you call it, suggested, without insisting, that I was annoying myself too much about affairs which did not really lie in my power, and that events might prove my worry quite senseless, which they did. There was neither definite prophecy nor promise. Had there been I should have said the 'ghost' was a pure swindle, my father having been a man so reserved that William the Silent was a chatterer to him. I've had worse worries and more serious troubles since, it is fair to say, which have neither been averted nor ameliorated by another visit from the 'vision.'"

A Ghost interested in the St. Leger. This story reminds me of one published by the Psychical Research Society, which from some points of view is even more remarkable than Mr. Dick's. It is not unnatural that a son should see his father, or thinks he sees him, for the human naturally broods over the memory of a much-loved parent, and some circumstance or train of thought may lead a sensitive medium to visualise his ideas. The apparition in the following story cannot be said to be due to any such personal sympathy, for the person who appeared, so far from being a near relation, was merely a man with whom the percipient had done business in the past in connection with horse-racing. The narrative, as received from Mr. William H. Stone, 1, Park Avenue, Slade Lane, Levenshulme, Manchester, and as printed in the " Proceedings," runs as follows :—

"I was going along from our office in rather a merry mood, to order from a stationer in P—— Street a quantity of catalogues wanted in our next Friday's sale, for we sold the hides and skin every Friday by auction, at half-past one o'clock to the minute, or nearly so. As I said, I was going along P—— Street, it might be some six or eight days before the great St. Leger day. I generally had a pound or two on the 'Leger,' and it was my intention, as soon as my little order was given, to see a friend about the horse I had backed. Crossing from left to right in P—— Street, whom should I meet (or as I thought met) but an old customer, as he had been for some years, of my father's. My father was formerly a brewer, and had supplied the party I thought I met with ale for some years, and I used to collect the accounts from him along with others in the same line ; he was a beerhouse keeper, or, as they then called them, a jerry-shopkeeper. I went up to him, called him by his right name and shook him by the left hand, for he had no right, it having been cut off when he was a youth ; he had a substitute for a hand in the shape of a hook, and he was, said he, very active with his hook when his services were required in turning any one out of his house that was in any way refractory. He was what you may call a jolly, good, even-tempered sort of man, and much respected by his customers, most of whom did a little betting in the racing line. He had a very red, countrified sort of face, and dressed quite in the country style, in a felt halt, something after the present style of billy-cocks, with thick blue silk handkerchief with round white dots on it, his coat a sort of chedle-swinger, and a gold watchguard passing over his neck and over his waistcoat ; his clothing was all of good material and respectably made. The moment he saw me his face shone bright, and he seemed much pleased to meet me, and I may say I felt a similar pleasure towards him. Mind, this occurred in broad daylight, no moonlight or darkness, so essential an accompaniment to ghost stories ; many people were passing and repassing at the time. You may be sure I did not stand in the middle of the street for about seven minutes, talking and shaking hands with myself. Some one would have had a laugh at me if that had been the case. I almost at once, after the stereotyped com-pliments of the day, launched into the state of the odds respecting the St. Leger, and into the merits and demerits of various horses. He supplied me with what information I required, and we each went our way. He was a man supposed to be well posted up in such matters, had cool judgment and discrimination ; in fact, he was one of those who would not be led away by what are called tips. I made a memorandum or two, shook his hand again, and passed on about my business, ordered my catalogues, etc.

" I came back sauntering along towards the office, not now intending to see the party I had previously intended to see. As I got to the same part of P—— Street on my way back, I suddenly stood still, my whole body shook, and for a moment I tried to reason with myself. The man I had been speaking to was dead some four years before ! Could it be possible that he had been buried alive ? This is horribly shocking to think about, but such things have happened. Decomposition being the only certain indication of death, might he not have been prematurely buried ? But if so, what had I to do with it ? I had nothing to do with his death, but I am sorry now I do not recollect or know the particulars of his death or burial. I certainly saw his funeral. (We have failed to obtain the certificate of death or burial.) As I stood in the street I tried to give utterance to my thoughts and feelings ; but no, I felt a sort of dumbness, and fairly gasped for breath. I felt a cold shiver come over me although the day was warm ; the hair of my head seemed as if it would force my hat off my head ; my very blood seemed to object to perform its duty.

" The question might be asked, was I unwell? Had I been indulging too freely in stimulants ? In both cases I answer, No. Was it an optical delusion, for nothing is so deceptive as optical delusions ? Certainly not. We sometimes believe we see what we do not see ; but in this case it was nothing of the sort ; nor could it be somebody like him, it was him ! As I said before, he had but one hand, and his right hand was his left hand in a sense. I had business transactions with him for many years. He had entirely slipped out of my memory for a length of time. That he was in or out of existence it never occurred to me for one moment till now ; and the thought never presented itself during the interval of my going and coming, and perhaps never would have done had I not gone back by way of P—— Street, and passed the identical spot. It may be asked am I, or was I, superstitious ? I say, No, emphatically."

If this story be credited, it is totally different from all pre-conceived notions of the subject of ghosts. Whatever else disembodied spirits have been accused of doing in the past, this is the first time they have been credited with even a passing interest in the fortunes of the St. Leger.

A Clergyman's Narrative. Ever since the leading case of Baalam's ass, it is understood that animals have a plainer perception of the invisible than human beings. In out-of-door ghosts, it is usually the horse which discovers the uncanny visitant before the human biped who rides or drives him. Here is a story in which a pony plays a conspicuous part. It is sent me by the Rev. D. Holland Stubbs, of Penwortham Vicarage. It is as follows :—

"I am a clergyman of the Church of England, holding a small country living in one of the prettiest localities in the western portion of the diocese of Manchester.

"It was just at the end of a day in the autumn of 1889, when the sun had set, that I proceeded in my pony trap to conduct a Bible Class in a small schoolroom in a distant corner of my extensive parish. I set off from the vicarage about half-past six o'clock, and had proceeded about a mile and a half on my way, down a long lonely lane, with cottage-farms at some distance apart, and had arrived just opposite a strange-looking, square-built house, with heavy, overhanging roof and curiously shaped windows, embedded in dark, gloomy looking trees. Several times on previous occasions my good wife had shuddered when passing this strange abode, though in the open daytime, and had once made the remark, 'I don't like the look of that house; there is something uncanny about it.' Ordinarily she is not of a superstitious turn of mind, nor of a highly nervous temperament. However, on the occasion referred to I was alone and progressing at a fairly rapid rate. I arrived at the spot mentioned, when suddenly and unaccountably my pony stopped, causing me to be thrown forward and to nearly fall over the dash-board; at the same time setting his ears and stretching his neck as though he saw something in front. We were just about entering a part of the road which was thickly covered with trees, upon which still lingered a few leaves unremoved by the September gales, so that the place was very gloomy. The more distant part of the road appeared to be in pitchy darkness. Unfortunately, I had no lamps lighted at the time. I urged on my steed with whip and voice. He proceeded cautiously, still craning his neck and listening intently, as though he saw and heard something which I certainly could not, though I strained my eyes and ears to do so. One or two smart cuts with the whip made him move on more rapidly until we were right under the trees. Again he stopped, and this time wheeled right round, and with difficulty I prevented myself being landed with the trap on top of me in a deep and wide land-drain. After a little persuasion he headed round again and ran on. Another start and stoppage, and this time the pony trembled in every limb, shaking the harness and trap. Fear, they say, is infectious, and I, too, began to be somewhat alarmed, although I could see nothing to cause fear. Looking, however, intently ahead, I perceived a figure in white, moving along silently on the grass border of the road, about ten yards in front. Thinking it was a farm servant girl in print dress and white apron, I laid on with the whip, in order to come up with her. The pony went on cautiously, stopping whenever the figure stopped. I called out, but no response was given. Mustering up all my courage I urged the animal forward. The figure went on rapidly, and as I was just about to overtake it, it turned at right angles and disappeared through the hedge. The conclusion I came to was that it must have been some farm servant, and having been surprised and not wishing to be overtaken and recognised, she made a short cut across the field to the farm-house near at hand. After passing on a little way until I came to a cross road, I stopped and got out to soothe my frightened animal, and found him bathed in a cold sweat, which literally ran off him. He was trembling violently, and appeared so weak that I feared he could not go much farther. For some minutes I let him rest, talking to him the while, and comforting him. After he had somewhat quietened down I proceeded to my destination, determining, on the first occasion, to examine that portion of the road, and see whether I could learn the cause of our fright. The opportunity pre sented itself in a day or two after, and with the noonday brightness I carefully inspected the road, and particularly that portion of the hedge through which the figure disappeared. To my astonishment, though I had marked the spot and knew it well, there was no gap in the hedge, as I had expected to find—no, not even one so small that a slight person could have squeezed through. The hedge for the whole length was an exceptionally good one, without gap or mend. Who or what the figure was I have never, from that day to this, been able to learn. Certain it is, it could not have been a farm girl, for no one could possibly have got through or over a hedge like that. Further information than this I cannot give, nor can I offer any explanation, but merely state the bare facts as they certainly happened, with the effects they caused upon both myself and pony."

A Ghost on the Hambleton Hills. In the next story, which is sent me by a solicitor of Teeside, the horse, oddly enough, did not seem the least scared at the ghost. My correspondent had ridden to Bilsdale, on business to Thirsk, across the Hambleton Hills :—

"In returning after dinner he reached the brow of the Hambleton Hills, and began to make the steep descent. There was a vast expanse of land to be seen, covered with closely cropped turf; but the whole scene looked 'as wild as an hawk.' It may be as well to mention that I was in splendid health, having been out travelling for months; and my spirits were buoyant, or I think the scene of desolation would have depressed me. I had not proceeded far in the descent, when I observed the tall figure of a lady draped in black, in advance of me, and walking in the same direction, but on the turf and on my right. I must say it occasioned me surprise to see a lady alone in so dreary a region. Obedient to my first impulse, I put my heel to the horse to come up abreast with her. My attention was divided between the lady and my horse, lest he should come to grief, the road being both steep and rough. I had the object thus several times in view, but I did not seem to be advancing upon it. I am not long-sighted, but there were no trees or shrubs on this part of the ground, nor any mist that could have occasioned a mistake. After awhile, we neared the bottom of the hill, the road turning then along its base, and bounded on the right by a large and ancient wood. Near this turn, the object vanished! I expected to find a stile into the wood through which the lady had entered, but there was no stile, neither was there a gap in the hedge, which was of immense growth. On the left hand was a very high wall, but no stile through it. I pulled up my horse and listened, but there was no sound. Had any one asked me if I would swear I had seen a lady in black descending the hill I would have done so without hesitation. I must say I was surprised at the disappearance, and thought (and most likely said) to myself, 'Well, this is a rum go!' Riding on, I shortly afterwards came to a picturesque hamlet which appeared almost imbedded in the ancient wood. I had a strong disposition to pull up here and make some inquiries, but I resolved not, lest the good people, hearing my extraordinary statement, should laugh at me for a fool. Proceeding on my journey I afterwards passed a high and massive wall that appeared to protect the garden or grounds of some old ruin, and in due course I reached Thirsk, having had a very enjoyable day. A busy life has left me little time to give to subjects of this kind, but after some years had gone, I was taking a quiet cup of tea with an old friend in the county of Durham, when he introduced the subject of apparitions. Having heard what he had to say, I remarked that never but once in my life had I seen anything I could not account for, and I related to him the statement I am now making, and nearly in the same words. My friend paid great attention, and when I had concluded said, ' Now let me put to you two questions : Did you ever hear anything of what you have been telling me ? ' ' Never,' was my answer, ' I was a perfect stranger to the place and the people.' He continued, ' Did you ever read anything about it ? ' ' Never.' ' Then,' he said, ' it is a most extraordinary statement you have made, for it confirms a pamphlet I have somewhere in my house, that gives a similar account of what has been seen in that neighbourhood. Had you called at the hamlet and made an inquiry, so far from laughing at you as a fool, you would have been quietly told that you had seen My Lady ; and you would have found that they are familiar with the sight. The tradition is that many years ago a gentleman and his wife lived at the hall—the old ruin of which you passed—and that he was worked up to fit of jealousy by some Iago of a character and destroyed his wife, hiding the body in that massive garden wall. Restless, he fled to France, and was ultimately murdered by the same Iago.'

"To prove to you that I am not morbidly curious on subjects of this kind, I may say that I never made a point of seeing my friend's pamphlet, and he is now dead ; but, not unlikely, a copy of it may be found in some old household. I have never again visited the scene, though I have sometimes been as near to it as Thirsk. The account I am giving has scarcely been named beyond the range of my own family, and this is the first time I have put pen to paper about it.

" I send you my name, but not for publication."

The Murdered Miller on the Grey Horse. The next story is sent me by one of the leading townsmen of Cowes, in the Isle of Wight. The horse was not frightened in the least, although in this case there was a spectral horse as well as a horseman :—

"On a fine evening in April, 1859, the writer was riding with a friend on a country road. Twilight was closing down on us, when, after a silence of some minutes, my friend suddenly exclaimed, ' No man knows me better than you do, J. Do you think I am a nervous, easily frightened sort of man ? ' ' Far from it,' said I ; ' among all the men I know in the wild country I have lived and worked in, I know none more fearless or of more unhesitating nerve.' ' Well,' said he, ' I think I am that, too ; and though I have travelled these roads all sorts of hours, summer and winter, for twenty years, I never met anything to startle me, or that I could not account for, until last Monday evening. About this time it was. Riding old Fan (a chestnut mare) here on this cross (a four-way cross road), on my near side was a man on a grey horse, coming from this left-hand road. I had to pull my off rein to give myself room to pass ahead of him; he was coming at a right angle to me. As I passed the head of his horse I called out 'good-night.' Hearing no reply, I turned in my saddle to the off-side, to see whether he appeared to be asleep as he rode, but to my surprise I saw neither man nor horse. So sure was I that I had seen such, that I wheeled old Fan round and rode back to the middle of the cross, and on neither of the four roads could I see man or horse, though there was light enough to see two hundred or three hundred yards, as we can now. Well, I then rode over to that gate' (a gate at one corner opening into a grass field), 'thinking he might have gone that way; looking down by each hedge I could see nothing of my man and horse; and then—*and not until then*— I felt myself thrill and start with a shuddering sense that I had seen something uncanny, and, by Jove! I put the mare down this hill we are now on at her very best pace. But the strangest part of my story is to come,' said he, continuing. 'After I had done my business at the farm-house here, at foot of this hill, I told the old farmer and his wife what I had seen, as I have now told you. The old man said, " For many years I have known thee, M——, on this road, and have you never seen the like before on that cross?" " Seen what be-fore?" I said. " Why, a man in light-colour clothes on a grey horse," said he. " No, never," said I; " but I swear I have this evening." The farmer asked, " Had I never heard of what happened to the miller of L—— Mills about forty years ago?" " No, never a word," I told him. " Well," he said, " about forty years ago this miller, returning from market, was waylaid and murdered on that cross,. pockets rifled of money and watch. The horse ran home, about a mile away. Two serving-men set out, with lanterns, and found their master dead. He was dressed, as millers often do in this part of the country, in light-coloured clothes, and the horse was a grey horse. The murderers were never found. These are facts," continued the farmer. " I took this farm soon after it all happened, and, though I have known all this, and have passed over that cross thousands of times, I never saw any-thing unusual there myself; but there have been a number of people who tell the same story you have now told mother and me, M——, and describe the appearance of a man on grey horse, seen and disappearing , as you have done to-night." '

"Four evenings after all this occurred my friend related it to me as we were riding along the same road. He continued to pass there many times every year for ten years, but never again saw anything of the sort."

" He has seen the White Horse ! " "An Afrikander" sends me the following graphic description of a South African ghost. He says :—

"I'm not a believer in ghosts—no, never was ; but, seeing you wanted a census of them, I can't help giving you a remarkable experience of mine. It was some three summers back, and I was out with a party of Boer hunters. We had crossed the northern boundary of the Transvaal, and were camped on the ridges of the Lembombo. I had been out from sunrise, and was returning about dusk with the skin of a fine black ostrich thrown across the saddle in front of me, in the best of spirits at my good luck. Making straight for the camp, I had hardly entered a thick bush when I thought that I heard somebody behind me. Looking behind, I saw a man mounted on a white horse. You can imagine my surprise, for my horse was the only one in camp, and we were the only party in the country. Without considering, I quickened my pace into a canter, and on doing so my follower appeared to do the same. At this I lost all confidence, and made a run for it with my follower in hot pursuit, as it appeared to my imagination ; and I did race for it (the skin went flying in about two minutes, and my rifle would have done the same had it not been strapped over my shoulders). This I kept up until I rode into camp right among the pals cooking the evening meal. The young Boers about the camp were quick in their inquiries as to my distressed condition, and regaining confidence, I was putting them off as best I could, when the old boss (an old Boer of some sixty-eight or seventy years) looking up from the fire said, 'The White Horse ! The Englishman has seen the White Horse.' This I denied, but to no purpose. And that night, round the camp fire, I took the trouble to make inquiries as to the antecedents of the White Horse. And the old Boer, after he had commanded silence, began. He said, 'The English are not brave, but foolish. We beat them at Majuba, some twenty-five seasons back. There was an Englishman here like you ; he had brought a horse with him against our advice, to be killed with the fly, the same as yours will be in a day or two. And he, like you, would go where he was told not to go; and one day he went into a bush (that very bush you rode through to-night), and he shot seven elephants, and the next day he went in to fetch the ivory, and about night his horse came into camp riderless, and was dead from the fly before the sun went down. The Englishman is in that bush now; anyway, he never came back. And now anybody who ventures into that bush is chased by the White Horse. I wouldn't go into that bush for all the ivory in the land. The English are not brave, but foolish; we beat them at Majuba.' Here he ran into a torrent of abuse of all Englishmen in general and in particular. And I took the opportunity of rolling myself up in my blankets for the night, sleeping all the better for my adventure. Now, Mr. Stead, I don't believe in ghosts, but I was firmly convinced during that run of mine, and can vouch for the accuracy of it, not having heard a word of the Englishman or his white horse before my headlong return to the camp that night. I shortly hope to be near that bush again; but, like the old Boer, I can say, I wouldn't go into that bush again for all the ivory in the land.

"P.S.—A few days after we dropped across a troop of elephants without entering the fatal bush, and managed to bag seven, photographs of which I took, and shall be pleased to send for your inspection if desired."

The Ghosts of Animals. The ghosts of horses are not very numerous, but they exist. Mr. Kendall, in his Diary, has several instances of this kind. Two Cumberland farmers, who had broken their necks in riding home drunk from market, are occasionally seen riding along the high road, and suddenly disappearing on the spot where they met their deaths. There is also a very good story of a spectral pony that was seen on New Year's morning. But the best story of all about a spectral horse is that found in the "Proceedings of the Psychical Research Society."

A weird story from the Indian Hills. It is told by General Barter, C.B., of Careystown, Whitegate, Co. Cork. At the time he witnessed the spectral cavalcade he was living in the hills in India, and when one evening he was returning home he caught sight of a rider and attendants coming towards him. The rest of the story is in his own words :—

"At this time the two dogs came, and, crouching at my side, gave low, frightened whimpers. The moon was at the full·—a tropical moon—so bright that you could see to read a newspaper by its light, and I saw the party before me advance as plainly as if it were noonday. They were above me some eight or ten feet on the bridle road, the earth thrown down from which sloped to within a pace or two of my feet. On the party came, until almost in front of me, and now I had better describe them. The rider was in full dinner dress, with white waistcoat, and wearing a tall chimney-pot hat, and he sat a powerful hill pony (dark brown, with mane and tail) in a listless sort of way, the reins hanging loosely from both hands. A syce led the pony on each side, but their faces I could not see, the one next to me having his back to me and the one farthest off being hidden by the pony's head. Each held the bridle close by the bit, the man next me with his right and the other with his left hand, and the other hands were on the thighs of the rider, as if to steady him in his seat. As they approached, I, knowing they could not get to any place other than my own, called out in Hindustani, ' Quon hai ?' (who is it?) There was no answer, and on they came until right in front of me, when I said, in English, ' Hollo, what the d—l do you want here ? ' Instantly the group came to a halt, the rider gathering the bridle reins up in both hands, turned his face, which had hitherto been looking away from me, towards me, and looked down upon me. The group was still as in a tableau, with the bright moon shining upon it, and I at once recognised the rider as Lieutenant B., whom I had formerly known. The face, however, was different from what it used to be ; in the place of being clean shaven, as when I used to know it, it was now surrounded by a fringe (what used to be known as a Newgate fringe), and it was the face of a dead man, the ghastly waxen pallor of it brought out more distinctly in the moonlight by the dark fringe of hair by which it was encircled ; the body, too, was much stouter than when I had known it in life.

" I marked this in a moment, and then resolved to lay hold of the thing, whatever it might be. I dashed up the bank, and the earth which had been thrown on the side giving under my feet, I fell forward up the bank on my hands. Recovering myself instantly, I gained the road, and stood in the exact spot where the group had been, but which was now vacant : there was not a trace of anything. It was impossible for them to go on, the road stopped at a precipice about twenty yards further on, and it was impossible to turn and go back in a second. All this flashed through my mind, and I then ran along the road for about 100 yards, along which they had come, until I had to stop for want of breath, but there was no trace of anything, and not a sound to be heard. I then returned home, where I found my dogs, who on all other occasions my most faithful companions, had not come with me along the road.

" Next morning I went up to D. who belonged to the same regiment as B., and gradually induced him to talk of him. I said, 'How very stout he had become lately, and what possessed him to allow his beard to grow into that horrid fringe?' D. replied, 'Yes, he became very bloated before his death. You know he led a very fast life, and while on the sick list he allowed the fringe to grow in spite of all that we could say to him, and I believe he was buried with it.' I asked him where he got the pony I had seen, describing it minutely. 'Why,' said D., 'how do you know anything about all this? You hadn't seen B. for two or three years, and the pony you never saw. He bought him at Peshawur, and killed him one day riding in his reckless fashion down the hill to Trete.'

" I then told him what I had seen the night before.

" Once, when the galloping sound was very distinct, I rushed to the door of my house. There I found my Hindoo bearer, standing with a tattie in his hand. I asked him what he was there for. He said that there came a sound of riding down the hill, and 'passed him like a typhoon,' and went round the corner of the house, and he was determined to waylay it, whatever it was." (Vol. V. p. 471.)

That such a story as this can be gravely told by a British General in the present day helps us to understand how our ancestors came to believe in the wonderful story of Herne the Hunter.

A suicide's Ghost by the Wayside.

My concluding story is at least fifty years old. It is sent me by the son of a Cornish poet, who certainly does not allow his tale to suffer in the telling :—

" In a certain town in the West of England dwelt Mr. V——, whom I will call William Foster, a young man of ability, acknowledged to be one of the best local preachers in his native country.

" One day he received an invitation to preach in a village chapel, being warmly urged to undertake its anniversary services. Readily he acceded to the request, and promised to be present on the date specified, on condition that a horse should be placed at his disposal in the evening to convey him

a part of the way home.   The loan of a horse being arranged
for, Foster prepared to fulfil his promise.

"About a week before the Sunday arrived on which he was
to go to P—— he had a remarkable dream.   In his dream
he saw himself riding along a moonlit road on a bay horse.
Suddenly, without any warning, his horse stopped, and he
barely saved himself from falling over the animal's neck.
Struggling, he awoke, and found himself in a profuse perspiration.   In his imaginary fall over the horse's head, he
had acted so vigorously that his good wife was awakened
from a sound sleep, and wonderingly asked whether he had
lost his reason.   The dream was repeated.   This time he
clung to the horse's mane, and awoke, as before, in a state
of mental disquietude.   Again sleeping, he was for the third
time visited by the same dream.   This time he fell from the
horse over his neck on the road.   So vividly was the whole
circumstance brought thus before his mind, and so exactly
did the details correspond, that it was some time before he
could be convinced he had really been dreaming.   He
thought it very singular.   On narrating the dream to his wife,
she persuaded him not to go on horseback anywhere again on
any account: he would certainly be killed; the dream was a
warning.   But little did Foster heed his better-half's specula-
tions, and by the time the appointed Sabbath came round he
had forgotten his dream altogether.   He went and preached,
and set off home.

"Nothing remarkable occurred for the first half-hour.   The
moon was shining brightly.   By-and-by the route went
straight through a cutting where the hedges were a little
higher than ordinary.   On arriving at this point he noticed
that the horse changed his easy trot into a walking pace, and
seemed somewhat uneasy.   However, the cutting was passed,
and again they were on the moonlit road, which he could see
stretching away in front over the undulating hills.   Cantering
along they had not proceeded far before the animal dropped
into a walk again.   Encouragement and caresses were vain,
walk he would.   Suddenly the horse came to a dead halt in
the middle of the road.   The suddenness of stopping nearly
unseated the rider, but he urged the animal forward.   The
horse was induced to walk on again, although apparently very
uneasy.

"They had not gone many yards before the horse stopped
again so suddenly that he had to clutch the animal's mane to
prevent being thrown headlong upon the highway.   What was

the meaning of such strange behaviour? Then there flashed
through his mind the circumstances of his dream. Yes, there
were all the accompaniments of his picture—the bay horse,
the moonlit road, the sudden stoppages. `Surely it was a
warning. Twice had the creature halted, and he recollected
his dream made him the third time fall head foremost on the
road. He got off, and, throwing the bridle over his arm,
coaxed the horse to move onward. He noticed that the
animal was covered with perspiration, as if after a hard gallop,
and that he was trembling violently. Repeatedly, too, he
glanced searchingly at the hedges. What could be the
matter?

"The strange conduct of the horse became yet stranger.
More suddenly than before the animal came to a dead halt.
The animal was in deep distress. His nostrils were distended; sweat covered his limbs; his eyes were bent in one
direction, with every symptom of terror. Not seeing anything remarkable at first in the direction in which the
horse was gazing, Foster tried to urge him onward: in vain!
Passing round to the other side of the animal's head, Foster
was induced to look more closely towards that portion of the
somewhat low hedge which the horse so intently regarded.

"There in the moonlight, hanging, bending limp and apparently lifeless over the hedge, was the body of a tall man.
With arms outstretched, the figure seemed touching the ground
with its fingers, the legs being on the other side of the hedge.
What was his horror to see the body move! Slowly, mechanically, the long arms were outstretched, uplifted; the body
swayed, up, up; and there in the bright moonlight was the
man's face. How ghastly it looked! The glassy eyes were
staring at the young man, whose blood seemed chilling in his
veins. Motionless, upright as an elm, with outstretched arms,
stood the gaunt spectre. Its throat was cut.

"There stood the group. The horse terrified; the young
man speechless, terror-stricken, and the hideous something
seemingly regarding them with his stony gaze, while blood
appeared to flow from its lacerated throat. How long he
remained Foster could not afterwards tell; but after an
interval that seemed an age, the horrible vision began, as
slowly and mechanically as before, to bend its erect body
forward, until it resumed its former position, hanging over the
hedge.

"With a mighty effort the young man induced the horse to
move on once more; but, on looking back, he was startled

again to see the erect figure of the nocturnal spectre—uplifted arms, ghastly features, and blood-red throat. Just as slowly as before, the tall body bent forward ; the arms dropped down, down, until some intervening bushes shut out the horrible apparition from view.

"The horse seeming more composed, Foster mounted and urged him on rapidly. In due time R—— was reached, and here he found a lad awaiting him to take the horse back to his owner. No such vision was seen by the boy, nor was anything noteworthy remarked in the conduct of the horse during the return journey.

"Foster reached home near midnight. Afterwards, he learnt that a man had been murdered on the very spot where he had seen the tall figure."

Pursued by a Ghost's Spectre.

The Rev. H. Elwyn Thomas, 35, Park Village East, N.W., has kindly written out for me a very remarkable experience of his own which no one would care to have repeated. He says :—

"Twelve years ago I was the second minister on the Bryn-mawr Welsh Wesleyan Circuit, in the South Wales District. The circuit consisted of eight churches. The smallest were those of Llanelly, Crickhowell, and Llangynidr. It was my duty to preach in each of these once a month. I commenced at Llanelly, where the service was held at ten o'clock. I then proceeded to Crickhowell for an afternoon service, and finished off at Llangynidr at six in the evening. The distance between these places was about five miles, which I mostly did on foot.

"It was a beautiful evening in June when, after conducting the service at Llangynidr, I told the gentleman with whom I generally stayed when preaching there, that three young friends had come to meet me from Crickhowell in the afternoon, and that I meant to accompany them back for about half a mile on their return journey, so would not be home before nine o'clock. He lived about half a mile on the other side of the village.

"When I wished good-night to my friends, it was about twenty minutes to nine, but still light enough to see a good distance. The subject of our conversation all the way from the chapel until we parted was a certain eccentric old character who then belonged to the Crickhowell church. Many laughable incidents in his life had been related by my friends for my amusement, at which I laughed heartily again and again. I walked a little further down the road than I intended, in

order to hear the end of a very amusing story about him and
the vicar of a neighbouring parish. Our conversation had no
reference whatever to ghosts or ghostly things. Neither were
we in a mood befitting a ghostly visitation. Personally, I was
a strong disbeliever in ghosts, and invariably ridiculed those
who I then thought superstitious enough to believe in
them.

" When I had walked about a hundred yards away from my
friends I saw on the bank of the canal (which runs parallel
with the road for six or seven miles) what I thought at the
moment was an old beggar. The spot was a very lonely one.
The nearest house was a good quarter of a mile away. The
night was as silent as death. Not a single sound broke upon
the silence from any quarter. I couldn't help asking myself
where this old man had come from to such a place. I had
not seen him in going down the road.

" I then turned round quite unconcernedly to have another
look at him, and had no sooner done so than I saw within
half a yard of me one of the most remarkable and startling
sights I hope it will ever be my lot to see. Almost on a level
with my own face I saw that of an old man, over every
feature of which the putty-coloured skin was drawn tightly,
except the forehead, which was lined with deep wrinkles. The
lips were extremely thin, and appeared perfectly bloodless.
The toothless mouth stood half open. The cheeks were hollow and sunken like those of a corpse, and the eyes, which
seemed far back in the middle of the head, were unnaturally
luminous and piercing. This terrible object was wrapped in
two bands of old yellow calico, one of which was drawn under
the chin and over the cheeks and tied at the top of the head,
the other was drawn round the top of the wrinkled forehead,
and fastened at the back of the head. So deep and indelible
an impression it made on my mind, that were I an artist I
could paint that face to-day, and reproduce the original (excepting, perhaps, the luminous eyes) as accurately as if it were
photographed.

" What I have thus tried to describe in many words I saw at
a glance. Acting on the impulse of the moment I turned my
face again towards the village, and ran away from the horrible
vision with all my might for about sixty yards. I then stopped,
and turned round to see how far I had distanced it, and, to
my unspeakable horror, there it was still face to face with me,
as if I had not moved an inch. I grasped my umbrella and
raised it to strike him, and you can imagine my feelings when

I could see nothing between the face and the ground, except an irregular column of intense darkness, through which my umbrella went as a stick goes through water !

" I am sorry to confess that I again took to my heels with increasing speed. A little further than the place of this second encounter, the road which led towards my host's house branched off the main road, the main road itself running right through the centre of the village, in the lower end of which it ran parallel with the churchyard wall. Having gone a few yards down this branch road, I reached a crisis in my fear and confusion when I felt I could act rationally : I determined to speak with my strange pursuer whatever he was, and I boldly turned round to face him for the third time, intending to ask him what he wanted, etc.

" He had not followed me after I left the main road, but I could see the horribly fascinating face quite as plain as when it was close by. It stood for two or three minutes looking intently at me from the centre of the main road. I then realized fully it was not a human being in flesh and blood ; and with every vestige of fear gone I quickly walked towards it to put my questions. But I was disappointed, for no sooner I made towards it than it moved quickly in the direction of the village. I saw it moving along, keeping the same distance from the ground until it reached the churchyard wall ; it then crossed the wall, and disappeared near where the yew-tree stood inside. The moment it disappeared I became unconscious. When I came to myself two hours later, I was lying in the middle of the road cold and ill. It took me quite an hour to reach my host's house, which was less than half a mile away, and when I reached it I looked so white and strange that my host's daughter, who had sat down with her father to await my return, uttered a loud scream. I could not say a word to explain what had happened, though I tried hard several times. It was five o'clock in the morning when I regained my power of speech ; even then I could only speak in broken sentences. The whole of the following week I was laid up with great nervous prostration.

" The strangest part of my story yet remains to be told. My host, after questioning me closely in regard to the features of the face, the place I had first seen it, and the spot where it disappeared, told me that fifteen years before that time an old recluse, answering in every detail to my description (calicoes, bands, and all), lived in a house whose ruins still stand close by where I first saw it, that he was buried in the exact spot in the churchyard where I saw the face disappearing, and that he was a very strange character altogether.

"I should like to add that I had not heard a syllable about this old man before the night in question, and that all the persons referred to in the above story are still alive."

A Ghostly attack on a Ghostly Laager. The following narrative, which appeared in the *Orange Free State Magazine* of ten or eleven years since, is sent me by a correspondent in South Africa :—

"Some years ago a gentleman was travelling through a part of the then newly-founded Orange Free State in South Africa. Farmhouses and places of accommodation were at that time far apart, and one had often to travel for miles before reaching any of them. Railways were unknown—almost unheard of in the country—and the only means of conveyance the two-wheeled Cape cart, or the lumbering ox-wagon, drawn by its team of from fourteen to sixteen huge animals, yoked to it by heavy wooden yokes. It possessed one advantage, however, and that was where you had to travel for miles and miles through an almost wild country, infested with wild animals, sparsely populated, and often through the midst of savages. You found yourself provided with a moving *home*, like a ship at sea ; you could carry all you required with you, and even be ready on the defensive in case of an attack by the enemy. Our traveller, however, had chosen a two-wheeled cart, drawn by a couple of horses. He found one day to his dismay that, after crossing a river and ascending the steep bank on the opposite side, his horses had become too jaded to proceed further in order to reach the nearest farmhouse before night set in, as it was still some miles away. He had therefore to make up his mind for a night's binnar on the river's bank until morning. The horses were soon unharnessed, and after slaking their thirst in the river, and having a roll to stretch their stiff and wearied limbs, they were tethered to the vehicle. His native servants, with their usual aptitude in these things, soon had made every preparation for the evening meal, and the fragrant coffee was steaming most invitingly in the kettle by the hastily improvised kitchen-fire. The traveller, being tired with the long day's journey, soon sought repose under the shelter of his vehicle, in order to protect himself from the heavy night-dews so common in this country. It was a brilliant night ; but, unfortunately, our traveller courted sleep in vain. Whether it was the unusual sensation of sleeping in the open, but he felt restless and uncomfortable, probably the effects of too strong a cup of coffee. At last he determined to get up and walk about, to try what a little exercise would do. What was his surprise to find that not far from his bivouac there was a fierce battle going on, and that a large Boer laager[1] was being furiously attacked by hordes of savage Kaffirs, who seemed to swarm like ants, and were as fiercely repulsed from within the laager. The flash of the rifles were distinctly seen, but not a sound could be heard. While he was standing transfixed at the strange sight, a more than usually fierce onslaught was made by the Kaffirs, who desperately tried to clamber over the piled-up branches between the wagons —yea, and even over the wagons themselves—when they were met by a volley of no uncertain aim, which laid several in the dust, whilst the rest fled with the greatest precipitation. As the traveller was watching the black mass in full retreat, the laager, or camp, seemed to open on one side, and out came a number of armed and mounted men in full pursuit of the enemy. They passed so close to where the traveller was standing that he could distinguish the horses, and in his excited state gave them a cheer, although no sound of horses' hoofs reached his ear. He soon retired to rest again, and after a couple of hours of troubled sleep he found that it was broad daylight, and soon prepared for a start; but where was the large camp of the previous evening, and where were the warriors bold and their gallant steeds? All, all had disappeared as a *vision of the night*. He soon pursued his journey, and reached the farmhouse whither he had been bound the previous evening. The homestead was reached after a couple of hours' drive, and so impressed was he with what he had experienced that he told his host the whole affair before allowing himself even to partake of any refreshment. To his surprise, ' mine host ' seemed in no way surprised or discomfited, but told him that *his* was no isolated case, as the phantom laager, and the fierce attack on it, and pursuit by the defenders, had been witnessed by former travellers in that same place, and that the general belief was— in fact it was a certainty—that in the days of the first pioneers into the country a large camp had stood on that very spot, that it had often been attacked, and had been the scene of many a bloody onslaught, and that ever since, at certain times of the year, the camp was seen, and the bloody campaign fought over again by the phantom bands who took part in it in the

---

[1] A roughly fortified camp formed of heavy ox wagons drawn into a square, the interstices filled up with the boughs of trees. The women and children inside, also the cattle at night.

early years. Perhaps the shrill whistle of the railway which now runs through those parts may have scattered them, and succeeded in laying their ghosts. We hope so."

"Dead or Alive." Mr. R. D'Onston sends me the following communication :—

"To those instances in 'Real Ghost Stories' of ghosts who have kept promises made in life to appear to those dear to them, may I add my own experience? The incident occurred to me some years ago, and all the details can be substantiated. The date was August 26th, 1867, at midnight. I was then residing in the neighbourhood of Hull, and held an appointment under the Crown which necessitated my repairing thither every day for a few hours' duty. My berth was almost a sinecure ; and I had been for some time engaged to a young North-country heiress, it being understood that on our marriage I should take her name and 'stand for the county,' or rather for one of its divisions.

"For her sake I had to break off a love affair, not of the most reputable order, with a girl in Hull. I will call her Louise. She was young, beautiful, and devoted to me. On the night of the 26th of August we took our last walk together, and a few minutes before midnight paused on a wooden bridge running across a kind of canal, locally termed a 'drain.' We paused on the bridge, listening to the swirling of the current against the wooden piles, and waiting for the stroke of midnight to part for ever. In the few minutes' interval she repeated, *sotto voce*, Longfellow's 'Bridge,' the words of which 'I stood on the bridge at midnight,' seemed terribly appropriate. After nearly twenty-five years I can never hear that piece recited without feeling a deathly chill and the whole scene of two souls in agony again arising before me. Well! midnight struck, and we parted ; but Louise said : 'Grant me one favour, the only one that I shall ever ask you on this earth: promise to meet me here twelve months to-night at this same hour." I demurred at first, thinking it would be bad for both of us, and only re-open partially-healed wounds. At last, however, I consented, saying: 'Well, I will come if I am alive !' but she said, 'Say alive or dead !' I said, 'Very well then, we will meet, dead or alive.'

"The next year I was on the spot a few minutes before the time ; and, punctual to the stroke of midnight, Louise arrived. By this time, I had begun to regret the arrangement I had made ; but it was of too solemn a nature to be put aside. I therefore kept the appointment, but said that I did not care to renew the compact. Louise, however, persuaded me to renew it for one more year, and I consented, much against my will ; and we again left each other, repeating the same formula, ' Dead or alive.'

" The next year after that passed rapidly for me until the first week in July, when I was shot dangerously in the thigh by a fisherman named Thomas Piles, of Hull, a reputed smuggler. A party of four of us had hired his 10 ton yawl to go yachting round the Yorkshire coast, and amuse ourselves by shooting sea-birds amongst the millions of them at Flamborough Head. The third or fourth day out I was shot in the right thigh by the skipper Piles ; and the day after, one and a quarter ounce of No. 2 shot were cut out therefrom by the coastguard surgeon at Bridlington Quay (whose name I forget for the moment), assisted by Dr. Alexander Mackay, at the Black Lion Hotel. The affair was in all the papers at the time, about a column of it appearing in the *Eastern Morning News*, of Hull.

" As soon as I was able to be removed (two or three weeks) I was taken home, where Dr. Kelburne King, of Hull, attended me. The day—and *the* night—(the 26th August) came. I was then unable to walk without crutches, and that for only a short distance, so had to be wheeled about in a Bath chair. The distance to the trysting place being rather long, and the time and circumstances being very peculiar, I did not avail myself of the services of my usual attendant, but specially retained an old servant of the family, who frequently did confidential commissions for me, and who knew Miss Louise well. We set forth ' without beat of drum,' and arrived at the bridge about a few minutes to midnight. I remember that it was a brilliant starlight night, but I do not think that there was any moon, at all events, at that hour. ' Old Bob,' as he was always affectionately called, wheeled me to the bridge, helped me out of the Bath chair, and gave me my crutch. I walked on to the bridge, and leaned my back against the white painted top rail, then lighted my briar-root, and had a comfortable smoke.

" I was very much annoyed that I had allowed myself to be persuaded to come a second time, and determined to tell ' Louise ' positively that this should be the last meeting. Besides, *now*, I did not consider it fair to Miss K., with whom I was again negotiating, *en rapport* to a certain extent. So, if anything, it was in rather a sulky frame of mind that I awaited Louise. Just as the quarters before the hour began to chime I distinctly heard the ' clink, clink,' of the little brass heels, which she always wore, sounding on the long flagged causeway, leading for 200 yards up to the bridge. As she got nearer I could see her pass lamp after lamp in rapid succession, while the strokes of the large clock at Hull resounded through the stilly night.

"At last the patter, patter of the tiny feet sounded on the woodwork of the bridge, and I saw her distinctly pass under the lamp at the farther end—it was only twenty yards wide, and I stood under the lamp at my side. When she got close to me I saw that she had neither hat nor cape on, and concluded that she had taken a cab to the farther end of the flagged causeway, and (it being a very warm night) had left her wraps in the cab, and for purposes of effect had come the short distance in evening dress.

" ' Clink, clink,' went the brass heels, and she seemed about passing me, when I, suddenly urged by an impulse of affection, stretched out my arms to receive her. She passed *through* them, intangible, impalpable, and as she looked at me I distinctly saw her lips move, and form the words, ' Dead or alive.' I even *heard* the words, but not with my outward ears, with something else, some other sense—what, I know not. I felt startled, surprised, but not afraid, until a moment afterwards, when I *felt*, but could not see, some other presence following her. I could *feel*, though I could not hear, the heavy, clumsy ' thud ' of the feet following her; and my blood seemed turned to ice. Recovering myself with an effort, I shouted out to ' Old Bob,' who was safely ensconced with the Bath chair in a nook out of sight round the corner. ' Bob, who passed you just now?' In an instant the old Yorkshireman was by my side. ' Ne'er a one passed me, sir !' ' Nonsense, Bob,' I replied, ' I told you that I was coming to meet Miss Louise, and she just passed me on the bridge, and *must* have passed you, because there's nowhere else she *could* go ! You don't mean to tell me you didn't see her?' The old man replied, solemnly, ' Maister Ros, there's something uncanny aboot it. I heerd her come on the bridge, and off it, I'd knaw them clicketty heels onywhere; but I'm dommed, sir, if she passed me. I'm thinking we'd better gang.' And ' gang ' we did; and it was the small hours of the morning (getting daylight) before we left off talking over the affair, and went to bed.

"The next day I made inquiries from Louise's family about her, and ascertained that she had died in Liverpool three months previously, being apparently delirious for a few hours

before her death, and our parting compact evidently weighing
on her mind, as she kept repeating 'Dead or Alive! Shall I
be there?' to the utter bewilderment of her friends, who could
not divine her meaning, being of course entirely unaware of
our agreement."

A Curious
Sign of
Shipwreck.
The Rev. T. E. Lord, Vicar of Escomb, in reply
to an enquiry from me, wrote as follows :—
"My sailor boy, on his return home from
Australia, brought with him a painting of the ship *Shannon*,
which afterwards hung in his grandmother's bedroom.   My
son left London for Calcutta on the 17th January, 1885.   On
the 2nd of May, Mrs. Bowness, my mother-in-law, who kept
house for me since the death of my wife in 1872, was sitting in
her room with one of my daughters, aged seventeen, when
suddenly the picture became enveloped in a bright cloud, and
for a moment the vessel was lost to sight.   My daughter,
alarmed, rushed out of the room and called for me.   Unfortunately, I was out at the time.   When I returned and went
into the room nothing unusual was to be seen.

"My mother-in-law, who died about three years ago, at the
ripe age of eighty-eight, was a remarkably calm woman.   After
telling me what had happened, she said, 'If Jack's ship is lost,
it is lost to-day,' and she made one of my daughters write on a
slip of paper, 'Light on ship, May 2nd, 1885, Saturday evening, between six and seven p.m.   Seen by Grannie and Kattie.'
This she placed in her Prayer-Book, and there it has been
ever since.

"Knowing that the *Shannon* was not expected to arrive at
Calcutta for two or three weeks at the soonest, I laughed at
their fears.   The ship, however, was never heard of afterwards.
The vessel had a large amount of gunpowder on board, and I
sometimes think the powder became ignited and destroyed
the vessel.

"I enclose Board of Trade report, which, after you have
read, please return."

The Board of Trade Report is numbered 2,822, and is
signed by H. C. Rothery (Wreck Commissioner), on February
12th, 1886.   His report is to the effect that the *Shannon* left
this country in January, 1885, in good and seaworthy condition, but that she was not sufficiently manned.

From the Annex to the Report it appears that the *Shannon*
left the East India Docks on January 17th, 1885, with a crew
of twenty-eight hands all told, and a cargo of about 2,200 to
2,250 tons of general merchandise, including 5 tons of gun-

powder. She was spoken when forty-two days from London by a vessel called the *Senator*, a little to the north of the line. The ships remained in company for five or six days, but then they parted, and since that time the *Shannon* has never been seen or heard of. The Commissioner reports that it is quite impossible to say what may have caused the loss of the vessel.

CHAPTER XI

EVIL SPIRITS AND PHANTASMS WHICH TOUCH

" . . . We cannot doubt that evil spirits in some way are always about us ; and I had comfort in the feeling that whatever was the need, ordinary or extraordinary, I should have protection against it.

" . . . How can people say what is or is not natural to evil spirits? What is a grotesque manifestation to us may not be so to them. What do we know about an evil spirit? "—*Life of Cardinal Newman* (Mozley, 334).

THIS is a difficult and disagreeable subject, but none of our English ghosts which touch can be compared for a moment with the ghastly horror of the vampire, whose existence is still in Eastern Europe an article of popular faith. Upon that grisly subject there is no need to speak here.

The most remarkable of all the stories which I have heard concerning ghosts which touch is one that reaches me from Darlington. I owe this, as I owe so many of the other narratives in this collection, to the Rev. Henry Kendall, of Darlington, whose painstaking perseverance in the collection of all matters of this kind cannot be too highly praised. Mr. Kendall is a Congregational minister of old standing. He was my pastor when I was editing the *Northern Echo*, and he is the author of a remarkable book, entitled, " All the World's Akin." The following narrative is quite unique in its way, and fortunately he was able to get it at first hand from the only living person present on the occasion. Here we have a ghost which not only strikes the first blow, hitting a man fair in the eye, but afterwards sets a ghostly dog upon his victim and then disappears. The narrative, which was signed by Mr. James Durham as lately as December 5th, 1890, is as follows :—

" I was night watchman at the old Darlington and Stockton Station at the town of Darlington, a few yards from the first station that ever existed. I was there for fifteen years. I used to go on duty about 8 p.m. and come off at 6 a.m. I had been there a little while—perhaps two or three years— and about forty years ago. One night during winter and about twelve o'clock or 12.30, I was feeling rather cold with standing here and there; I said to myself, 'I will away down and get something to eat.' There was a porters' cellar where a fire was kept on and a coal-house was connected with it. So I went down the steps, took off my overcoat, and had just sat down on the bench opposite the fire, and turned up the gas, when a strange man came out of the coal-house, followed by a big black retriever. As soon as he entered my eye was upon him and his eye upon me, and we were intently watching each other as he moved on to the front of the fire. There he stood looking at me, and a curious smile came over his countenance. He had a stand-up collar and a cut-away coat with gilt buttons and a Scotch cap. All at once he struck at me, and I had the impression that he hit me. I up with my fist and struck back at him. My fist seemed to go through him and struck against the stone above the fire-place, and knocked the skin off my knuckles. The man seemed to be struck back into the fire, and uttered a strange unearthly squeak. Immediately the dog gripped me by the calf of my leg, and seemed to cause me pain. The man recovered his position, called off the dog with a sort of click of the tongue, then went back into the coal-house, followed by the dog. I lighted my dark lantern, and looked into the coal-house, but there was neither dog nor man, and no outlet for them except the one by which they had entered.

"I was satisfied that what I had seen was ghostly, and it accounted for the fact that when the man had first come into the place where he was sat I had not challenged him with any inquiry. Next day, and for several weeks, my account caused quite a commotion, and a host of people spoke to me about it; among the rest old Edward Pease, father of railways, and his three sons, John, Joseph, and Henry. Old Edward sent for me to his house and asked me all particulars. He and others put this question to me, 'Are you sure you were not asleep and had the nightmare?' My answer was quite sure, for I had not been a minute in the cellar and was just going to get something to eat. I was certainly not under the influence of strong drink, for I was then, as I have been now for forty-nine years, a teetotaler. My mind at the time was perfectly free from trouble.

" What increased the excitement was the fact that a man a number of years before, who was employed in the office of the station, had committed suicide, and his body had been carried into this very cellar. I knew nothing of this circumstance, nor of the body of the man, but Mr. Pease and others who

had known him, told me my description exactly corresponded
to his appearance and the way he dressed, and also that he
had a black retriever just like the one which gripped me. I
should add that no mark or effect remained on the spot where
I seemed to be seized.

(Signed)   "JAMES DURHAM."

"December 9th, 1890."

Commenting upon this case Mr. Kendall says :

" Mr. Durham has attended my church for a quarter of a
century, and I have testimony going back that length of time
to the effect that he has given the same account of the extraordinary experience. It is a long time since he retired from
the post of night watchman, and he has since become a
wealthy man. He is one of the strongest men I have met
with, able to do his forty miles a day, walking and running
with the hounds, and not feel stiff the day after. He takes
great pleasure in country life, and is a close observer of the
objects which belong to it, walking and fishing forming his
principal occupations. I forwarded his strange narrative to
Prof. Sidgwick, the president of the S.P.R., who expressed a
wish for fuller assurance that Mr. Durham was not asleep at
the time of the vision. I gave in reply the following four
reasons for believing that he was awake :—First, he was
accustomed as watchman to be up all night, and, therefore,
not likely from that cause to feel sleepy. Secondly, he had
scarcely been a minute in the cellar, and, feeling hungry, was
just going to get something to eat. Thirdly, if he was asleep
at the beginning of the vision, he must have been awake
enough during the latter part of it when he had knocked the
skin off his knuckles. Fourthly, there is his own confident
testimony. I strongly incline to the opinion that there was an
objective cause for the vision, and that it was genuinely ap-
paritional. At the same time I see that it was shaped and
coloured to some extent by the percipient's own temperament,
as apparitions often are. Mr. Durham, with the habit of a
watchman, when he sees anything in the least degree suspicious, is immediately on the alert, doubtful and inquiring till
he obtains satisfaction ; and it is significant that when the
apparition entered the cellar they immediately eyed each
other and continued doing so all the time, while the apparition moved on to the front of the fire.

" Again, Mr. D. is a believer in physical force, prompt,
decisive, not disposed to brook any delay, but wishing a man
to come to the point with him there and then ; and it corres-

ponds with the quality in him that the man all at once
struck out at him, and that he struck back again, and that
the dog gripped him, and was then called off and immediately retired with his master. It is the only instance which
I remember in which an apparition attempted to injure,
and even in this solitary instance there was no real harm
done."

Writing on October 22nd, this year, Mr. Kendall says :—

"To-day I have visited the scene of the battle with the
ghost, under the guidance of an old official who was at the
North Road Station during all the period in question. The
porters' room down the steps is still there, and the coal house
and even the gas bracket. A person could get out of the
coal house if he tried. My guide remembers the clerk who
committed suicide, and he showed me the place where he
shot himself with a pistol. His name was Winter. He left
a wife, but no children. He was no doubt in trouble, from
which he fled by suicide. He dressed and had a dog as
described. The explanation accepted by the stationmaster
and men at the time was that Mr. D. had had a five-minutes'
nap. This was, of course, a gratuitous supposition on their
part, as they were not there, and Mr. D., who was, declares he
was wide awake. Even if he had dozed, there would still
remain the remarkable correspondence between what was seen
and the habits of the suicide when living, and which were
unknown to the percipient."

Three days later Mr. Kendall wrote me again, sending
a plan of the scene of this strange nocturnal combat. The
fireplace is now bricked up, and this is the only change. He
writes :—

"After looking at both sides, I must say the accuracy of
Mr. D.'s account seems to remain unimpeached, though, of
course, it is not evidential after the high standard of the
Psychical Society. A strong, sober man is likely to know
whether he was asleep or not at such a crisis.

"One objection has been made to this effect : Mr. D. had a
cabin at the level crossing, and there was his post. What was
he doing down in the porter's room at the station? But it
was long since he left the crossing. For fifteen years he was
watchman at the station and round about it, and during that
time the porters' room was his proper place if he wanted to sit
down by a fire and take some refreshment.

"The room is not used by the porters now. The station is
homely and old-fashioned, but interesting as successor of the

first that ever was, which was a few yards away across the Durham Road. The No. 1 engine, run on the day of opening, with George Stephenson as driver, stands in front, exposed to wind and weather."

A Russian Ghost.   Mr. W. D. Addison, who dates from Riga, sends me the following curious personal experience of a struggle with a ghost, which may be read as a pendant to the fight with the ghost at Darlington :—

"It was in February, 1884, that the incidents which I am about to relate occurred to me, and the story is well known to my immediate friends.

"Five weeks previously my wife had presented me with our first baby, and our house being a small one, I had to sleep on a bed made up in the drawing-room, a spacious but cosy apartment, and the last place one would expect ghosts to select for their wanderings.

"On the night in question I retired to my couch soon after ten, and fell asleep almost the moment I was between the sheets.

"Instead of, as I am thankful to say is my habit, sleeping straight through till morning, I woke up after a short, dreamless sleep with the dim consciousness upon me that some one had called me by name. I was just turning the idea over in my mind when all doubts were solved by my hearing my name pronounced in a faint whisper, 'Willy!' Now the nurse who was in attendance on the baby, and who slept in the dressing-room adjoining our bedroom, had been ill for the past few days, and on the previous evening my wife had come and asked me to assist her with the baby. As soon, therefore, as I heard this whisper, I turned round, thinking, 'Ah! it is the baby again.'

"The room had three windows in it ; the night was moonless but starlit ; there was snow on the ground, and, therefore, 'snowlight,' and the blinds being up the room was by no means dark.

"The first thing I noticed on turning round was the figure of a woman close to the foot of my bed, and which, following the bent of my thoughts, I supposed was my wife. 'What is up?' I asked, but the figure remained silent and motionless, and my eyes being more accustomed to the dimness, I noticed that it had a grey-looking shawl over its head and shoulders, and that it was too short of stature to be my wife. I gazed at it silently, wondering who it could be ; apparitions and ghosts were far from my thoughts, and the mistiness of the outlines of this silent figure did not strike me at the moment as it did afterwards.

"I again addressed it, this time in the language of the country, 'What do you want?' Again no answer. And now it occurred to me that our servant girl sometimes walked in her sleep, and that this was she. Behind the head of my bed stood a small table, and I reached round for the match-box which was on it, never removing my eyes from the supposed somnambulist. The match-box was now in my hands, but just as I was taking out a lucifer, the figure, to my astonishment, seemed to rise up from the floor and move backwards towards the end window; at the same time it faded rapidly, and became blurred with the grey light streaming in at the window, and ere I could strike the match it was gone. I lighted the candle, jumped out of bed and ran to the door: it was fastened. To the left of the drawing-room there was a boudoir, separated only by a curtain: this room was empty too, and the door likewise fastened.

"I rubbed my eyes. I was puzzled. It struck me now for the first time that the figure from the beginning had been hazy-looking, also that my wife was the only person who called me 'Willy,' and certainly the only person who could give the name its English pronunciation. I first searched both drawing-room and boudoir, and then, opening the door, stepped into the passage, and went to my wife's door and listened. The baby was crying, and my wife was up, so I knocked and was admitted. Knowing her to be strong-minded and not nervous, I quietly related my experience. She expressed astonishment, and asked me if I was not afraid to return to my bed in the drawing-room. However, I was not, and after chatting for a few moments went back to my quarters, fastened the door, and getting into bed, thought the whole matter over again quietly. I could think of no explanation of the occurrence, and feeling sleepy, blew out the light and was soon sound asleep again.

"After a short but sound and dreamless slumber, I was again awake, this time with my face towards the middle window; and there, close up against it, was the figure again, and owing to its propinquity to the light, it appeared to be a very dark object.

"I at once reached out for the matches, but in doing so upset the table, and down it went with the candlestick, my watch, keys, etc., making a terrific crash. As before, I had kept my eyes fixed on the figure, and I now observed that, whatever it was, it was advancing straight towards me, and in another moment retreat to the door would be cut off. It was not a comfortable idea to cope with the unknown in the dark, and in an instant I had seized the bed-clothes, and grasping a corner of them in each hand and holding them up before me, I charged straight at the figure. (I suppose I thought that by smothering the head of my supposed assailant I could best repel the coming attack.)

"The next moment I had landed on my knees on a sofa by the window with my arms on the window-sill, and with the consciousness that 'it' was now behind me, I having passed through it. With a bound I faced round, and was immediately immersed in a darkness impalpable to the touch, but so dense that it seemed to be weighing me down and squeezing me from all sides. I could not stir; the bed-clothes which I had seized as described hung over my left arm, the other was free, but seemed pressed down by a benumbing weight. I essayed to cry for help, but realised for the first time in my life what it means for the tongue to cleave to the roof of the mouth; my tongue seemed to have become dry and to have swelled to a thickness of some inches; it stuck to the roof of my mouth, and I could not ejaculate a syllable. At last, after an appalling struggle, I succeeded in uttering, and I knew that disjointed words, half prayer, half execrations of fear, left my lips, then my mind seemed to make one frantic effort, there seemed to come a wrench like an electric shock, and my limbs were free; it was as if I tore myself out of something. In a few seconds I had reached and opened the door and was in the passage listening to the hammerings of my heart-beats. All fear was gone from me, but I felt as though I had run miles for my life and that another ten yards of it would have killed me.

"I again went to the door of my wife's room, and hearing that she was up with the baby, I knocked and she opened. She is a witness to the state I was in : the drops were pouring down my face, my hair was damp, and the beatings of my heart were audible some paces off.

"I can offer no explanations of what I saw, but as soon as my story became known, the people who had occupied the house previously told us that they had once put up a visitor in that same drawing-room, who had declared the room to be haunted and refused to stay in it.

"The previous summer, while staying at the seaside, we

had left a respectable, staid old woman as caretaker, and she now came forward with the story that one evening in June of that year (1883), as she was fastening up the windows of this drawing-room before going to bed, something which she could not describe passed through the room, and at the same moment an indescribable panic seized her, causing her to flee headlong from the room. So alarmed was she that she went outside the house, and dared not re-enter it, but as she could not leave it unprotected she sat on the door-step all night.

"I may state that the drawing-room is 35 ft. from the ground, and so there is no question of the appearances in question being the shadows of passers-by; moreover, the house is in private grounds, the gate of which is closed at night, and in possession of a watchman.

"I had better conclude by saying that I am not nervous, and often have occasion to sleep in a large empty house with not even a servant in it. I do not suffer from any affection of the heart, and am perfectly sound in every way. Friends who have listened to my tale have invariably favoured me with some kind explanation of their own, but not one of which met the case. Some said ' Nightmare ' ! My story distinctly disproves anything of the sort. I woke up quietly, thinking I had been called by name, and when the call was repeated I turned round, thinking my wife wanted me to help her with the baby. When, too, I saw the strange figure, I did not immediately think—' Hollo, here is a ghost ! ' but reasoned to myself that it must be the servant walking in her sleep; in fact, all through the first experience I was clear-headed and calm, and even when the figure vanished I still sought for some ordinary explanation of the occurrence.

"I know that people sometimes wake up suddenly in the night in an unaccountable state of fear, but which lasts only a few moments while they are collecting their thoughts which have been disturbed by some dream which, perhaps, they cannot even call to mind.

"Some friends who study neither almanack nor sky argued that it was the shadow of a cloud passing over the moon, but there was no moon in the sky that night.

"As for my food on the evening in question, I had dined at 6.30 on clear soup, roast mutton, and apple soufflé, washed down with half a bottle of Lager beer, and topped by a single glass of sherry.

"In the evening, before turning in, I had been reading *Charles O'Malley* over again for the second time.

"W. D. ADDISON."

A Soldier's Story. The phenomenon of being touched or grasped by a ghost is by no means unusual. Here, for instance, is a very curious story sent me by Major C. G. MacGregor, who writes from Donaghadee, County Down, Ireland. Major MacGregor is not a believer in ghosts, and, according to his own account, is without any physical fear or nervousness. He has furnished me with the names and addresses necessary to complete the story, which is as follows :—

"In the end of the year 1871 I went over from Scotland to make a short visit to a relative living in a square on the north side of Dublin.

"In January, 1872, the husband of my relative, then in his eighty-fourth year, took paralysis, and having no trained nurse, the footman and I sat up with him for sixteen nights during his recovery. On the seventeenth night at about 11.30 p.m., I said to the footman, 'The master seems so well, and sleeping soundly, I shall go to bed ; and if he awake worse, or you require me, call me.' I then retired to my room, which was over the one occupied by the invalid.

"I went to bed and was soon asleep, when some time afterwards I was awakened by a push on the left shoulder. I was at the time lying on my right side facing the door (which was on the right side of my bed, and the fireplace on the left). I started up and said, 'Edward, is there anything wrong?' I received no answer, but immediately received another push. I got annoyed, and said, 'Can you not speak, man, and tell me if anything is wrong?' Still no answer, and I had a feeling I was going to get another push, when I suddenly turned round and caught (what I then thought) a human hand, warm, soft, and plump. I said, 'Who are you?' but I got no answer. I then tried to pull the person towards me, to endeavour to find out who it was, but although I was nearly thirteen stone I could not move whoever it was, but felt I myself was likely to be drawn from the bed. I then said, 'I will know who you are,' and having the hand tight in my right hand, with my left I felt the wrist and arm, enclosed, as it seemed to me, in a tight sleeve of some winter material with a linen cuff; but when I got to the elbow all trace of an arm ceased. I was so astonished I let the hand go, and just then the house clock struck 2 a.m. I then thought no one could possibly get to the door without my catching them ; but, lo ! the door was fast shut as when I came to bed, and another thought struck me : when I pulled the hand I heard no one breathing, though I myself was puffed from the strength I used.

" Including the mistress of the house, there were five females, and I can assert the hand belonged to no one of them. When I related the adventure the servants exclaimed, ' Oh, it must be the master's old aunt Betty, who had lived for many years in the upper part of that house, occupying two rooms, and had died over fifty years before, at a great age.' I afterwards learned that the room in which I felt the hand had been considered haunted, and many curious noises and peculiar incidents occurred, such as the bed-clothes torn off. One lady got a slap in the face from some invisible hand, and when she lighted her candle she saw as if something opaque fell or jumped off the bed. A general officer, a brother of the lady, slept there two nights, but he preferred going to an hotel to remaining a third. He never would say what he heard or saw, but always said the room was uncanny. I slept for months in that room afterwards, and was never in the least disturbed. I never knew what nervousness was in my life, and only regretted my astonishment caused me to let go the hand before finding out the purpose of the visit. Whether it was meant for a warning or not, I may add the old gentleman lived three years and six months afterwards."

An Eerie Story from the Shetlands. Mr. Athol Murray sends me a curious tale from the very far North, which is unique in its way. I do not quote it as having any evidential value, but only as a sample of the narratives repeated in good faith by the superstitious inhabitants of these remote islands. Mr. Athol Murray's story is to this effect : that one day in 1830, a fisherman of the name of Grey found that when returning from fishing his boat stopped without any apparent cause. In vain he strained at the oars ; it would not move a foot. He looked over the prow, thinking he might have got entangled in seaweed, but the water was clear. He thought he might have struck on a hidden shoal, and rocked the boat. She rocked freely, showing there was water under her keel. Grey then looked over the stern, and to his horror he saw a man, whom he knew had been dead for six months, holding on to the stern post. This man was one with whom he had had some little quarrel, and Grey besought him to free the boat, saying that he had hoped that death would have cancelled all enmity between them. Without replying, the man still held on, and at last, in despair, Grey took his axe and hacked off the stern post, when the boat at once shot forward. The man, however, cried out that he and Grey should meet again in six weeks. Grey, in great fear, hastened home and told his family and friends of the occurrence. In six weeks, at the exact time the dead man had named, Grey was found in the morning dead in bed. A son of Robert Grey, who saw the mutilated boat come in, was, at any rate as late as 1875, keeping a sailors' boarding-house in Antwerp ; but there are many in the Shetland Isles who well remember the circumstances, and seeing the boat with the stern post cut off.

The Touch of a Vanished Hand. I have received many strange communications, but the following, which was sent me by Mr. J. McDowall, of 48, Clyde Street, Calton, Glasgow, is one of the strangest, both from the narrative itself and the voucher which accompanies it. The voucher, signed by Mr. McDowall, is as follows :—

"This short sketch I believe to be literally true on the ground of my grandmother's word. My mother was conversant with the matter from her youth, with hearing her mother tell the story. I am myself a spiritualist, and for many years I have enjoyed open communion with the spirit world by means of a clairvoyant whom I put to sleep, when the other world becomes as visible to him then as this world is to our ordinary senses. I only wish to say that through this clairvoyant I sent for the spirit of my grandmother, and read to her a first draft of this sketch. She corrected it in one or two points, and said that it is correct."

Here is the communication :—

" About the middle of the first decade of this century, there lived in the little seaport town of Girvan, in South Ayrshire, a young man and his sister ; they were warmly attached to each other. My grandmother, from whom I heard their story, was intimately acquainted with the young woman. The brother followed the precarious and dangerous avocation of the fisher, and our story begins with the loss of his life by the swamping of his boat in a storm.

" For a week or two his sister was inconsolable ; her mind dwelt in imagination on the loved form of her brother tossed amongst the weeds and ooze on the bed of the ocean, the food for fishes, and the dwelling place for creeping things.

" One night, about a fortnight after the sad accident, there came to the town, in the pursuit of his calling, a pedlar ; he sought and obtained lodgings for the night, and had for a bedfellow a native of the town.

"Whether he had informed the pedlar of the sad event or no, I could not say, but any way the pedlar could not get to sleep for a persistent dream or vision, which anon turned up as he was on the point of falling off to sleep. In the vision he saw a stretch of rocky shore, and, oh, horror! amongst the rocks, and rising and falling as the waves advanced or receded, was the mutilated form of a man. He awoke his companion and told him the dream, the physical characteristics of which were conspicuous because of a hill which rose up almost from the shore. His bedfellow, being a native of the place, identified the description with a place on the beach about half a mile north of the harbour, and when daylight broke together they went to the place, and found the dream confirmed by finding the body of a man, much decomposed, and with the right hand missing. The body was identified as that of the young woman's brother; and if the vague imaginings of her mind put daggers into the hands of her grief, the spectacle of the mutilated form of her brother drove them home to her very heart. The loss of the hand seemed to give point and force to her sorrow; her mind, perhaps, was entangled in the labyrinths of a physical resurrection, and could not see how the missing hand was to be restored. Anyway, ever and anon, she would burst out into a fit of weeping, wringing her own hands, and bewailing the loss of her brother's hand.

"This continued for about a week, until one night, preparatory to going to bed, she had undressed; but before she had got into bed, overcome by the force of her emotions, she threw her face on the pillow and burst out weeping, and bemoaning the lost hand, but scarcely had she done so when, with a cry of fear, she sprang from the bed.

"Her cries soon brought the other inmates of the house to her room, and when questioned, she informed them that when she had thrown herself on the bed, she felt some one give her a slap on the back, as if with the open hand; and that the place where she was struck was still pricking from the effects of the blow, and put her hand over her shoulder to point out the place she was struck.

"They examined the place, and over the shoulder blade, in livid blue, was the impression of a man's right hand.

"J. McDOWALL.

"48, Clyde Street, Calton, Glasgow."

Mr. Thomas Mayfield, of Godmanchester, Hants, sends me

the following account of a ghost with a very disagreeable
method of making its presence felt :—

"Charles Mayfield was sleeping in the Bell at Stukeley,
three miles from Huntingdon, in the year 1833. In the night
my father felt some one pulling the bedclothes off, and looking
up saw the landlord tugging away at the bedclothes. Upon
being spoken to the apparition vanished, and afterwards my
father discovered that the landlord, Joseph Kendall, died in
the next room at that hour."

The Grasp of a Spectral Hand. In this connection I will only quote a single
case from the "Proceedings of the Psychical Re-
search Society." It is a very remarkable one,
because the ghost in this case was minus the middle finger,
and was unknown to the person whom he touched :—

"We went upstairs together, I being perhaps a couple of
steps behind my friend, when, on reaching the topmost step,
I felt something suddenly slip behind me from an unoccupied
room to the left of the stairs. Thinking it must be imagination, no one being in the house except the widow and servant,
who occupied rooms on another landing, I did not speak to
my friend, who turned off to a room on the right, but walked
quickly into my room, which faced the staircase, still feeling
as though a tall figure was bending over me. I turned on the
gas, struck a light, and was in the act of applying it when I felt
a heavy grasp in my arm of a hand minus the middle finger.
Upon this I uttered a loud cry, which brought my friend, the
widow lady, and the servant girl, into the room to inquire the
cause of my alarm. The two latter turned very pale on hearing the story. The house was thoroughly searched, but
nothing was discovered.

"Some weeks passed, and I had ceased to be alarmed at
the occurrence, when I chanced to mention it whilst spending
the afternoon with some friends. A gentleman asked me if I
had ever seen a description or seen a 'carte' of the lady's
late husband. On receiving a reply in the negative, he said,
singularly enough, he was tall, had a slight stoop, and had lost
the middle finger of his hand. On my return I inquired of
the servant, who had been in the family from childhood,
if such were the case, and learned that it was quite correct,
and that she (the girl) had once, when sleeping in the same
room, been awakened by feeling some one pressing down her
knees, and on opening her eyes she saw her late master by the
bedside, on which she fainted, and had never dared to enter
the room after dusk since. I did not see anything. I may

say that I am not in the least nervous or superstitious, had been reading nothing of an excitable character, and whilst walking upstairs had my mind occupied in conjectures as to whether the key of my watch was upstairs or down. I had slept in the room for eight months and never before experienced anything of the kind." (Vol. V. p. 465.)

Some Pleasanter Touches.

I will close this chapter with some more agreeable experiences. All the way from Jerusalem a lady sends me an account of a hallucination of touch which was distinctly of a pleasurable nature :—

"About seven years ago I was in great trouble, and away from all near friends. One night, on retiring to rest, I was oppressed with a sense of my utter loneliness. About two or three o'clock I awoke, and was immediately conscious of some one standing at my head, and gently stroking my hair in a caressing manner, such as two dear friends, then dead, had been in the habit of doing. I felt no surprise nor fear, only a feeling of being loved and helped, and great comfort came to my sad heart. Then it ceased; and only then I began to wonder who or what it was."

Mrs. Woodcock has had a similar pleasant experience, although in this case it was not a stroking of the hair, but a mother's kiss. Her narrative is as follows :—

"My mother died on June 25th, 1879, at Driffield, in Yorkshire. Her death was a peculiarly painful one, and a great blow to us all. The same month in which she died we removed to Hull. In October of the same year I was suddenly awakened by feeling her kiss me on my mouth, and she smiled so sweetly, just as she used to do in life, and said, 'Get up, Sophia.' It was all so very natural that it was quite two minutes before I realised that my mother had been dead four months. As soon as she had spoken those three words she turned to go into her own bedroom, or what would have been her own bedroom if she had lived to go to Hull with us. I raised myself upon my elbow and watched her go down two short steps, then up five broader ones, along a few feet of landing, open her bedroom door, and shut it; all done naturally and deliberately. She had on her nightgown and a wrap thrown over her shoulders just exactly as a mother does look when she is popping about into her children's rooms in the early morning. Almost instantly I awoke my sister Mary, who slept with me, and told her that mother had been to our bedside; but it agitated her very much, she being a remarkably nervous girl, and she tried to persuade me I had been dreaming, but I can never think so; and it has been a great comfort to me to dwell upon that supernatural (in one sense) though most perfectly natural visit (in another)."

A great friend of mine, with whom I was discussing the question, informed me that at the moment when her father died—at a distance of some hundred miles—she was conscious of his presence with her; she felt as if he had taken her in his arms as he used to do when she was a little child, and a feeling of inexpressible joy filled her heart.

CHAPTER XII

DREAMS AND DREAMERS

" We are such stuff as dreams are made of, and our little life is rounded with a sleep."

" DREAMS, books, are each a world," says Wordsworth, but while of the world of books whole Alexandrian libraries and Bodleians have been written, how little attention has been devoted to the world of dreams! In Dreamland we spend all of us at least one-fourth, most of us one-third, ot our lives. But to consider the life we lead in Dreamland is regarded as a waste of time. He is supposed to be but half-witted who even thinks about his dreams. Yet, although there are multitudes and myriads of dreams, idle and vain and meaningless as the shapes of the mist of the marsh, it is not so with all dreams. We have all had "a dream which was not all a dream," and some have lived more vividly and intensely in dreams than ever they have lived in their waking moments. In dreams are the keys to many mysteries. Holy Writ is full of dreams. The New Testament opens with the dream of Joseph and closes with the apocalyptic vision of John in Patmos. After the Bible, the most popular book in the English language is the Dream of the Bedford tinker. But to-day no one seems to care for dreams, and it is assumed that the age of the dreamer is past, and that visions are no more.

One-third ot life. It is not so, and it never will be so as long as one-third of existence is spent in sleep. The lack of careful and intelligent study of dreams leaves the common people a prey to the ineffable folly of the dream-books—a form of literature much more widely circulated than the classics. A generation which finds itself repaid in the study—close, minute, and elaborate—of the habits of earth-worms, and the genealogy of the marine ascidian, may some day discover that Dreamland lies vacant and unexplored. In all the voluminous literature of scientific psychology is there one authentic human document wherein there is due note

and observation made of the dreams of a single student for a
year, for a month, or for even a week? In dreams the sub-
conscious soul asserts its existence. In dreams we see without
eyes, hear without ears, and transport ourselves without an
effort to the uttermost parts of the world. We are emancipated
from the slavery of the material senses. In dreams we have a
foretaste of the freedom and the capacity of spiritual existence.

A dreamer of dreams.   There are some souls which either never dream,
or which are so constituted that there is no bridge
of memory between their conscious and their sub-
conscious selves. But there are others who dream constantly,
and who remember their dreams. One such exceptionally
gifted dreamer is Mrs. Georgina F., whose vivid narrative of
how her dead lover kept his promise was one of the most
weird and pathetic of all the incidents in " Real Ghost Stories."
She has had all manner of dreams from her childhood up—
dreams of things to come, dreams of her own death, and
dreams, too, of the life after death, of heaven and of hell,
which seem to me almost unique, from their strange, homely
realism and their almost grotesque originality. Macaulay's
description of Dante, as the man who had been in hell,
recurs to the mind on reading these strange visions, told without an attempt at literary art, the things seen being jotted
down just as they occurred, with a minute particularity of
detail that is the best evidence that the writer is describing
what she saw, and not what she laid herself out to imagine.
Leaving over for the present her vision of her own corpse
and her dream of heaven, I will quote here from two of her
dreams, the first being a remarkable premonition of what she
afterwards saw on the other side of the Atlantic.

A foreseeing dream.   Let me disarm my critics by admitting without
reserve that I make no claim whatever for any
evidential value for this dream. I know that she
told me, some years before she went to America, that she had
dreamed of what she would see there ; and I know also that
when she got there she wrote and told me that she had found
everything as she had dreamed it. Knowing Mrs. F. for some
years, I do not doubt that she is speaking the truth, but my
belief is not evidence, and the legal evidence which I might
have had if I had taken notes or preserved letters is now
impossible. It is evident also that in some points she herself
was only conscious of the dream after she had visited the
place. This is a common experience. There are probably
few persons who have not, at some time or other, on arriving

at a strange place, found it strangely familiar. We feel we have some time or other been there before. All that, of course, is strictly subjective. We cannot prove it, we only know it, and it is but seldom that we can locate the dream in which we foresaw, in sleep, the place or the events which we witness again in the light of day. Without more preamble, here is Mrs. F.'s story :—

A dream with a preface. "During the year 1887, I decided on making a journey to Buffalo, the capital of Erie County, New York State, and close to Niagara Falls. I was prevented by other business affairs from carrying out my intention until the beginning of 1891. I did not know any person in Buffalo, had never read any description of the place, nor had I seen any picture of it. I tried all over London to obtain such but failed, and though I met many persons who had been in the States, I never could meet one who had been to or could tell me what the city of Buffalo was like. Between 1887 and 1891 I had three dreams, about a year apart, and each dream exactly the same. It was only on the first occasion, however, that I dreamed what I may call the preface to the dream. I dreamed of being in a strange country. I had just arrived. When I got ashore and a short distance from where I landed, I saw curious, very tall poles ; and in fact, on getting nearer, I saw they were very irregular trunks of trees, supporting what seemed to be telegraph wires. The neighbourhood was rough, street paving very bad, and I noticed advertisements all over everywhere. On crossing the road, I stopped a working man who was passing, and asked in which direction I should go to get to the central part of the city. He told me to keep straight on to the left, which I did. I then woke up and lay thinking for about five minutes.

The threefold dream. "I fell asleep again and dreamed the first of the three dreams proper. I did not seem now to have any knowledge or consciousness of where I had been in the preface to my dream, but I found myself walking about in a place I had never before been in ; I did not know if it was a city, town, or suburbs of a town. I fancied it the latter, as there were trees everywhere along the streets, and few people about. I remarked the particular nature of the soil in the roads. I walked along a street overarched by fine trees, and was looking for a particular number, where lived, as I had been told, the person I wanted to see on business. I saw a small house with about four steps up to the door. The door stood open ; I had my foot

on the first step, and was going to knock and ask where in the
street that number was, the street being a very long one, when
a woman in a white apron appeared at the door, and replied
to my question. I then walked down the street, found the
number, but on stopping opposite it I seemed to doubt that
it was really there the person I wanted lived. I passed on
and came to a turning down which I could see through a
long straight avenue of thick, green trees, what looked like
the sea or some large water, but it was a long way off, at the
very bottom of the avenue. The sun was shining; I thought
I had had a long journey, and that having so far reconnoitred
the place, as I was tired, I would return home and leave
further business till later on or next day. I was on my way
home when some person addressed me on the street, but in
my recollection of the dream, this item was very indistinct,
and I could not tell if male or female, or what they said.
In the dream I did not seem to know what country I was in,
nor the name of the city, nor where I came from, nor how I
got there ; I had a sort of feeling of having gone there before
fate intended me to have gone, but I felt, too, that I was not
responsible for being there, and had got to the place without
a conscious deliberate intention of going to it. I was somewhat surprised at finding myself there, and thinking how queer
to be there and not even know in what quarter of the world
I was in if any one asked me. I had also an indistinct
feeling that the business I had to go there on was not going
to get done during that visit, but that I should have to leave
and come another time ; still, this feeling was indistinct, and I
still intended calling on the person next day. I then ceased
dreaming. This dream was repeated in all its details three
times.

"On arriving in New York in 1891, a gentleman
Its fulfilment who was to have met me on my arrival failed to
in New York. do so, owing to the boat arriving at a different
time from what was expected. While waiting for my baggage
to pass the Customs, I stood looking out beyond the great
wide exit leading from the Customs office and landing stage
to the public street. I there saw the tall poles and other
things, and felt quite sure that I had been there before. The
place seemed all familiar, but I did not at that moment
remember my dream. I sent my baggage by the express to
an hotel, and then walked across the road to a corner of a
street, and seeing tram tracks and a car coming along in the
distance, I spoke to a man who was passing to ask him if

the cars went to any place close to the G.P.O., or Broadway, and if so in which direction the car I should take would go. Almost before he had replied, I seemed to recognise the man's face and red necktie, and then all my dream came suddenly to my mind as he replied : 'Yes, Miss, this car coming up will take you straight as you can go to Washington Market, and it is about —— blocks up —— Street to the Post Office.'

And in Buffalo. "The direction was, as in the dream, to the left, and in a straight line. I was so astonished at my unconsciously carrying out the dream by speaking to the man, and at seeing surrounding objects as in the dream, that I let the first car pass, and waited for the next one, so as to take a good look around from where I stood. I saw as I went along in the next car several points, places, and things, which I recognised from the dream. I went to my hotel, and remained some time in New York City before going to Buffalo.

It was near midnight when I first arrived in the latter city. I put up that night at an hotel beside the railway station. I was awake before 6 a.m. next (Sunday) morning. I got up, dressed, and went out to view the town, being anxious to see at once if it would turn out to be the same place I had thrice seen in my dreams. On getting to a central part I began to recognise first of all the soil and the trees, and all at once, on turning a corner, there, exactly as I dreamed it, was the long street arched by trees, and being so early, and on a Sunday, there were hardly any persons to be seen in the streets, just as I dreamed. There, too, on looking down Court Street, I saw the water I took in the dream to be the sea, but which was really Lake Erie, at the bottom of the avenue of trees. I could not see any one about to ask in which part of the street No. —— was likely to be in. The numbers seemed to be very irregular, and many houses were unnumbered. As I turned to go back I saw a woman with a white apron standing outside the open door on the top step of the very house of my dream. I crossed the road and asked her, and she sent me in the same direction for No. —— as in the dream. Now, the most curious part of all is that when I got to the number that I had been given by a Government official as being the residence of the person I had to call on, I walked past it two or three times, looking at it, and felt as good as certain, notwithstanding the street and number being correct, that the person wanted did not live in that house. I cannot tell by what instinct or second-sight I knew this, but I was so certain that I did not even go and ask, but instead I walked along, feeling that I would know when I got in front of whichever house he did live in that that was the right house. Well, I walked on till I came to a turning and a crossing, and although that particular street did not end there, but ran perhaps a couple of miles on further past that turning and crossing, still I felt as if I must cross over there and walk back again, but on the other side. So on I went, and in getting in front of a house within about two houses of being opposite to the one I felt he did not live in, I knew that I had found the right one. I noted the number, and being Sunday I decided I could do no business that day, so I started off, feeling quite satisfied about that house, to have breakfast at my hotel—it was only about 8.15 a.m. I halted and looked back and down streets as I went, and as I stood there came up to me a gentleman who offered to show me where the institutions were I wanted to see. I went along with him, as he was in any case going in my direction, and they were almost on the way to my hotel. This was the fulfilling of the person addressing me in the street on my way home in my dream. Next morning I called upon a City official connected with the matter in hand, and on asking if the person whose house I had been looking for the previous day was living at No. ——, he replied, 'Oh, no! That's their old residence; they left that house some couple of years ago, and are now living at No. ——, almost opposite.' So it turned out that I was right in both dream and reality, and in the latter, the house I felt certain he did reside in was the right one."

This vision of Buffalo from London, thrice-repeated with curious exactitude, was verified, it would seem, to the letter. The second thrice-repeated dream has not been verified, and cannot be verified in the nature of things on this side the grave. From whatever point of view it is regarded, it cannot be deemed to be a very sombre and original vision of the antechamber of Hell.

"I three times dreamed the same dream, once
At the Mouth of Hell. before marriage, once after marriage, and once during widowhood. In my dream I found myself seated on one of three irregular blocks of soft, yellowish, sandy-looking stone, situated about 6 ft. inside from the entrance, and on the right-hand side against the wall of a cave. How I came there I was not aware, neither had I any definite consciousness of *how* long I had been there, but it

did not appear to be a very long time, probably hours and not days or weeks. I seemed to be still in my material body, and in my usual out-of-door attire, and the stone I sat upon was damp, and the largest of the three, and the only one having a surface flat enough to make a resting place. The cave appeared to be about 25 ft. or 30 ft. wide and 13 ft. high at the entrance, but became more low and narrow the further you went into the interior. The edges of the entrance were very irregular indeed, quite sharp in some places and rugged in others, and soft and even, as if worn smooth, right on the central top edge of the entrance.

The Atmosphere. "I felt an unseen and immaterial weight pressing down my whole conscious being, a horrible, weird, paralysing deadweight or pressure. I seemed to begin to half realise that I was actually in the spirit world, and knew it to be a place where only lost and unhappy souls existed. The entrance of the cave abutted and joined on to and was on a level with what seemed to be an endless expanse of water and space, the atmosphere of which was composed of a most unearthly and peculiar, half-opaque, yellowish mist, or what might be described as like a rather dense light yellow fog. It had a feathery appearance, as if composed of half down and half thick, damp mist or heavy air. The yellow colour seemed to be of such a peculiar tint as was never seen on earth, and was created by, or really was, in fact, the light, if two-thirds darkness can be called light. Well, this light was such that one could not know for certain if it was day or night ; it did not seem to be either, for one of its characteristics was a sort of changing or shading, or intermittent transient alternation of colour from what one might call the light of a bad oil lamp to the weak attempt of the sun to make itself seen through the dense London fog.

The Sea. "For about fifty feet in front of the cave all was fine, feathery, shifting sand, and it seemed to extend and form a foreshore all along further than I could see through the mist. To the left and right of the cave entrance, away beyond the fifty feet of sand, was what seemed the great endless ocean of water, yet it could not be clearly seen to be actual water, but looked through the horrible light more like an endless expanse of undulating jelly of a very slight flesh colour or pink tint, the contrast with which the yellow light was made doubly horrible. There seemed to be a cloud of thicker atmosphere lying low between me and the ocean, and obscured my vision. The whole place, in and outside the cave, was all the same sort of light and atmosphere, but outside was about ten times as dense. I was going to get up and walk along to see what depth backwards the cave went, but I was stopped by a terrible pressure as of a hand on my head and became conscious, finally conscious, that there was no end to nor outlet to the other end of the cave, and I was told in the spirit that when once I insisted and penetrated further into it I would never be permitted to leave the regions of the lost.

The Sound of Sighing. "Now, there was all this time I was in this region a noise as of the sea—a dreadful, sad, undulating, sighing, hollow, subtle, penetrating, deep sound, a half far-away sound as you hear in a sea-shell. It seemed to come from the direction of that ocean. The sounds were modulated from time to time, and at times appeared like human voices in agony, mingling with the demoniac, scoffing laughter and groans of despair from other lost souls. I had been looking for a short time towards the interior of the cave, and as I was turning my face again to look out on the expanse in front, I saw something moving or floating along through the air. It floated close to the roof of the cave, and evidently had come from out of the far interior of the latter, where I was forbidden to enter. I looked up, and followed the object with my eyes. It was a round form about as large as a full-sized human head, and composed of what looked like a jelly-like substance inside a bladder, like such as toy balloons are made of, and of a cloudy, partly transparent yellow look or flesh colour, something like the ocean from where the voices came. It floated out into the great space, and in doing so it brushed against the smooth place I described at the top edge of the cave's entrance. I then saw that the whole space outside the cave was full of similar floating forms. I noticed about half a dozen more float out of the cave, and all touched the smooth edge of the cave in doing so. I said to myself that it was evidently the constant passing out of the forms I describe that had worn that part so smooth.

A Vision of Lost Souls. "I sat looking out at all the strange scenes, and was conscious of an inward trembling and wondering horror, for I saw now that inside each of the globular forms there could just be discerned, though indistinctly, human features. I saw the eyes, nose, and mouth much more distinct and defined than the whole face—still the outline was there, and there was a different face inside each of them ; and oh, the expression ! The expression in the eyes of each I can never, never forget ; indeed, no words I can think of would describe in anything like a graphic manner the intense and awful depth of agony, of remorse and consciousness of hopeless and eternal loss, and silent, immutable isolation of the soul, portrayed in those living eyes, all of which seemed to look out straight before them, and as if denied the power to even shift or move the eyeballs. Still, I could see in them not only the actual living light as seen in the eyes of those still on earth, but they possessed an unearthly light, as if the very spirit-fire was ready to burst through, but was not permitted, though on the verge of madness—a look of suppressed, horrible, speechless, conscious agony. Each mouth was closed tight, and had a strained, compressed look, as of a sick person suffering great physical pain. The hundreds of forms I could see (but I felt that all the unseen space over the ocean was all full of them too) kept on mingling and intermingling as they floated up and down and around through space ; but I noticed that none ever were permitted to touch each other, for each floated around all ; there was always a distance of two feet between them at least. I noticed, too, that as soon as these forms came in sight all the horrible noise as of voices ceased, and there remained only subdued, regular sound, as of the going out of the tide. There was no hair, ears, or neck discernible in these spirit faces, and in all cases it was the full front view of the face which was seen inside the balls, but the face was outside, and seen through the bladder-like outside surface. The tip of the nose being apparently about three and a half inches in from the surface, the part inside at the back of the features was not transparent enough to see through, but like a more dense, jelly-like substance than elsewhere. I felt a strange anxiety and doubt as to whether I would ever again get back into this world, and how I was convinced that the place I was in was really hell. I felt powerless and too horrified and disinclined to move or try to see further. After a long spell of horror I suddenly felt a sort of peaceful, hazy relief feeling steal over me, and I bent my head and saw that my own clothing was becoming indistinct, and all consciousness faded away and ended the vision. Each time I had this dream all details were exactly the same.

How the Vision came and went. "I always had the dream at the same time, that was just before getting up in the morning, and it occurred as follows :—I had slept well, as usual, and had awakened and was about to get up and dress when I felt a sort of half-conscious, dreamy, light feeling steal over me as if passing through air, or carried on the wind, then an interval of inaction, during which I was powerless to awake, although I could recognise and hear sounds and what was said or done in or near my room. I felt that I was not all there myself; I had a divided sensation, as if that part of my consciousness which had left me had taken all power of motion and will along with it in its flight; and as if only passive and weak consciousness remained. Eventually I felt a great shock, gave a deep sigh, and awoke, my whole self once more, and thereupon I was at once aware of having been two people or spirits, or divided, and knew I had been in two places and conditions at the same period. I can't describe to you how troubled and alarmed I was, for I believed the vision was given me as a warning, and that I would really go to hell after death. I thought so because I had been so often before, in dreams, in places I had no idea or knowledge of from either pictures or books or descriptions, but had really gone to them after and recognised them from the dream. I was so upset that I went and told my vision to the Rev. John Donor Powell, the pastor of my church in Lower Abbey Street, Dublin, and asked his advice and prayers. That was the first time I had the vision. I have had it twice since, with intervals of six years between each. If I ever have it again I shall know that my doom is sealed; but I believe I shall be saved from that."

Mrs. F. was good enough to write out for me a dream of heaven, which is quite as original in its way as this sombre dream of the mouth of hell. Milton and Dante both made more of the Inferno than of the Paradiso. My correspondent's vision of the celestial regions is, however, much more remarkable even than her weird vigil at the mouth of the cave between the bottomless pit and the sea of lost souls.

A foreseeing of Messina. The Count R. de Maricourt sends me the following account of a dream which anticipated events by three years, which bears some resemblance to Mrs. F.'s dream of New York and Buffalo :—

" About ten years of my childhood were spent in Italy —the most part at Naples, near my father, who was then *attaché* to the French Embassy (with the Duke de Montebello, ambassador at that time). When sent back to France for the last school studies, I felt like an exile and a prisoner in the college—always longing most sadly for Italy and dreaming ot it, crying the night in my bed. I was recovering from a severe illness when I dreamed that I was on sea, facing the well-known Neapolitan bay, the smoking Vesuvius, etc., etc. Then the landscape faded, and a new shore appeared. The outlines of the coasts were as if cut out with scissors into a rude scrap of grey paper and glued upon another dark paper, figuring stormy skies. I was almost paralysed by an unspeakable feeling of awe, looking at such an anomalously lugubrious coloration.

" But, soon relieved, I saw the rising sun illuminating a large, perfectly unknown town, white, surrounded with green hills. A strong, lively, good-faced, almost naked and sunburnt man took my trunk when arrived in the harbour. He was dressed with drawers only, and a Phrygian red woollen cap.

" When landed on shore, through far streets he led me to the front door of a palazzo, where waved the French flag. And soon here I was greeted by my father, my step-mother, and my young brothers. Now, I am quite an old man, and still the picture of the gloomy coast and sky remains printed on my brain.

" Three years later, when I had gained the bachelorship and was engaged in the first law studies, my father bade me rejoin him at Messina, where he was freshly appointed to the French vice-consulate ; he was unwilling to leave me alone at Paris in the middle of revolution (1848).

" Arriving at Naples, where I was landed by the French Marseilles steamer, I embarked on a very small old and bad Neapolitan ship. We were assailed by a gale in the night. A long and dismal journey through the lightning, I perceived and acknowledged the shapes of the Calabrian coasts, but not so gloomily as in the childish nightmare which so vividly had stricken me some years ago.

" At Messina I recognised perfectly, between the men carrying on shore the passengers' luggage, my appointed *facchino*. He, and no other, took my trunk on his naked shoulder. After some paces he asked me where I was going. At the first corner of a street I felt so perfectly sure I could not miss my way that I told him ' *Lasciami camminare innanzi ine ti vortero io dove voglio andare.*' And soon we arrived near the front door, the large archway entrance of the *palazzo*, with the French flag, and so on."

A Murder seen in a Dream. A correspondent in Chester sends me the following detailed story of what appears to be a trustworthy account of a murder actually witnessed in a dream in all its details by the brother of the murdered man. The names of persons and places are disguised. The dates, however, are correct. The murder took place in Cornwall. The report of the execution and of the trial can be traced in the local newspapers. The case is now being investigated by the Psychical Research Society. Sir A. Cockburn prosecuted on behalf of the Crown. My informant's relatives were the intimate friends of the murdered man.

On one of the slate tombstones in the churchyard of the Cornish village of St. Eglos is the following inscription :—

"SACRED TO THE MEMORY OF

HART NORTHEY,

Who was murdered on February 8th, 1840."

St. Eglos is situated about ten miles from the Atlantic, and not quite so far from the old market town of Trebodwina.

Hart and George Northey were brothers, and from childhood their lives had been marked by the strongest brotherly affection.

Hart and George Northey had never been separated from their birth, until George became a sailor, Hart meantime joining his father in business.

The Vision. On the 8th of February, 1840, while George Northey's ship was lying in port at St. Helena, he had the following strange dream :—

"Last night I dreamt my brother was at Trebodwina Market, and that I was with him, quite close by his side, during the whole of the market transactions.

"Although I could see and hear everything which passed around me, I felt sure that it was not my bodily presence which thus accompanied him, but my shadow, or rather my spiritual presence, for he seemed quite unconscious that I was near him.

"I felt that my being thus present in this strange way betokened some hideous hidden danger which he was destined to meet, and which I knew my presence could not avert, for I could not speak to warn him of his peril.

"Conscious as I was of impending danger, I hoped he would return early to his home with some of his neighbours.

"As the evening passed and his friends one by one left the market-town, my apprehension increased ; I became more and more assured that the threatened blow could not be averted. Hart remained hour after hour receiving amounts due to him from various accounts, so that it was fully forty minutes after the last of his townsfolk had left Trebodwina before he started on his homeward journey.

"It was a bright starlight night, but as there was no moon, objects on the roadside were only dimly discernible.

"My brother was on horseback, and, unconscious of danger, he rode smartly up the narrow old street of Trebodwina, past the asylum on the brow of the hill, then down between high hedges into the well-wooded vale of Trenmere; still on up the hillside of St. Didimus, until he arrived at the Half-Way Inn, three miles from his starting place.

"Up to this time (for I seemed to accompany him on his ride) I had seen nothing to warrant my anxiety, but yet I was more certain than ever that impending doom was awaiting him.

"His ride, so far, had been through a comparatively open country. He now entered on the loneliest and darkest part of the road. The stars, which had previously lighted his way, became obscured by overhanging trees. He now gradually descended into a very deep valley, with large woods on the hills which were parallel to the road on either side. The effect of these thickly-wooded hills was to render the darkness complete. My terror gradually increased as Hart approached the hamlet of Polkerrow, until I was in a perfect frenzy, frantically desirous, yet unable, to warn my brother in some way and prevent him going further.

"He had slackened speed to rest his horse during the latter part of his ride, and had now reached a spot about half a mile from Polkerrow.

"At this point a large excavation had been made by the roadside, in one corner of which there is a gateway which leads to a lonely orchard, through which runs a dark stream. This excavation caused the shadow of the hedge to cease, and there was at this point a faint light upon the road.

"Looking in its direction, I suddenly became aware of two dark shadows thrown across the road from the recess. I felt my brother's hour had come, and I was powerless to aid him !

"Two men appeared, whom I instantly recognised as notorious poachers, who lived in a lonely wood near St. Eglos.

"Even now my brother seemed to have no fear, and on being saluted by them stopped his horse.

"The men wished him 'Good-night, maister,' civilly enough. He replied, and entered into conversation with them about some work he had promised them. After a few minutes they

asked him for some money. It was not the first time he had
given them aid, and, without needing persuasion to a generous
deed, he handed them some silver. They were evidently dis-
satisfied, and asked for more, their demeanour meanwhile
altering from begging to demanding. Their further request he
refused, and they urged and threatened him in vain. The
elder of the two brothers, who was standing near the horse's
head, and said, ' Mr. Northey, we know you have just come
from Trebodwina market with plenty of money in your
pockets ; we are desperate men, and you bean't going to leave
this place until we've got that money, so hand over.' My
brother made no reply, except to slash at him with the whip
and spur the horse at him.

"The younger of the ruffians instantly drew a pistol and
fired. Hart dropped lifeless from the saddle, and one of the
villains held him by the throat with a grip of iron for some
minutes, as though to make assurance doubly sure, and crush
out any particle of life my poor brother might have left.

"The murderers secured the horse to a tree in the orchard,
and, having rifled the corpse, they dragged it up the stream,
concealing it under the overhanging banks of the water-course.
They then carefully covered over all marks of blood on the
road, and hid the pistol in the thatch of a disused hut close
to the roadside ; then, setting the horse free to gallop home
alone, they decamped across the country to their own cottage.

"The agony I had endured through this terrible scene,
utterly unable as I was to save him I loved most on earth,
became now quite insupportable. I tried to pursue the murderers, I shouted their names, I called on God to avenge my
brother, and I awoke ! "

"An awful dream, indeed ! " said one of the listeners,
"but surely you do not believe such a fate has befallen your
brother ? "

"I am absolutely certain Hart is dead ; that he was murdered on the Trebodwina Road last night, just in the exact
way I saw in my dream," replied George Northey.

The vessel left St. Helena next day, and reached Plymouth
in due course. George Northey had, during the whole of the
voyage home, never altered in his conviction that Hart had
been killed as he had dreamt, and that retribution was by his
means to fall on the murderers.

What actually happened. The following incident actually took place on
the night of the murder :—

"It was market day at Trebodwina, and the old
country town was bustle itself.

"Others among the crowd were Tom Marter, Henry Tresyons, and John Penpoll, all near neighbours of his, and these four gentlemen arranged to ride home together, if possible.

"This arrangement, however, could not be followed; each was obliged to leave the town at a different time; Hart Northey some while after the others.

"At midnight Mrs. Hart Northey was startled by the sound of a horse's gallop, which ceased outside her house. She had been waiting up for her husband, and now, hearing the horse go to the stable, she went to the rear of the house. 'Hart, dear, what news?' asked she. The only reply her question received was the champing of the horse's bit, as he stood at the door of the stable, patiently awaiting admittance. For an instant Mrs. Northey stood amazed, but gradually a dreadful fear came over her. There was the horse, riderless; and, looking closer, she saw the mane and saddle stained with a few drops of blood. Hart must have met with foul play upon the road, and when this conclusion with its attendant horror had fixed itself on her mind, her nerves failed her, and with a startling cry she fainted. Her scream roused the servants, and soon the sad news spread round the neighbourhood. Without waiting for daybreak the good folk of St. Eglos set out on the Trebodwina Road to find Hart Northey, dead or alive. Their search was futile; there was no trace to guide them towards the object of their quest, nor were signs of a struggle anywhere visible.

"The next day a ploughboy, as he was walking along the Trebodwina Road, determined to pick some of the watercress which grew in a brook running through an orchard close to the road.

"As he bent over the overhanging bank to look for the cress, he saw the body of a dead man lying cold and ghastly in the stream. Wild with fright, the lad rushed off and told his terrible discovery to others. The body was almost immediately identified as that of Hart Northey.

"The police of the neighbourhood entered at once into an investigation of the murder. The horror and indignation at the crime were widespread. The deceased was so well known and so popular that every one concurred in thinking that special efforts should be made to detect his murderer.

"A sum of £3,500 had meanwhile been presented to the widow as an expression of sympathy.

"At last suspicion fell on the brothers Hightwood, whose cottage was searched and blood-stained garments were discovered concealed in the roof, but no trace of the pistol was to be found which the younger brother admitted having had. He stated he lost it almost immediately after its purchase. The elder Hightwood denied all knowledge of the pistol.

" Both brothers were arrested and brought before the magistrates.

" The evidence against them was certainly not strong, but their manner seemed that of guilty men. They were ordered to take their trial at the forthcoming assizes at Trebodwina. They each confessed in the hope of saving their lives, and both were sentenced to be hanged.

" There was, however, some doubt about the pistol. Before the execution George Northey arrived from St. Helena, and declared that the pistol was in the thatch of the old cottage close by the place where they murdered Hart Northey, and where they hid it.

" ' How do you know ? ' he was asked.

" George Northey replied : ' I saw the foul deed committed in a dream I had the night of the murder, when at St. Helena.'

" A pistol was found, as George Northey had predicted, in the thatch of the ruined cottage."

CHAPTER XIII

SOME HISTORICAL GHOSTS

THE following collection presents a list of names—more or less well known—with which ghost stories of some kind are associated. The authority for these stories, though in many cases good, is so varied in quality that they are not offered as evidential of anything except the wide diversity of the circles in which such things find acceptance.

ROYAL.

Henry IV., of France, told d'Aubigné (see d'Aubigné, Histoire Universelle) that in presence of himself, the Archbishop of Lyons, and three ladies of the Court, the Queen (Margaret of Valois) saw the apparition of a certain cardinal afterwards found to have died at the moment. Also he (Henry IV.) was warned of his approaching end, not long before he was murdered by Ravaillac, by meeting an apparition in a thicket in Fontainebleau. ("Sully's Memoirs.").

Abel the Fratricide, King of Denmark, was buried in unconsecrated ground, and still haunts the wood of Poole, near the city of Sleswig.

Valdemar IV. haunts Gurre Wood, near Elsinore.

Charles XI., of Sweden, accompanied by his chamberlain and state physician, witnessed the trial of the assassin of Gustavus III., which occurred nearly a century later.

James IV., of Scotland, after vespers in the chapel at Linlithgow, was warned by an apparition against his intended expedition into England. He, however, proceeded, and was warned again at Jedburgh, but, persisting, fell at Flodden Field.

Charles I., of England, when resting at Daventree on the eve of the battle of Naseby, was twice visited by the apparition of Strafford, warning him not to meet the Parliamentary army, then quartered at Northampton. Being persuaded by Prince Rupert to disregard the warning, the King set off to march northward, but was surprised on the route, and a disastrous defeat followed.

Orleans, Duke of, brother of Louis XIV., called his eldest son (afterwards Regent) by his second title, Duc de Chartres, in preference to the more usual one of Duc de Valois. This change is said to have been in consequence of a communication made before his birth by the apparition of his father's first wife, Henrietta of England, reported to have been poisoned.

HISTORICAL WOMEN.

Elizabeth, Queen, is said to have been warned of her death by the apparition of her own double. (So, too, Sir Robert Napier and Lady Diana Rich.)

Catherine de Medicis saw in a vision the battle of Jarnac, and cried out, "Do you not see the Prince of Condé dead in the hedge?" This and many similar stories are told by Margaret of Valois in her Memoirs.

Philippa, wife of the Duke of Lorraine, when a girl in a convent, saw in vision the battle of Pavia, then in progress, and the captivity of the king her cousin, and called on the nuns about her to pray.

Joan of Arc was visited and directed by various Saints, including the Archangel Michael, S. Catherine, S. Margaret, etc.

LORD CHANCELLORS.

Erskine, Lord, himself relates (Lady Morgan's "Book of the Boudoir," 1829, vol. i. 123) that the spectre of his father's butler, whom he did not know to be dead, appeared to him in broad daylight, "to meet your honour," so it explained, "and to solicit your interference with my lord to recover a sum due to me which the steward at the last settlement did not pay," which proved to be the fact.

Brougham, Lord (see page 59).

CABINET MINISTERS.

Buckingham, Duke of, was exhorted to amendment and warned of approaching assassination by apparition of his father, Sir George Villiers, who was seen by Mr. Towers, surveyor of works at Windsor. All occurred as foretold.

Perceval Spenser (see page 47).

Castlereagh, Lord (who succeeded the above as Foreign Secretary), when a young man, quartered with his regiment in Ireland, saw the apparition of "The Radiant Boy," said to be an omen of good. Sir Walter Scott speaks of him as one of two persons "of sense and credibility, who both attested supernatural appearances on their own evidence."

Peel, Sir Robert, and his brother, both saw Lord Byron in London in 1810, while he was, in fact, lying dangerously ill at Patras. During the same fever, he also appeared to others, and was even seen to write down his name among the inquirers after the King's health.

EMPERORS.

Trajan, Emperor, was extricated from Antioch during an earthquake by a spectre which drove him out of a window. (Dio Cassius, lib. lxviii.)

Caracalla, Emperor, was visited by the ghost of his father Severus.

Julian the Apostate, Emperor (1), when hesitating to accept the Empire, saw a female figure, " The Genius of the Empire," who said she would remain with him, but not for long. (2) Shortly before his death, he saw his genius leave him with a dejected air. (3) He saw a phantom prognosticating the death of the Emperor Constans. (See S. Basil.)

Theodosius, Emperor, when on the eve of a battle, was reassured of the issue by the apparition of two men ; also seen independently by one of his soldiers.

SOLDIERS.

Curtius Rufus (pro-consul of Africa) is reported by Pliny to have been visited, while still young and unknown, by a gigantic female—the Genius of Africa—who foretold his career. (Pliny, b. vii. letter 26.)

Julius Cæsar was marshalled across the Rubicon by a spectre, which seized a trumpet from one of the soldiers and sounded an alarm.

Xerxes, after giving up the idea of carrying war into Greece, was persuaded to the expedition by the apparition of a young man, who also visited Artabanus, uncle to the king, when, upon Xerxes' request, Artabanus assumed his robe and occupied his place. (Herodotus, vii.)

Brutus was visited by a spectre, supposed to be that of Julius Cæsar, who announced that they would meet again at Philippi, where he was defeated in battle, and put an end to his own life.

Drusus, when seeking to cross the Elbe, was deterred by a

female spectre, who told him to turn back and meet his approaching end. He died before reaching the Rhine.

Pausanius, General of the Lacedæmonians, inadvertently caused the death of a young lady of good family, who haunted him day and night, urging him to give himself up to justice. (Plutarch in Simone.)

Dio, General of Syracuse, saw a female apparition sweeping furiously in his house, to denote that his family would shortly be swept out of Syracuse, which, through various accidents, was shortly the case.

Napoleon, at S. Helena, saw and conversed with the apparition of Josephine, who warned him of his approaching death. The story is narrated by Count Montholon, to whom he told it.

Blucher, on the very day of his decease, related to the King of Prussia that he had been warned by the apparition of his entire family, of his approaching end.

Fox, General, went to Flanders with the Duke of York shortly before the birth of his son. Two years later he had a vision of the child—dead—and correctly described its appearance and surroundings, though the death occurred in a house unknown to him.

Garfield, General, when a child of six or seven, saw and conversed with his father, lately deceased. He also had a premonition, which proved correct, as to the date of his death —the anniversary of the battle of Wickmauga, in which he took a brave part.

Lincoln, President, had a certain premonitory dream which occurred three times in relation to important battles, and the fourth on the eve of his assassination.

Coligni, Admiral, was three times warned to quit Paris before the feast of St. Bartholomew, but disregarded the premonition and perished in the massacre (1572).

MEN OF LETTERS.

Petrarch saw the apparition of the bishop of his diocese at the moment of death.

Epimenides, a poet contemporary with Solon, is reported by Plutarch to have quitted his body at will and to have conversed with spirits.

Dante, Jacopo, son of the poet, was visited in a dream by his father, who conversed with him and told him where to find the missing thirteen cantos of the Commedia.

Tasso saw and conversed with beings invisible to those about him.

Goethe saw his own double riding by his side under conditions which really occurred years later. His father, mother, and grandmother were all ghost-seers.

Donne, Dr., when in Paris, saw the apparition of his wife in London carrying a dead child at the very hour a dead infant was in fact born.

Byron, Lord, is said to have seen the Black Friar of Newstead on the eve of his ill-fated marriage. Also, with others, he saw the apparition of Shelley walk into a wood at Lerici, though they knew him at the time to be several miles away.

Shelley, while in a state of trance, saw a figure wrapped in a cloak which beckoned to him and asked, " Siete soddisfatto ? " —(Are you satisfied ?)

Benvenuto Cellini, when in captivity at Rome by order of the Pope, was dissuaded from suicide by the apparition of a young man who frequently visited and encouraged him.

Mozart was visited by a mysterious person who ordered him to compose a requiem, and came frequently to inquire after its progress, but disappeared on its completion, which occurred just in time for its performance at Mozart's own funeral.

Ben Jonson, when staying at Sir Robert Cotton's house, was visited by the apparition of his eldest son with a mark of a bloody cross upon his forehead at the moment of his death by the plague. He himself told the story to Drummond of Hawthornden.

Thackeray, W. M., writes, " It is all very well for you who have probably never seen spirit manifestations to talk as you do, but had you seen what I have witnessed you would hold a different opinion."

Mrs. Browning's spirit appeared to her sister with warning of death. Robert Browning writes, Tuesday, July 21, 1863, 'Arabel (Miss Barrett) told me yesterday that she had been much agitated by a dream which happened the night before— Sunday, July 19. She saw *her*, and asked, 'When shall I be with you ?' The reply was, 'Dearest, in five years '; whereupon Arabel awoke. She knew in her dream that it was not to the living she spoke." In five years, within a month of their completion, Miss Barrett died, and Browning writes, " I had forgotten the date of the dream, and supposed it was only three years, and that two had still to run."

Hall, Bishop, and his brother, when at Cambridge, each had a vision of their mother looking sadly at him, and saying she would not be able to keep her promise of visiting them. She died at the time.

Dr. Guthrie was directed, by repeated pullings at his coat, to go in a certain direction, contrary to previous intention, and was thus the means of saving the life of a parishioner.

Miller, Hugh, tells, in his "Schools and Schoolmasters," of the apparition of a bloody hand, seen by himself and the servant but not by others present. Accepted as a warning of the death of his father.

Porter, Anna Maria, when living at Esher, was visited one afternoon by an old gentleman—a neighbour, who frequently came in to tea. On this occasion he left the room without speaking, and fearing that something had happened she sent to inquire, and found that he had died at the moment of his appearance.

Edgworth, Maria, was waiting with her family for an expected guest, when the vacant chair was suddenly occupied by the apparition of a sailor cousin, who stated that his ship had been wrecked and he alone saved. The event proved the contrary—he alone was drowned.

Marryat, Captain—the story is told by his daughter—while staying at a country house in the north of England saw the family ghost—an ancestress of the time of Queen Elizabeth who had poisoned her husband. He tried to shoot her, but the ball passed harmlessly into the door behind, and the lady faded away—always smiling.

De Stael, Madame, was haunted by the spirit of her father, who counselled and helped her in all times of need.

L. E. L.'s ghost was seen by Dr. Madden in the room in which she died at Cape Coast Castle.

De Morgan, Professor, writes: "I am perfectly convinced that I have both seen and heard, in a manner that should make unbelief impossible, things called spiritual which cannot be taken by a rational being to be capable of explanation by imposture, coincidence, or mistake."

Foote, Samuel, in the year 1740, while visiting at his father's house in Truro, was kept awake by sounds of sweet music. His uncle was about the same time murdered by assassins.

MEN OF SCIENCE.

Davy, Sir Humphrey, when a young man, suffering from yellow fever on the Gold Coast, was comforted by visions of his guardian angel, who, years after, appeared to him again—incarnate—in the person of his nurse during his last illness.

Harvey, William, the discoverer of the circulation of the blood, used to relate that his life was saved by a dream. When a young man he was proceeding to Padua, when he was detained—with no reason alleged—by the governor at Dover. The ship was wrecked, and all on board lost, and it was then explained that the governor had received orders—in a dream —to prevent a person, to whose description Harvey answered, from going on board that night.

Farquhar, Sir Walter, physician (made a baronet in 1796), visited a patient at Pomeroy Castle. While waiting alone a lady appeared to him, exhibiting agony and remorse (who proved to be the family ghost) prognosticating the death of the patient, which followed.

Clark, Sir James, Wife of, while living in their house in Brook Street, saw the apparition of her son, Dr. J. Clark, then in India, carrying a dead baby wrapped in an Indian shawl. Shortly afterwards he did, in fact, send home the body of a child for interment, which had died at the hour noted; to fill up the coffin it was wrapped up in an Indian scarf.

Herbert of Cherbury, Lord, one of the first to systematise deism, when in doubt whether he should publish his "De Veritate," as advised by Grotius, prayed for a sign, and heard sounds "like nothing on earth, which did so comfort and cheer me, that I took my petition as granted."

Bacon, Francis, was warned in a dream of his father's approaching end, which occurred in a few days.

THEOLOGIANS.

Luther, Martin, was visited by apparitions,—one, according to Melancthon, who announced his coming by knocking at the door.

Melancthon says that the apparition of a venerable person came to him in his study and told him to warn his friend Grynaeus to escape at once from the danger of the Inquisition, a warning which saved his life.

Zwingli was visited by an apparition "with a perversion of a text of Scripture."

Oberlin, Pastor, was visited almost daily by his deceased wife, who conversed with him, and was visible not only to himself, but to all about him.

Fox, George, while walking on Pendle Hill, Yorkshire, saw his future converts coming towards him "along a river-side, to serve the Lord."

Newman, Cardinal, relates in a letter, January 3rd, 1833,

that when in quarantine in Malta he and his companions heard footsteps not to be accounted for by human agency.

Wilberforce, Bishop, experienced remarkable premonitions, and phenomena even more startling are attributed to him.

Saints.—The stories of visions, apparitions, etc., which are told in connection with the saints are far too numerous to quote. The following, however, may be referred to as of special interest :—

1. *Phantasms of the Living.*—St. Ignatius Loyola, Gennadius (the friend of St. Augustine), St. Augustine himself, twice over (he tells the story himself, Serm. 233), St. Benedict and St. Meletius, all appeared during life in places distant from their actual bodily whereabouts.

2. *Phantasms of the Dead.*—St. Anselm saw the slain body of William Rufus, St. Basil that of Julian the Apostate, St. Benedict the ascent to heaven of the soul of St. Germanus, bishop of Capua—all at the moment of death. St. Augustine and St. Edmund, Archbishops of Canterbury, are said to have conversed with spirits. St. Ambrose and St. Martin of Tours received information concerning relics from the original owners of the remains.

3. *Premonitions.*—St. Cyprian and St. Columba each foretold the date and manner of his own death as revealed in visions.

MISCELLANEOUS.

Harcourt, Countess, when Lady Nuneham, mentioned one morning having had an agitating dream, but was met with ridicule. Later in the day Lord Harcourt—her husband's father—was missing. She exclaimed, " Look in the well," and fainted away. He was found there with a dog, which he had been trying to save.

Aksakoff, Mme., wife of Chancellor Aksakoff, on the night of May 12th, 1855, saw the apparition of her brother, who died at the time. The story is one very elaborate as to detail.

Rich, Lady Diana, was warned of her death by a vision of her own double in the avenue of Holland House.

Breadalbane, May, Lady, her sister (both daughters of Lord Holland), was also warned in vision of her death.

The Daughter of Sir Charles Lee.—This story, related by the Bishop of Gloucester, 1662, is very well known. On the eve of her intended marriage with Sir W. Perkins, she was visited by her mother's spirit, announcing her approaching death at twelve o'clock next day. She occupied the intervening time with suitable preparations, and died calmly at the hour foretold.

Beresford, Lady, wife of Sir Tristam, before her marriage in 1687, made a secret engagement with Lord Tyrone, that whichever should die first would appear to the other. He fulfilled his promise on October 15th, 1693, and warned her of her death on her forty-eighth birthday. All was kept secret, but after the fated day had passed, she married a second time, and appeared to enter on a new lease of life. Two years later, when celebrating her birthday, she accidentally discovered that she was two years younger than had been supposed, and expired before night. The story is one of the best known and most interesting in ghost-lore.

Fanshaw, Lady, when visiting in Ireland, heard the banshee of the family with whom she was visiting, one of whom did in fact die during the night. She also relates (in her " Memoirs," p. 28) that her mother once lay as dead for two days and a night. On her return to life she informed those about her that she had asked of two apparitions, dressed in long, white garments, for leave, like Hezekiah, to live for fifteen years, to see her daughter grow up, and that it was granted. She died in fifteen years from that time.

Maidstone, Lady, saw a fly of fire as premonitory of the deaths, first, of her husband, who died in a sea-fight with the Dutch, May 28th, 1672, and second, of her mother-in-law, Lady Winchilsea.

Chedworth, Lord, was visited by a friend and fellow-sceptic, saying he had died that night and had realised the existence of another world. While relating the vision the news arrived of his friend's death.

Rambouillet, Marquis of, had just the same experience. A fellow-unbeliever, his cousin, the Marquis de Précy, visited him in Paris, saying that he had been killed in battle in Flanders, and predicting his cousin's death in action, which shortly occurred in the battle of the Faubourg St. Antoine. (Quoted by Calmet from "Causes Célèbres," xi. 370.)

Lyttleton, Lord (third), died November 27th, 1799, was warned of his death three days earlier, and exhorted to repentance. The story, very widely quoted, first appears in the *Gentleman's Magazine*, vol. lxxxv. 597. He also himself appeared to Mr. Andrews, at Dartford Mills, who was expecting a visit from him at the time.

Middleton, Lord, was taken prisoner by the Roundheads after the battle of Worcester. While in prison he was comforted by the apparition of the laird Bocconi, whom he had known while trying to make a party for the king in Scotland, and who assured him of his escape in two days, which occurred.

Balcarres, Lord, when confined in Edinburgh Castle on suspicion of Jacobitism, was visited by the apparition of Viscount Dundee—shot at that moment at Killiecrankie.

Holland, Lord (the first), who was taken prisoner at the battle of St. Neot's in 1624, is said still to haunt Holland House, dressed in the cap and clothes in which he was executed.

Montgomery, Count of, was warned by an apparition to flee from Paris, and thus escaped the Massacre of St. Bartholomew. (See Coligni.)

Shelburne, Lord, eldest son of the Marquis of Lansdowne, is said, in Mrs. Shimmelpenninck's Memoirs, to have had, when five years old, a premonitory vision of his own funeral, with full details as to stoppages, etc. Dr. Priestley was sent for, and treated the child for slight fever. When about to visit his patient (whom he expected to find recovered) a few days later, he met the child running bareheaded in the snow. When he approached to rebuke him the figure disappeared, and he found that the boy had died at the moment. The funeral was arranged by the father, then at a distance, exactly in accordance with the premonition.

Eglinton, Lord, was three times warned of his death by the apparition of the family ghost, the Bodach Glas—the dark-grey man. The last appearance was when he was playing golf on the links at St. Andrews, October 4th, 1861. He died before night.

Cornwall, The Duke of, in 1100, saw the spectre of William Rufus pierced by an arrow and dragged by the devil in the form of a buck on the same day that he was killed. (Story told in the "Chronicle of Matthew Paris.")

Chesterfield, Earl of (second), in 1652, saw, on waking, a spectre with long white robes and black face. Accepting it as intimation of some illness of his wife, then visiting her father at Networth, he set off early to inquire, and met a servant with a letter from Lady Chesterfield, describing the same apparition.

Mohun, Lord, killed in a duel in Chelsea Fields, appeared at the moment of his death, in 1642, to a lady in James's Street, Covent Garden, and also to the sister (and her maid) of Glanvil (author of "Sadducismus Triumphatus").

Swifte, Edmund Lenthal, keeper of the Crown jewels from 1814, himself relates (in "Notes and Queries," 1860, p. 192) the appearance, in Anne Boleyn's chamber in the Tower, of "a cylindrical figure like a glass tube, hovering between the table and the ceiling" visible to himself and his wife, but not to others present.

PART II

HAUNTED HOUSES

CHAPTER I

SOME HAUNTED CASTLES

THERE is a certain uncanny fascination about haunted houses, but it is one of which it may emphatically be said that distance lends enchantment to the view. There is something much more thrilling in looking at a haunted house from the outside and reading of it at a distance of many miles, than spending a sleepless night within its walls. It has never been my good fortune to sleep in a haunted house, but on one occasion I went to sleep in the ruins of a haunted castle, and was awakened with a shuddering horror that I shall never forget as long as I live.

Haunted Hermitage. It was in Hermitage Castle, Hermitage, that grim old border stronghold which stood in Liddesdale, not many miles from Riccarton, that most desolate of railway junctions. I visited it when I was just out of my teens, with a mind saturated with legendary lore of the Scotch border. I made a pilgrimage to Brankesome Hall, taking Hermitage on my way. I write this, not to maintain the objectivity of any ghostly haunting of Hermitage Castle, but to show that although it may all have been the merest delusion of a subjective character, I have at least gone through an experience which enables me to understand what it feels like to be in a haunted house.

Hermitage Castle, one of the most famous of the Border keeps in the days of its splendour, retains to this day a pre-eminence among the castles of the Scotch border :—

" Haunted Hermitage,
Where long by spells mysterious bound,
They pace their round with lifeless smile,
And shake with restless foot the guilty pile,
Till sink the mouldering towers beneath the burdened ground."

Lord Soulis, the evil hero of Hermitage, made a compact with the devil, who appeared to him, so runs the legend, in the shape of a spirit wearing a red cap, which gained its hue from the blood of human victims in which it was steeped. Lord Soulis sold himself to the demon, and in return he could summon his familiar whenever he chose to rap thrice on an iron chest, on condition that he never looked in the direction of the spirit. Once, however, he forgot or ignored this condition, and his doom was sealed. But even then the foul fiend kept the letter of his compact. Lord Soulis was protected by an unholy charm against any injury from rope or steel; hence cords could not bind him and steel would not slay him. When, at last, he was delivered over to his enemies, it was found necessary to adopt the ingenious and effective expedient of rolling him up in a sheet of lead and boiling him to death.

> " On a circle of stones they placed the pot,
>   On a circle of stones but barely nine ;
>   They heated it red and fiery hot,
>   And the burnished brass did glimmer and shine.
>   They rolled him up in a sheet of lead—
>   A sheet of lead for a funeral pall ;
>   They plunged him into the cauldron red,
>   And melted him body, lead, bones, and all."

That was the end of Lord Soulis's body, but his spirit still lingers superfluous on the scene. Once every seven years he keeps tryst with Red Cap on the scene of his former devilries :

> " And still when seven years are o'er,
>   Is heard the jarring sound,
>   When hollow opes the charmèd door
>   Of chamber underground."

When I visited Hermitage Castle I was all alone, with my memory teeming with associations of the past. I unlocked the door with the key, which I brought with me from the keeper's cottage, at a little distance down the valley. As it creaked on its hinges and I felt the chill air of the ruin, I was almost afraid to enter. Mustering my courage, however, I went in and explored the castle, then lying down on the mossy bank I gave myself up to the glamour of the past. I must have been there an hour or more when suddenly, while the blood seemed to freeze down my back, I was startled by a loud prolonged screech, over my head, followed by a noise which I could only compare to the trampling of a multitude of iron-shod feet through the stone-paved doorway. This was alarming enough, but it was nothing to the horror which filled me when I heard the heavy gate swing on its hinges with a clang which for the moment seemed like the closing of a vault in which I was entombed alive. I could almost hear the beating of my heart. The rusty hinges, the creaking of the door, the melancholy and unearthly nature of the noise, and the clanging of the gate, made me shudder and shiver as I lay motionless, not daring to move, and so utterly crushed by the terror that had fallen upon me that I felt as if I were on the very verge of death. If the evil one had appeared at that moment and carried me off I should have but regarded it as the natural corollary to what I had already heard. Fortunately no sulphureous visitant darkened the blue sky that stretched overhead with his unwelcome presence, and after a few minutes, when I had recovered from my fright, I ventured into the echoing doorway to see whether or not I was really a prisoner. The door was shut, and I can remember to this day the tremour which I experienced when I laid my hand upon the door and tried whether or not it was locked. It yielded to my hand, and I have seldom felt a sensation of more profound relief than when I stepped across the threshold and felt that I was free once more. For a moment it was as if I had been delivered from the grave itself which had already closed over my head. Of course, looking back upon this after a number of years, it is easy to say that the whole thing was purely subjective. An overwrought fancy, a gust of wind whistling through the crannies and banging the door close were quite sufficient to account for my fright, especially as it is not at all improbable that I had gone to sleep in the midst of the haunted ruins.

So I reasoned at the moment, and came back and stayed another hour in the castle, if only to convince myself that I was not afraid. But neither before nor after that alarm did any gust of wind howl round the battlements with anything approaching to the clamour which gave me such a fright. One thing amuses me in looking back at a letter which I wrote at the time, describing my alarm. I say, "Superstition, sneer you? It may be. I rejoiced that I was capable of superstition; I thought it was dried out of me by high pressure civilisation." I am afraid that some of my critics will be inclined to remark that my capacities in that direction stand in need of a great deal of drying up.

An Irish Castle and its Ghosts. If the foregoing narrative may be regarded as little better than a second cousin to an authentic ghost, this cannot be said of the story of another haunted castle which I will proceed to relate. In this case the castle is undoubtedly haunted, and the lady of the castle, who is a great friend of mine, is my authority for the narrative. Mrs. D—— is the only friend in a tolerably large circle of acquaintances who has not only seen a ghost, but has been touched by one. She is a young English lady of considerable force of character and originality. She rides to the hounds, is a good shot, and is the last person in the world whom you would suspect of morbid fears on the subject of the supernatural. The best proof that she is not timid is shown by the fact that, notwithstanding her visible and tangible experience of the spectre, she continues to live in the castle which it frequents, and after she got over the first shock of its acquaintance contrived to find existence quite supportable under the same roof. L—— Castle, in Ireland, is one of the most famous haunted castles in the three kingdoms. As far back as the sixteenth century it was famous for its ghosts, and it remains famous to this day. It has its haunted chambers, its murder hole, its dungeons, and a family of spectral inhabitants which for eleven months in the year go about the castle in a harmless and inoffensive manner. In the month of November they wax obstreperous, and for the last ten years at least no member of the family has been able to face the November ghosts. Tradition has it that in the month of November some ancient Irish notable, I believe called O'Callaghan, murdered his wife in L—— Castle, and ever since that date that ill-omened month has been set apart for a kind of demoniac high jinks, which render the place almost uninhabitable. In the other eleven months of the year its normal complement of ghosts is two, one a little old man in green, the other the conventional ghost in whitish grey. It was the latter ghost, Mrs. D—— informs me, whose acquaintance she made within the last year or two. There is one very curious phenomenon which distinguishes this haunted castle from all others, namely, the regularity of the visits of the apparition of its ghostly inmate. Spiritualists maintain that there is nothing so punctual as your ghost; he is never late for an appointment, and you may be always certain that the spectre will be on time. Every night, year in and year out, all the dogs in a certain wing of the castle howl, at half-past eleven, after the fashion of dogs when they see ghosts. So well established is this that the howling of the dogs has become to be regarded as a kind of Greenwich time gun, a kind of daily, or rather nightly, check upon all the watches and clocks of the establishment, a very convenient arrangement which, it is hardly necessary to observe, can only be found in Ireland ! One night after eleven Mrs. D—— had gone to her own room, where she had been joined by her husband, but after some conversation he had gone down stairs again. At half-past eleven o'clock his wife came to the stair-head, and, leaning over the balustrade, called out for him to come upstairs. Nothing was further from her mind than the ghosts whom she had up to that time never seen, although, of course, she had heard the family legend of their existence. As she was looking down into the hall she was suddenly conscious of two hands being placed upon her shoulders, and looking round to see who it was, she was horrified to find herself looking into the face of a figure about her own height which had placed one of its hands upon each of her shoulders. Whether it was in male or female shape she could not say, but what she saw beyond all possibility of mistake was a human figure, looking as if it were made of grey cotton wool, which had placed its hands upon her shoulder and looked straight into her face. In an agony of fear, if the stair rails had not been in the way, she would have flung herself into the hall, but as it was she ran down stairs to her sister's room, where she fainted. On recovering she stated what she had seen. She had received such a fright that it was a fortnight before she had recovered from the nervous shock. Her testimony is perfectly clear and unmistakable ; she has never seen a ghost in her life either before or since. She was not in the least nervous, nor was she thinking of the possibility of any apparition appearing when she was startled by the sudden pressure of the spectre's hands upon her shoulder. The ghost did not speak, but simply touched her, and confronted her when she turned round. What came of it she does not know, nor has she seen it again, although it is taken as a matter of course that it is still going its rounds in the castle.

Castles, especially ancient ruined feudal castles, are remarkable as the natural habitat of the conventional ghost. " Beneath these battlements, within these walls, no end of foul crimes were perpetrated by these robber chiefs." And it is but in the fitness of things that the ghosts of these ancient chieftains should wander desolately round the ruins which witnessed in ancient times their deeds of violence and crime. At the same time, it must be admitted that it is seldom that the ghost which haunts the battlements is the perturbed spirit of the wicked lord. It is, perhaps, more frequently that of some humble retainer, or some hunted priest, or sometimes that of some injured victim of the vanished oppressor.

Some North-umbrian Castles. Tyneside abounded with stories of haunted castles, but with the doubtful exception of Dilston, where Lady Derwentwater was said to revisit the pale glimpses of the moon, to expiate the restless ambition which impelled her to drive Lord Derwentwater to the scaffold, none of them were leading actors in the tragedies of old time. There is, for instance, the ghost of Callaly Castle, of which a Northumbrian correspondent sends me the following account :—

" In August I was with the Society of Antiquaries at Callaly Castle, the seat of Major A. H. Browne, and Mrs. Browne told me a ghost story about the place. In the older part of the castle, which was the pele-tower of the Claverings, there was known to be a room walled-up. During Major Browne's absence —I think he was taking a trip to India—Mrs. Browne, with the curiosity of her sex, had the wall broken into, but the room was found to be quite empty. She says, however, that she let a ghost out who is known as ' The wicked Priest.' Ever since they have been annoyed with the most unaccountable noises, which are sometimes so loud that you would think the house was being blown down. There are tramplings along the passages and noises in some of the bedrooms. I believe the ghost has been seen—it is a priest with a shovel hat. Mrs. Browne showed me the chamber, which is close to the roof. Probably it was one of those ' priests' hiding-holes ' of post-Reformation times. I am sorry I did not make notes of all Mrs. Browne told me."

Then there is the seat of the Trevelyans, where there is a haunted chamber. A lady who spent several nights in it gave me a very graphic account of her experiences. She was a Northumbrian, with a nerve which was quite proof against all spectral terrors ; but her motherly heart was grieved to hear all through the night the incessant wailing of a spectral child. No baby was on the premises, as the old squire particularly objected to the presence of children ; but all the same, all night through, the cry of the baby, as if in pain, was distinctly audible in the haunted room. In the middle of the night, also, the door which was between the bedroom and dressing-room moved mysteriously to and fro, as if persons were passing through it, and at a certain hour of the night there was heard a heavy fall in the adjoining room, as if some one had fallen heavily on the floor. When inquiring next morning as to the origin of these mysterious sounds, they were told in whispers that those rooms were haunted, and that in the room where the fall of the heavy body had been heard, a member of the family many years before had committed suicide. The ruins of Seaton Delaval Castle are said to be haunted, but of this I can find no authentic record. Churton Hall, at one time the seat of the Duke of Argyle, has marked Tyneside with the ghost of the Duke's mistress, who is locally known as "Silky." She was seen last by a nephew of Mr. Skipsey, the miner poet, who has been kindly interviewed for me by a correspondent in the North.

Writing on December 7th, 1891, my correspondent says :—

"I called upon Mr. Skipsey's nephew last Saturday. His name is Robert R——. He lives at Churton. He is a man of about forty, as fine a specimen of a Northumbrian miner as you could meet. He struck me as being a quiet, steady-going, intelligent man, very matter-of-fact in his statements. The account that Mr. Skipsey gave me of R——'s meeting with 'Silky' was inaccurate in one point. R—— was not proceeding towards the Balk Well, but towards the river. On my asking him whether he had had anything to drink, he admitted calling at the Hopewell Pit Inn and having two glasses of beer. He assured me, however, he was perfectly sober. He had been seeing his sweetheart, and was certainly not thinking of 'Silky' as he went down the lane ; in fact, I understood him to say that, being a comparative stranger in the district, he knew nothing about the phantom lady. 'Silky' came out of the hedge on the left-hand side of the road, and stood right before him. She came so close to him that he could distinctly see her face. She was a tall, elderly woman —he thought her age was between fifty and sixty—and she wore a bonnet, 'something like what the Salvation Army lasses wear,' he said. (This item of information is valuable. She was evidently a lady of the eighteenth century.) On her right was a 'black cur dog.'

"She raised her arm above R——'s head, and he fancies she must have touched the top of his head, as he felt a peculiar sensation run through him. He was too astounded to speak. He had both his hands in his pockets, but, such was her effect on him that, though he tried, he could not draw them out. She glided back into the hedge. A sound like a twig snapping made him fear she was coming back, and in a state of great fear he took to his heels.

"I asked him if her dress made a rustling sound. He said no. The dress was a black one. The apparition seemed to him like a shadow. Personally, I should be disposed to consider that he had been frightened by the shadow of a waving branch, had he not been so explicit about the face and bonnet."

A Haunted Castle in Wales. I close this very brief chapter with the following narrative of a haunted castle in Wales, sent me by a correspondent in the Principality, who supplements his narrative by the names and addresses, which I am only permitted to indicate by initials :—

"At the Assizes held at C——, in the spring of 1859, a case was tried in which one D—— W——, a solicitor's clerk, was tried, on the accusation of a man named D—— G——, on the charge of suborning a witness. Public sympathy in the Vale of C—— was universally on the side of the accused, the other party being a man of a very low moral type, who was eventually imprisoned for a year and a half for writing a threatening letter, and who was also strongly suspected of murdering his housekeeper. In stopping the case at an early stage the judge stated that, in his opinion, the positions of the accuser and accused ought to be reversed. To show their appreciation of the verdict, the inhabitants of the little market town of L——, and the neighbouring village of Trefino, determined to celebrate the event with illuminations and fireworks. Amongst others who were highly delighted with D—— W——'s acquittal was Miss M——, lady housekeeper at the noble castle of G——, who had business transactions with and highly appreciated D—— W——'s honesty and integrity. She, together with her niece, a Miss S——, in order to see the illuminations, etc., sat up till about midnight at a window commanding the town. Wishing also to see the F—— display, she left her niece and went along a passage which led to the north side of the house. She had not proceeded many yards when, to her surprise, she noticed a figure standing in the middle of the passage. Her first impression was that J—— F——, the old gardener, had taken to masquerading in honour of the event. In retreating before her the figure had to pass one of the windows, through which the moon shone brilliantly, and then she saw what appeared to be the presentment of a gentleman of the early part of the seventeenth century. She described him as being dressed in dark velvet, with knee breeches, silk hose, and buckled shoes. His hair hung in long curls over a large point-lace collar. The face reminded her of the portraits she had seen of Charles I. She followed him as far as the cross passage leading to the (reported) haunted room, the figure continuing to beckon to her. Here her terror overcame her, and, rushing back to her niece, she swooned. Her hair, previously showing a few streaks of grey, she declared turned perfectly white in that one night of terror. This was her first and last experience of the supernatural during her thirty-five years' residence in the beautiful but rather melancholy-looking castle of G——. Some members of the G—— family, residing at the magnificent family mansion of G——, in L——, having heard of her adventure, requested her attendance there, so that they might hear her own narrative of the affair, as she declared she could not identify the figure with any of the family portraits of the Dukes of A——, the W——s, of G—— (by Lely, Sir Joshua Reynolds, and other artists), which were at the castle. After giving full particulars, she was requested to visit the splendid picture gallery, to see if she could recognise any one of the portraits as representing the unearthly visitor. After looking over the endless collection for some time, she stood opposite one representing a member of the W—— family, who, she said, lived at G—— between 1630 and 1640, but she did not mention his name."

CHAPTER II

WILLINGTON MILL

ALL these hauntings of castles and halls fade into in-
significance compared with the famous haunting of Willington Mill.

I spent my boyhood within a mile of this mill, which is one
of the most famous haunted houses in existence. My father's
deacon, Mr. Edward Elliott, one of the most excellent and
sober-minded of men, lived in the house, and the stories of
the hauntings were familiar to me from my childhood. I well
remember the awed feeling with which I felt myself alone in
the house when I was a very small boy, but I saw nothing and
heard nothing. Of the reality of the apparitions which were
seen and the noises which were heard no rational person can
doubt, unless it be a sign of rationality absolutely to reject
the concurrent testimony of a number of credible witnesses,
many of whom approached the subject in the spirit of utter
scepticism.

The story of Willington Mill has so often been referred to
in a more or less fragmentary fashion by all of those who have
been interested in the subject of the haunting of houses, that
it may be well to take advantage of the present opportunity to
place on record the exact truth so far as it can be known at
the present time.

The Mill on
the Gut.
Willington Mill stands on what is locally known
as Willington Gut, a sluggish tidal stream which
empties itself into the Tyne between Willington
Quay and Wallsend. The valley is crossed by a railway
viaduct. The mill itself is said to have been built upon the
site of a cottage occupied a hundred years ago by a witch,
but that is a hazy and nebulous tradition which has never
been verified. The best account of the mill and its hauntings was published by the *Newcastle Weekly Leader*, the
writer being an old acquaintance of mine, Mr. Robert
Davidson, of Rose Hill, Willington. Mr. Davidson is the

son of a housemaid who spent eight years in the haunted house in the service of Mrs. Proctor, and he is, therefore, the natural heir and depositary of the local legends on the subject. The house which adjoins the mill was formerly occupied by Mr. Proctor, a member of the Society of Friends, an upright man, diligent in business, and universally respected by all who knew him. He had a partner of the name of Unthank, and when Mr. Davidson begins his story, some forty or fifty years ago, the Mill House was made so uncomfortable by unaccountable noises that Mr. Proctor and Mr. Unthank made arrangements to occupy it alternately four years at a time. Mr. Unthank did not believe in the ghost, and he got through his four years pretty comfortably. He is said to have heard a mangle going all night shortly after his arrival in the house, and on ascertaining that no mangle was on the premises, he became judiciously silent as to his unbelief in the hauntings of the mill.

When Mr. Unthank had done his four years, Mr. Proctor came to live at Willington, and brought with him Davidson's mother, then a servant girl of the name of Mary Young. She, like the Proctors, was a pious and trustworthy witness, and whatever she may at first have thought of the haunting, she seems to have become acclimatised. During the eight years' service with Mrs. Proctor, Mary Young only "saw something" on three occasions. One Whit-Monday, after dinner, while washing up the dishes in the kitchen, she heard a footstep on the passage, and saw a lady in a lavender-coloured dress pass the kitchen door, go upstairs, and enter one of the upper rooms. She at once informed Mrs. Proctor that a lady had gone upstairs, and entered the room over the sitting-room. Mrs. Proctor replied that she expected no visitors, but that she had heard a great noise in that room, "nor will I stay any longer, but go with thee into the kitchen."

The Lady in Lavender.

The second occasion on which she saw anything was more curious, and as the sight was shared by Mr. Davidson's father, who was at that time courting the maid of the mill, I quote it from the narrative :—

(1) Cat
(2) Rabbit
(3) Sheep.

"On one occasion, during the period that Thomas was courting Mary, he was standing at the window outside (no followers being allowed inside, lest fabulous reports were sent abroad). He had given the usual signal. The night was clear, and the stars beamed forth their light from a cloudless sky. Suddenly something appeared which arrested my father's attention. Looking towards the mill, which was divided from the house by an open space, he beheld what he supposed was a whitish cat. It came walking along in close proximity to his feet. Thinking Miss Puss very cheeky, he gave her a kick ; but his foot felt nothing, and it quietly continued its march, followed by my father, until it suddenly disappeared from his gaze. Still the ghost was not thought of by him. Returning to the window, and looking in the same direction, he again beheld it suddenly come into existence. This time it came hopping like a rabbit, coming quite as close to his feet as before. He determined to have a good rap at it, and took deliberate aim ; but, as before, his foot went through it and felt nothing. Again he followed it, and it disappeared at the same spot as its predecessor. The third time he went to the window, and in a few moments it made its third appearance, not like unto a cat or a rabbit, but fully as large as a sheep, and quite luminous. On it came, and my father was fixed to the spot. All muscular power seemed for the moment paralysed. It moved on, disappearing at the same spot as the preceding apparitions. My father declared that if it was possible for 'hair to stand on end,' his did just then. Thinking for once that he had seen sufficient, he went home, keeping the knowledge of this scene to himself."

Next day he called at the mill, and told Mr. Proctor what he had seen. Mr. Proctor listened to his story, and then told him he had seen the same thing himself on another occasion, on the front of the house. These were the only two apparitions visible to either Mr. or Mrs. Thomas Davidson. If they saw little they heard much.

Mysterious Noises. The noises that went on intermittently in the mill were only too frequent and unmistakable. Mr. Proctor did his level best to ascertain what caused the noises, but it was all in vain. The floors of the house were taken up, but nothing was found ; then the floors were covered with meal, in order that the footmarks might be detected ; but the ghost of Willington Mill trod with too light a step even to leave a trace upon the flour-strewn floor, and the utmost diligence of the inquirers was baffled. Sometimes the noises were very violent. On the Whit-Monday on which Mrs. Davidson saw the lady in the lavender silk dress, the uproar in the house was the worst that was known during the eight years. Noises were kept up so violently all night that neither the family nor the servants got a wink of sleep.

About midsummer in the year 1840 Mr. Edward
The Report of Drury, of Sunderland, asked Mr. Proctor to be
Mr. Drury. allowed to remain in the house all night with no
other companion than his watch dog, upon whose courage and
fidelity he said he put more reliance than on any three gentlemen known to him. Mr. Proctor accepted Mr. Drury's offer,
and on the 3rd of July Mr. Drury with pistols and a Mr.
Thomas Hudson, whom he had substituted for his dog, made
arrangements to spend the evening in the house. Mr. Proctor
was also in the house. After the doors had been locked, Mr.
Drury and Mr. Hudson examined every room most minutely,
and satisfied themselves that there was no one in the house
except themselves and Mr. Proctor. It was ten days before
Mr. Drury sufficiently recovered from the experiences of that
night to be able to write out an intelligible report of what had
happened. It seems that Mr. Drury, although he had a brace
of pistols in his pocket, had not loaded them. After the
examination of the house he and Mr. Drury sat down on a
third-story landing, about eleven o'clock at night. At ten
minutes to twelve they both heard a noise as if a number
of people were pattering with their bare feet upon the floor.
A few minutes afterwards they heard a noise as if some one
was knocking with his knuckles amongst their feet; then they
heard a hollow cough from an adjoining room, and a sound as
if a person was rustling against the wall coming upstairs.

At ten minutes to one o'clock Mr. Drury took
The Lady in out his watch to ascertain the time, and on look-
Grey. ing up from it his eyes became rivetted upon the
closet door, which he distinctly saw open. From the open
door appeared the figure of a female attired in greyish
garments, with the head bending downwards and her left
hand pressed against her chest; the right hand was extended
towards the floor with the index-finger pointing downwards.
Mr. Hudson had gone to sleep, and the grey lady advanced
cautiously across the floor, extending its right hand towards
him. At that moment Mr. Drury rushed at it, giving a most
awful yell, but instead of grasping it he fell upon his friend,
and recollected nothing distinctly for nearly three hours afterwards. Mr. Proctor, who heard the shriek, carried him downstairs. Mr. Drury was beside himself with fright, crying out
in agony, "There she is. Keep her off. For God's sake,
keep her off!" For nearly three hours he kept on saying
this, after which he came to himself, and said that not for
£10,000 would he put his foot across the door-step of that

house again. Mr. Hudson, who was asleep and was awakened by the shriek, saw nothing. Writing upon what he called "that horrid and most awful affair," Mr. Drury said that no one could have gone into that house more disbelieving in respect to anything happening, but that no one could be more satisfied than himself.

By the Mouth of Thirty Witnesses. "I am persuaded," he told Mr. Proctor, "of the horrid apparition, that I would affirm that what I saw with my own eyes was a punishment to me for my scoffing and unbelief." "Happy," he added, "are those that believe and have not seen." Mr. Proctor wrote to him in acknowledging this letter as follows :—

> "WILLINGTON, 7th mo.
> "9th, 1840.

"RESPECTED FRIEND, EDWARD DRURY,—

"Having been at Sunderland I did not receive thine of the 6th till yesterday morning. I am glad to hear that thou art getting well over thy unlooked-for visitation. I hold in respect thy bold and manly assertion of the truth in the face of that ridicule and ignorant conceit with which that which is called the supernatural in the present day is usually assailed. I shall be glad to receive thy detail in which it will be needful to be very particular in showing that thou couldst not be asleep, or attacked by nightmare, or mistake a reflection of the candle as some sagaciously suppose.

"I remain, thine respectfully,
"JOSEPH PROCTOR.

"P.S.—I have about thirty witnesses to various things which cannot be satisfactorily accounted for on any other principle than that of spiritual agency."

Mr. Joseph Proctor was acclimatised to the ghost, but his family were less bold, and the visitation caused great terror in the household, and no wonder, for the noises were enough to try the nerves of the boldest.

The Noises. Sometimes, says Mr. Davidson, the noise was like a paviour at work with his rammer thumping on the floor, making all things rattle and shake that were not fixtures. Again it was like a donkey galloping round the room overhead ; at another time it was as if a shovelful of scrappy iron had been thrown upon the fireplace and fender. It was very difficult to get servants to remain in the house. Heavy footsteps were heard going up and down stairs, door handles turned, doors creaked as. if they were opening, occasionally the room would be filled with bluish smoke. Sticks would crackle as if they were burning, but when the closet door was opened no fire was to be seen. At other times it was as if newspapers were being crumpled and trampled about football fashion. On one occasion Mr. Davidson's mother counted 120 taps on the wash-table, as if some one were striking it with a pencil. On another occasion the spirit made itself so fearfully palpable in Mr. Proctor's bedroom, that he adjured it in the following words :—" If thou art a good spirit, why not stay in thy own place? if thou art a bad spirit, why torment me and my house?" With a great noise the spirit took its departure for that night. Next night, however, it was as busy as ever. But it was not only by noises that it inconvenienced the denizens.

One Ghost seen by Two at one time. When two of Mrs. Proctor's sisters were staying at the mill on a visit, their bed was suddenly violently shaken, the curtains hoisted up all round to their tester and then as rapidly let down again, and this again in rapid succession. The curtains were taken off the next night, with the result that they both saw a female figure of mysterious substance and of a greyish blue hue come out of the wall at the head of the bed and lean over them. They both saw it distinctly. They saw it come out of and go back again into the wall. After that they refused to sleep any more in the mill, and no wonder. Mr. Davidson's sister-in-law had a curious experience on one occasion. One evening she was putting one of the bedrooms right, and looking towards the dressing-table, she saw what she supposed was a white towel lying on the ground. She went to pick it up, but imagine her surprise when she found that it rose up, and went up behind the dressing-table over the top, down on the floor across the room, disappeared under the door, and was heard to descend the stairs with a heavy step. The noise which it made in doing so was distinctly heard by Mr. Proctor and others in the house.

Another Ghost seen by Four. I have never been able to make out exactly whether there was only one ghost or several in the mill. If only one it could assume various shapes. On one occasion, Mr. Mann the old mill foreman, with his wife and daughter, and Mrs. Proctor's sister, all four saw the figure of a bald-headed old man in a flowing robe like a surplice gliding backwards and forwards about three feet from the floor, level with the bottom of the second story window; he then stood still in the middle of the window, and the part of the body, which appeared quite luminous, showed through the blind. While in that position the framework of the window was invisible, while the body was as bright as a star, and diffused a radiance all around; then it turned a bluish tinge, and gradually faded away from the head downwards. On one occasion Mr. Robert Davidson's father spent a night in the house. He saw nothing, but at midnight a noise began which continued about fifteen minutes, and gradually became louder and louder, until it became so deafening that it was as if rivetters were at work on a boiler in the room. His companion was asleep, Davidson nudged him, said "Jack," instantly the noise ceased. When Jack went to sleep again the noise began worse than ever in half an hour; the building seemed to shake to its very foundations. The bed curtains shook, the rings rattled; this continued for a long time; again he said "Jack," and the noises ceased.

The Door Unlocked and Unbolted. There was one feature of the Willington ghost which was peculiar. Most ghosts pass through doors, and even when they seem to open them, the doors are found locked as before. The Willington ghost, however, not merely passed through doors, but left them open. On one occasion, when family prayers were being conducted by Mr. Proctor, a noise began in the room above, a heavy footstep descended the stairs, passed the room door, and then proceeded to the front door, then the bar was removed, the lock turned, two bolts drawn back, the latch lifted, the door flung open, and the footsteps pass into the front garden. Mr. Proctor ceased reading, went out into the passage, and, behold, the door was wide open. Mrs. Proctor was almost fainting, and Mr. Proctor filled himself with gloomy reflections as to the opportunities which such ghostly habit would afford to burglars.

Spectral Animals. In November, 1841, Mr. Carr paid a visit to the house, when the figure of an animal about two feet high appeared in the window of the blue room. They made a careful search, but found nothing, although Mr. and Mrs. Mann, who were outside, saw the animal in the window without intermission for half an hour, then it began to decrease in size and gradually disappeared. That night Mr. Davidson's aunt felt a heavy blow on the chair-back as she was sitting in the nursery with the children; then the night-table was moved from one side of the room to the other without any one apparently touching it. The disturbances were so con-

tinuous that one of the millers was sent for, and he sat up all
night. Mr. Carr had a terrible night of it, and left next morning, saying that he could never come back again. The next
night Mr. Davidson's aunt and Bessy Mann saw a whitish
figure glide downstairs, cross the nursery floor, and enter a
closet, from which an hour before they had heard a prolonged
groan. Occasionally the ghost assumed the shape of an animal.
A two years' old boy saw it in the shape of a "bonny pussy,"
while Mr. Davidson's aunt thought it looked like a white
pocket-handkerchief knotted at the four corners, which kept
dancing up and down, sometimes rising as high as the first
floor window. One day, when his aunt was cleaning boots by
the kitchen table, she was suddenly startled by the bark of a
dog, and two paws were heavily laid upon her shoulders, so as
to make her lay hold of the table for support. Mrs. Proctor
ran into the kitchen, but no dog could be found, and all the
doors were shut, and there were no dogs in the house. Rev.
Mr. Caldwell, my father's predecessor at the Congregational
Church, Howden, sat up all night with another minister, but
saw nothing, although they heard noises as if bass mats were
being drawn over the floor.

Mr. John Richardson, an old and trusty servant
The Ghost and the Bible. of Mr. Proctor's, on one occasion sat up with an
old Quaker gentleman who had come to discover
the cause of the disturbances. The old Quaker asked Mr.
Richardson to get a Bible, and he would read a chapter. No
sooner did he begin to read than the candle began to jump in
the candlestick and to oscillate to such an extent that the
Quaker could not see to read. The moment he stopped, the
candle became quiet. The old Quaker looked at Mr. Richardson, and said, "Strange!" He began to read again, and again
the candle began to sway from side to side. "Art thou afraid,
John?" said the Quaker. "No," said John, "but I feel a
peculiar sensation which I cannot describe." "Let us pray,
John," said the Quaker. Immediately a terrific noise arose in
the room, all the furniture seemed to be driven from its place,
the candlesticks rattled on the table, newspapers seemed to be
scattered to and fro in great profusion, the whole building
seemed shaken. So terrible was the hubbub that John could
not hear a single word of the Quaker's petition. The moment
the Quaker arose from his knees everything became quiet.
Another Quaker, who faced the intruder with a bold "Who
art thou? In the name of the Lord, I bid thee depart," was
received with a mocking sound which Mr. Davidson says only

can be described as a spasmodic suction of the air through the teeth.

The Ghost with Eyeholes but no Eyes. The children, however, were the chief ghost-seers. No one was allowed to tell them anything about the ghost, and any servant who told a fairy tale in Willington Mill was instantly dismissed. No conspiracy of silence, however, would prevent the children from seeing the ghost. On one occasion one of the little girls came to Mrs. Davidson and said, "There is a lady sitting on the bed in mamma's bedroom. She had eyeholes, but no eyes; and she looked so hard at me." On one occasion a little girl told Mrs. Davidson that on the previous night a lady had come out of the wall and looked into the glass; she had something tied over her head; she had eyeholes, but no eyes. On another occasion a boy of two years old was charmed with the ghost; he laughed and kicked, crying out, "Ah! dares somebody, peepee, peepee." On several occasions the children would have much amusement in chasing up or downstairs a "funny cat or a bonny monkey," which they saw before them.

The Ghost that Snuffed the Candle. On one occasion his mother saw through the bed curtain a figure cross the room to the table on which the light was burning, take up the snuffers and snuff the candle, then cross the room towards the bed, laid its hand upon the curtains all round the bed, and then strike the side table with such force that she thought the furniture seriously damaged, but when she examined it, it was uninjured. The last time the apparition was seen was quite recently, and I well remember the story being told at Sunday School by my scholars. It was long after the Proctors had left the mill, and the manifestations, it was noticed, were always worst when a member of the Proctor family was on the premises.

The Last Apparition. On this occasion the mill was working night and day, when the engine-man, on going into the engine-house at midnight, saw the eyeless woman sitting there. With a wild scream he flung himself out of the window into the Gut, plunged through the mud and water to the opposite side, and never stopped until he reached home at Shields, some three miles off. Such at least was the story which was reported in the village. Since then the glory seems to have departed from the haunted mill. A converted rabbi inhabited the house for some time, and during his stay the manifestations partially returned; since then it has been cut up into tenements, and when I was in Newcastle Mr. Davidson informed me that there were strange sounds heard, but nothing to compare to the infernal charivari which went on fifty years ago.

Such is the story of the haunted house at Willington. Mr. Proctor has lost the diary which he kept of the strange occurrences in that undesirable residence. Mr. Edward Elliott, my father's senior deacon, was a sober, pious, most veracious old gentleman. He was loath to speak about the apparitions at the mill. Personally, he had never seen anything, but he had heard plenty. His wife and only daughter also bore witness as to the reality of the commotion made by their invisible fellow-denizens. The usual explanation is entirely out of the question, that of rats. Not all the rats that followed the Pied Piper of Hamlin to destruction could make the row which occasionally disturbed the peace of Willington Mill. From time to time various explanations were invented to account for the phenomenon of the objective reality of the manifestations of which there can be no doubt unless all the most reliable human evidence is to be regarded as worthless. But no explanation held water. The mill remains to-day, as heretofore, an insoluble mystery, with its lady in lavender, eyeless old woman, its mysterious animals, its bald-headed surpliced clergyman, and heavy footfalls, apparently produced without any visible cause.

An Unsolved Mystery.

The following is Mr. Edmund Proctor's latest information on the subject, dated October 5th, 1891 :—

" I fear I cannot help you. Tomlinson's ' Guide to Northumberland,' or the Appendix to ' Quaker Records—the Richardsons of Cleveland,' by Mrs. Boyce, contain the references to all that is published in regard to the Haunted House at Willington.

" Of what is unpublished there is little, if anything, except my father's diary, which I am under promise to send to Mr. Myers for the ' Journal of Psychical Research,' but which is not ready yet.

" The house is not pulled down, but is outwardly a wreck, and inwardly divided into tenements. There have, I believe, been no disturbances of any sort for many years.

" When the house was unoccupied, perhaps ten years ago, I visited it twice—once with a well-known ' medium,' once with a party of five, who sat up alone till 5 a.m.—and both cases were without result worth record.

" I made inquiries of the present tenants a few months ago, but they have absolutely nothing to tell."

There was an attempt made in 1853 to find out
the secret of the mystery of the mill by clairvoyance. The record of this interesting experiment
is included in Mrs. Henry Sidgwick's paper " On
the Evidence for Clairvoyance," published in the eighteenth
part of the " Proceedings of the Society for Psychical Research,"
in April, 1891. The clairvoyant was a pitman's wife in the
county of Durham, and the record of her visions collected by
Mr. Myers is one of the most extraordinary and convincing
pieces of evidence for the reality of clairvoyance in the
mesmeric state that is to be found in the archives of the
Psychical Research Society. This good woman, Mr. Myers
informs us, never received any fee, and never made any
exhibition of her powers, fearing to be suspected of being a
witch. How many rare and invaluable talents have thus been
lost to the world ! Dr. F. mesmerised her for sleeplessness,
and discovered that, when in the mesmeric state, she was
wonderfully clairvoyant.

The narrative in Mr. Sidgwick's paper is chiefly
composed of his notes. " Jane," as the clairvoy-
ante was termed, could in her mesmeric state visit
any part of the world in thought, and describe accurately places
which she had never seen, such as the interior of St. Paul's,
the building of St. Peter's in Rome, the tent of Dr. Livingstone
in Africa. " Jane " was a remarkably refined woman, sweet and
gentle-looking, with delicately cut features, and wavy dark hair.
She was very religious, conscientious, and resigned. But her
Second Self, when liberated by the mesmeric sleep, was quite
a different personality. She always spoke when in trance of
her body as " we's girl," regarding her as something quite distinct from herself, who troubles her to give her pains in her
side and face, for Jane suffered from very bad health. Her
body was without feeling when in the sleep. She could read
the thoughts of those present, and when tired would read what
she saw in the mind of the mesmeriser instead of taking the
usual journeys to which he was wishing her. The following is
the record of Dr. F.'s notes of Jane's attempt to solve the
mystery of the mill. It is interesting not merely on account
of the mill story, but as an illustration of the methods of clairvoyance. The narrative is considerably condensed.

" After sleep was produced, I said : ' We are on
a railway, and can see a large building like a mill ;
where is it?' ' Is it a mill for grinding food?' she
replied. I said, 'Yes.' She then asked, ' May we go into

the mill?' and upon my giving her leave she described the interior of the building, when I stopped her and told her to leave the mill and enter the house near it. She said a gentleman lived in the house, but directly afterwards corrected herself, and remarked he was not a gentleman, but a gentleman had formerly lived in it. She now seemed very much puzzled, her face accurately expressing the perplexity of her mind. 'Why did the gentleman leave this pretty house?' 'Oh, yes, it is something about a lady.' At last she said, in a low tone, 'Now we see it was not this gentleman's wife, for she's alive; it was a vision that frightened him away.' I now told her that I brought her to that house for the purpose of finding out why the lady haunted the house. I said she had better go back to the time when the gentleman lived in the house. She directly answered, 'Yes, we will. Now I see the gentleman has a wife and a family, and I see the vision standing before him; but why does it make these noises? Why does it now frighten them all? and why does it frighten the servants in that way so that the gentleman is forced to leave? She thinks he has no right to be there, but why has he no right to be there? It cannot be an angel of light, can it? It must be an angel of darkness, and to find out an angel of darkness we will have to go a long way to a bad place.'"

That was the beginning of it. It will be noticed that nothing was said as to the place. Dr. F. thought of the mill, and she at once went to it, and saw it, corrected her mistakes—for instance, he thought that was a large garden, in reality it was a small one—and described exactly what was to be seen. Then occurred a curious thing. Dr. F. told Jane she had better find out the gentleman. She at once said, " Shall we go again upon the railway?" and there and then went first to a town (Shields), and then to a village where after a little hunting about, she saw—always in clairvoyant-trance—Mr. Joseph Proctor, whom she had never seen or heard of before, but whom she accurately described. Jane, I should mention, had never heard of the haunted mill; she had once passed over Willington Bridge by rail, but knew absolutely nothing about the story which she was wished to unravel.

On July 21st, 1853, another experiment took **A Vision of the Ghosts.** place. This time Jane was mesmerised by a lady, Mrs. Frazer, Dr. F. being present and taking notes. On this occasion she had a very clear and accurate vision of the spirits which haunted the mill.

" 'It looks like a vision. It is a lady.' 'What is it like?'

asked the operator. 'It has a face, but not like we's face. It is very white, but she moves about so quick; she has eyes, but no sight in them; she is like a shadow.' 'Has it a name in its head?' asked Mrs. Frazer. 'No, she has no name and no brains; she is just like a shadow, and flits about so quickly from place to place. We don't care about the lady. We want to go into the house and downstairs. We want to go into the cellar. Is there a way to the sea in this house? We will go downstairs into the lowest part and take a candle. We are not a coward. We will examine and find a place to the sea. Let us look—there is a cellar Could not the gentleman examine the cellar? He must have stronger people than we to look into them, we are too weak. We can't see any place of conceal- ment. Tell him to bring somebody to look down. There must be a place of concealment. Like it ran down to the sea, and people came up for some bad purpose. It seems like something about the sea. We'll tell the gentleman with the broad hat about this. We's not afraid; there must be some- thing concealed there, and it might be found out in this cellar, and we will come and help him. Let us go to the gentleman. We want this place looked into, and, mind, not a slight exam- ination, for something will be found there.' 'Are they real people, then?' asked Mrs. Frazer. 'Well, she is a strange one, and walks about so quietly.' 'Has it spoken?' said the operator. 'Yes, it has spoken. But there are so many, there are two or three kinds of animals, We's only a coward after all.' 'What are the animals like?' inquired Mrs. Frazer. 'We won't be afraid,' was the reply. 'Do we like to look? One is like a monkey, and another like a dog. Had the lady dogs and monkeys? They go all about the house. She has got funny things, has she not? We don't like her. What is that other one? Do we know what we call it? It is not a pussy, it runs very fast, and gets amongst feet. It is a rabbit, but a very quick one.' 'Are they real animals?' said Mrs. Frazer. 'We don't touch them to see,' replied she; 'we would not like a bite. What a violent woman she is! She wants to stay all alone in that house, but we can't see into her, she is so strange. We have never seen her eat any supper nor anything else.' 'Has she a name in her head?' inquired Mrs. Frazer. 'No, she has no brains. She is now going upstairs, and it is so dark. She has no light with her, but we have light.' 'Are the animals with her now?' said Mrs. Frazer. 'No, they are not. She is all white: it is loose, not a dress like we's, but something loose thrown over her. She disturbs everybody.'

'Why don't they catch her?' asked Mrs. Frazer. 'Because she moves so quickly. But the mischief is in the cellar, and tell the gentleman to look there.'"

[Here again she slept.]

"Upon awakening she said, 'We won't have her for ours.' 'Is she always the same?' inquired the operator. 'We will look,' was the reply. 'Now she is coming downstairs again to go her rounds. She makes me feel cold. Now she is as dark as the devil. It is very strange; we don't like her.' 'Look and see what her dress is like,' said Mrs. Frazer. 'We will. It is not like we, for it is all dark. Where have we seen anything like it before? It is not like we's English ladies' dress. Where has she got that? It is like the dress we saw in foreign countries—a Spanish lady kind of dress. They are rich things she has on; it rustles like silk. Is it not strange? She is just like a devil.'"

July 28*th* or 29*th*, 1853.

Dig in the Cellar. "She was again sent to see the 'haunted house,' when she said she saw the figure of a man who also troubled them. Mrs. Frazer asked her if it was not a real man she saw. Could it not be the person who now lived there? but she said, 'No, it is a vision; he has no brains in his head; he looks very fierce, his eyes flash like a tom cat's—like a tiger's; he has a white dress on like a surplice. Oh, how angry he is! he is so indignant at being disturbed; he does not want the gentleman to find out what he is there for. It is the *man* who makes the noises in the house; he goes stamping about. We did not like the woman, but the man is far worse. Oh, how angry he is! What a commotion there is in the cellar! They have not made the hole large enough; it is not close enough to the wall. They must make a wide, deep hole close to the wall, and they should take down the wall.' Mrs. Frazer said, 'But perhaps the house will fall if they take the wall down.' She replied, 'Never mind, if they only find it out.' She said that the woman walked about with her hands upon her breast as if in pain; but the man goes stamping about very angry. 'Oh! how indignant he is that the gentleman is digging in the cellar.'"

It is noteworthy that Jane described exactly the phenomena which Mr. Davidson declared actually existed. Jane had no conceivable motive for deceiving any one. She knew nothing about it, and was completely unconscious, when she came out of the mesmeric state, of what she had seen or said.

Mr. Proctor caused excavations to be made in the cellar,

and found nothing. Local gossip, however, always asserted that when the men dug down to a certain depth they came upon a huge stone or slab, beneath which they believed the mystery lay. At that point, however, Mr. Proctor, so said Willington rumour, interfered, saying that to remove the stone would endanger the foundation of the mill, and so the mystery remains unsolved to this day.

I have an impression that Mr. Proctor denies the truth of this story. If so, there is not even a shadow of a clue to the solution of the mystery.

CHAPTER III

BROOK HOUSE

MR. RALPH HASTINGS, of Broadmeadow, Teignmouth, wrote me on October 1st, 1891, stating that some years ago he was a spectator of extraordinary occurrences in a so-called haunted house, and noted them in his diary. He adds :—

"I have often thought of making a fair copy of the same, but have been deterred by various reasons, notably the evil influences that even at this lapse of time seem to stretch towards me when I go back to them in imagination. However, if they are ever to be committed to writing, here is apparently an opportunity. Should you desire my 'relation,' perhaps you will kindly state when you will require it."

Mr. Hastings wrote on October 23rd, enclosing his MSS. He said :—

"I herewith enclose the communication. I am sorry for the delay, but, as you can imagine, it has taken a considerable time to extract from my diary and present in a readable form.

"The relation I have here set down is taken from notes of occurrences that I recorded faithfully in my diary at the time, and which, if not sensational and highly coloured as similar narrations often are, possesses at all events the advantages of being a perfectly truthful one.

"I was spending some months of the summer of '73 at a favourite watering-place on the S.E. coast. One afternoon (the 19th June) I went to visit some friends who had lived many years in an old-fashioned house which stood in a quadrangle, and was approached from the church by a narrow lane on a declivity. Brook House was a commodious red-bricked structure of three stories, faced by a court, and with its ground-floor windows unseen from the outside by reason of the lofty wall that encircled them, and which was continued sloping downwards till the base of the hill was reached. Local tradition gave it the foremost place for antiquity in a town at that

276

time abounding in old houses, but now, alas, mostly replaced
or modernised. The 'tenants at will' were an old lady, the
widow of a captain in the 79th Highlanders, and her daughter.

"On the day in question, as I approached the
First Sight of house from Church Lane, I happened to glance
the Ghost. at the window to the right on the second floor.
There I saw to my astonishment the apparent figure of Miss
B. standing partially dressed, arranging her hair, and looking intently at me. On entering the house I was at once shown into
the drawing-room, which was on the right-hand side of the door,
the dining-room being on the left. I found Miss B. sitting
reading ! Some days after (July 3rd) I called again. In the
course of conversation I asked Miss B. whether she had been
long in the room when the servant admitted me on my previous
visit. 'More than an hour,' she replied. Observing my
astonishment, she inquired the cause. 'What did I mean?'
I then told her what I had seen. In a tone of distress she replied, 'It is useless to conceal from you that strange things do
take place here. I have been observed seemingly by others
than yourself. I have not been in the room you refer to
for weeks, nor has it been occupied for years.' My curiosity
was now aroused, but scouting the idea of anything supernatural, I proposed we should go up into the room in question.

"On entering, I went to the window looking on
The Haunted to the gardens ; there were three, the third looking
Room. on to the hill at the side of the house. Throwing
up the window, the afternoon being sultry, and sitting on the
ledge, I began talking of other subjects than the matter in
hand. After some ten minutes I remarked, 'Nothing happens
when you are expecting it.' The door was open, the words
were hardly out of my mouth when a fearful sound as of a
raging crash of bells filled the air around us ; it lasted about
half a minute. There was formerly a bell in the servant's
room, which divided this from a corresponding one, but it had
long been removed, as it used to ring of its own accord.
Another singular circumstance was that about five minutes
previously we had heard distinctly some one come upstairs and
go into the room adjoining ; then we heard the servant's voice
exclaiming from down-stairs (we had heard her, or her double,
come up and go into her room, as above related, and Miss
B. had called out, 'Are you there, L.?' and she had replied)
'Did you hear those bells, Miss; they are none of ours?'
The bells ! they had literally rang in our ears as if swung
by invisible hands, and then, without a last tinkling vibra-

tion, stopped with curious suddenness. I had had enough
for one day, and shortly afterwards left. Before leaving Miss
B. related an extraordinary circumstance which took place the
night before. Having retired to rest—she occupied a room
on the first floor—on turning her face to the wall, not being
able to sleep, she saw a gossamer veil, as it seemed, thrown
over her head. Terrified, she turned, and after a little time,
thinking she had been deceived, turned again to the wall; it
was repeated.

The Legend of
Brook House. " I should like to speak here of the former history
of the house, so far as it could be learnt. In the
year 1815, just before Waterloo, some officers were
quartered in the town, and one here at Brook House ; there
was a lady, young and beautiful (so report said), with him, his
wife or otherwise was not known ; she used to be seen pacing
up and down the room with a child in her arms, apparently in
great distress ; suddenly she disappeared, and was never again
seen. Although anticipating the narrative in detail, I may
here say that, one summer afternoon, whilst in the garden, I
saw this lady distinctly walking backwards and forwards in the
room above mentioned, and, no less distinctly, I saw the child
in her arms. More than this, I then saw a figure apparently
ascend some steps in the centre of the room and suspend something from the beam that stretched athwart it.

Who Shut the
Window ? " My curiosity being now fully aroused, I went
to the house the next day, July 4th, accompanied
by a lady, a mutual friend. We went up into the
room, threw the window open—it being very hot—looking on
to the garden, and then went downstairs into the drawing-room,
where we had some music. We went up again in about half
an hour's time. Miss F. would not come, but went into the
garden. We stayed a few minutes, when we had reached the
first floor, and went into a room, a spare one, opposite to
Miss B.'s. She showed me some valuable Indian jewellery
which her father had brought her the year of the suppression
of the Mutiny. We then went upstairs, the window was *shut*,
we sat there for some time, throwing it wide open. When
we went down Miss F. said that whilst she was in the garden
and we were in the room on the first flight looking at the
jewellery she saw that the window was *shut*, and then a bulky
form came up to it ; she then left. We went down the garden,
and on looking up beheld the window shut and hasped.
Again we went upstairs ; a suffocating hot dead air pervaded
the room. On our way Miss B. had exclaimed, and, on my

inquiring the cause, said she had felt the momentary grasp of a hand round her right ankle. Wild with a fevered curiosity, and in spite of her remonstrances, I unhasped the window, flinging it open once more; we went down quickly into the garden, to the middle walk, leading to the gardener's house, whence we could command a full view of the window; it was still open.

The Ghost in Daylight. "Presently, to our horror, a figure appeared resembling Miss B., yet most unlike her; its fearful eyes were gazing at me without movement and totally expressionless. What, then, caused the arresting of the heart's pulsation (as it felt) and blood, that the moment before had burnt as it coursed madly through the veins, to be chilled to ice? This—one was face to face with a spirit, and withered by the contact. Those eyes—I can see them—I can feel them—after the lapse of nearly twenty years. Miss B. had incontinently fainted when she saw the shoulders (as she afterwards described it) of the figure. I continued gazing spellbound; like 'The Wedding Guest,' I was held by the spirit's eye, and I could not choose but look. The dreadful hands were lifted automatically; they rested on the window-sash. It came partly down, stayed a moment, then noiselessly closed, and I saw a hand rise and hasp it. I gazed steadfastly throughout. What impressed me strangely was this peculiarity, that as soon as the sash had passed the face, the latter vanished—the hands remained; the unreality of the actual movement of the window as it descended also seemed to contradict me: it suggested the (for want of a better comparison) mechanical passage of stage scenery, and some sorts of toys that are pulled by wires: it made no noise whatever. Now I distinctly recognised the shape as that of Rhoda, Miss B.'s elder sister, who had been dead some twelve years. I had never seen her during life, but I at once knew her by the resemblance to a portrait in the drawing-room, even (let cavillers laugh!) to the red bow which she always wore. The following afternoon, being July 5th, I went to Brook House, and we—*i.e.*, Miss B. and myself—went up into the room. I threw the window up. We then went into the garden, and sat in the summer-house. Presently we looked out and saw two hands at the window. They drew it a little down, then vanished to the right, as if annoyed at our seeing them. After some time we looked again, and saw the backs of two hands on the *outside* of the window, but they did not move it.

The Lady Headless. "We then went in, coming out again almost directly, and saw the window nearly closed; then upstairs into the room; and again I flung the window as wide open as it would go, and before leaving set the door open, with a heavy chair against it, but previous to this (I omitted to mention), as we were looking up at the window after the appearance of the hands, we saw a horrible object come from the right (the apparitions invariably did): it resembled a large white bundle, called by Miss B., who had before seen it, 'The headless woman'; it came in front of the window, and then began walking backwards and forwards. After the lapse of half an hour we went upstairs again, and found the chair by the window, and the door closed; thereupon I wrote ' It ' a letter to this effect: Miss B. . . . and Mr. H. present their compliments to the Lady Headless and request her acceptance of this fruit from their garden; they hope it will please, as she has often been seen admiring it. A reply will oblige, but the bearer does not wait for the answer. We put the chair once more against the door, placing the fruit and note on it; two or three times we went up, but nothing was changed.

Writing to a Ghost. "We then went and stood outside the summer house, whence a clear view of the window could be obtained; presently there came forward the headless figure, and distinctly bowed two or three times, then immediately afterwards a deafening slam of the door. The apex of this figure, which was rotund, i.e., that is neckless, once or twice dilated, and we feared seeing something, we knew not what; it then vanished, and we saw a beautiful arm come from the curtain and wave to us. Upstairs again, the door was shut; on entering we saw the chair overturned in the middle of the room, the fruit scattered in all directions, and to our horror the note, which I had folded crosswise, was charred at each corner. I took it up; but lacked the courage to open, and perhaps find a possible reply. Placing it in a plate I burnt it. The process was a very slow one, and it distilled a dark mucus.

Holy Water and the Bible. "July 6th.—At this period of my life I was a Roman Catholic, having had, *inter alia*, the efficacy of holy water duly impressed on me. Having procured some from the priest of the Mission, and promising to acquaint him with the result, I went to Brook House. We went up into the room (we found the window shut and hasped, which I opened). I then exorcised it, reciting the Lord's Prayer, and then sprinkling it with 'L'eau Santé.' Miss B. on her part placed more reliance on the Protestant Bible, which she placed on the table. July 10th.— To Brook House in the afternoon, prevailed on Miss B. to take the Bible out of the room. It was now habitually kept there, and assuredly acted as a talisman in contradistinction to the 'Aqua Sancta,' which proved of no efficacy whatever; then into garden, found the window closed, reopened it, had tea, then heard a deafening noise from upstairs. L. came down dreadfully frightened; she had been sitting in her room working, when the *other* door slammed to, and she had heard the window rattling down; into garden, and saw it was shut.

Bell Ring- ing.

"July 12th.—To Brook House in afternoon, up into the room, and removed the Bible; whilst at tea three tremendous thuds as with a steam ham- mer resounded on the ceiling above our heads, followed by two slammings of a door in quick succession. N.B.—Door and window had both been closed. A few minutes after ensued some jangling sounds as if all the basement bells had been set dancing; we found the three centre ones oscillating, those at each end were motionless, the three had communica- tion with the rooms on the first floor. We went upstairs, and I then put the door of the room wide open, setting a chair against it, placing another on the top of it, and went down again. In the course of a minute or two a loud crash was heard. We ran up and found both chairs lying on their sides, the door was not closed. At the first manifestation, during which the door and windows were closed, the big flower-stand was thrown down, and the chair on which the Bible rested when it remained in the room, was lying on its side. July 18th.—To Brook House in afternoon, opened the window of the room, leaving the Bible, but nothing happened. July 19th.—I took a friend, a Mr. S., to see the manifestations. Having removed the Bible, I threw up the window and placed a chair faceways to the large flower-stand in the window. Nothing occurred, however, so we left. I returned in the evening. Miss B. had been into the room, and found the chair removed a little to the right of the stand She was frightened and replaced the Bible. I went up; the chair was in the position she had stated.

A Startling Manifesta- tion.

"The whimsical idea now possessed me to ar- range the room like a theatre; the armchair and others I placed facing the stand; on them I laid antimacassars and books for programmes. We then went

down to the end of the garden which commanded a view of
the room, and looked: blank space, nothing more—stay! a
curious filmy vapour begins to float in the air, which slowly
coheres, evolves vague phantasms; they unite, and gradually
assume a definable shape. The headless woman fronts us at
the window, she vanishes, and an immense sheet is waved
twice or thrice from the right side of the window, something is
flung out, we walk quickly up the garden, and there under
the window lies one of the books. What had hastened our
steps was the frantic gesticulating of the servant; she was
frightened out of her senses by the peculiar sounds proceeding
from the room, but could not describe them, but that there
seemed to be a terrible hurrying to and fro, accompanied by
strange noises. Even Mrs. B., recovering slowly from a second
paralytic attack, had looked inquiringly upwards. We took
the Bible and entered the room, which was in disorder: the
flower-stand was thrown down, the two chairs widely apart,
one of the antimacassars was tightly folded up under the re-
cumbent towel-horse, the other with the towel were airing
themselves on a gigantic tree some seven feet from the win
dow.

"July 21st.—To Brook House in the afternoon,
up to the room, took 'it' or 'them' some tea in a
handless cup (which, I remarked, was the fashion
of that period), and two small slices of bread and butter, into
which L. stuck a pretty rose, half-opened; I added some
shrimps; these were put in an old saucer, and the whole set
on a small tray: it was placed in a recess of the window. I
then put the stand at a right angle with the centre of the
window, flanking it with a chair on either side; I placed a
book on one and a small box on the other; in the stand I
deposited the *Daily Telegraph*, and a bunch of keys. We
then left, removing the Bible, and shutting the door. Suddenly we heard a tremendous smash on the gravel walk, close
to our heads by the way. We were standing in the portico.
What had been the saucer was now disintegration; the tray lay
adjacent, whilst the cup was half imbedded in some ·loose
earth, but unbroken; the rest of the articles lay strewn
around. We went up into the room: the armless chair was
slightly moved, and my keys were on the floor, but that was
all. Stay! our eyes strayed to the bed, and we saw what
certainly had not been there before—a great impression—as of
some huge 'thing' having sat or lain upon it.

Tea and
Shrimps for
the Ghost.

A Ghost Breathing in the Bed. "On closer inspection, we distinctly saw the coverlet gently moving, resembling the very feeble respiration of a body beneath. We, *i.e.* L. and myself, then returned to the garden, having thrown open the window. After waiting a long time we saw what looked like a hand appear to sit on the centre of the window-sill, then from the curtain came the white figure. It disappeared, then after a moment or two the hand also ; but there must have been a ' something ' besides crouching under the window, for it heaved upwards, and seemed to fill the window for an instant. It then sank, the hand vanished, and we saw no more. We waited a long time till I spoke of going. I had noticed as a curious thing that almost always, when I had wearied of looking, seeing nothing and about to leave, something was sure to appear.

The Spectral Mother and Child. "On this occasion there suddenly presented to our view the figure of a fine tall woman, walking majestically backwards and forwards, attired in *crêpe de chine*. I saw the arms through their semi-transparent covering. I also noticed something white, as it seemed, hovering around her ; a child lay across her shoulder, and she gently caressed it with her hand ; they passed away. Then the white figure returned and distended its arms beneath its fearful drapery. Then, as ' it ' also went, we saw the right-hand curtain wrenched away ; I saw a hand in the act of drawing it away. Thinking we had seen enough for one day, we walked towards the house, and were about halfway when Miss B. came rushing to meet us (her eyes dilated with terror) and implored us to come in, as she was frightened out of her life by sounds overhead (the first floor), as of ponderous furniture being dragged about, and her mother had asked what it all meant.

Who Locked the Door? "I must here mention an incident or two I had forgotten. When we left the room the last time I had proposed turning the key, but was dissuaded. On our way upstairs we encountered an unexpected obstacle, to wit, the armchair : it was lying on the first floor landing, having been unceremoniously dropped over. On reaching the room I turned the handle of the door. It was locked ! and the key gone ! We fetched the one from the room opposite, which fitted, and entered ; the book lay open on its face, and the bottom drawer of a large wardrobe was wide open, the windows apparently as we had left them. The search for the missing key was a fruitless one ; it was *not* on the ledge over

the door, where, when last lost, it was found. I forgot also
to mention that the first time we went down we shut the door,
and on remounting found it open.

"July 23rd.—To Brook House in afternoon.
The Ghost and the Dolls. L. fetched two big dolls that had belonged to Miss
B. and her sister Rhoda. I placed them upright in
the flower-stand, with the armchair behind, then left the room,
not omitting the precaution of taking the key, thence to the
garden L. and T. All at once we saw the dolls fall backwards,
as if struck by lightning. On approaching the house, Miss B.
came running to meet us, and in a voice of terror told us that
whilst with her mother she had heard Fanny from outside the
door. Before she had recovered her composure it was repeated; it bore no resemblance to a natural voice, instead of
an articulation. It seemed an uttered breath. It came a
third time; then Mrs. B. said slowly, ' It is beginning again.'
We went upstairs (the Bible being on the balustrade); the door
was locked! I wondered vaguely whether with the missing
key L. produced the duplicate one, and we entered. The
dolls lay in the overthrown stand, and the armchair was also
on its side. We put things straight and then left. As Miss
B. and myself were sitting in the room later on, the Bible being
outside, I saw the curtain detach itself, falling and enfolding
her. That was sufficient for that day.

"August 13th.—Miss B. told me that whilst
Oh, Fanny, Fanny! sitting alone this afternoon reading, she heard 'Oh,
Fanny, Fanny !' Thinking it might have been her
mother, she went upstairs, but found her asleep. She related
how that about an hour after midnight, a tremendous knock at
the front door resounded through the house; of course there
was no one there, the outside gate of the court being locked
as usual. August 15th.—To Brook House in afternoon; up
to room, Miss B., Miss A., a friend staying in the house, and
myself. I sat with my back to the window, looking on to
Frog Hill; Miss A. in the armchair fronting window overlooking garden; Miss B. sat on the bed. I took the Bible outside.

"All at once we were startled by the sharp rap,
Miss B.'s Hair Singed. as of the knob of a stick, against the wooden
panel at the foot of the bed. Then Miss B. lost
her scissors, and after a time we saw them lying distended near
the door—no one had left their seats—then she missed her
cotton reel, this was not recovered; suddenly we smelt the
unmistakable fumes of fire, and we saw distinctly that some

of Miss B.'s hair had been singed away. We had not recovered from this fright, when a tremendous knock at the
door of the room, as with a heavy stick, startled us, followed
by a sound as if it were falling down the stairs. I rushed out
on to the landing, to the stairs, some fifty feet distant. I saw
nothing, then the phantom voice again called 'Fanny!' I now
fetched some apples, putting them in a box, and placing it in
the stand with a note to the effect that I was sorry they were
not ripe, but it was too early in the season, ending with
kindest regards. We then went down and stood in the porch.
Suddenly a rushing sound, as of something falling through the
branches of the huge tree past our heads. We found the
apples lying on the ground, and, on re-entering the room,
were assailed again with a faint smell of burning. Near the
bed I discovered the ashes of my note; the box was on the
window sill *open*.

The Ghost Dances. "August 18th.—To Brook House, and up into
the room. Almost directly a sound as of heavy
lumber rolling about in the attic overhead warned
us that 'activity' had commenced, and the door of the room
opposite closed with a terrific bang. After an interval, L. and
I volunteered to go up and explore. We closed the door, and
I had nearly gained the top step (L. was there already) when
the clanging as of a heavy railway bell filled the air; the others
came rushing out; we descended the stairs, went into the
garden and stood against the railings at the end. The white
figure appeared, bowed low, extending its arms still shrouded,
then seizing a chair, tossed it out of the window. 'It' next
commenced dancing madly about the room, then slowly seated
'itself' in the armchair.

From Realms of Sulphur. "We retraced our steps to the house, passing
the chair which lay on the lawn, up into the room.
The armchair and stand were lying on their sides.
Miss A. and myself then arranged to stay in the room, whilst
the others went into the garden. They were to wave their
handkerchiefs if they saw anything. I have omitted to mention
that although I never saw anything intangible when in the
room, yet I was always conscious when it was disturbed, by a
sense of suffocation, caused by a peculiar denseness which
suffused the chamber and seemed to pervade everything. On
this occasion I became aware, from the usual symptoms, that
'something' was breathing the same air with ourselves. Al-
mostly directly we saw Miss B.'s handkerchief waving, and she
rushed on to the lawn, imploring me to come down, if I wished

to escape serious injury. When we had descended, she told
us she had seen a vivid flame poised or hovering over my head,
and between us she distinguished, though indistinctly, as it was
more in the background, the headless lady. We essayed a
further instance, but this time L. remained with me ; the same
phenomena were presented.

"This ends my personal experiences. My health became impaired, and for upwards of two years I was invalided, but as
time wore on and the impressions waned, I gradually recovered.
I often wander back in imagination to the many mysteries
that in the 'long ago' held sway at Brook House.

Addendum. "I will relate one curious episode (as it was
told to me) in this account of the 'Haunters and
the Haunted.' Some years before (in Captain B.'s time), he
being at home on furlough, a child was staying in the house,
about eight years of age. One morning the captain was in
his room, when a tap was heard at the door, and on opening,
it admitted the scared figure of the boy; seeing something
was wrong, he asked what it was. It appeared the child had
wandered down into the breakfast room on the basement,
when from behind the door, a boy, seemingly of the same age,
had suddenly emerged, and apparently wanted to play with
him. Disguising with discretion his surprise, the captain
inquired, 'Well, why would you not play with him?' to which
the child answered, 'I was frightened, he was so very
white!'"

"All True, The extraordinary nature of this narrative led
every Word!" me to write to Mr. Hastings and ask him whether
he could produce any confirmatory evidence of
the statements which he made. He wrote in reply October
28th :—

"I have not drawn on my imaginative faculty in the slightest
degree. There was no necessity for doing so. I vouch for
the truthful reality of each and every occurrence as set down
in my MS., wherever it professes to be my personal experience,
but even the instance or two which I received at first hand I
have no hesitation in accepting, having known (names in confidence) the B.'s for many years. Mrs. B. is dead ; her
daughter married one of the N.'s of Jersey. Verification !
Facts are stubborn things, and my narrative bristles with them.
Alas ! there are more St. Thomases than believers in the
world, I am afraid. 'Unless I shall see . . . I will not
believe.' Faith is not credulity. I send you an extract from
the diary of the year in question, as far as it relates to the

subject in hand. The late Mr. Gurney, as I think I told you, asked me to draw out this relation (presumably for the Society), but I have always 'shirked' it, and I ejaculated a prayer of thankfulness as the last line was penned prior to the day of my forwarding it to you.

Explosions and Rumblings. "There was a curious episode one evening at Brook House, which I omitted to chronicle at the time, and consequently forgot to embrace in my description. One evening at supper, the day had been overcast and lowering, and the gloomy clouds which had long been hanging threateningly over our heads, at last had given way, emitting jagged and blinding flashes, followed in quick succession by deafening thunderclaps, resembling the discharges from heavy artillery; an avalanche of rain had then succeeded. Such days were always pregnant with mischief at Brook House. 'The tenants' seem to revel in the disorganisation of nature, and some mad freak was sure to happen to express their approval. On the evening in question the storm had lulled, and we had supped. I rose from my seat, took one step forward, and the sound as of a match exploding was heard. We had hardly recovered from our bewilderment, when another report took place, and then another, and yet another, came in quick succession. We were by this time considerably disturbed, and lost no time in considerately leaving the room to its 'would-be possessors.' One Sunday I met Mr. B., the uncle of Miss B., at dinner; he had come over from Sandwich, where he resided. Between the courses and some desultory conversation, a sound as of heavy shot falling and rolling was heard overhead. It was simply appalling in its vibratory action, and it gradually ceased with a slow sullen murmur. Now, had it been natural, we must have been impacted then and there, and flattened out amidst the ruins of our surroundings. Mr. B. was the first to regain the power of speech. 'Good God, Fanny, what was that!' An explanation was forthcoming, but it was a lame one, and I assisted Miss B. in diverting the conversation into a safer channel. But Mr. B. was not altogether to be thwarted. Some time after, 'That noise at dinner, Fanny, reminds me of some inexplicable sounds that disturbed me during the night, when I stayed here last summer. I slept, if you remember (for one night only), in such a room (naming the one in question); but that I knew it was nothing of the sort, I could have sworn it was 'haunted.'" Seeing we were in for it, I begged him to go on.

"It appeared that he could not sleep, yet he was naturally a sound sleeper ; some vague, indefinable feeling kept him awake ; the sensation gradually became stronger ; it was fear, it intensified, a horror sprang to life within him, it fought for the mastery and subdued him, quenching probability and reason together. He was not alone ! There was a 'Presence,' of what nature he knew not, but it was surely there ; it seemed to enter and fill his very being, pervading his senses and permeating the nerve tissues of the body. He was voiceless, he was powerless, an agonised mind in a paralysed frame. How long this lasted he knew not ; then the strain seemed somewhat lifted, and a fresh impression awaited him. The sound as of a woman's voice, wailing quietly, but with unutterable sorrow, came sighing to his ear. He listened acutely, and words unspoken, borne on the drowsy air, seemed to whisper their reflected meaning to his senses. They died away, and faint sounds as of 'far away' music, most mournful and soul-saddening, appealed to him. They sang, or seemed to sing, the 'Story of the House.' The Æolian strains rose higher, as if the long-drawn-out and pent-up agony of years would burst its bonds. Then, as if constrained by the Master Hand, they faltered, sobbed, then ceased. Nature thereupon reasserted her sway, and when he awoke it was bright morning. Do not call this a whimsical rhapsody. I have simply endeavoured to delineate the impressions as they were conveyed to me. Yet one or two last instances. One afternoon I went into the room, and was surprised to see the number of bees on the window looking over Frog Hill. An hour or two later I re-entered—they were all dead. A flower-stand figures in this history : formerly it held flowers in pots. One day a 'baleful breath' swept over them, poisoning their life's source ; it blighted and destroyed them ; it had gone, leaving a tainted odour, which clung to their disfigured petals.

"When Miss B. was asked by some friends how they liked their new house, she had replied, 'Oh, very much, but we do seem to hear the footsteps on the hill so plainly.'

"Some years after they (the B.'s) had gone, I, curious to hear the subsequent history (if any) of the house, called on the new people and made guarded inquiries. They were not imaginative people, and the house suited them, but there was one peculiarity not quite agreeable that puzzled them, the sound of a footfall that seemed to 'drop' beside them. *Crepitu modo pedis audito.*

"I find on examination of my diary, that these experiences and my private concerns are so interwoven that I must ask you to be contented with a specimen page of the year in question.

Some additional Details.

"One afternoon, Miss B. turned the handle of the drawing-room door and essayed to enter. No! Was it locked? Certainly not. Did it give at all? No! Another push, and yet another, with the same result. Aid was invoked; but it was insufficient. Additional help was forthcoming, swelling the attacking party to three in number. Suddenly, yet quickly, the door yielded, or rather collapsed, precipitating them into the room, and a 'Laugh' yawned in the air; but they had already fled in confusion.

"For this next instant, I hardly expect credence—still it is true! While sitting and conversing one afternoon, a 'peculiar' sound was heard outside. Opening the door, a 'phenomenon' (or what shall I term it?) was revealed. A 'pounce box' leisurely descending the stairs.

"Lastly, one night, William B. went up to his room at 11.30 p.m., when he recollected having left his watch on the mantel downstairs.

"He returned; but as he went by the half-opened door, to his amazement, there, in the armchair drawn to the fire (he had replaced it before leaving against the wall), and gazing intently or vacantly—which?—at the smouldering embers, sat his dead sister Rhoda, or rather her 'appearance.' Pulling himself together he passed the door, and entered. 'It' had gone, but the chair witnessed to what he had seen. He then remembered that it was the anniversary of her death."

Two other Haunted Houses.

Mr. Hastings sends us the following notes concerning two other haunted houses known to him :—

Copley House.

"Copley House, erected probably about the same period as Brook House, resembled it to some extent in outward appearance, the court and walled gardens excepted. As long as I could remember anything, it had a fascination for me on account of a tradition respecting it. This (affecting me nearly as a descendant) related how that in a certain year, when the reign of George III. had slipped a decade, an ancestress, while sitting in a room overlooking the street, suddenly saw a 'something.' The moment after, leaping from the window, she was outside. I now take up the thread in our own times. In 1871 I was staying in the town and occasionally met the ancient lady

that lived alone in this large house, with her servant; she was
always attired the same—a dress of amber satin and a 'poke'
bonnet. I never passed the house but I looked up to one of
the topmost windows, where, on the sill, always in the same
position, and apparently never touched from year to year,
stood some childish toys—a wooden horse and a yellow
canary. I used to wonder what sort of a child he was that had
once played with them, and my mind pictured strange fancies,
tinged with a sadness. I was with the solitary boy, and I
tried to interest myself in his lonely play, which never varied
in its sad monotony; a childish quarrel, or less, a difference,
would have been welcomed, suggesting, as it would have done,
a companion, but the dreary days came and went and he was
still alone. At length a day came when they were untouched.
He was dead! the toys—they remained. Rumour, 'painted
full of tongues,' affirmed that the tenant of Copley House held
it in 'seizin' by a curious wording in the deed; as long as
the child was above ground, so it ran—therefore report had it
that he was 'kept' in that room. This by the way : one
afternoon in this year 1871 I called on some friends who were
full of news respecting Copley House. Dr. —— had been
called in. It appeared that on the afternoon of Sunday, her
mistress being at church, the servant was reading in a room
on the ground floor, when, suddenly, without a warning note,
there rose an uproar, which increased to such a pitch that
'pandemonium' itself appeared to have risen and established
itself here. This babel of sounds was all in a moment
tinctured with hellish laughter, then a rush as for dear life
raced up the stairs, followed immediately by a headlong descent. The door of the room fell or was flung open, showing
two heads, the one topping the other, contorted with an
horrific expression, and each appealing in its malignity. The
girl fell from one fit into another, in which condition she was
found, and the doctor feared for both life and reason."

Angle House. "This, unlike Copley House (altered almost
beyond recognition), still retains, I believe, its
old-time look; but even when I knew it early in the seventies,
it had already lost its high estate, and showed 'apartments to
let.' This surely in all conscience was matter of fact enough,
but yet there were 'whispers!' I do not think they became
much more; it would have injured the letting of the house,
and this the tenants and owners in one could not afford, but
they seemed to have a coherence which claimed a hearing,
and I heard 'one of them,' a lodger, coming down to break-

fast, complain of an unwarrantable intrusion into his room early that morning. When he awoke he was staggered at beholding 'an old woman' apparently bending over a drawer in a chest which she had opened. One of my relatives having a lot of young people came down to —— at this time, and took rooms at Angle House. Late one evening after supper I rose to go ; I had my back to the fireplace fronting the door, the table being between. We were cramped for space, the room being a small one of awkward shape, and many of us. However, some one opened it (the door), when I was chilled, or, vulgarly speaking, 'struck all of a heap,' at seeing an 'old woman' in a great shovel-bonnet which shrouded her features, bending across, as it appeared, in the act of listening. As I looked—it was but an instant—she had vanished. I then called to mind the 'whisperings.' "

CHAPTER IV

HAUNTED PARSONAGES

IT would be difficult to find a better story of a haunting ghost than that which relates to the family of the Wesleys at Epworth Parsonage. Both as to phenomena and evidence, the story is nearly all that a ghost story ought to be. If anything is wanting it is some indisputable, explanatory coincidence, although of theories, more or less plausible, we have enough and to spare. If only the Wesley family could have filled up one of the census papers circulated with " Real Ghost Stories," what excitement would have been caused to the Society for Psychical Research ! Their experiences were visual, audible, sensitive ; they had opportunities for observing psychical movement—their evidence was collective, independent, contemporary, What could Mr. Innes or Mr. Ernest Hart themselves want more?

The Epworth Ghost. The whole story was published by the Rev. John Wesley, in the *Arminian Magazine* for October, November, December, 1784, sixty-eight years after date, by which time the story was what the S.P.R. would call " remote," and though as the best known representative of his family his account has a special interest, yet we are glad to have it confirmed by various letters, written while the phenomena were in progress.

The Ghost's Debut. The first of these is from Mrs. Wesley to her son Samuel, in London (January 12th, 1716–17), expressing great pleasure at hearing from him, as certain recent occurrences had made her anxious as to distant friends. " We have various conjectures what these may mean," she writes. " For my own part I fear nothing now you are safe at London hitherto, though sometimes I am inclined to think my brother is dead." Mr. and Mrs. Wesley seem to have been open-minded upon the question, and to have looked at it from all sides, though—till he himself was favoured with a visitation—the vicar was, like other people limited to their own experience, inclined to pooh-pooh the whole thing. But when he himself heard knockings nine times just by his bed, and afterwards heard, as did the whole household, noises " like the winding up of a jack . . like a carpenter plaining (*sic*) boards," he was at last moved to speech and asked the ghost, "if it were Sammy, to knock again," after which it was for that occasion silent.

Sammy apparently did not think much of the story, and suggested tricks, cats, rats, and dogs as possible explanations. " Wit, I fancy, might find many interpretations—wisdom, none "—is his conclusion. Acting on this suggestion, Mrs. Wesley has a horn blown all over the house to scare away rats, or even—a still more remote possibility—weasels. This has no effect, and the ghost appears to be gathering force, for on January 25th Mrs. Wesley describes a new phenomenon.

The Ghost Comes to Prayers. The ghost has taken to coming to family prayers, and the good lady, utterly disconcerted, declines conjecture and observes enigmatically, " Secret things belong to God."

Miss Susannah Wesley is more explicit, and relates details which point to the presence of a disembodied Jacobite, who remonstrates with violent knockings at the words " Our most Gracious Sovereign Lord," when applied to King George I She adds that from the first to the last of a lunar month the noises have continued—groans, squeaks, tinglings, knockings, and " my father's particular knock, very fierce."

It Appears and is named. She then carries the mystery a step further. "To conclude this, it now makes its personal appearance, but of this more hereafter." This must have been rather tantalising for Samuel, and the reader shall not be made to share his impatience. We learn from a subsequent letter that "Something has been thrice seen." Mrs. Wesley saw IT, " like a badger." The man-servant also saw the same animal " sat by the dining-room fire," but when he chased it into the kitchen it was like a white rabbit, " which," says Emily Wesley, who takes up the tale at this point, " seems likely to be some witch." Emily was specially anxious to have the mystery explained, because at an early stage her father had suggested " lovers," which she says " made me desirous of its continuance." She it was who gave IT a name—Jeffrey.

J. W. Wesley seems to have relegated the lover hypothesis to the oblivion shared by the rats and weasels, and speaks of the phenomena with absolute certainty. " I have been thrice pushed by an invisible power," he writes. " I have followed the noise into almost every room in the house, both by day and night, with lights and without, and have sat alone for some time, and when I heard the noise, spoke to it to tell me what it was, but never heard any articulate voice, and only once or twice two or three feeble squeaks a little louder than the chirping of a bird, but not like the noise of rats, which I have often heard."

Jeffrey's Political Opinions. Susannah tells us that when her father first discovered that Jeffrey objected to the State prayers, he decided for the future to have three collects instead of two, which showed that he had not only courage, but the courage of his political convictions. One Friday night when they had attended service in church the family devotions were shortened by the omission of the "Prayer for the Royal Family," and no knocking occurred, which Mr. Wesley considered good evidence. "Always at the name of the king it began to knock, and did the same when I prayed for the Prince. This was heard by ten persons."

What Samuel Thought. Samuel's comment upon this is worth recording :—" As to the devil being an enemy of King George, were I the king myself I should rather old Nick should be my enemy than my friend."

Samuel is always practical, and writes with an absence of passion for which his distance from the scene may account. Alluding to a story told by his mother, he asks, "Have you dug in the place where the money seemed poured at your feet?"

The Ghost's Electivity. To disarm possible criticism on the point it is only fair to mention that we have evidence outside the Wesley family of the existence of their lad. A Mr. Hoole, the Vicar of Haxby, described by John Wesley as an eminently pious and sensible man, gives us his evidence at some length, agreeing in every particular with that of Mr. and Mrs. Wesley, Susannah and Emily, as does that also of the household servants. Hetty, another sister, is reported to have been the ghost's personal favourite, but she has left us no independent account. For some time the nursery was the place of his liking, but when Mr. Wesley called him a dumb and deaf spirit, and accused him of frightening innocent children, instead of behaving like a man —Jeffrey took to the vicar's study, which, on the whole, served him right. To Mrs. Wesley he was more courteous. On being informed that she specially desired quiet between five and six he was always silent at that hour. It is worth noticing, as further evidence of that electivity so familiar to the student of ghost literature, that " John and Kitty Maw, who lived over against us, listened several nights in the time of the disturbance, but could never hear anything."

Effect of Familiarity. As usual, we find—even on such delicate, not to say spiritual, ground—that familiarity breeds contempt. By February 11th we find Mr. Wesley saying, " All quiet now "—an assumption which proved to be premature — and adding with an interesting prescience of " More Ghost Stories," " It would make a glorious penny book ! "

The ladies of the family began to get bored. On March 27th Susannah complains, " We are secluded from the sight or hearing of anything, except Jeffrey." And about the same date Mrs. Wesley exclaims piteously, " I am quite tired with hearing or speaking of it."

Jeffrey's Predecessors. Among the Wesley correspondence communicated by the Rev. S. Badcock, and edited in 1791 by Joseph Priestley, we find a rather interesting " Memorandum of Jack's," from which we gather that five months of Jeffrey's presence was not the only supernatural experience of the Wesley family. He says : " The first time my mother ever heard an unusual noise at Epworth was long before the disturbances of old Jeffrey. My brother, lately come from London, had in the evening a sharp quarrel with my sister Sukey." Then followed knockings, " doors and windows rung and jarred," and these phenomena were reproduced in all times of family excitement and before death, which accounts for Mrs. Wesley's anticipation of misfortune to Samuel.

John Wesley's Explanation. Jack—whom it is at first not easy to identify with the saintly and truly Reverend John Wesley —had a theory of his own as to the Jeffrey disturbances :—

" As both my father and mother are now at rest and incapable of being pained thereby (he writes in the *Arminian Magazine*), I think it my duty to furnish the serious reader with a key to this circumstance. The year before King William died, my father observed my mother did not say *Amen* to the prayer for the King. She said she could not, for she did not believe the Prince of Orange was King. He vowed he would never cohabit with her till she did. He then took his horse and rode away, nor did she hear anything of him for a twelvemonth. He then came back and lived with her as before, but I fear his vow was not forgotten before God."

A North of England Haunting. The only drawback to the Epworth Ghost is that it dates from last century. The following story of another haunted parsonage is quite recent, the event described having occurred only last year.

Mr. C. W. Dymond, F.S.A., dating from 3, Forefield Place, Lyncombe Hill, Bath, writes me as follows :—

"I am glad to be able to send you the account (received only this morning) of the haunting at a parsonage in the north of England.

"Perhaps you will kindly return it to me when done with, as I believe the gentleman who handed it to me wishes to have it again. The haunted family are friends of his daughter.

"The following occurrences took place during the week commencing Monday, January 5th, 1891, when a clergyman, his wife, and another lady, whom we will call respectively A., B., and C., were living in a retired country house in the north of England. The servant had left a day or two previously, and her successor had not yet come; the lady whom we call C. had arrived on a visit about eleven o'clock on the morning of Monday.

The First Bell Rings. "Soon after dinner on that day, in the early dusk of a winter's afternoon, a bell was sharply rung in the house, and one of the ladies, thinking it was a visitor, went to the front door. There was no one there. Somewhat startled, she at once examined the bells (which are hung about ten feet from the ground close to the hall door in a passage leading to the kitchen), and said that the one still vibrating was not the front door bell at all, but one connected with the servants' bedroom, in which no person had been that day. However, the ringing was put down to mice, and was not thought much about that evening. But on the next night, Tuesday, from about seven o'clock to ten, nearly all the bells in the house rang at very frequent intervals in violent peals and clashings with a force that neither rats nor mice could exert; and the wires were heard clanging and seen moving as if violently pulled. On Wednesday morning a bedroom bell was rung loudly as early as seven o'clock, and all the rest rang at intervals throughout the day.

The Bells Muffled. "Between four and five in the afternoon the rings became much more frequent, and it was then decided to muffle the bells. This was done, the front door bell alone being left free, as it was thought very undesirable that these curious proceedings should become

known in the village. After this the unmuffled bell was constantly rung, and the dull thud of the muffled clappers was also
heard. It was then suggested by one of the party that the
rings might be produced in some way by electrical action, and
accordingly some of the wires were cut close, a few only being
allowed to remain. The uncut wires were pulled, if anything
more vigorously than before, and on going into the drawing-
room, which had not been used for a day or two, whose bell
had been peculiarly active, the bell tassel was found wrenched
off and lying in the middle of the floor!

Knocking. "Next day, Thursday, the bells were constantly
sounding, and, in addition, knocks of all sorts were
heard every few minutes by all three inmates of the house.
For the most part they were sharp, quick knocks, such as
would be caused by the rapping of knuckles on a door; but
sometimes they were loud and violent thuds, such as might be
made by a heavy piece of timber directed with some force
against the main beams of the house. As evening drew on,
more startling phenomena began.

Lamps Put Out. "The house was lighted by small oil lamps, hung
or standing in various places, and it now became
exceedingly difficult to keep these lamps alight.
They were in no draught, oil was abundant, wicks perfect, but
they went out every few minutes, and on going to them it was
discovered that the screw of the wick had been turned down!
No human hand had been near them. A., the clergyman, was
appointed custodian of the lamps, and for two hours or more
he was mainly occupied in going through the house, re-lighting
the lamps when out, and rescuing them when on the point of
extinction. All this time the bells and knocks continued as
usual.

A Laughing Imp. "Next morning, Friday, the bells began as
before and, with the knockings, continued at very
frequent intervals during the day. On this afternoon there happened, if possible, a greater wonder than ever.
A. was downstairs in the dining-room, B. and C. upstairs in
one of the bedrooms, when B. and C. heard a slight 'click'
as of metal clashing against tin. On going into the adjoining
bedroom it was found that a pair of trousers had been removed from a chair and dashed into a bath of water in the
middle of the room; the 'click' being evidently caused by
one of the buttons dashing against the metal bath. A. heard
a peal of laughter, which was quite refreshing, and on going
upstairs learned the cause. This incident was quite reassuring.

The party had been slightly alarmed by what had been occurring, but this affair of the trousers looked like the act of a
naughty young imp who had sufficient sense of humour to
appreciate a practical joke, and a sort of fellow-feeling seemed
to be established. About the same time as before, between
four and five in the evening, the bells sounded more frequently,
and the lamps on being lighted were turned out again and
again. In order to keep them lighted A. found it again necessary for two hours or more to act as peripatetic lamplighter,
spending nearly all this time in going from lamp to lamp in a
sort of race with these curious sprites. This evening wonder
after wonder occurred.

"A closet door, though locked again and again,
**Doors
Unlocked.** the key being left in, was again and again thrown
half open, as wide as a movable shelf would allow,
no one being near it. Once during this time, B., the clergyman's wife, said in an emphatic tone, as she again locked the
door, 'You shall keep shut!' and on the instant there was the
clashing of a bell so violently as to startle all three. Now
there came a fresh marvel. The front door had been fastened
by means of a latch and a chain slipping in a groove. Again
and again, when no human hand was near, the latch was
raised, the chain was slipped along to the end of the groove
so as to release it, and the door was opened about five or six
inches. A. thinks he once saw the chain moving along; at
any rate, he caught it in the nick of time, just as it was on the
point of setting the door free. Thus this evening there were
the bells, the knocks, the turned-down lamps, the closet, and
front doors opened; these occurring at no regular intervals,
but altogether making, perhaps, not less than fifty marvels in
the course of a few hours. Whilst these were going on another
phenomenon occurred. A., B., and C. were all in another
part of the house, and all heard a strange, dull thud, which
they could not account for, but on going into the back kitchen
it was found that a wooden bar, which is used to bar the
shutters, fitting in a square staple and fastener, had been
taken out and thrown on the kitchen floor three yards off!
After this there were the usual accompaniments of bells,
knocks, etc., and though the three inmates of the house had
fairly good nerves, and were not easily frightened, they were
beginning to wish that they might be left alone. Once during
this evening the closet door was opened almost before their
very eyes, when all three were close to it, but no one touching it.

"Depart in the Name of Christ!" "A. dashed the door wide open, and finding, as was expected, no one inside, he fell on his knees, the others following his example, and in a loud voice prayed, or rather commanded, all spirits in the name of Jesus Christ to depart. It may have been excited nerves, but they had an impression that other beings were within hearing, and that they recognised a power whose commands they must obey. A., B., and C. also believe that from that time the visitations became both less frequent and less violent. It became necessary for two of the party to go out that night into the back-yard, and as they crossed it, a loud crash was heard ; something was thrown from the roof as if hurled at them. On making an examination it was found that a stone blacking-bottle had been violently hurled against a wall with such force as to break it into a score pieces ! It is their impression that this was thrown at their heads, but fortunately missed them. Bedtime came, and, as on previous evenings, no sound reached them at night, a parting bell perhaps sounding as they passed to go upstairs. These phenomena continued at intervals on Saturday, but no fresh wonders were observed, and those that took place became less frequent. On coming from church on Sunday evening one of the lamps was observed to be strangely swinging, and there was a very strong smell of oil in the room, but both these were mere trifles. Sunday evening was comparatively quiet; bells, knocks, lamps and doors, though occasionally manifesting, were, on the whole, approaching their normal state. On Monday morning early there were a few bells, and bells and a knock or two during the day. On Monday evening they began slightly and for a short time, the last bell being heard as the knock of a new servant at the back door announced that she had arrived.

"Since that time some of them have a few times heard a bell, and occasionally things not readily explained take place. But these are trifling and may admit of explanation.

The Witnesses. "All three of those concerned, A., B., and C., are fairly sensible and clear-headed, honest and veracious. Collusion or conspiracy, or any known human agency causing these wonders, is out of the question. Notes were made by B. in a small diary of the occurrences, and that diary still exists. All three also are prepared to verify, if necessary, these statements upon oath, and to submit to separate cross-examination. There might be slight discrepancies in their statements as to the exact *order* of the events narrated, but concerning the main facts there can be no

question.   Other matters, it may be remarked, went on during
that time just as they were wont—the world seemed turned
upside down, and all notion of natural laws with unvarying
operation cast to the winds, but only as respects these phenomena
—and in all other matters the brains of A., B., and C. found
the world just as other people find it.   There was, of course,
intercourse with the outside world during that time, visits were
made, and a few neighbours called.

"It should be remarked that once, about fifteen months
before, a bell was heard by A. and B. when they only were
in the house; this bell was the same that first rang on the
Monday evening.

"A copy of the diary is appended—this is the best authority
as to the precise *order* of the occurrences.

"Copy Diary.

	1891.	31 Days.	January.
5.	Mon.	'C.' came. 'A.' drove her from station — one bell rang.	
6.	Tu.	'A.' went to tea at ——— many bells rang—'A.'s' birthday.	
7.	Wed.	'A.' cut bell wires—still they rang.	
8.	Th.	Knocks at several doors—lamps went out.	
9.	Fri.	Bells, knocks, 'A.'s' trousers thrown in bath. Street room door opened. Lamps went out. L. called about place. Cupboard under stairs opened several times.	
10.	Sat.	All wires continued.	
11.	Sun.	Dg. window opened — all others continued till evening when abated.	
12.	Mon.	Only bells—the last about 4 o'clock. L. came. 'C.' went on the hills.	
13.	Tu.	'C.' went away. 'A.' drove her to———."	

CHAPTER V

SOME HAUNTED HOUSES IN THE COUNTRY

MR. E. D. WALKER, formerly mayor of Darlington, the W. H. Smith & Son of the Stockton & Darlington Railway, contributes to the *Northern Echo* the following narrative of a ghost that haunted his own home when he was a child. His father was a coastguardsman who married a farmer's daughter in Sussex, and subsequently was appointed to the little village of Goldsborough, five miles north of Whitby. Mr. Walker writes :—

"When we reached this place it was found that there was no house of any kind available as a habitation for us, but after making numerous inquiries we found shelter in the wing of a farm-house which for some time previously had been unoccupied.

A Haunted House near Whitby.

"We had not been in this particular house more than about a month, when one night my father— coming in, as was his nightly custom, between eleven and one o'clock, as his rounds permitted—was sitting in the little kitchen, and was about to take from the oven his coffee and toast for supper, when, just as he was reaching to the oven, the fender upon which one of his feet was resting lifted up from the hearthstone three times and fell again with a loud bang. Concurrently with this action on the part of the fender, one-half of a double-doored long closet opened three times also and slammed to again, louder, my father always said, than he could have done it himself. Mother, who was sleeping in a room on the same level, called out to father, 'James, what is that?' He replied, 'Betsy, I don't know; it's very strange.' However, they heard no more that night, and father finished his coffee and had his pipe, and went out again. He came in in the morning, and said to his wife, 'That was a very strange thing last night, Betsy.' She rejoined : 'It was ; it is very strange. What could it be?' He said: 'I don't think it meant anything,' and then, 'Did James [my eldest brother] hear it?' Mother replied, 'Yes he did.' That made my

father think it still more strange, but nothing further was said,
and for many nights he went about his business as usual.

The Lifting of Beds and Pistol Shots. "About a month afterwards, however, when he was out one night, and about half an hour before the time he generally came in, my mother, who was lying in bed asleep with me in her arms, felt the bed lifted three times and banged down again with a loud noise. Simultaneously with the bed lifting there were three distinct and very loud sounds of pistol shots fired over the bed. My mother screamed out, as also did my brother James upstairs, and she then lay in bed almost paralysed with fear, praying, as she said she never prayed before, for father to come in. When he came she told him and said, 'I dare not stay in the house; you must see and get out of it as soon as possible,' and he replied, 'I will do so.' After she had told him this, and while he was sitting having his pipe, he heard, and she also heard distinctly, outside the window, what seemed to them like two dogs in deadly combat, fighting and tearing each other to pieces. Father said, 'Do you hear that?' She said, 'Yes,' and then he also began to get a little scared. He got his cutlass and went to the front door, but could see nothing; and he made up his mind then that he would inquire about the matter, having up to this time kept his own counsel. A Mrs. Bewick, a widow, who was living in the other portion of the farmhouse, told him that the last people who had lived there said there was something wrong about the house, but she personally knew nothing, although only separated by a wall. Within a week or two of this father was down on the sands one day with mother (I was just able to walk), and were making their way from the top of the cliff, when they met Lord and Lady Normanby, on their way to the Lady's Walk, where there was a beautiful grotto in which they used to sit. Father raised his hat to the Marquis of Normanby, who said, 'I suppose you are the new coastguardsman?' He said, 'Yes, my lord,' and told him his name. The Marquis said, 'Have you got a comfortable house?' and he then told his lordship briefly this story. His lordship said, 'I have heard something about that before. It is very strange that there is anything in it,' and father repeated the story. The Marquis then said, 'You shall not stay there any longer than it is possible to provide you with some other place. I will get my steward to at once put a cottage in the village in order for you.' In a little time after this my father got into the cottage which the Marquis speedily had made ready for him. But meanwhile, after father had spoken to the Marquis, and while the cottage was being prepared, it was found necessary by the owners of the farmhouse, on father's representation, to bring a joiner in from Whitby to make some repairs in an upstairs bed-room.

A Male Figure Draped in White. "My brother James, then twelve years of age, was upstairs with him, and whilst the man was busy at the window—he knowing nothing, and having no suspicion of the building—all at once a male figure, draped in white, appeared, coming apparently from nowhere, crossed the room, and vanished. The joiner, affrighted, threw his tools down and rushed downstairs, followed by the boy James, who was screaming at the top of his voice. Father was downstairs, and the joiner told him what they had seen. Nothing could induce him to go and fetch his tools, and ultimately my father had to go for them. We lived in the house in the village for some years, and then my father was promoted again, and sent to Coatham, near Redcar. After we had been there a few years, and I had grown up to be thirteen years of age, my father, on the invitation of a Mr. Watson—who farmed the principal farm on the estate of the Marquis of Normanby, near Goldsborough—again visited the neighbourhood, and took me with him. Amongst other subjects that naturally came up in conversation between them was the question of the haunted farmhouse. My father asked, 'Did those who went into the house after us have any similar experiences to what we had?' Mr. Watson replied, 'I am glad, James, that you have named that. A few years after you left, Mrs. Bewick, who had the other part of the house, died, and the house was repaired and done up and let in its entirety to another man.

The Skeleton under the Hearthstone. "'Before he entered into possession the new tenant had the interior very much modernised, and amongst other things the flagged floor in the kitchen was taken up, and of course the hearthstone along with it, and under the hearthstone was found a human skeleton.'

"Now my father was a man who would be one of the least likely to imagine anything of the kind. He had been the first in time of need to man the lifeboat, no matter how great the peril, and his occupation being principally carried on at night made him know no fear. During that terrible and never-to-be-forgotten Whitsuntide storm which strewed the entire north-east coast with wrecks, and sent scores and hundreds of poor sailors to a restless ocean grave, thirty or thirty-one years ago, he was the first to get a lifeboat crew together at Redcar and go out to the Salt Scar through a sea that was unprecedented for its mountains of broken water, and bring off the crew of fourteen men of a three-masted vessel which had struck there. My mother died only eight months ago, at the age of eighty-four, and told this story up to the time of her death, and had no doubt whatever as to the terrible reality of her experience."

How uninhabitable a house may become when
The Haunted   haunted we have an example in the following
No. 8.
narrative, which is sent me by a lady who says that she has carefully abstained from any embellishment, and that she is willing to give dates, names, and addresses of witnesses who will corroborate her narrative in every detail.

" Some years ago I one day met a lady, with whom I was slightly acquainted, who told me that she was on the eve of making a change of residence. She added that her husband had taken a three years' lease of a house in —— Road, and when she described the costly improvements which were being carried on in order to make the abode luxuriously habitable, I remarked that the alterations were more in keeping with a long rather than a short lease. My surprise, therefore, was great, when a few months later I heard that the family, whom I will here call the Smythes, had removed not only from the house in question but from the vicinity altogether. About four years later we removed to a house in the same road—No. 8, the house formerly occupied by the Smythes, being then a very dismal-looking residence. The hinges of its heavy gate were coated with rust, the front garden and approach covered with wild growth, while the massive portico and sills wore a hopelessly blackened complexion, and I again wondered why the Smythes had removed so suddenly. About this time I received a visit from a lady whose acquaintance I had made a month or two previous, and she began at once to discourse on the merits of the houses composing our road. ' I always liked the terrace,' she said, ' and you may judge we must have been terribly unnerved to leave No. 8 as we did.' I started, and looked astonished. ' Did you not know,' she continued, ' that we lived for nearly a year at No. 8? We took an expiring lease of the house from a Mr. Smythe. The family had only been in it a few months when they left very hurriedly, although no expense had been spared in the way of improvements to the house itself. Every one was surprised ; but Mr. Smythe told me that his "wife was suffering from great nervous depression, and the doctor had ordered her immediate removal at any cost ; " ' and, she added, 'After we had been in the house a little time I ceased to wonder at her nervous depression, or the sudden removal of the family ; for the probable cause developed all too speedily in our own daily lives.' She went on to say, ' I am not at all superstitious, but it is a fact that long before we were settled in our new abode every one became conscious of an eerie, uncanny feeling pervading the house and seeming almost atmospheric.' My friend then entered very fully into gruesome detail. She said that apart from the sense of the ghostly depression of which she had spoken, nothing was seen or heard for two or three weeks before their arrival.

Knockings. "When one evening, while sitting in the dining-room with her husband, an Australian captain, they were suddenly startled by a loud knocking in the fireside recess ; a few minutes later the knocking was repeated in the recess on the other side, and after a time was repeated also in recesses in the back room. My friend, whom I will here call Mrs. A., immediately sent to the adjoining house to know if any one was knocking for aid, but the answer returned was that Mr. and Mrs. —— were in the dining-room, the former being confined to the couch by indisposition. On several occasions a peremptory knocking at the dining-room door was heard, but when, on more than one occasion, the door was quickly opened from the inside, no one was visible. One evening, soon after the captain's departure for Australia, Mrs. A. was sitting alone in the breakfast-room, this room being in the basement ; no one else was in the house, for the children were at a juvenile gathering in the neighbourhood, and the servant had gone to bring them home. My friend was busily engrossed in writing, when suddenly she was startled by the tread of slippered feet across the dining-room floor, and she also distinctly heard a leather chair moved some distance along the ground, and she at once concluded that thieves were in the house.

What did the Dog see? "A dog which lay on the rug also heard the sounds, for he pricked up his ears and barked. Without a moment's delay she flew to the door, calling the dog to follow her, intending as she did so to open the hall door and call for assistance ; but the dog, though an excellent house dog, crouched at her feet and whined, but would not follow her up the stairs, so she carried him up in her arms, and, reaching the door, called for assistance ; when, however, the dining-room doors were opened the rooms were in perfect order and destitute of any signs of life. The servant told her afterwards that, as she sat in the kitchen, she repeatedly heard footsteps overhead at times when she knew the rooms were perfectly empty.

"After the family had been in the house a few weeks, a white rabbit made its appearance. This uncanny animal would suddenly appear in a room in which members of the family were seated, and after gliding round and slipping under chairs and tables, would disappear through a brick wall as easily as through an open door. Mrs. A. then related another incident which had evidently made a profound impression on her. She said that as the captain was so seldom at home, and the house was very large, she was solicitous that the children should, if possible, be kept in happy ignorance of their weird surroundings.

The White Rabbit.

"Ghostly possibilities were never alluded to in their presence ; she was therefore horrified one evening, when sitting in the dining-room in company with her young daughter—a child of nine years—at seeing her suddenly spring to her feet from her seat on the rug, and exclaim, 'Mamma, look at that boy creeping round the wall !' The mother looked in the direction to which her hand pointed, but saw nothing. She then endeavoured to divert the child's attention, assuring her that it was only her nervous fancy. She partially succeeded, although the little one seemed much agitated. A few minutes after, however, she sprang to her mother's side the second time, again exclaiming, 'There is that boy again ! Look, mamma, he has slipped under the table.' She was greatly terrified, and begged to be taken from the room.

"That Boy Creeping Round the Wall !"

"By Christmas time a gruesome spell had brought the entire family under its sway, and my friend said it required quite an effort to enter with zest into the gaieties of the season. She, however, decided to give a party in the New Year. The house was full of merry guests, fires flung hospitable gleams on bedroom and parlour wall, and bright gaslight shone—surely no ghost could live in such an atmosphere of brightness. Three or four of the guests were to stay till the next day. One lady, however, on leaving the house to catch a last train arrived at the station just in time to see it steaming out, and as there were no other facilities for effecting her homeward journey she returned to the merry party she had just left, and begged that she might be allowed the use of the couch in the dining-room for the night. Mrs. A. started at the request. The skeleton of her house for

A Christmas Party.

the first time that evening rose up before her, and she at once left the room to confer with her faithful domestic on the matter. Jane, though an excellent servant, was at all times subservient to her surroundings, and her advice to her mistress was in perfect keeping with the mirth and music in the upper rooms. 'I should let her be on the couch, ma'am ; no visitors will trouble us to-night, that you may depend. She knows nothing of the things that do go on, and perhaps, after all, our fancy plays us tricks.' So Mrs. A. returned to her guests, and told Miss —— that the coveted couch was at her disposal. After the lapse of another hour or two, good-nights were said, the guests dispersed, lights were put out, and she was left in undivided possession of the room. 'I hope you will sleep well, but burn the gas all night,' were her hostess' last words. Feeling tired, she speedily sought her couch ; but forgetting her friend's warning with regard to the gas, she first turned out the lights and had not lain long when she was awoke to clearest consciousness by the sense of a presence in the room.

The Ghost enters. "Some one was evidently moving about in the further end of the front room. She lay for a moment or two and listened, then thought she heard a chair move. This sound decided her: some one had evidently entered the room either to play her a trick, or in quest of something they imagined they could find in the dark ; so sitting up she exclaimed, 'Who is it ? What do you want ?' On receiving no reply however she hastily rose, and after feeling about in the darkness for the matches for several trying seconds, found them and lit the gas, but to her dismay the rooms were empty ; she searched under the table and behind the window curtains, but in vain ; she was the room's sole occupant. The gas-light was reassuring, and under its rays she reasoned with herself: she had evidently, she concluded, been dreaming when she thought herself awake, and her impressions belonged to the realm of dreams. So adopting this comfortable reflection, she again addressed herself to repose, but in vain ; for scarcely had she fallen into slumber when she was once more aroused by her former impressions. She said afterwards that she saw nothing, and indeed dared not look round the rooms again, but burying her head in her pillow, she lay trembling violently, but utterly powerless to move.

The Ghost moving unseen. "She at the same time was perfectly conscious of the movements of the ghostly intruder, knew one moment that it stood in the vicinity of the front window, then felt it was standing by the fire-place, then she knew that it moved again, and was now pausing at the head of the couch on which she was lying ; but she knew no more, for she had lost consciousness, and when she came to herself the morning light was contending for supremacy with the lighted gas jets, and the sound from the kitchen regions told her that another day's duties had begun. She sought her hostess who, in relating this incident to me, said, ' I never shall forget how I felt when, bursting into tears, she said, " Mrs. A. ! Mrs. A. ! why did you put me in that awful room last night ? it has almost killed me." ' She then proceeded to relate the experience which I have already given. ' That winter,' said my friend, ' was the most terrible one I have ever spent. I was powerless to make any change in our abode in my husband's absence, and the strange and ghostly incidents were now of such constant occurrence, concentrating their forces not only in the dining-rooms, but in one or two of the bedrooms as well, that at last we all slept together in one bedroom my servant, on several occasions, being compelled, through sheer terror, to share the room as well. After Captain A.'s return home we lost no time in effecting our removal, but even now I never think without a shudder of our dreadful sojourn at that No. 8.'

The White Rabbit returns.
"Some years have now elapsed since the incident I have now related took place, and again, in response to orders given by the enterprising landlord of the property, the long-closed doors and windows have been thrown open, and painters and paperhangers have brought their skill to bear upon gruesome rooms and halls ; the house is once more inhabited, this time by a widow lady and some grown-up sons. These tenants came from a distance, and are entirely strangers both to the neighbourhood and the former history of the house, but, to use her own words, the mistress ' cannot understand what ails the house,' her sons insist on sleeping together in one room, and the quiet of the house is constantly being broken in upon by the erratic appearances of a large white rabbit, which the inmates are frequently engaged chasing but are never able to find."

Persistent Spectres.
In compiling this chapter I have not drawn in any way upon the haunted houses which are reported in the Psychical Research Society's proceedings. The narratives have been supplied me by various correspondents, who have written me from all parts of the land. Of haunted chambers, whose occupants have experi-

enced weird and creepy feelings, there are enough and to
spare. But I need not allude to them, as a sensation which is
purely subjective does not supply material for investigation and
verification. It would be improper, however, not to include in
this chapter several familiar haunting ghosts which do no
harm to anybody, but which cling with a strange persistency
to some spot associated with a crisis in their former lives. A
very good example of this is sent me by Mrs. Doby, of 1,
Forbes Place, Paisley. She says that the following account
of a ghost which visited her father and mother is absolutely true. They both saw the ghost at different times,
and had no doubt whatever as to its reality. The house
is now pulled down, so that the ghost has probably disappeared.

A Dunfermline Ghost Story. Mr. James Doby put up at an old commercial
hotel at Dunfermline. He occupied a bedroom
close to a sitting-room, and found it was a very
uncomfortable place to sleep in. He was restless and fever-
ish, and being unable to sleep, he lay turning from side to side,
when to his great surprise he saw the door open. Thinking that
it was a thief, he prepared to defend himself, but to his astonishment he saw a little old gentleman dressed in the costume of
the last century, with lace ruffles at his wrists, knee breeches,
a rapier by his side and his hat under his arm, cross the room to
a large old chest. Taking a key from his pocket, he opened it
and lifted the lid, and searched the chest. After looking for a
long time, he closed the chest with a look of disappointment,
and left the room by the door through which he had entered.
Finding, next morning, that the door had been locked all night,
Mr. Doby concluded he had been dreaming, and dismissed the
subject from his mind. Next month he occupied the same room,
and, as morning approached, he woke up and again saw the old
man come in and go through the same search. He was quite
awake, and the moment his visitor turned to go he jumped
out of bed to follow him, but found to his astonishment the
door locked, which a moment before he had seen open. He
unlocked the door and went out upon the landing, but could
see no one. A third time he occupied the room the old
gentleman came again. Whenever he came a brilliant light
filled the room, which obscured the light of a small jet of gas
which was burning. He tried to speak to it, but failed; he
could never find his voice. After the third visit he gave up
sleeping in that room. Two years afterwards he again visited
the inn, this time with his wife, to whom he had never men-

tioned the fact of the apparition. As no other room was
available, his wife and he were quartered in the haunted room.
In the middle of the night he was awakened by a brilliant
light, and he saw his wife get out of bed and try to open the
door. She was very much excited, and describing the old
gentleman, said that he had entered the room, gone to the
chest, and then had gone out again.

A Spectral
Searcher for
the Missing
Will.

On making inquiries at the inn, he found that
the old chest, which was always opened by the
ghost, belonged to an old Roman Catholic family,
who had once lived within a few miles of Dunfermline. When the family became extinct the effects were
sold, and this box bought by the landlord of the inn. It seems
that the old laird had quarrelled with his son for marrying his
gardener's daughter, and had made a will leaving the estates
to a nephew, but afterwards, finding that his nephew was a
loose character, he made another will restoring his son to his
inheritance. His son, however, was abroad when the father
died, and the nephew possessed himself of the property and
made away with the second will. The housekeeper, however,
knew of the will and told him that his father had left the
property by a will which was deposited in the old charter box.
When, however, the son came to look for the will he could not
find it. His health was failing and his intellect was weak, and
for some weeks he searched daily in that chest for the missing
will, and failing to find it, he died, and since that time his
ghost seems to have haunted the spot, and when the box was
transferred from the hall to the inn he went with the box.
This is a very curious case, and it would have been very interesting to have tried to photograph the defrauded heir when he
came, night after night, to open the box and look for the missing will. A Kodak ready for instantaneous use, and provided
with flash light, ought to solve the question as to whether such
ghosts possess sufficient objectivity to leave an impression of
their existence upon a sensitive plate. This is a type of a
numerous family of ghosts of whose existence the phonograph
may give us some hint by way of analogy. You speak into
the phonograph, and for ever after as long as the phonograph
is set in action it will reproduce the tone of your voice. You
may be dead and gone, but still the phonograph will reproduce
your voice, while, with it, every tone will be audible to posterity. So it may be in relation to ghosts. A strong emotion
may be able to impress itself upon surrounding objects in such
a fashion that at certain times, or under certain favourable

conditions, they reproduce the actual image and actions of the person whose ghost is said to haunt.

The Policeman's Story. Here is a capital story from Wales, told by a veteran policeman :—

"I was born in M—— the year 1819. I joined the M—— police force at twenty-five years of age, and have served for forty-six years through all the grades from P.C. to Superintendent, most of which time I have been stationed in the small market town of Ll——t. I have now been superannuated under the new County Council regulation. During the many years I spent in the Force I have had some rough experiences in street rows, night poaching affairs, etc., and my worst enemies would hardly charge me with lack of pluck under sometimes dangerous circumstances. However, I must admit that I was on three occasions thoroughly unnerved, and as you requested, through the medium of the late number of the *Review of Reviews*, particulars of any supernatural visitation, at first hand or otherwise, I venture to give particulars of my adventures on the above-mentioned occasions.

Captain H. "The scene of the said adventures was an old-fashioned mansion know as G., situated about eight miles from this town (and now used by the noble owner as a shooting-box). A Captain H., R.N., occupied the place for some years, and I became intimately acquainted with him, and found him particularly kind and liberal. He was very popular in the neighbourhood, and took great interest in agriculture. His household consisted of a few female servants and a niece, who acted as his housekeeper. The latter was married to a Capt. L., who was a worthless spendthrift. His wife's uncle supplied him with money for a time, but eventually got tired of his extravagance, and turned him adrift, at the same time giving his wife a home at G.

His Death. "On November 10th, 1871, I was grieved to get a note from Mrs. L., who stated that her uncle had died suddenly of apoplexy on the previous night, and earnestly requesting me to come and stay in the house until his friends and relations should come over for the funeral. Of course I was only too glad to accede to her request. She informed me that her husband was somewhere in the neighbourhood, and she was afraid he might make a descent on the house and possess himself of valuables and documents he might come across. She requested me to examine carefully all the doors and windows before going to bed, as she was very nervous. I retired about eleven o'clock, having had a very slight supper, and feeling very comfortable. At about one o'clock in the morning, as near as I could tell, I woke with an undefinable sensation, and I could not help feeling that something was going to happen. I listened intently for a few moments, when I could hear a door open and a step approaching. At first I thought some one was going to one of the rooms in what they called the tower—past my bedroom.

His Ghost.   " However, when the steps appeared at my door, it was gently pushed open, and to my horror in came my poor (late) friend the Captain, dressed as I had often seen him at this market, in a brown suit and ' knickerbockers.' He held in his hand a large, antique brass candlestick, in which was a ' mould ' candle. He passed up to the chimney-piece, about two yards from the bed, and took up a large meerschaum pipe, which I had not noticed previously, and after examining it intently replaced it on the chimney-piece. He then went to the dressing-table, took down some trinkets, etc., from the looking-glass frame, and returned them in the same way. He then approached the bed, and appeared to draw aside the curtains. I do not know how long he stood there looking me straight in the face with his old benevolent smile. All this time I was sitting up in bed, and staring in terror. At last *he* (or it) leisurely left the room, and I could hear his footsteps going towards the room where the poor gentleman was lying in his coffin. Next morning I considered the matter over, and finally decided to tell no one of the matter but my wife, as it might prejudice the letting of the house, and that would not suit any one in the neighbourhood. I told my wife that nothing on earth could induce me to spend such another night, but she laughed at me, and said I had had a heavy supper, etc., and that it was all imagination. Finally, I was shamed into going back the next night. The second night the same occurrence took place. The third night was a repetition of the first and second, with the difference that I had made up my mind, if possible, to speak to the apparition, but totally failed to open my mouth. On the fourth day some members of the family arrived from the eastern counties. On that night I slept peaceably until daylight, when I was very glad finally to bid adieu to the place. For two or three years afterwards I never ventured to return late alone from the C. Petty Sessions by the road passing the house, but always took the upper mountain road. I shall never forget the sensations of those three nights, and, although not naturally superstitious, I have never been able to account for the appearances on natural grounds."

Mr. J. B. Killen, B.L., 31, Lower Gardiner Street, Dublin, sends me the following account of an experience which befell him more than twenty years ago, when he was residing in the city of Cork—in that part of it known as Sunday's Well—a sort of suburb situated upon the lofty slopes on the north side of the city :—

Three Quaker Ghosts at Cork.

" I was quite familiar with the locality, having lived in it for nearly two years while a student of the Queen's College attached to the city where I was at the time I refer to. It was in the month of November, shortly after the opening of the college session. The day was disagreeable in more senses than one. For some trivial reason a difference had arisen between my landlady and myself, the consequence of which was that I abruptly left my lodgings. Towards evening I secured another place, near where I had been staying, on the recommendation of a lady of my acquaintance (whom I shall call Mrs. M.), and it was on the first and only night of my staying there that the phenomenon to which I have referred occurred.

" There was nothing exciting or sensational in the transactions of the day ; they were prosaic and commonplace in the extreme. A domestic dispute which did not last more than ten minutes, a search for another shelter, which could scarcely have occupied more than an hour, the removal of impedimenta almost too trifling to deserve the name, perhaps five minutes, chat with a friend I may have casually met—that was all. When the day was nearly over, I found myself seated by the fire in the sitting-room of my new lodgings.

" I sat far into the night, smoking and reading Lytton's strange novel, ' A Strange Story,' by the fire alone. It was near two o'clock when, lighting my bedroom candle, I crossed the hall and entered the room. Having locked the door and extinguished the candle, I went to bed and soon fell asleep. I could not have slept more than half an hour when I suddenly awoke, and in the faint glimmer that came through the chinks of the shutters from the lamp outside, or from some other light for the presence of which I cannot account, I distinctly saw the bedroom door open, and three male figures enter, one immediately after the other. A few steps brought them alongside my bed, where they halted, and looking at me intently, with eyes horribly blue and glassy, they each simultaneously raised its right arm slowly and solemnly extended it towards me. The figures were of the full stature of men, the foremost being the tallest of all three, and were dressed in the Quaker costume of two hundred years ago, a kind of dress I had never seen except, perhaps, in pictures. For a moment I was stunned, and for the first time in my life I felt the sensation of horror. Recovering the use of my voice, I asked, hoarsely enough I must confess, 'Who are you?' No reply was given, but immediately the words were spoken, the figures, still keeping their great blue eyes fixed upon me, and fixed upon me with an expression of the deepest sadness, not to say pain, began slowly to move, and passed, as it seemed to me, into the wall at the end of the little room. I got up at once, lit my candle, and examined the door. Everything was as I had left it, nor, though I listened intently in the hope of hearing some human sound, did anything reach my ears except the moaning of the wind among the sad-looking trees opposite, and the faint rush of the river in the hollows below.

"I went to bed again, extinguished the candle, and fell into a sort of slumber. Suddenly and soon I awoke again, and with even more distinctness than on the previous occasion the door seemed to open, the apparitions, in every respect the same, entered, crossed the floor in precisely the same deliberate way, stopped in front of my bed, raised their arms and looked at me in the same solemn and pitiful manner, then passed into the wall as before. This time I was more collected, and, besides putting my former question, asked what they wanted and could I do anything for them? From these questions it is pretty evident, whatever my cooler judgment may have inclined to afterwards, that I had a suspicion at the time that the apparitions were really of a ghostly character. This, however, by the way. To my questions I received no reply, so having lit the candle, I examined the room and door, but found everything as I had left them. After a short delay I extinguished the candle, and returning to bed, fell into a disturbed slumber as before. Again, and after no great length of time, the same thing occurred, alike in every particular to the phenomena that had preceded, but, if possible, more distinct. This time my sensations of horror were getting mixed up with a certain feeling of sensation at being so frequently and so unmeaningly disturbed by visitors who refused, when civilly spoken to, to give any answer, or to tell the object of their visit, and my voice sounded quite sharply in the stillness of the room as I put my questions with some additions to them as before, and with the same result. Lighting my candle quickly on the disappearance of the figures, I got up, unlocked and opened the bedroom door, and going into the hall, looked 'with all my eyes' into the darkness and called out in a loud tone of voice, 'Is any one there?' There was no reply of any kind, and the only sound besides that of the wind and the river which broke the silence, came from the heavy breathing of some sleeper, who, I suppose, was the old woman in the apartment below.

"Returning to my bedroom I locked the door as before, but this time I did not put out the candle, nor did I go to sleep. It had little more than burned down to the socket when the day began to break and I arose. There had been no reappearance of the apparitions, but, judging from the face I saw in the glass, they had been with me often enough. It was deadly pale, haggard, and almost wild in expression, and seemed fully ten years older than it had been the night before. I left the house at once. I heard afterwards that it had the reputation of being haunted.

" Neither time, reflection, nor the opinions of the many to whom I have repeated the story, have made it less a mystery. There was nothing in my previous experience, or the then condition of my mind or body to throw a ray of light upon it. I was in my usual good health at the time. I had not been thinking, or reading of, or speaking to, any member of the Society of Friends, nor had I ever more than a casual acquaintance with any member of the body in my whole life, much less seen any of them in the costume in which the apparition appeared. Moreover, this appearance was so unmeaning, so entirely, as it would seem, without aim or object (unless, —which is an absurd if not impossible supposition—to cause me a temporary inconvenience), that, if ghosts at all, we must believe them to have been ghosts who had lost any little common sense they may have had when in the flesh. What makes the matter still more mysterious is that I am not, as some people profess to be, in the habit of meeting with any such experiences. The one I have referred to was the first and last I ever had."

CHAPTER VI

HAUNTED HOUSES ABROAD

MRS. TALBOT COKE, the editor of *Hearth and Home*, whose husband is on the staff of Lord Wolseley in Ireland, has had the good fortune to see a ghost no fewer than three times. Her narrative is very straightforward, and it would be interesting to know whether the hotel in question still keeps its famous haunted chamber shut up from the general public. If so, it might be worth while for some benevolently disposed person to ascertain what the ghost wanted Mrs. Coke to do. Mrs. Coke writes as follows :—

" It was the year of the Franco-Prussian war ; my husband (a soldier) and I were staying at the peaceful little Felsenthor Pension, half-way up the Righi mountain, when war was declared.

" Captain Coke's leave of absence was so nearly run out that we deemed it advisable to start homewards at once, knowing that the railway service would be much upset by the sudden movement of troops.

" We therefore hastened down the mountain, "The Three wiring on to the Trois Rois Hôtel at Basle for Kings." rooms (the hotel to which we had sent on our heavy baggage some weeks before).

" Arriving at Basle we found the Trois Rois in a chaotic ferment, luggage of flying tourists piled nearly to the roof of the big hall. [Those who know the hotel will remember it was, hundreds of years ago, a nobleman's palace ; those who do not will please note the fact, as the common or garden hotel is not a good *mise en scène* for a ghost.] The frenzied manager knew nothing of rooms for us, nothing of our baggage ; but we were firm in saying, as they had our boxes, we must sleep in the hotel that one night. Then ensued an excited argument in German, by which I learnt that one man advocated a certain room, while another, with exclamations and gestures of horror, objected.

A Haunted Room. " Being nothing if not practical, my thoughts flew to small-pox (then prevalent on the Continent), and I pictured a corpse being hastily removed from the proposed room, so stepping forward I told them German was to me as my own tongue, and that I insisted on knowing whether there had been illness in the proposed room.

" I mention this to show no thought of any *other* objection to it even crossed my matter-of-fact mind.

" They assured me, so far from that, that the room had not been used since they could remember, but that it was dirty, unfurnished, and quite unfit for the ' Hochgeborene gnädige Herrchaffen.'

" Disposing of all these polite scruples, we decided to take the room—a long narrow attic up several flights of stairs—with a squalid-looking little bed at either end, a bare boarded floor, a white-tiled china stove, a couple of chairs, and the skimpiest of washing necessaries, and windows looking on the river. We had a merry dinner, went out afterwards to a *café chantant*, and at last climbed to our eyrie, and went thankfully to bed.

The Little Pale-faced Woman of Thirty. " I was wakened by the feeling of some one bending over me, and sat up to see a little pale-faced woman of about thirty close to me. She wore a dark dress, on the bodice of which was a curious square of gold and coloured embroidery. She had faded-looking brown hair, which hung in two plaits down her back, and was slightly deformed ; the face had the pathetic appealing look often seen on people thus afflicted. At first, so real was the presence, I thought it was one of the Swiss chambermaids, but when I saw she carried no light, and that the room was pitch dark, save for a halo round her figure (something like a bad magic-lantern), I—being, as before said, a practical woman—thought ' the hot sun coming down the Righi has upset my liver,' turned over with my face to the wall, and went to sleep again, but only to experience the same feeling that some one was bending over me.

Again ! " This time she stood between me and the wall, and I noticed with surprise that though she looked exactly like a real person, she was yet so transparent that when, determined to investigate matters, I laid my hand on her shoulder (need I say I only felt the cold wall ?) I could see the gleam of my wedding ring through her quaint embroidery. The moment I touched her she seemed to slip down between the bed and the wall, and the last thing I saw were wan hands clasped as if in entreaty. I feel I should be telling the story far better if I could say the 'blood froze in my veins, my hair stood on end, vainly I tried to cry out,' etc., but, to be truthful, I, though somewhat staggered, was not frightened, but more annoyed at being again awakened. Thinking it might be the heat which affected me, I dragged the mattress under one of the little windows, and was soon once more asleep.

And Yet Again! " But again the forced awakening. This time the figure stood at the bottom of the mattress, and the strange indescribable look of *solid* transparency—which I can see to this day—showed the gleam of the white-tiled stove through the figure which stood out complete and perfect in its weird halo.

" Her right arm pointed to the door ; her face with the sad eyes (which yet seemed to see nothing), sadder than ever, seemed asking me to follow ; but here I confess my courage failed, and, sitting up, I watched her fade gradually away, chased, perhaps, by the coming dawn which soon after came in cold and pale at the little windows.

" I have never yet told this true tale without the question, 'Why didn't you wake your husband?' Common sense again, because I knew he was tired, and the visitant was not of a nature to alarm. Had it been that of a truculent-looking man with a dagger, I might perhaps have been beguiled into the orthodox 'shriek of terror.'

" Beyond plentiful enquiries from employés downstairs, ' Ob die gnädige Frau wohlgeschlafenhat ?' and no attempt at comment or denial when I stated that I quite understood why the room was not used, there was no sequel to the adventure.

" Another frequent suggestion from auditors is that I was ' the victim of a freak with a magic lantern from a house opposite,' but any one knowing the quaint old hotel knows the height the top floor is above the broad river which stretches between the Trois Rois and other habitations ; nor would any slide have thrown those wan, passionately clasped hands, or that gesture, between entreaty and command.

" No ! the proper explanation of what I saw, and why, has yet to be offered me."

A Ghost in the Law Court. It is not often that ghosts are brought into a court of law, but in the following case, which is sent me by an Anglican clergyman, the ghost formed the matter of a lawsuit. The judge, however, ruled that ghosts could not be admitted to exist, and the person who refused to pay his rent, on the ground that the apartments were already tenanted, lost his case.

"During the Nice season of 1858-9, I was staying there with some of my family in a house near the old town, but on the opposite side of the river. It is much changed there now. We occupied a part of the Rue de Chausée. Exactly over our apartment was a set of rooms that were not let during any part of the season, although I was told by the landlady that they were good rooms and well furnished; but she never offered to show them to me, nor did I ever see them during the six months I remained in the house.

"However, the house was large, and adjoining the said rooms, the best for sun, etc., in the house, by their position, were other rooms on the same floor, and to these rooms came a German lady and her two sons, to lodge for the winter. The elder of the sons was a young musician, in the habit of playing the piano far into the small hours of the night when he first arrived.

"It was soon reported to us that the German family was troubled with a ghost. We heard different tales about their being much alarmed; and at length it was whispered that the whole family, their servant included, had been so frightened that they all slept in one room.

"Affairs were thus when, one morning, the landlady, a Mademoiselle Rose, an aged lady who had been a fashionable dressmaker in her time, and was well known in Nice, which was then Italian, entered our rooms in violent agitation, holding a large key in her hand. She said the German lady and her son were about to leave the house that very day, because they alleged that the night before, while a lady and gentleman, both artists of Nice, were spending the evening with them, a monk had passed through a door of the room in which they sat, which door communicated with the under apartment, that the monk had crossed the room and filled them with terror. I do not remember how they said he got out of the room, nor could the landlady tell how he got in. 'How could the monk have got through that door?' exclaimed Mademoiselle Rose, holding up the key, 'for here is the key of it, that I have had all along in my possession; and there is a bureau against the door on the other side.'

"Ghosts, by all accounts, have done even more curious things than that. Only the landlady did not call it a ghost,

but a monk. The German lady was as good as her word.
They all left the house that day, and took lodgings elsewhere.   What is more, the German lady refused to pay the
rent.   The consequence was the landlady sued her in court.
The case was in the newspapers—I saw it there.   The Judge
decreed that, as the law did not recognise ghosts, the German
lady must pay the rent for the season.   If I remember right,
the younger son of the German lady acknowledged that
his brother had seen a ghost before, which ghost was also
a monk.

" We were never incommoded during our stay of six months
by any apparition."

Mr. William Paterson Henry, writing from Old
A Haunted   Bank House, Macduff, N.B., sends me the fol-
Bungalow.   lowing account of a haunted Ceylon bungalow.
He says :—

" At the time of the occurrence I am about to relate we were
living on the Black Forest tea and coffee garden in the island
of Ceylon.   Our family consisted of my wife, self, and two
children, with the usual staff of servants.   Our bungalow was
situated on the spur of a hill which ran at a right angle across
a large valley, comprising some hundreds of acres under tea
and coffee.   The bungalow, forming three sides of a square,
consisted of the main building with a frontage of about ninety
feet, and a back wing at each end ; the one on the north side
containing nursery and children's bath and dressing rooms,
and on the south, dining-room, pantry, and scullery, only
removed by a few yards from the kitchen and servants' rooms.
A ten-feet wide verandah ran along the entire length of the
house in front, and was continued round the north end as far
as the nursery door.

" One night after we had visited the nursery
The Ghost   and seen that all was right we retired to our own
Knocks.   room, and were soon in bed and asleep.   I had
slept, as I afterwards ascertained, for about a couple of hours,
when I slowly awoke with a dim consciousness that there was
some one in the room.   Seeing nothing, I lay down again.
Hardly, however, had I done so, when I was aroused by
a loud sound of knocking—six distinct knocks I counted—
and had no difficulty in tracing the sound to the door of the
children's dressing-room, removed but a few feet from my back
window.   I lay quite still, listening intently, and half expecting to hear the door open, but instead of this the knocking
was again repeated.

"My wife then came in from her room. On comparing notes I found she had been awakened in exactly the same manner, and had then heard the six distinct knocks twice repeated. I was already dressed in pyjamas, and hastily encasing my feet in a pair of slippers, I went out to see what caused the knocking.

The Ghost Flies. "I was completely puzzled to account for the disturbance, and was just on the point of returning to the bungalow baffled, when my attention was suddenly arrested by a white form crouching under a Hibiscus shrub within three feet of where I then stood. Immediately on being discovered it assumed the upright form, and bolted along the path in front of me. I promptly gave pursuit for ten or a dozen paces, but the distance between us was so speedily increased that I gave up the chase, and was fain to content myself by hurling threats of shooting, etc., after the retreating figure. I stood in the road and turned the full light of the lamp on it for a distance of some eighty yards, until a bend in the path hid it from my sight. On my return to the bungalow, in reply to my wife's inquiries, I described what I had seen as a figure having the appearance of a native man considerably above the average height, with a huge white turban encircling his head, while all the upper part of his body, and as far down as the middle of the thigh, was enveloped in a loose flowing robe of Madras muslin, the end of which fluttered over the right shoulder as the form retreated. As I was proceeding with my description, it suddenly struck me that not only were the lower limbs invisible, but there was not the faintest sound of footsteps as it sped along the road.

"It's only the Ghost!" "Next day, when I returned to the bungalow for my mid-day breakfast, I found that my wife had been ventilating our previous night's experience amongst the servants with a view to obtaining some light on the matter, and was not a little astonished to discover the matter-of-course manner in which her circumstantial account of our midnight visitor was received. 'Why, that's the *ghost*,' they exclaimed with one voice. 'Master and lady have seen the *ghost*; that's all.' 'Twas '*only the ghost*,' they reiterated, and there was therefore not the slightest cause for alarm. It seemed, then, that the ghost was quite an old acquaintance of theirs. I was somewhat amused with the explanation, but thinking it might lead to something, I summoned our servants, who were partly Tamils from the Malabar Coast, and

partly Singhalese natives of the country, and subjected them
one by one to a most severe cross-examination in their respective languages in my office. With some insignificant and
immaterial details, all their descriptions agreed in a manner
that was at once striking and startling.

"The gardener, who came to work in the grey
dawn of the morning, had *frequently* seen the
'Ahvie or Pezazi' (ghost or devil) loitering twixt
the dining-room and nursery doors. The first time he saw it,
he supposed it to be a coolie from some neighbouring estate,
who had arrived over-night with a letter—a thing of frequent
occurrence—and passed by to begin his day's duties without
remark. The following morning, on finding the figure again
in the same place, he accosted it with the question, 'What
estate do you come from?' He received no reply, and again
passed on towards the kitchen. On the third morning he
again perceived the same figure, and on this occasion summoned up courage to put out his hand, with the idea of seizing
what he had concluded was some person there for no honest
purpose. To his astonishment and horror, his hand grasped
nothing, and he hurried along to the kitchen in a state of the
utmost fear and excitement. On recounting his experiences
of the past three mornings to the inmates, he was good-
naturedly assured that there was no cause for alarm. 'You
have only seen the ghost. Don't be afraid.' 'What Ghost?'
'Why, the bungalow ghost, to be sure. Master's ghost!'
The cattle-keeper and groom had much the same account
to give; the former had many times seen the figure loitering
on the road leading to the cattle-shed in the early dawn, while
the latter had often seen it standing in the stable door. The
head servant, the cook, the kitchen-matey, and the bungalow
boy all gave like testimony to its appearance, viz.—that it was
that of a very tall man, dressed in a large white turban and
loose flowing robes of white Madras muslin.

"On the ayah's return a few days later I took
the earliest opportunity of examining her, and
before there was time for any collusion with the
other servants. Oh, yes, she had many, many times been
aroused from sleep by loud knocking on the nursery door,
generally about midnight, and often had she gone and opened
the door, sometimes to see nothing at all, and at other times
to see the tall figure of a man dressed in flowing white robes.
'Was there anything peculiar about the knocking? Was
it a double or a single knock?' 'Six distinct single knocks!'

*The Gar-
dener's Story.*

*What the
Ayah Said.*

'Always the same number?' 'Always the same.' 'When did she last hear it?' 'Quite recently, but she really could not fix a date, as it was of such frequent occurrence that she had ceased to pay any attention to it.' All subsequent inquiry led up to the same point—ample corroboration, but not a scintilla of explanation—but not one step beyond. In very truth an insolvable mystery!

"The Pezazi continued to favour us, or, at least, our domestics, with his visits from time to time, but unless specially questioned no one made any mention of his appearance outside the kitchen walls. For months after I used every means I could think of to throw light upon it, but all in vain. Four or five years have passed away since then, but nothing whatever has occurred to throw any light on the circumstances set forth, and I am utterly at a loss for any explanation."

A Gruesome Horror in Georgia. The following story reaches me from across the Atlantic. It appeared in the San Francisco *Examiner*, November 29th, 1891. If it is not true it is at least well invented, the item about the cat being in itself sufficient to justify its reproduction here. The authority for the story is a correspondent of the Chicago *Press*, in Statesborough, Georgia. The occurrences are said to have begun about the first week in November, in a house occupied by a farmer of education, named Walsingham, in Oakville, on the Savannah river. Not believing in ghosts, the Walsinghams at first attributed the disturbances to mischievous neighbours. This explanation, however, soon had to be abandoned :—

The Dog's Neck Broken. "These disturbances generally took the form of noises in the house after the family had retired and the light extinguished—continual banging of the doors, things overturned, the door-bell rang, and the annoying of the house dog, a large and intelligent mastiff.

"One day Don Cæsar, the mastiff, was found in the hallway barking furiously and bristling with rage, while his eyes seemed directed to the wall just before him. At last he made a spring forward with a hoarse yelp of ungovernable fury, only to fall back as if flung down by some powerful and cruel hand. Upon examination it was found that his neck had been broken.

The Cat and the Ghost. "The house cat, on the contrary, seemed rather to enjoy the favour of the ghost, and would often enter a door as if escorting some visitor in, whose hand was stroking her back. She would also climb about a chair, rubbing herself and purring as if well pleased at the presence of some one in the seat. She and Don Cæsar invariably manifested this eccentric conduct at the same time, as though the mysterious being was visible to both of them.

"The annoying visitant finally took to rousing the family at all hours of the night by making such a row as to render any rest impossible.

"This noise, which consisted of shouts, groans, hideous laughter, and a peculiar, most distressing wail, would sometimes proceed, apparently, from under the house, sometimes from the ceiling, and at other times in the very room in which the family was seated. One night Miss Amelia Walsingham, the young lady daughter, was engaged at her toilet, when she felt a hand laid softly on her shoulder. Thinking it her mother or sister, she glanced in the glass before her, only to be thunderstruck at seeing the mirror reflect no form but her own, though she could plainly see a man's broad hand lying on her arm.

An Infernal Charivari.

"She brought the family to her by her screams, but when they reached her all sign of the mysterious hand was gone. Mr. Walsingham himself saw footsteps form beside his own while walking through the garden after a light rain.

"The marks were those of a man's naked feet, and fell beside his own as if the person walked at his side.

"Matters grew so serious that the Walsinghams became frightened and talked of leaving the house, when an event took place that confirmed them in this determination. The family was seated at the supper-table with several guests who were spending the evening, when a loud groan was heard in the room overhead.

"This was, however, nothing unusual, and very little notice was taken of it until one of the visitors pointed out a stain of what looked like blood on the white tablecloth, and it was seen that some liquid was slowly dripping on the table from the ceiling overhead. This liquid was so much like freshly-shed blood as to horrify those who watched its slow dropping. Mr. Walsingham, with several of his guests, ran hastily upstairs and into the room directly over the one into which the blood was dripping.

Blood Dripping from the Ceiling.

"A carpet covered the floor, and nothing appeared to explain the source of the ghastly rain; but, anxious to satisfy themselves thoroughly, the carpet was immediately ripped up, and the boarding found to be perfectly dry, and even covered with a thin layer of dust, and all the while the floor was being examined the persons below could swear the blood never ceased to drip. A stain the size of a dinner-plate was formed before the drops ceased to fall. This stain was examined next day under the microscope, and was pronounced by competent chemists to be human blood.

The Ghost Faced for a Wager. "The Walsinghams left the house the next day, and since then the place has been apparently given over to spooks and evil spirits, which make the night hideous with the noise of revel, shouts, and furious yells. Hundreds from all over this county and adjacent ones have visited the place, but few have the courage to pass the night in the haunted house. One daring spirit, one Horace Gunn, of Savannah, however, accepted a wager that he could not spend twenty-four hours in it, and did so, though he declares that there is not enough money in the county to make him pass another night there. He was found the morning after by his friends with whom he made the wager in an insensible condition, and was with difficulty brought out of the swoon. He has never recovered from the shock of his horrible experience, and is still confined to his bed suffering from nervous prostration.

An Icy Breath Blows out the Light. "His story is that shortly after nightfall he endeavoured to kindle a fire in one of the rooms and to light the lamp with which he had provided himself, but to his surprise and consternation, found it impossible to do either. An icy breath, which seemed to proceed from some invisible person at his side, extinguished each match as he lighted it. At this peculiarly terrifying turn of affairs Mr. Gunn would have left the house and forfeited the amount of his wager, a considerable one, but he was restrained by the fear of ridicule of his story not being believed in. He seated himself in the dark with what calmness he could, and waited developments.

An Invisible Chase. "For some time nothing occurred, and the young man was half dozing, when, after an hour or two, he was brought to his feet by a sudden yell of pain or rage that seemed to come from under the house. This appeared to be the signal for an outbreak of hideous noises all over the house. The sound of running feet could be heard scurrying up and down the stairs, hastening from one room to another, as if one person fled from the pursuit of a second. This kept up for nearly an hour, but at last ceased altogether, and for some time Mr. Gunn sat in darkness and quiet, and had about concluded that the performance was over for the night. At last his attention was attracted by a white spot that gradually appeared on the opposite wall from him.

A Ghastly Head. "This spot continued to brighten, until it seemed a disc of white fire, when the horrified spectator saw that the light emanated from and surrounded a human head, which, without a body or any visible means of support, was moving slowly along the wall, about the height of a man from the floor. This ghastly head appeared to be that of an aged person, though whether male or female it was difficult to determine. The hair was long and grey, and matted together with dark clots of blood, which also issued from a deep jagged wound in one temple. The cheeks were fallen in and the whole face indicated suffering and unspeakable misery. The eyes were wide open, and gleamed with an unearthly fire, while the glassy balls seemed to follow the terror-stricken Mr. Gunn, who was too thoroughly paralysed by what he saw to move or cry out. Finally, the head disappeared and the room was once more left in darkness, but the young man could hear what seemed to be half a dozen persons moving about him, while the whole house shook as if rocked by some violent earthquake.

Grasped by Icy Hands and Throttled. "The groaning and wailing that broke forth from every direction was something terrific, and an unearthly rattle and banging as of china and tin pans being flung to the ground floor from the upper storey added to the deafening noise. Gunn at last roused himself sufficiently to attempt to leave the haunted house. Feeling his way along the wall in order to avoid the beings, whatever they were, that filled the room, the young man had nearly succeeded in reaching the door when he found himself seized by the ankle and was violently thrown to the floor. He was grasped by icy hands, which sought to grip him about the throat. He struggled with his unseen foe, but was soon overpowered and choked into insensibility. When found by his friends his throat was black with the marks of long, thin fingers, armed with cruel, curved nails.

"The only explanation that can be found for these mysterious manifestations is that about three months ago a number of bones were discovered on the Walsingham place which some declared even then to be those of a human being. Mr. Walsingham pronounced them, however, to be an animal's, and they were hastily thrown into an adjacent limekiln.

It is supposed to be the outraged spirit of a person to whom they belonged in life that is now creating such consternation."

CHAPTER VII

A PARTING WORD

> " There are more things in heaven and earth, Horatio,
> Than are dreamt of in your philosophy."—HAMLET, Act i. sc. 5.

THAT quotation is the most hackneyed in the language. That is why I have used it. I have hardly found one individual to whom I have told the " Real Ghost Stories " who has not taken refuge in Shakespeare's familiar couplet. The tritest reflection is the most general. But the perusal of " Real Ghost Stories " may convert what has hitherto been but a meaningless phrase into a solid and abiding conviction.

If this be the case, the reader will ask, what are these " more things "? If he does not ask it, the phrase for him is still only a phrase with no soul in it. For if it be a fact that, as our other great poet affirms,—

> " Millions of spiritual creatures walk the earth
> Unseen, both while we wake and when we sleep,"

it is impossible not to feel a natural and healthy curiosity as to what these creatures may be. Nor do I think it possible to read all the evidence massed within the covers of this book, without having a deeper sense of the reality and the nearness of the Invisible World borne in upon the mind.

The net result of the study of the most fascinating subjects, if I test it by its effect upon my own mind, cannot fail to be for good and almost only for good. I began the compilation of this volume somewhat lightly, little dreaming that I should close it with so serious a sense of the enormous importance of the subject, and so deep a conviction as to the results likely to follow a revolution in the attitude of the popular mind towards the phenomena of the occult world. These results are both scientific and religious, and between them they include almost the entire range of human thought.

Without claiming that any finally conclusive demonstration has yet been afforded us of any of the phenomena described in the foregoing chapters—from telepathy to the return of the ghosts of the dead—there seems to be indubitably sufficient testimony to justify a suspension of that popular judgment which hitherto has been so definitely hostile to the hypothesis of the objective reality of these phantasmal apparitions. All that I claim is, not that any one should admit that apparitions actually appear, but only that the evidence in favour of that hypothesis is too strong to justify any impartial person in refusing to consider and to investigate. That attitude of mind is irrational, and therefore unscientific ; and as this prides itself upon being a scientific age, it may be hoped that the initiative so boldly taken by Professor Oliver Lodge at the last meeting of the British Association may be resolutely and persistently followed up. Of one thing we can fortunately feel no doubt. When scientific men include the unexplored region in the domain of their investigations, they will not make the silly complaint that no phenomena are genuine because there is an enormous overgrowth of pseudo-phenomena due to fraud and folly. Practical men never refuse to mine for gold, although, in order to extract an ounce of the precious metal, they have to crush a ton of worthless quartz. The proportion of genuine to merely imaginary or fraudulent phenomena is certainly not so small as that which exists between the pure metal and the reefs of auriferous stone in Australia, California, or the Transvaal. Neither will men of science object on the score that many of the phenomena are in themselves trivial and sometimes almost imbecile. They will remember the ridicule the scientists of his day poured upon Galvani for his experiments with frogs, and they will reflect that " the frog's dancing-master," together with one Benjamin Franklin, who experimented with kites on Boston Common, are to-day revolutionising the mechanical world. The objection, that if there had been anything in these occult manifestations it would not have been left to us to find it out, will not even occur to those who remember that water had hissed when boiling into steam since fire and water first came together, but it was not till last century that James Watt saw in the power that lifted the kettle-lid the motor of commerce and the sceptre of civilisation. Telepathy, or thought transference without the use of the organs of sense, may be destined to play as great a part in the world as steam and electricity. That remains to be seen, and one solid practical good that will come out of this book will be the impetus which it will give to telepathic experiments. Anything that increases the mastery of mind over the limitations of matter and space tends to the upward evolution of Man.

After telepathy, the most practically useful truth that is

suggested by the " Real Ghost Stories " is that of the existence
of the Double. This ancient belief bids fair to be scientifically
demonstrated as an actual fact. The day when a Double is
photographed under test-conditions will mark the dawn of a
new era of scientific discovery. The instantaneous transporta-
tion of the Thought Body, instinct with consciousness, tangible, capable of speech, and preserving memory of its flight
from place to place, is a conception so stupendous as to
stagger the most daring imagination. It is as if we were transported into space of four dimensions. Yet who can read the
record of the appearance of Doubles, both before death and
at other times, without feeling that the possibility of such
latent powers existing in at least some human beings can no
longer be dismissed as unthinkable? Whether or not the experiments which I am conducting with a Double turn out
successfully or not—they were not concluded in time for publication in this Number—there seems to me sufficient evidence
to justify a belief that in these phantasms of the living we have
a clue to a great and as yet unworked mine of latent human
capacity, which, if, like all other human faculties, it be capable
of development by education and exercise, may yet prove an
enormous agency in transforming society.

The importance of the Double from a theological point of
view was long ago recognised by the Fathers of the Church.
Of this there is a familiar instance in the story told by S.
Augustine about his friend Gennadius, a physician well-known
at Carthage, who had a vision of a young man who conveyed
him to a distant city, where he showed him many things. He
appeared to him again at a later date, and was greeted by
Gennadius, who reminded him of their former meeting.
" Where is your body now? " the apparition inquired. " In
my bed." " Do you know that now you see nothing with the
eyes of your body? " " I know it." " Well, then, with what
eyes do you behold me? " As Gennadius hesitated and knew
not what to reply, the young man said to him, " In the same
way that you see and hear me now that your eyes are shut and
your senses asleep, thus after your death you will live, see,
hear, but with eyes of the spirit; so doubt not that there is
another life after the present one."

It is rather curious to learn that this strange, incredible, and
altogether preposterous phenomenon of the Double, if established, will merely be the scientific verification in the nineteenth century of the old Catholic doctrine of Bi-Location.
When engaged in writing this chapter a German Doctor of

Divinity, who had been on a mission to the United States, arrived in London on his way back to the Vatican. I had known him two or three years ago before he had entered holy orders, while he was still studying at Rome. Learned, enthusiastic, and keenly intelligent, he listened with polite attention to the discussion of the so-called Thought Body. Then he said, "All this has been settled long ago. Why are you disturbing yourselves about it?" "Now, how," said I, "and when?" "If you will read the Roman Catechism, or the works of St. Thomas Aquinas, or even the Decrees of the Council of Trent, you will find that the Church has spoken, and there is nothing more to be said." "Well, what has the Church said about astral bodies?" I said, rather curiously. "The teaching of the Church is that the phenomenon of bilocation is not natural, but is occasionally permitted by special grace, as in the case of certain well-known saints, or sometimes for other inscrutable reasons which are less advantageous to those who are the recipients of the favour, which is not natural, but distinctly supernatural. There you have a case of this phenomenon of Thought Body recorded in the history of the Church in connection with two of her most famous saints. Francesco Mariani tells us, in his 'Life of Loyola,' that, ' At the time that Ignatius was living at Rome, he appeared to Leonardo Clesselis at Cologne. Leonardo was a Fleming, and an aged old man, who was the first rector of the college in that city, and who governed it a long time with great reputation of sanctity. He had a most fervent desire again to see the holy father, and to have the happiness of speaking with him ; he informed him of this desire in a letter, and begged, as a great favour, that he might journey over the 300 leagues which lay between them on foot. Ignatius answered that the welfare of others required his stay at Cologne, so that he must not move, but that perhaps it might please God to content him in some easier way. While he still remained at Cologne, one day when he was not asleep, the holy father showed himself to him alive and held a long conversation with him. He then disappeared and left the old man full of the greatest joy at the accomplishment of his desires in so marvellous a way.'

"S. Athanasius—in his Life of S. Anthony—relates that while that saint was preaching in the Cathedral (presumably of Milan) he suddenly became entranced and on his return to consciousness stated that he had been attending the funeral of S. Martin of Tours, who, it was afterwards ascertained, had died at the time."

"Then," said I, "may I take it for granted on your authority that the Catholic Church has stamped its *imprimatur* upon the doctrine of the dual body?" "Not upon the doctrine of the dual body," said the theologian, "but upon the doctrine of bi-location." "Which," said I, " is the same thing." "No, not quite," he said. "So near as to make no matter," said I. "But tell me, does bi-location allow the bi-located person to be intelligently conscious in both places at the same time?" "No," said the doctor, "because the soul is one and not two." "But what about our dual personality?" "That is all nonsense. The so-called dual personality is simply two phases of the one personality. No sound, sane psychologist, from the days of Aristotle to our own, has ever advocated such a figment as the duality of the soul. There may be on rare occasions, by Divine grace permitted, a duality of body, but a duality of soul, no, that is impossible!"

A Catholic priest writes to me as follows :—

The Doctrine of the Catholic Church. "With regard to bi-location, or double personality, there is a great deal of very interesting matter in S. Thomas of Aquin, and also in Cardinal Cajetan's "Commentaries of S. Thomas." I had been hoping I should have had time to go through it—give you a good deal in modern English expressions—so as to make it interesting and intelligible to your readers, but I have not had the time. However, the substance of the principles is this :— *Bi-location properly* so-called, is defined by the scholastics as the perfect and simultaneous existence of one and the same individual in two distinct places at the same time. This *never* does and never can happen. But bi-location, improperly so-called, and which S. Thomas terms *raptus*, does occur, and is identical with the *double*, as you call it, in the cases of Gennadius, S. Ignatius, etc.

"S. Thomas quotes as illustrations or instances, S. Paul being taken up to the Third Heaven. Ezekiel, the prophet, was taken by God and shown Jerusalem, whilst at the same time he was sitting in the room with the ancients of the tribe of Judah before him (Ezekiel viii.), etc. In which the soul of man is not wholly detached from the body, being necessary for the purpose of giving life, but is detached from the SENSES of the body. S. Thomas gives three causes for this phenomenon : (1) Divine power ; (2) the power of the Devil ; and (3) disease of the body when very violent sometimes.

"Cornelius à Lapide, in his 'Commentaries on the Scripture,' has some interesting comments on this subject."

The third benefit from this study has been the wonderful actuality which it gives to the familiar text, which says, " There is nothing hidden which shall not be revealed, and that the secrets of the innermost chamber will be proclaimed upon the housetops." The great invisible camera obscura on which there seems to be imprinted, as imperishably as in a mirror, all the words and acts of our life, what is it but the semblance of the books which, it is written, shall be opened at the Day of Judgment? The clairvoyant vision of things past as if they had been actually in progress, and of things thousands of miles distant as if they had been in the street below our windows, gives one a wonderfully vivid realisation of the possibilities of the great day of final account.

The greatest gain, however, that is likely to accrue from the study of the phenomena to which this volume is devoted, will arise from the deepened certainty which it gives as to the permanence of the individual after death. Of immortality I say nothing. That cannot, from the nature of things, be demonstrated. But of a life after death—a life in which those who live on this side of the grave retain their identity in the other world—that may yet be demonstrated by tests as exact and as conclusive as any of which the science of psychology admits. The evidence and experiments of the Psychical Research Society have already shattered, for one at least of our acutest scientific minds, all purely materialistic hypotheses. When dust returns to dust and ashes to ashes, the Ego lives on ; the personal identity, the consciousness of the individual, does not seem to even be momentarily impaired. It does not seem to be too bold a speculation to believe that the patient methods of inductive science, the careful examination of evidence, and the repeatedly renewed experiments of investigators, will before long completely re-establish the failing belief in the reality of the world beyond the grave, and leave us with as little room for doubt as to the existence of the spirit after death as we have now for doubting the existence of Behring Straits or of the Pyramids. It is possible that this bringing of life and immortality to light, or at least the establishment of the certainty of a future life upon impregnable scientific foundations, may seem to some by no means an unmixed blessing. To many it would undoubtedly add a new terror to death. The thought of a prolonged existence in a more spiritual sphere, where you would witness the working out of the dread consequences of the breach of laws and of the neglect of responsibilities, is often anything but attractive to the mind of man.

To rest, and that for ever, even in the grave, seems sometimes the boon of boons. It would seem to be an unattainable one. For if the testimonies of many credible witnesses may be believed, there is no death. The form—the vesture—perishes, but the soul, the Ego, the essential principle, lives on. Revelation has always affirmed this. It seems as if Science were once more to vindicate her claim to be regarded as the handmaid of Religion by affording conclusive demonstration of its reality. Whether we like this or dislike it is immaterial. The supreme question is, What is the truth? And whatever drawbacks there may be to the theory of the future life, there is at least one enormous compensating advantage in knowing that the accounts between man and his Maker are not finally closed when he ceases to breathe on earth, and that the Almighty has still the infinite expanse of eternity in which to vindicate the justice of His dealings with every human soul.

INDEX

A.

Abel the Fratricide, Apparition of, 241.
Abercrombie on Dreaming, 81.
Addison, W. D., 214.
African Ghosts, 128, 194, 203, 243.
Aimless Doubles, 39.
Aksakoff, Mme., Apparition to, 248.
Alternating Personality, Instance of, 7.
Angle House, Ghosts in, 290.
Animals:
  Apparitions of, 192, 210, 258, 262, 267, 268, 269, 293, 306, 308.
  Fighting, Ghostly sounds of, 302.
  Perception of the Supernatural in Animals stronger than in Human Beings, 129, 188, 195, 198, 255, 305, 323.
  Phantoms Killing, 323.
  [See also Names of Animals.]
Anne Boleyn's Chamber in the Tower, Apparition in, 251.
Ansel Bourne and A. J. Brown— Instance of Alternating Personality, 7.
Archer, Mr., 150.
Armenian Magazine, 292.
Armstrong Trial—W. T. Stead's presentiment of sentence, 74.
Artabanus, Apparition to, 243.
Astral Body [See Title Thought Body, or Double].
Atmosphere, Denseness of, Ghostly presences announced by, 216, 231, 285.
Australian Tragedy seen in Ireland, 123.

B.

Baby crying, Spectral sound of, 257.
Backman, Dr., 60.
Bacon, Francis, Dream of, 247.
Badcock, Rev. S., 295.

Badger—Apparition, 293.
Balcarres, Lord, Apparition to, 250.
Banshee heard by Lady Fanshaw, 249.
Barrett, Miss, Apparition to, 245.
Barter, General, 195.
Battles seen in Visions, 242, 244.
Baumgarten, Dr., 68.
Beds, Ghosts using, 282.
Bees killed by a " baleful breath," 288.
Bells rung by invisible agency, 277, 281, 296, 298, 299, 300.
Ben Jonson, Apparition to, 245.
Beresford, Lady, Apparition to, 249.
Beresford, Lord Charles, 120.
Besant, Mrs., Thought Body, Theory of, 30.
Best Beloved in Life, Spirit of, attending Death-bed, 183.
Betting Man converted by a Dream, 91.
Bi-location, Doctrine of:
  Roman Catholic Church, Teaching of, 330.
  Scriptural instances supporting, 332.
Bible:
  Family prayers, Ghost at, 293, 294.
  Phantoms respecting, 281.
  Reading aloud, spectral disturbances during, 268.
  Scriptural commands, Ghosts obeying, 154, 299.
Birkbeck Double, 133.
Bite of a Spectral Dog, 211.
Black Spirit—Instance of Diabolical Possession, 164.
Blackham, Mr., Prediction of, 82.
Blacking-bottle, Ghost flinging, 299.
Blood dripping from a Ceiling, 324.
Blows, Ghosts dealing, 210, 221, 267, 326.
Blucher, Apparition to, 244.

Georgina, F., 108, 226.
Georgia, Horrors in, 323.
"Glimpses of the Supernatural," 134.
Göethe :
Grandfather of, Visions, of, 76.
Premonitory vision of his own double, 245.
Goldsborough Farmhouse, Ghost in, 301.
Green, Mrs, 123.
Grellet, Stephen, Visions of, 80.
Grey Lady in Willington Mill, 264.
Grey, Robert, Warning of death to, 219.
Groans, Spectral, 268, 324, 326.
Gunn, Horace, 325.
Gurney, Mr. 33, 48, 128, 287.
Guthrie, Dr., Coat pulled by ghost, 246.

H.

Hair :
Singed by Phantoms, 284.
Stroked by Phantoms, 34, 223.
Hall, Bishop, Apparition to, 245.
Hambleton Hills, Ghost on, 190.
Hamilton, T. A., 91.
Hands :
Apparitions, 246.
Spectral, 279, 283.
[See also Title Touch.]
Happerfield, C., 179.
Harcourt, Countess, Vision of, 248.
Harford, John, Ghost of, 179.
Harvey, William, Dream saving life of, 247.
Hastings, Ralph, 276, 286, 289.
Haunted Houses [See Title Houses].
Headless Lady in Brook House, 280, 286.
Heads and Faces, Floating, 152, 155, 156, 201, 232, 290, 326.
Hell, Vision of, 230.
Henry, William Paterson, 320.
Henry IV. of France, Apparitions to, 241.
Herbert of Cherbury, Lord, and the sign, 247.
Hermitage Castle, Ghosts in, 253.
Highland faculty of Second Sight, 67, 88.
Holland, Lord, Apparition of, 250.
Holy Water, Ghost despising, 280.
Horses :
Apparitions, 192.

Perception of the supernatural in, stronger than in human beings, 129, 188, 198.
Hotels, Ghosts in, 222, 309, 316.
Houses, Haunted :
Angle House, 290.
Brook House, 276.
Copley House, 289.
Goldsborough, Farmhouse at, 301.
Möttlingen, Cottage at, 159.
No. 8, 304.
Parsonages, 292, 296.
Willington Mill, 261.
Howitt, William, 158, 163.
Hypnotism :
Myers, F. W. H., on, 21.
Thought Body, Mystery of, explained by, 47.
Unconscious personality set free by, 6, 9.

I.

Ignatius, Double of, 248, 331, 332.
Indian Hills, Spectral Cavalcade descending, 195.
Inglewood Advertiser, 124.
"Intellectual Powers," 81.
Intelligent action of Ghosts, 170, 242, 243, 244, 245, 309.
Irish Castle and its Ghosts, 254.
Irish Outrage seen in a Dream, 58.

J.

Jacobite Ghost, 293, 294.
James IV. of Scotland warned by apparition, 241.
"Jane"—Clairvoyant Visions of, 271.
Janet, M. Jules, 6, 13, 17.
Jarnac, Battle of, seen in a vision, 242.
"Jeffrey" the Epworth Ghost, 293.
Joan of Arc, Visions of, 242.
Johnson, Rev. Mr., 77.
Jonson, Ben, Apparition to, 245.
Journeys, Dream, afterwards fulfilled, 226, 234.
Julian the Apostate—Apparitions, 243, 248.
Julius Cæsar, Apparition to, 243.

K.

Kaffirs attacking Laager, Apparition of, 203.

[This Index has been compiled by Miss Nancy Bailey, Indexing Office, 7, Great College Street, Westminster, S.W.]

Library of the Mystic Arts
A LIBRARY OF ANCIENT AND MODERN CLASSICS

ANIMAL GHOSTS by Raymond Bayless. With a Foreword by Robert Crookall, B.Sc. (Psychology), D.Sc., Ph.D. 5⅜ x 8″ $5.95   PSYCHICAL RESEARCH

In this significant volume, Raymond Bayless presents a methodical, scientific analysis of animal ghosts, and other paranormal and psychic phenomena found with certain animals.

With engaging skepticism, the author separates the "mediumistic chaff" from authentic paranormal experiences to present a remarkable series of verified case histories of animal ghosts and hauntings. In twenty-one fascinating chapters, he explores such topics as: Animal Hypnotism . . . Mysterious Abilities . . . Psychic Photography . . . Thinking and Communicating Animals . . . Animals and Mediums . . . Pseudo-Mediums and Mediumistic Chaff . . . Animals and Astral Projection . . . Materialization and Animals . . . Hauntings and Animals . . . Composite Phantoms . . . The Tweedale Haunting . . . A Mysterious Barking . . . Animal Ghost Stories . . . The Poltergeist . . . Witchcraft . . . Objectivity and Apparitions.

Bayless brings a delightful candor and humor to his investigations, as when he exposes a fraudulent medium, in Chapter VIII: "We were treated to endless messages from our departed relatives, . . . and this incredible communion with our dead became all the more awesome and majestic since our dear departed were all very much alive at the time."

The author demonstrates how psychic abilities and phenomena exhibited by human beings are also possessed by certain animals—and he points out the distinctive differences between the animal and human phenomena.

The distinguished scientist, Dr. Robert Crookall, lauds *Animal Ghosts* as a "really worthwhile book . . . the first comprehensive survey of the possibilities of animal extrasensory perception (ESP) and animal survival of death . . . a great service in giving us an authoritative review of this intriguing area."

Animal Ghosts is an exciting, provocative work—offering solace to animal lovers, food for thought to the general reader, and important new vistas to the serious student of the occult sciences and psychical research.

INTRODUCTION TO AFRICAN CIVILIZATION by John G. Jackson, introduction and additional bibliographical notes by John Henrik Clarke. 384 pp. bibliography, illustrations. 5⅜ x 8″ 75-92360 $10.00   ANTHROPOLOGY

With painstaking, objective, brilliant scholarship, John G. Jackson presents a portrait of a human heritage infinitely more rich and colorful and varied than is generally understood.

This book challenges all of the standard approaches to African history and will, no doubt, disturb the large number of overnight "authorities" on Africa who will discover that they do not really know the depth of African history and the role that the Africans have played in creating early human societies.

Star-gods, moon-gods, sun-gods, Osiris, the zodiac, the lost continent of Atlantis—the impact of the myths and legends of ancient man upon human history is analyzed here: *"Since the lore of astronomy and the calendar were the basis of much of the mythology, ritual, and religion of ancient Egypt, which in turn has profoundly affected all the great religious systems of later days,"* observes the author, *"we deem it proper to discuss . . . these ancient African cults and creeds, and their effects on other cultures."*

What must be one of the most tragic instances of near-genocide in all the ages is told in Jackson's devastating, poignant chapter, "The Destruction of African Culture": *"All told, the slave trade was responsible for the death of one hundred million Africans. The modern reader may find it hard to imagine the desolating impact of the slave trade on African society."*

John G. Jackson has examined rare, musty tomes and universal classics, obscure studies and celebrated works of ancient philosophers and modern scholars—men like Homer, Herodotus, Darwin, Haldane, Frobenius, Morgan, McCabe, Freud. He has drawn from the work of distinguished anthropologists, archaeologists, geologists, sociologists, evolutionists, psychologists, as well as conventional historians, to present a vivid history of man's origin, his barbarisms, his glories in the vast continent of Africa.

THOMAS JEFFERSON VS. RELIGIOUS OPPRESSION by Frank Swancara 160 pp. appendices. 5⅜ x 8″ 70-105440 $5.95   POLITICS/RELIGION

This volume tells of the laws and decisions outside of Virginia before and after the American Revolution which imposed various civil disabilities for nonconforming opinion, *e.g.,* making the "Infidel" incompetent to testify in court, even against a murderer. It also contains a review of cases where criminal penalties, sometimes capital, were inflicted for avowal of disbelief in established doctrines or narratives of biblical miracles.

Here are the prelatic, priestly, and mobbish cruelties, impostures and coercions committed to aid orthodoxy and enable ecclesiastics to retain pelf and power.

Here too are observations on how it became possible in 1786 (and then only in Virginia) to obtain a Statute which would free from state **penalties or interfer**ence every opinion or speech "in matters of religion."

OUT-OF-THE-BODY EXPERIENCES: A FOURTH ANALYSIS by Robert Crookall 208 pp. Appendices. 5½ x 8¼″ 79-97822 $4.95   PSYCHICAL RESEARCH

From the dawn of history to the present time, people have claimed to have left their bodies in various circumstances, to have retained consciousness, and subsequently to have reentered their bodies.

In *Out-of-the-Body Experiences: A Fourth Analysis,* a distinguished scientist applies the same rigorous procedure, on a psychological level, to such claims as he uses in a microscopic investigation of a petrified stem.

Robert Crookall, B.Sc., D.Sc., Ph.D., using scholarly, unsensational investigative techniques, has made detailed analyses of the testimonies of hundreds of individuals who have reported out-of-the-body experiences. *His investigations have revealed a remarkable pattern of events in out-of-the-body experiences.*

Crookall notes the extraordinary contrast in experiences of those who "died" forcibly or suddenly, as contrasted with those who "died" naturally or gradually. He compares the experiences of two different kinds of people: ordinary folk and those of a mediumistic bodily constitution. He describes in detail two distinct stages reported in some testimonies of out-of-the-body experiences.

Throughout this important volume appear significant insights and implications with regard to the concepts of Hades and Paradise, the question of life after death, the presence of "ghosts," and the meaning of the "silver cord" of the Scriptures.

MODERN AMERICAN SPIRITUALISM by Emma Hardinge. With an introduction by E. J. Dingwall. 5½ x 8¼" $5.95

An extraordinary document by an incredible woman, *Modern American Spiritualism* is a twenty-year record of Spiritualism in mid-nineteenth-century America.

In this volume, first published in 1870, Emma Hardinge sketches the events preceding the birth of modern Spiritualism in the United States. She describes the varied work of the exponents of Mesmerism, electro-biology, and phreno-magnetism.

Chronicled here are the life and writings of Andrew Jackson Davis, "the Poughkeepsie Seer," whose works Emma Hardinge viewed as the beginnings of Spiritualism proper.

In her comprehensive record of what she calls "the communion between earth and the world of spirits," the author quotes generously from nineteenth-century documents and pamphlets, which today are virtually unobtainable.

She traces the curious phenomena known as the Hydesville rappings, which ushered in what believers call the first Spiritual Telegraph. She describes the course of events during the investigation of the Fox sisters, and charts the growth of Spiritualism in the city and state of New York, as well as New England and throughout the United States up to the end of the Civil War.

E. J. Dingwall, in his Introduction to this work, discusses the amazing events in Emma Hardinge's early life that inspired her lifelong Spiritualistic activities. In an age when "woman's place was in the home," this courageous woman journeyed over three continents, lecturing, writing, and serving as a medium.

Besides *Modern American Spiritualism,* Emma Hardinge wrote *The Electric Physician* and *Nineteenth Century Miracles;* translated and edited two books of mysterious authorship called *Art Magic* and *Ghost Land;* collaborated in compiling a hymnal, *English Lyceum Manual;* saw to publication of two volumes of her lectures; edited *The Christian Spiritualist;* and founded and edited three journals— *The Western Star, Two Worlds,* and *The Unseen Universe.* She was also an accomplished musician and composer, and became Directress of Music at Dodsworth's Hall in New York.

Recounted here are Emma Hardinge's astonishing experiences as a medium and magnetic subject, her supernatural experiences with table tipping and rapping, her participation in a Spiritual Telegraph, and her involvement in an extraordinary and disturbing courtship having occult ramifications.

Both *Modern American Spiritualism* and the story of its fabulous author provide the reader a fascinating panorama of a remarkable era in the history of American Spiritualism.

THE BUDDHIST PRAYING-WHEEL. A Collection of Material Bearing Upon the Symbolism of the Wheel and Circular Movements in Custom and Religious Ritual by William Simpson, R.I., M.R.A.S., F.R.G.S., Hon. Assoc. R.I.B.A. x + 303 pp. index. Illustrated. $7.95   RELIGION/BUDDHISM

Why is the circular motif common to so many religious rituals?

This book traces the underlying symbolism of the wheel, the movements of worshippers and the religious dances of many races and religions, to a common solar origin in which the turning of a prayer-wheel or the motions of ceremonial all express the basic mystery of the sun's movement.

WILLIAM SIMPSON (1823-1899) was a well-known artist, journalist, author, and archaeologist. As special artist of the "Illustrated London News" he was present at many wars, coronations, and other important events. He travelled throughout India, Kashmir, Tibet and Europe, and published various works on architecture and archaeology.

Here he reviews the design of temples, the ceremonies amongst Egyptians, Mohammedans, Jews, Greeks, Gauls, Teutons, and Celts, and shows the importance of sunwise movement in pagan and Christian custom and folklore. The special significance of the anti-sunwise direction "Widdershins" is also discussed. The symbolism of the wheel is shown to be the most meaningful basic movement in the religions and folk customs of mankind from earliest times.

This book throws light on comparative religion and has special value today in view of modern interest in rituals and Oriental religion. "The truth of his main theory seems . . . fully established by the facts he has collected about the symbolism of the wheel, and the universality with which a sunwise direction has been associated with circular movements in religious ritual or ceremonial from time immemorial."—THE ATHENAEUM (London).

THE HISTORY OF MAGIC; to which is added an Appendix of the Most Remarkable and Best Authenticated Stories of Apparitions, Dreams, Second Sight, Somnambulism, Predictions, Divination, Witchcraft, Vampires, Fairies, Table-Turning, and Spirit Rapping by Joseph Ennemoser, translated by William Howitt. 2 vols. xvi + 741, 518 pp. Index. $25.00   MAGIC/HISTORY

The first comprehensive history of Magic, and still one of the best overall surveys.

DR. JOSEPH ENNEMOSER (1787-1854) was a distinguished physician who held the Chair of Medicine in the University of Bonn in 1819, esteemed as a lecturer on pathology and medico-philosophical subjects. He was one of the first reputable investigators of the new science of Animal Magnetism which flourished in the nineteenth century, eventually displaced by Medical Hypnotism.

In his encyclopedic survey of Magic, Dr. Ennemoser sought an underlying rationale to marvels and miracles, which he found in the concepts of Animal Magnetism—a fusion of Mesmerism and the occult, which has since became a neglected chapter of medicine and magic which deserves revival. Ennemoser was not only a theorist, but also a brilliant practitioner of the system, and many remarkable cures are ascribed to him.

This great history covers Visions, Ecstasies, Clairvoyance, Seership, Somnambulism, Bleeding Wounds, Healing by Touch, Talismans, Influence of Stones, Exorcism, and a score of other occult phenomena from the most ancient nations to nineteenth century Europe, with sections on great magicians and mystics, and their philosophies.

WILLIAM HOWITT (1792-1879), the translator, was a prominent literary figure of nineteenth century England who became a leading Spiritualist in the early days of great mediums like Daniel Dunglas Home and Florence Cook. Nearly half the second volume is taken up by a marvelous selection of true supernatural stories selected by Mary Howitt, the translator's wife.

This English translation, first published 1954, has long been a scarce collector's item. It is now reissued as a basic reference work, and as an inexhaustible survey of the miraculous and uncanny for the general reader.

"It is the best work of its kind yet published, and we would advise all who feel interested in the subjects of which it treats to make themselves acquainted with its pages."—THE ZOIST (London).

CITED IN: *The Best Books* by W. S. Sonnenschein, 3rd ed.

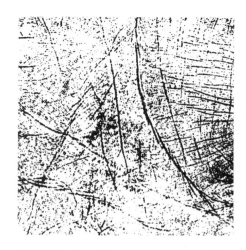

NAD: A Study of Some Unusual "Other-World" Experiences by Scott Rogo. Postscript by Dr. Robert Crookall. 5½ x 8¼" 71-114147 $5.95   PSYCHICAL RESEARCH

Here, for the first time in any book, is a full-bodied, critical appraisal of the extraordinary phenomenon known as NAD—a Sanskrit term signifying transcendental, celestial, astral, psychic, or paranormal music.

One hundred and one remarkable case histories, including those of the great English poet John Milton, author Bayard Taylor, the well-known parapsychologist Raymond Bayless, and authoress Rosamond Lehmann, illustrate the wide diversity of circumstances in which transcendental music has been heard by reliable witnesses.

There is an amazing correlation, the author has discovered, between certain bodily constitutions and vocal and instrumental paranormal music.

In his systematic presentation, D. Scott Rogo discusses these provocative aspects of the NAD phenomenon:

- NAD and out-of-the-Body Travel
- NAD in Normal States of Consciousness
- NAD — Related to Death
- NAD, Hauntings, and the Psychic Ether
- NAD, Mystics, and Mediums
- NAD and Its Relevancy to the Survival Issue

Also included in this volume are a masterly comparative study of *The Supreme Adventure* and the *Tibetan Book of the Dead* (Appendix A), and a comprehensive survey of literature on the out-of-the-body experience (Appendix B).

NAD: A Study of Some Unusual "Other-World" Experiences is an "interesting book," a "compact, well-reasoned study," and "the job has been well worth undertaking," says the distinguished scientist, Dr. Robert Crookall. It offers exciting avenues of exploration to all laymen and scientists who seek new light on the mysteries of psychic manifestations.

RAGNAROK; THE AGE OF FIRE AND GRAVEL by Ignatius Donnelly. vi + 720 pp.
$12.50   SCIENCE/SCIENTISM

More than half a century before Velikovsky's best-selling *Worlds in Collision,* Donnelly's *Ragnarok* put forward the same basic concept that a comet passed close to or struck the earth in prehistoric times, causing catastrophic changes remembered only dimly in mythologies, scriptural history, and the idea of divine judgment upon a sinful world.

IGNATIUS DONNELLY (1831-1901) was a farmer-politician who became lieutenant-governor of Minnesota, then a State Senator; before his death he had been nominated for the position of Vice-President of the U.S. His literary works were powerful and original—an amazing book on Atlantis, forerunner of the later works of Lewis Spence, two novels condemning social and racial injustice, and an extraordinary contribution to the Bacon-Shakespeare controversy.

The word "Ragnarok" comes from Norse mythology and describes the cataclysmic Twilight of the Gods that convulsed the earth during a Titanic conflict between gods and giants.

Less scientific than Velikovsky, and working within the limitations of his time, Donnelly nevertheless produced the precursor of many comet-catastrophe works, now valued for its inspired presentation of legends and mythologies from Hindus, Persians, Britons, Chinese, Greeks, Scandinavians, Central Americans, North and South American Indians, Aztecs, Toltecs, Quiches, Peruvians, Babylonians, Egyptians, and Arabians, with terrifying stories of disaster by fire, hail, frost and darkness, changes in climate, and legends of enormous dragons and other monsters.

Whether as a first expression of the Velikovsky theme, a stimulating analysis of doom legends, or simply science-fiction, this book is enthralling reading.

"It will be understood, therefore, that 'Ragnarok' is a strong and brilliant literary production, which will command the interest of general readers, and the admiration and respect, if not the universal credence of the conservative and the scientific."—THE DIAL (Chicago).

OCCULT SCIENCE IN INDIA AND AMONG THE ANCIENTS. With an Account of their Mystic Initiations and the History of Spiritism by Louis Jacolliot, translated from the French by William L. Felt. 275 pp. $5.95   OCCULT

This incredible eyewitness account of personal experiences amongst the wonder-working fakirs of India has been extensively cited in many standard works on Spiritualist phenomena.

LOUIS JACOLLIOT (1837-1890) was a French judge who became better known as an author of remarkable books. He travelled throughout the East and was appointed Chief Justice of Chandenagur (French East Indies) and of Tahiti. A certain amount of mystery and prejudice surrounded Jacolliot because some of his writings were sexological studies of Eastern life; they are still quietly suppressed by great libraries.

The present book of mysticism contains a translation of a little-known Indian treatise on initiations and magic, which the author compares with Kabbalism and other occult traditions. The second section of the book is a personal account of the most astounding occult demonstrations which the author claimed to witness. While it is now impossible to prove or disprove these wonders, it is only fair to say that they are typical of similar reports by other travellers in India during the late nineteenth and early twentieth centuries, and similar to phenomena produced by psychic mediums. In view of the author's important position as Chief Justice his accounts must rank higher than mere traveller's tales.

CITED IN *The Best Books* by W. S. Sonnenschein, 3rd ed.

MODERN MYSTICS by Sir Francis Younghusband, K.C.S.I., K.C.I.E. viii + 316 pp. index. $7.95   MYSTICISM

There are mystics in modern times, as well as in the romantic past. This book shows that the exalted states of awareness associated with the true mystic may be found in a variety of individuals from both East and West, regardless of race, creed, or country.

The author describes the lives of recent mystics as widely different as a Moslem merchant in Persia, a Hindu villager in India, a Roman Catholic nun in France, and a Baptist miner in Wales, but each sharing a higher consciousness beyond the demands and ambitions of everyday mundane life. In the lives of The Bab, Keshub Chander Sen, Sri Ramakrishma, St. Therese de Lisieux, Evan Roberts, and others, the characteristic pattern of the mystic can be discerned.

There was much of the mystic in the author himself, a famous soldier, diplomatist, explorer, geographer, and writer. He was the moving spirit behind the first three Everest expeditions, headed a historic mission to Lhasa in 1903, and travelled throughout India, Kashmir, Tibet, Hunza, and Turkestan. In 1936 he founded the World Fellowship of Faiths, devoted to the underlying truths of all different religions. He claimed that the mystical experience is the indicator of man's true evolution in the Universe, and need not be confined to a few rare individuals. Many may attain it by proper training and meditation, and inspire the rest of mankind to fulfill a divine destiny.

Rasputin—Saint or Devil?

GRIGORY EFIMOVITCH RASPUTIN, the great enigma of Tsarist Russia, was a man with two faces. Many people thought him the most evil occult monster of the age; others claimed that he was a saintly man of destiny! There can be no doubt of his almost supernatural powers, and he certainly became the real ruler of pre-revolutionary Russia. He was murdered December 29, 1916. After reputedly resisting poison, bullets, stabbing and battering, his body was thrown into the icy waters of the Neva.

Here are two key books on the legendary Rasputin. Take your choice of two violently conflicting views, both well documented. Better still—read both sides of the question and make up your own mind.

RASPUTIN. PROPHET, LIBERTINE, PLOTTER by T. Vogel-Jorgensen, translated from the Danish by William Frederick Harvey. 143 pp. index $5.00   BIOGRAPHY

One of the first biographies, published soon after the fantastic murder of Rasputin, this important work was compiled from Russian printed sources, including both moderate and radical newspapers. The author reviews Rasputin's strange personality and rise to power, his political influence, and the plots that gathered around him until his death. While many facts are still disputed, this book remains the best guide to what was said and printed about Rasputin in his own time.

MY FATHER by Maria Rasputin. 157 pp. $5.00   BIOGRAPHY

Many years after a flood of books and even films depicting Rasputin as a depraved and evil genius, his daughter Maria Rasputin wrote this powerful and outspoken defense of her father, condemning his killers as assassins of a saintly martyr. She tells the story of Rasputin's peasant background, his vision of the Holy Virgin of Kazan, his wanderings as a religious pilgrim, his strange magnetic powers of healing, his life as a "Man of God" at the court of the Tsar. This book also prints in full an English translation of the only work Rasputin himself wrote—*My Thoughts and Meditations*. In this he speaks with ecstasy of his visits to holy places at Constantinople, Ephesus and Jerusalem, the blessings of the Sabbath, and the power of divine love.

IS THE BIBLE TRUE?   THE CASE FOR FREETHOUGHT

Ever since Tom Paine's daring *Age of Reason,* Freethinkers have sought a rational non-mystical view of the universe, and their arguments against dogmatic Christianity have often been reinforced by appeals to pagan religions which contain myths paralleling the New Testament stories and throwing doubt on their priority or historicity. Banned for many years by narrow-minded bookshops and libraries, freethinkers wrote aggressive attacks on dogma.

Nowadays the cause for literary freedom and tolerance demands that the Freethought case be properly heard. But more than that, enlightened thinkers also find that the comparison of pagan myth and Christian story reveals a common *mystical* foundation, and that the case against a narrow doctrinaire Christianity could also become a powerful argument for the underlying mystical and ethical truth of all religions.

The following two Freethought classics stem from the shattering impact of Godfrey Higgins' masterpiece *Anacalypsis* (reissued in limited edition by University Books, Inc.) and present a Freethought case that could also be interpreted in favor of the archetypal mysticism of all religions.

THE WORLD'S SIXTEEN CRUCIFIED SAVIORS or Christianity Before Christ by Kersey Graves. 436 pp. $10   RELIGION

First published 1875, this is a popular discussion of the Saviors, Messiahs, or Sons of God preceding the Christian era, and the rituals and religions which surrounded them. A vigorous criticism of the Christian position which has been a best seller for nearly a century.

BIBLE MYTHS AND THEIR PARALLELS IN OTHER RELIGIONS; Being a Comparison of the Old and New Testament Myths and Miracles with Those of Heathen Nations of Antiquity, considering also their Origin and Meaning by T. W. Doane. + 589 pp. index. With numerous illustrations. $10   RELIGION

A monumental comparison of the basic elements of all religions, proving that the main details of the Christian story have parallels in pre-existing religions. The writer concludes that all religions are elaborations of myths relating to natural phenomena. Whether or not one agrees with this general thesis, this great compilation is an indispensable source book for comparison of the archetypal basis of religions old and new.

THE ORIGIN AND PROPERTIES OF THE HUMAN AURA by Oscar Bagnall. xii + 160 pp. illustrated, index. 5½″ x 8¼″ 79-76329 $5.00

MEDICAL/PARAPSYCHOLOGY

Ever since we published a new edition of *The Human Aura* by Walter J. Kilner, readers and scientists have sought further information or help in their own researches. We are now issuing an important book which continues the work of Dr. Kilner and presents further evidence in support of it. For thousands of years, saints and gods were represented with a halo of similar luminous aura; gifted seers claim today to see a subtle aura surrounding ordinary individuals. Dr. Kilner, a physician at St. Thomas' Hospital, London, claimed the reality of the human aura as a physical fact which could be viewed through a special screen using a rare and expensive coal-tar dye known as dicyanin. Kilner declared that the aura changes in various conditions of health.

Twenty-six years after first publication of Dr. Kilner's book, Oscar Bagnall, B. A. (Cantab.) checked the Kilner experiments and confirmed the reality of the human aura, adding new findings. Bagnall claims the aura is in the ultra-violet wave band, and describes techniques for sensitizing the eyes to perceive it. He has developed a cheaper viewing screen, using the dye pinacyanol. His book provides important data for future experiment.

"The late Dr. Walter Kilner . . . described a process of retinal sensitization which he claimed would render the human aura visible to ordinary observers. Mr. Bagnall has continued this work and now presents evidence in support of Kilner's remakarble assertions."—TIMES (LONDON) LITERARY SUPPLEMENT

MAGIC AND MYSTICISM. Studies in Bygone Beliefs by H. Stanley Redgrove, B.Sc. (Lond.), F.C.S. xvi + 205 pp. With numerous illustrations. $5.95

MAGIC/MYSTICISM

Readers who admired Dr. Redgrove's fine study *Alchemy: Ancient and Modern* which we issued last year will welcome this further work by the same author.

This wise and scholarly study of the magic and mysticism of ancient times includes chapters on: *Mediaeval Thought—Pythagoras and His Philosophy—Medicine and Magic—Superstitions concerning Birds—The Power of Sympathy—Talismans—Ceremonial Magic—Architectural Symbolism—The Quest of the Philosopher's Stone—The Phallic Element in Alchemical Doctrine—Roger Bacon—The Cambridge Platonists.* The author shows profound understanding and sympathy with the philosophy that animated bygone magical beliefs, and shows what we may still find valuable in modern times. The book is copiously illustrated with many reproductions of quaint engravings and old magical symbols.

H. STANLEY REDGROVE, B.Sc. (London), F.C.S. (1887-1943) was a noted authority on chemistry and cosmetics, and also Acting President of the Alchemical Society. He was a leading spirit in the revival of serious scientific interest in Alchemy.

"A work of surpassing interest and value."—BRISTOL TIMES.

THE SHROUD OF CHRIST by Paul Vignon, D.Sc. (Fr). 171 pp. 9 plates and 38 illustrations in text. $5.95

RELIGION

Is there a photograph of Christ, printed by chemical reaction on the Holy Shroud preserved in the cathedral of Turin?

Although this sacred relic had been venerated for centuries, even religious dignitaries had doubts about it, until in 1898 a photographer discovered that his negative plate revealed a perfect image of a noble and majestic face with forehead wounds suggesting a crown of thorns, and a body with wounds in the hands and side with marks of scourging.

Dr. Paul Vignon, Professor of Biology at the Institut Catholique, Paris, made the first scientific investigation of the Holy Shroud. The results were presented before the French Academy of Science by his agnostic friend and co-worker Dr. Yves Delage, and published in a full-length book by Dr. Vignon. This English translation of an epoch-making book is the first unshakeable vindication of the authenticity of the Holy Shroud and its amazing image. Whether one believes that the individual laid in this Shroud many centuries ago was the crucified Savior of mankind, or a great mystic and saintly reformer of the period, Dr. Vignon's famous book still presents an unanswerable case, as convincing today as when first published nearly seventy years ago.

Reissue of this scarce full-length study, the first of its kind and still the definitive work, will be welcomed as a major contribution to the ever-growing literature on this extraordinary subject.

MAGIC, WHITE AND BLACK or The Science of Finite and Infinite Life, containing Practical Hints for Students of Occultism by Franz Hartmann, M.D. 298 pp. $7.95

MAGIC

There are many books on the symbols and rituals of Magic, but few on the underlying philosophy and meaning.

This is one of the best expositions of the mystical basis of Magic, and an authoritative guide to the special purification and insights that must develop before practicing the operations of Magic. Without this preliminary training, all magical practices become dangerous or perverse.

DR. FRANZ HARTMANN (1838-1912), famous occult writer, was prominent in the Rosicrucian and Theosophical movements. Born in Bavaria, he was a descendant of the old Irish kings of Ulster. He travelled widely in the U.S.A., acted as coroner in frontier towns during the fast shooting days of the Wild West, prospected in the Rocky Mountains, and investigated leading spiritualist mediums of the time. Upon returning to Bavaria, he studied mysticism under a secret Rosicrucian sect and developed occult gifts himself. He wrote many important books, drawing upon Eastern and Western mystical traditions.

The present book, first published over seventy years ago, went through seven editions before becoming a scarce out-of-print item. In the light of increasing modern interest in the occult by irresponsible cultists, this book makes a welcome reappearance as a classic explanation of the real meaning and purpose of Magic.

CITED IN *The Best Books* by W. S. Sonnenschein, 3rd ed.

COMPLETE MANUAL OF OCCULT DIVINATION. Two books in one set: vol. 1 A Manual of Cartomancy, Fortune-telling and Occult Divination; vol. 2 The Book of Destiny. Both by "Grand Orient" (pseudonym of Arthur Edward Waite). 2 vols. $15

DIVINATION

The largest and most complete compendium of ESP games ever compiled. This intriguing collection of mystical card and other divination systems includes: *The Oracle of Human Destiny—Cagliostro's Mystic Alphabet of the Magi—The Golden Wheel of Fortune—The Art of Invoking Spirits in the Crystal—Divination by Dreams—Astrological Prediction—The Occult Science of Jewels—The Wheel of Wisdom*—and dozens of other fascinating and uncanny occult secrets for the man in the street. Over sixty traditional systems of divination are listed, from *Aeromancy* to *Xylomancy,* in a complete lexicon of these strange arts.

The author was a world-famous British authority on Magic and Mysticism, but wrote these divination manuals under the pseudonym "GRAND ORIENT" for the amusement and entertainment of the general public—and as an easy introduction to the occult arts. Although these are popular volumes, there is an undercurrent of thoughtful and wise advice which prepares the reader for Waite's more imposing works like *Ceremonial Magic—The Holy Kabbalah—The Holy Grail*—all available from University Books, Inc.

SUPERNORMAL FACULTIES IN MAN An Experimental Study by Eugene Osty, M. D. translated by Stanley de Brath. new introduction by Felix Morrow. xvi + 245 pp. index. 6⅛ ″ x 9¼ ″ 69-16360. $6.95. CLAIRVOYANCE

This book is a study of clairvoyants and the nature of clairvoyance; it sums up the author's experiments with sensitives and mediums during a period of 15 years. It will introduce those who do not read French to the best work of the "golden age" of French psychical research.

EUGENE OSTY (1874-1938), an eminent physician, became interested in the paranormal in 1909 when he happened to witness the work of a palmist who accurately described the character of subjects known to Dr. Osty but not to the palmist. Intensive study of palmistry convinced Dr. Osty that looking at the palm merely focussed an intuitive ability and that it was "intuition" or clairvoyance which enabled the palmist to acquire information without the help of known sensory channels. From 1909 to 1924 Dr. Osty divided his time between medicine and experiments with clairvoyants. He published the present work in 1925. From 1924 until his death in 1938 he was the director of the Institut Métaphysique International, the French counterpart of the Society of Physical Research in England and America. His closest collaborators were the physiologist Charles Richet and the philosopher Henri Bergson. Dr. Osty was the first to use infrared and ultra violet photography in darkened seance rooms.

This book reports about a hundred experiments in which clairvoyants "see" at a distance, or on the telephone; describe the character and events in the lives of people unknown to them; foretell events which come to pass; "see" and "hear" the dead and describe what they were like and did when living. In some of the experiments the sensitive responds to a specimen of the subject's handwriting or a piece of clothing. Dr. Osty usually hypnotized the clairvoyant. This is one of the most impressive books of cases in the whole history of parapsychology. This is the first American edition.

FREUD: CHARACTER AND CONSCIOUSNESS by Israel Rosenfield, M.D., Ph.D.
160 pp. 5½ x 8¼" 75-107370 $5.95   PSYCHOLOGY

Israel Rosenfield examines Freudian theory through a detailed analysis and critique of Freud's writings. He shows that the concept of the unconscious lacks a solid theoretical basis and that it is not confirmed by therapeutic experience. Notions such as "wishfulfillment," "displacement," and "condensation" are, the author says, arbitrary descriptions of important psychological events. The existence of unconscious motivation, itself, is questioned since the unconscious is, according to Freud, a structure devoid of verbal content. In addition, suggestion is found to play an important role in the success of psychoanalysis, but its effectiveness is considered short-lived. Ultimately, Freud's attempt to rationalize unconscious behavior fails. The author argues that the irrational element in behavior may result from physiological rather than psychological factors.

Freudian social theory emerges as an inconsistent, ahistorical extension of his individual psychology. In his analysis, the author points out that Freud recognizes the importance of calculation in social activity, and that such calculation is often socially, rather than psychologically, determined. This raises serious questions as to the validity of contemporary applications to the study of society.

MUDRAS. THE RITUAL HAND-POSES OF THE BUDDHA PRIESTS AND THE SHIVA PRIESTS OF BALI by Tyra de Kleen. Introduction by A. J. D. Campbell. 42 pp. text + 62 plates. $5   RELIGION/BUDDHISM

Mudras are the sacred hand gestures which are symbolic of *Mantras*—the magical formulae of Hindu and Buddhist religions. *Mantras* are only fully expressed by a threefold combination of mental concentration, sound utterance, and physical gesture. In India, where the tradition originated, *mudras* are also found in the elaborate hand language of *Bharata Natyam* religious dance.

The Buddhist and Hindu religious gestures illustrated in this remarkable book were preserved by tradition in greater purity in the island of Bali than in any other part of the East. Special implements are associated with the temple rituals of *mudras*—censer, chalice, rosary, hand-bell, lamp, and holy water—rather like the Western traditions of magical practice.

In 1920, Miss Tyra de Kleen, a Swedish artist and traveller, sketched these rare Hindu and Buddhist *mudras* from life, thus preserving a permanent record of an ancient tradition that has faded since the recent political upheavals in the Republic of Indonesia, of which the small island of Bali is now a part.

These beautiful *mudras* are a mystic language of the priests, part of elaborate religious observances known only to initiates.

"Miss de Kleen's drawings are very well done and possess great interest in themselves. They should certainly be studied by all who are interested in modes of spiritual expression which they illustrate."—THE OCCULT REVIEW (London).